The Church Music
of Heinrich Biber

Studies in Musicology, No. 95

George J. Buelow, Series Editor

Professor of Music
Indiana University

Other Titles in This Series

The Church Music
of Heinrich Biber

by
Eric Thomas Chafe

U·M·I Research
Press

Ann Arbor, Michigan

Produced and distributed by
UMI Research Press
an imprint of
University Microfilms, Inc.
Ann Arbor, Michigan 48106

Library of Congress Cataloging in Publication Data

Chafe, Eric Thomas, 1946-
The church music of Heinrich Biber.

(Studies in musicology ; no. 95)
Bibliography: p.
Includes index.
1. Biber, Heinrich Ignaz Franz, 1644-1704—Criticism
and interpretation.   I. Title.   II. Series.
ML410.B586C5   1987   783'.02'60924   86-30866
ISBN 0-8357-1770-4 (alk. paper)

To my mother, Mary Elizabeth Chafe,
and the memory of my father, Leslie Victor Chafe

Contents

Preface

Heinrich Biber is today recognized as one of the great originals of the late seventeenth century. In the realm of instrumental music he stands apart from his contemporaries in South Germany and Austria as the composer who most combines the elements of folk and programmatic "entertainment" music with the more durable Italian styles of the period and the time-honored, contrapuntal values. As composer for the violin his achievement is unique, unrivalled even by the other great virtuosi of the time such as Johann Jakob Walther and Johann Paul Westhoff, who were his equals or near equals in technique. In Biber the German violin school of the seventeenth century reaches its peak. And the violin is unquestionably the key to understanding the remainder of his music as well. Yet, although Biber's amazing advances in the area of string playing and composition pervade his entire corpus, they have been accompanied by a shadow side, in that not only has the remainder of his work been largely ignored, but even the instrumental works are in danger of appearing overly concerned with immediacy of effect. Biber's cultivation of folk and program elements as well as the violin *scordatura* have contributed to a sense that pieces such as the *Battalia* typify most clearly the composer's work. And they are, in fact, close to the heart of Biber's *oeuvre,* not because of gimmicks such as the famous dissonant quodlibet or the imitation of battle sounds in themselves, but because of Biber's great understanding of the importance of instrumental idioms and the larger question of sonority in music of all types. This is one of the great themes of the baroque style in music as identified by Bukofzer, and it goes vastly deeper into the nature of the style of the age than is commonly recognized. [1]

Biber's church music, surveyed here for the first time in print, is balanced between the pictorialism and effectiveness it shares with the instrumental works and the traditional contrapuntal arts and techniques that were rooted in the *stile antico.* The former element makes a fascinating study in itself, because it involves a dialectic comprising on the one side an unusually fixed and ostentatious set of performance conditions in Salzburg and on the other the highly original mind of a composer rooted in instrumental music with a decided leaning towards folk music. Biber's career shows clearly a moving away from its early emphasis on the folk and program elements, even to some extent from instrumental music, and towards the more "public" genres of opera and church music, especially after the mid-1680s. While this direction involved him in the composition of more and more compositions of large scale both in terms of performance time and scoring, including polychoral Masses of mammoth dimensions, it by no means produced a musical hardening of the arteries as a result of the composer's capitulation to the formal requirements of his position. It is true that we do find indications in his biography of a desire, in the last decade or so of his life, to separate what must have been a life of numerous external demands from the more personal, private character of musical composition. Reflections of musical performances in the protocol books of the Benedictine convent at Nonnberg (which his musically gifted daughter, Maria Anna

Magdalena, entered in the mid-1690s) suggest a musical life that was to some extent separate from the pomp of cathedral festivities. Yet, within the framework of numerous C-major compositions with festive orchestration dominated by trumpets, the voice of the violin innovator and pious south German individual can be heard. Biber was able, through his church music, to suggest the bridging of social levels that were outwardly incompatible. The *Requiem in F minor,* written probably in the last decade of his life, is a work in which meditation on the universality and inevitability of death takes on a deeply affective character suggestive of both public and personal dimensions.

This study offers the fullest biography of the composer attempted to date (chapter 1), and the first systematic catalog of all his works. One chapter is devoted to performance conditions at the Salzburg cathedral (chapter 2) and another comprises an introduction to the repertoire of seventeenth-century church music in Salzburg (chapter 3). The remainder of the book constitutes a stylistic study of all the surviving church works, both vocal and instrumental. Biber's style stands forth from that of any of his contemporaries to a sufficiently clear extent that the question of authorship in the case of a work such as the *Missa in Albis* (ascribed only to "H. B.") becomes a relatively straightforward matter; and those of the *Missa Salisburgensis* and *Missa Bruxellensis,* formerly attributed to Orazio Benevoli, can be confirmed to a still greater extent than hitherto. [2] The nature of this study will not be to argue for authorship in the case of the latter two works but to suggest, on the basis of a broad consideration of Biber's style, that no other attribution is possible. These compositions must be cataloged as "of doubtful authorship," but their styles point as unmistakably to Biber as that of *Il ritorno d'Ulisse in patria* does to Monteverdi. And, in fact, a basic truth about Biber's style that will be taken up here is expressed in the fact that the *Missa Salisburgensis* could have been taken for a work of the first half of the seventeenth century for so long.

Any attempt to list here the literally hundreds of libraries and archives and individuals who responded to my search for Biber's music would run to many pages. I am particularly grateful to the following institutions: the Konsistorial Archiv, Salzburg (especially Dr. Hans Spatzenegger); the Salzburg Government Archives (Dr. O. Pagitz); the Museum Carolino Augusteum, Salzburg (Dr. Frederike Prodinger); the library at the Benedictine monastery of Michaelbeuern, Salzburg; the Austrian National Library, Vienna; the Allgemeine Verwaltungs Archiv, Vienna; the music archive of the Minoritenkonvent, Vienna; the Sächsische Landesbibliothek, Dresden; the Bayerische Staatsbibliothek, Munich; the archive of the Benedictine monastery of Seitenstetten, Lower Austria (especially Father Benedikt Wagner); Kloster Einsiedeln, Switzerland (Father Kanisius Zünd); the Benedictine monasteries at Kremsmünster and Göttweig, Upper Austria; the music libraries of Syracuse and Columbia Universities, and the Library of Congress, Washington. Special thanks are due to Sister Maria Theresia Bolschwing of Stift Nonnberg, Salzburg, who made it a pleasure to work with the convent's music manuscripts and archive materials. Dr. Jiří Sehnal of the Moravske Museum, Brno, gave me much information concerning the Biber manuscripts in Czechoslovakia, helped me to procure copies of the Kroměříž manuscripts and alerted me to valuable secondary literature. Dr. Ernst Hintermaier of the University of Salzburg has been especially kind in several different ways, including getting me photocopies of the Biber manuscripts in Salzburg, allowing me to see the manuscripts at a time, several years ago, when the archive was generally inaccessible and undergoing a new cataloging, and giving me the results of his research into the Salzburg watermarks. Dr. Sibylle Dahms, also of the University of Salzburg, let me have information concerning Salzburg musicians from her dissertation. And Prof. Nikolaus Harnoncourt gave me assistance of various kinds (including the loan of scores), not least of which was the inspiration from his wonderful Biber performances. I gratefully acknowledge financial assistance from the Canada Council, Ottawa, Wilfrid Laurier University, Waterloo, Ontario, and Brandeis University. Prof. Rika Maniates of the University of Toronto was of great assistance in getting an earlier incarnation of this book into shape. Armand Qualliotine and Patrick Jordan copied the musical examples. And finally, my wife Patricia has lived with this project for years; without her support there would be no book at all.

A Note on Orthography, Italics, Capitalization, and Pitch Designation

Certain usages in orthography, italics, and capitalization that may appear inconsistent must be explained. These involve the titles of manuscript works and of movements, sections, and passages of texts within larger compositions.

Wherever possible capitalization follows the form found on the title pages of works. Certain titles have been modernized with respect to capitalization and spelling. For example, *Requiem ex F con terza min[ore]* will be referred to as *Requiem in F minor*. Others in more common use (for example, *Sonata* and *Fantasia*) have been retained in their original form but with the addition of distinguishing key indications, the latter not italicized (*Sonata* in E major).

In some cases the original spelling and capitalization of manuscript titles have been retained because they may reflect some of the character of the work (for example, *Sonata à 6 die pauern-Kirchfarth genandt*).

The five major sections of the Mass Ordinary and the corresponding sections of Requiem masses are not italicized, nor are references to sections within the major movements. However, references to portions of the text within those sections appear in quotation marks when they refer only to a specific passage, and do not constitute self-contained sections.

The Catalog preserves original forms of titles for both prints and manuscript works. Corresponding references within the text of the book may use shortened forms. Thus, *In Festo Trium Regium, Muttetum Natale à 6* will be referred to in the text simply as *Muttetum Natale*, and *Fidicinium Sacro-Profanum, tam Choro, quam Foro, Pluribus Fidibus concinnatum, et concini aptum* will be identified in the text as *Fidicinium Sacro-Profanum*.

Pitch is indicated according to the following system:

C   c   c′ (middle c)   c″   c‴

Heinrich Biber at Thirty-Six Years of Age
(Salzburg, Museum Carolino Augusteum)

Heinrich Biber: A Seventeenth-Century Musical Life

Early Years (1644–1668)

Heinrich Ignaz Franz Biber, the greatest German violinist-composer of the seventeenth century, was born in the small town of Wartenberg (Straz pod Ralskem), near Reichenberg (Liberec) in northern Bohemia, and baptized there on August 12, 1644. The baptismal entry, which still survives, gives us the names of his parents, Martin and Maria, as well as his father's occupation—that of "Schützen," translated variously as huntsman, guncharger, or field guard.[1] The exact duties of Martin Biber's position are not known; but it is likely that, as Paul Nettl surmises, he was employed—probably as a gamekeeper—on the estate of the local overlord, Count Christoph Paul von Liechtenstein-Kastelkorn.[2] The names Ignaz and Franz, which do not appear on the baptismal record, are typical of the time. They reflect the spirit of the Counter-Reformation, prevalent in Bohemia and Austria as in most Catholic countries in the period of the Thirty Years' War.

All we know about Biber's early years is that he was brought up in humble circumstances. As might be expected, the events of his life are more readily and securely documented from the time of his achieving local, and ultimately European renown. From the years of his employment in Salzburg (1670–1704) we possess enough data to form a picture of his activities as a musician, even to afford us a glimpse into his domestic life. His sojourn in Kroměříž, from around 1668 to 1670, is now illuminated to some extent by contemporary records and compositions; and it appears that he was perhaps in connection with the Kroměříž music chapel as early as 1663. Newer evidence, unfortunately clouded by uncertainty with respect to dates, reveals that he held at least one, and probably two other positions before 1668. But when we try to work backwards to his early musical instruction we are left with no firm ground of documentary evidence; we cannot even determine when he first left Wartenberg.

Paul Nettl made much of a suggestion by the Wartenberg historian Wilhelm Feistner that Biber's first teacher was the local organist, schoolteacher and cantor, Wiegand Knöffel (or Knöstel), a drunkard and rabblerouser.[3] Although this assertion is by no means secure, it receives support from the fact that Biber must have spent his earliest years in his native town. It would have been exceedingly unlikely for a family of the social standing of Martin Biber's to have moved; and, in any case, we know that Biber's mother died in Wartenburg in 1684 and that his brother Michael was "Rentschreiber" there in 1692.[4] It may well be, therefore, that Biber learned the rudiments of music under Knöffel. But he could not have gone very far there; there is no indication that the Wartenberg organist was a skilled string player. And Biber's musical upbringing certainly included competent, probably expert instruction on the violin and viola da gamba, for he was undoubtedly master of both these instruments by the early to mid 1660s.[5] Whatever the circumstances of his introduction to the instrument that turned out to be of central importance in his development, his musical ability must have been remarked by someone with the means of providing for his further training. The most likely figure in that position was Count Maximilian von Liechtenstein-Kastelkorn, who inherited the local estate in 1648. As Nettl suggests, Biber in his youth might have entered the employ of the count as a servant and musician.[6] Such a circumstance, common at the time, would account for Biber's later connections with two other members of the count's family. We know that all the members of the Liechtenstein-Kastelkorn family were great lovers of music and that Biber was later employed by both Count Maximilian's son (Christoph Philipp) and his brother (Prince-Bishop Karl). A nobleman such as Count Maximilian would certainly have been aware of promising young musical talent within his area. It is easy to imagine that the count at some point took over responsibility for Biber's education, ensuring that he have the quality of musical education his abilities obviously merited, and later arranging the positions that Biber held under other members of his family.

Where and with whom Biber studied composition and violin, not to mention viola da gamba, have long been subjects for conjecture. Prague, Reichenberg, Dresden and Vienna have all been suggested as places, while Antonio Bertali and Johann Heinrich Schmelzer have been put forth as possible teachers.[7] These two composers were both prominent at the Vienna court, Schmelzer eventually becoming the first German *Kapellmeister* in a chapel that was dominated by Italians in the seventeenth century.[8] Although, as we will see, there are indications that Biber did indeed have close ties with Vienna at an early stage of his career, and probably studied there, it does not follow that he went there as a boy. The first real documents that we possess after his baptism come from Kroměříž in the year 1663: a manuscript *Salve Regina à 2* for soprano, obbligato viola da gamba and continuo, the earliest dated work of Biber's, a *Sonata à 4 violis* attributed to "H. B." and preserved in manuscript along with a sonata of Antonio Bertali's, and a *Congregamini Omnes Populi* of "H. B." Although the latter two compositions are of uncertain authorship, the violin writing in the sonata bears such a striking resemblance to Biber's and the style of composition compares so closely to certain other early works of Biber's that it is difficult to imagine whom else the initials could represent. On the basis of handwriting and paper analyses of these and other related manuscripts from the Kroměříž archive, Jiří Sehnal has drawn the following conclusions concerning Biber's activity around the year 1663.[9] Biber was at that time already in communication with someone at Kroměříž, most likely Pavel Josef Vejvanovský, the leader of the chapel, who was in the bishop's employ from 1660 or 1661. Biber was apparently acquainted with one Philip Jakob Rittler as well, since the copyist of Biber's *Salve Regina,* if not Rittler himself, served as copyist of a block of twenty-five music manuscripts at Kroměříž, mostly from the year 1663, among which five of Rittler's compositions appear. Rittler, seven years older than Biber, was a composer known at the Kroměříž chapel for some time before 1663; some of his works there are dated as early as 1660. Rittler knew Vejvanovský from Troppau, where Vejvanovský had studied at the Jesuit school from 1656 to 1660. Biber might have met Vejvanovský through Rittler, or the three musicians might all have studied in Troppau. Since the copyist of Biber's *Salve Regina* used chiefly paper made in Glatz (and therefore more likely to have been used in Troppau than in Kroměříž), Sehnal concludes that Biber might have studied in Glatz or Silesia rather than in Austria.[10]

That Biber was known in Kroměříž by 1663 or even earlier seems very probable when we consider that Biber's future employer there, Karl Liechtenstein-Kastelkorn, who did not actually become bishop until 1664, represented by proxy the thirteen-year-old bishop (Josef Karl, died 1664) in the diocese from the year 1662.[11] In all likelihood Biber became known to Bishop Karl through the bishop's brother, Count Maximilian, or the count's son, Christoph Philipp. A letter of Biber's to Bishop Karl (unfortunately undated) has survived, in which the composer thanks the bishop for sending the discharge certificate (*Losbrief*) from his master,

Christoph Philipp, and asks for a "Testimonium peracti Servitii" as well.[12] It is possible, however, that Biber wrote this letter from Salzburg after 1670; his statement that he needed the *Testimonium* for the "better advancement of himself and his family" suggests this.[13] If so, then the *Testimonium* would have referred to his period of employment in Kroměříž from 1668 to 1670. Nothing further concerning Biber's service under Christoph Philip has come to light.

Another position that Biber apparently held before 1668 is mentioned in a letter from Schmelzer to Bishop Liechtenstein-Kastelkorn dated December 24, 1670, a few months after Biber had left Kroměříž for Salzburg. The bishop had written Schmelzer seeking a replacement, and Schmelzer recommended Johann Jakob Prinner, saying that Biber's abilities were very well known to Prinner, since the two men had worked together at the court of the younger prince of Eggenberg in Styria (Graz).[14] At the time of Schmelzer's letter, Prinner was out of work because of the dissolving of the music chapel in Graz. Nettl suggested that Biber, too, lost his position as a result of the breaking up of the Eggenberg chapel, and that he went to Kroměříž at that time.[15] This, however, cannot have been the case, for the chapel in Graz was apparently dissolved in 1670 and not at the time that Biber began his service at Kroměříž, which was no later than 1668.[16] Another name familiar from Kroměříž that crops up in the Eggenberg archive is that of Philip Jakob Rittler again, who was employed in Graz from at least 1669 until 1673 as "fürstlicher Hoffcaplan," and in that position survived the dissolving of the chapel.[17] Although Rittler's presence at Graz before 1669 is not documented, and Biber was certainly not there after 1668, it is still possible that the two men worked together for a time at the Eggenberg court.[18] We assume that at some point Rittler and Biber had close contact; and it might be that Biber's Graz period goes back to the time that his Kroměříž *Salve Regina* was copied, in the early 1660s. In 1675 Rittler returned to Kroměříž and served as the Bishop's chaplain until 1677.[19] Virtually nothing of his music is known today, although he is one of the more interesting and best-represented composers in the Kroměříž collection. A work of his that was formerly known only from an anonymous manuscript, the *Sonata à 6 Campanarum* (1666), was attributed to Biber on stylistic grounds by Nettl, an ascription upheld also by Sehnal until a second manuscript turned up.[20] The work resembles Biber's program music in its imaginative treatment of the strings to depict the sound of bells.

Facts are also scanty concerning Biber's relationship to his other supposed colleague at Graz, Johann Jakob Prinner. A manuscript music treatise by Prinner has survived (*Musikalischer Schlissl*, 1677), but it offers no information concerning either Biber or its author's period of employment at the Eggenberg court.[21] Prinner apparently was not a prolific composer, since his surviving output is not comparable in quantity or scope to that of either Biber or Rittler; several manuscripts of "Balletti Francesi" by him are preserved at Kroměříž along with a few other pieces. What we know of his music today is confined to some songs for solo voice and basso continuo of a decidedly folk-like character; this might have been Prinner's milieu as a composer despite the broader knowledge of music that comes through in the treatise.[22] In any case, Biber used the melody of one of Prinner's songs, "Nambli wol kann ich ietzt glauben," in two of his instrumental works. Sehnal points out that it is one of the eight different tunes that sound simultaneously in the dissonant quodlibet movement of the well-known *Battalia* or *Sonata di Marche* of 1673, and I have found it in the last movement of a *Pastorella* for violin and continuo of Biber.[23] This latter work, a deliberately rustic piece, is most likely an early work of Biber's, and exhibits such an interesting relationship to a work of Schmelzer's as well that a consideration of its provenance and connections to Viennese musical circles is in order.

The *Pastorella* is preserved in Vienna in a late seventeenth-century manuscript of over a hundred violin sonatas by ten known composers and a number of anonymi, all presumably either Germans or Italians working in the Germanic lands.[24] This important collection can be divided into three categories that probably reflect the transmission of the works therein. First of all, the book contains copies of sixty sonatas made from four printed collections of the late seventeenth century; this is the least valuable part of the collection.[25] In addition, there appear eighteen solos by nine musicians, among whom Vienna-centered composers, such as Schmelzer and Bertali, figure prominently. Finally, there are twenty-four anonymous solos, all in styles comparable to the works in the preceding category. The copies from printed sonatas are grouped in succession (Nos. 7–66), while the unprinted works mix anonymous solos with those of known composers, with some internal subgrouping of works according to styles and composers. One surmises that the book was prepared from individual copies (perhaps largely from a single collection) of compositions available in Vienna in the late seventeenth century, some of which were relatively recent while others went back thirty or more years. Besides the *Pastorella* (No. 79) one other work appears under Biber's name, a *Sonata* in E major (No. 84), the only solo sonata of Biber's in that key, and a work that is arguably the most technically advanced of all his sonatas; it was presumably written after his move to Salzburg and a copy sent to Vienna. But there are also two anonymous pieces in the Vienna manuscript that are identifiable as works of Biber. One is a *Sonata* in C minor (No. 75) that is clearly recognizable as an older version of one of the sonatas from the *Sonatae Violino Solo* of 1681. The other appears among a group of anonymous solos in similar style to this early version (Nos. 3 through 6 of the manuscript): it is an older form of the D-major fourth sonata from the same Biber publication (No. 3; now entitled *Fantasia*). In the case of these two pieces the immature style characteristics they exhibit as well as the relationships between the two versions are particularly interesting and suggest that the Vienna pieces come from a much earlier period in the composer's life.[26] In the 1681 set the two sonatas that derive from them are the only ones to utilize *scordatura,* an indication that Biber's attachment to that device does indeed go back to his earliest known compositional period.[27] The presence of such markedly early versions in a manuscript of Viennese provenance, and furthermore amongst a group of composers several of whom worked chiefly in Vienna, suggests that Biber had close ties to the imperial city early in his career. The style of the *Fantasia* in particular is very similar to that of both the 1663 *Salve Regina* and the *Sonata à 4 violis* of "H. B." that is preserved at Kroměříž along with a sonata of Bertali's. Moreover, the group of anonymous sonatas that follows immediately in the Vienna manuscript (Nos. 4–6) seems almost certainly to contain early works of Biber's as well; No. 4 has almost identical musical characteristics—especially the same immature style, as the *Fantasia.*[28] The group is then followed immediately by a manuscript copy of the eight *Sonatae Violino Solo* (Nos. 7–14). Besides these works the manuscript contains one further sonata by Biber (No. 80), but this time attributed to Schmelzer, who is otherwise represented in the collection by two sonatas. This fifth Biber piece is the "Crucifixion" sonata from the so-called *Mystery Sonatas,* the violin notated at the same pitch, but the *scordatura* and basso continuo a tone higher; the Vienna copy also has programmatic titles referring to the Turkish siege of Vienna as well as an extra chorale-like movement at the end (entitled "Victori der Christen"). This sonata follows immediately after the *Pastorella* in another group made up chiefly of anonymous solos of which some might well be works of Biber.[29] It appears, in fact, that sonatas from several different periods in Biber's life are represented in the Vienna manuscript: two early pieces from his youth, the *Pastorella,* which in all likelihood was written at Kroměříž (see the following discussion), the *Sonata* in E, the print of the *Sonatae Violino Solo,* and probably also the "Crucifixion" sonata from Salzburg.

It is the *Pastorella,* however, that provides the best evidence for Biber's close musical association with Schmelzer. This piece bears an intimate relationship to a *Pastorella* for two violins and basso continuo of Schmelzer's preserved in the Paris manuscript of over three hundred early German violin works known as the "Recueil de Rost," one of the major early sources for the German violin school.[30] Biber's and Schmelzer's works share the same brief ritornello-like passage that begins and ends the two pieces and marks internal section divisions, as well as certain other material having the character of passage-work (ex. 1-1).

Example 1-1. *Pastorella* Excerpts
(a)   Johann Heinrich Schmelzer, Beginning of *Pastorella* for Two Violins and Basso Continuo

(b)   Schmelzer, *Pastorella,* mm. 22–29

(c)   Biber, Beginning of *Pastorella* for Solo Violin and Basso Continuo

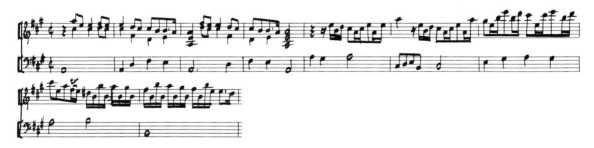

Biber's piece develops the common material more extensively than Schmelzer's. Both works have, of course, the obligatory triple-meter section that characterizes the pastorale (Schmelzer's has two). But, as indicated above, in Biber's work this section is an arrangement of Prinner's song "Nambli wol kan ich ietzt glauben." And Biber's setting makes an unmistakable musical association between the ritornello of the two *Pastorelle* and the second phrase of Prinner's song (ex. 1-2). It appears that Biber has drawn together ideas from two men who were probably of central importance to his early development, pointing up motivic interrelationships that lay dormant in Schmelzer's piece.[31] The true underlying connection

Example 1-2. Biber, Beginning of Final Section of *Pastorella*

among all these works that Biber's *Pastorella* makes explicit, however, is the folk music derivation of particular theme types that crop up frequently in seventeenth-century Austrian music. In this case the primary melodic pattern resembles numerous popular songs of the time in addition to well-known English tunes such as "Old MacDonald" and "Jack and Jill." It also figures prominently in the early version of Biber's D-major sonata in the Vienna manuscript, and the particularly "hoedown"-like beginning of a Kroměříž string sonata that Biber published years later as the ninth of his *Sonatae, tam Aris, quam Aulis servientes* (Salzburg 1676).

The relative dates of the two *Pastorelle* cannot be established with absolute confidence; the Rost collection is unquestionably older than the Vienna manuscript and represents on the whole an earlier stage in the German violin school. But the Biber *Pastorella* certainly goes back to an earlier period than that of the copying of the Vienna manuscript. One particularly interesting fact of relevance here is that in 1669, while Biber was at Kroměříž, three compositions of Schmelzer were sent to Bishop Liechtenstein-Kastelkorn and mentioned in a single letter to the Bishop from his contact at the Vienna court: the *Fechtschuele,* a *Pastorella* and another piece entitled *Vogelgesang.*[32] All three of these works have very close counterparts in Biber's *oeuvre* (see the following paragraph). The *Vogelgesang* has apparently not survived, but reference to it in a later letter from the same author indicates that, like Biber's *Sonata violino solo representativa* (subtitled *Representatio Avium*) of the same year, it represented the cries of various birds and animals. Schmelzer's *Pastorella* might have been written well before 1669, of course; but the *Vogelgesang* was being composed as the exchange of letters took place, in early 1669.[33] The most likely explanation of the relationship is that Biber's works were all produced after Schmelzer's, perhaps in response to Bishop Liechtenstein-Kastelkorn's request; for, as we will see, the bishop was especially fond of music of this kind and wrote the Vienna court regularly for more. In some cases, however, the musical influence between Biber and Schmelzer might have worked the other way around. A few years later, in 1673, the Bishop was especially delighted to receive a "Ciaconna ohne ferneres accompagniomento" from Schmelzer; in the seventeenth century the Kroměříž archive had a chaconne for solo violin by Biber, and it is quite possible that the well-known *Passacaglia* for unaccompanied violin that concludes the *Mystery Sonatas* was written for Bishop Liechtenstein-Kastelkorn.[34]

As far as biographical matters are concerned, it cannot be established that Biber experienced the musical life of the capital of the empire in his youth. It is probable, however, that he did, most likely in the early to mid 1660s. After detailed study of Biber's single surviving opera, Constantin Schneider concluded that the chief influences on its style came from Vienna, especially Cesti's *La Dori,* which was produced there in 1663, a striking fact when we consider that over a quarter of a century lies between the two works.[35] Connections to Schmelzer are numerous and well known in a general way. Besides the two *Pastorelle,* almost every instrumental work of the one composer has a counterpart in the *oeuvre* of the other: *Fechtschuel/Battalia; Ciaconna ohne ferneres accompagniomento/Passacaglia* for unaccompanied violin; *Sonata à 7 Flauti/Sonata pro Tabula; Die Polnische Sackpfeiffe/Sonata à 6 die pauern-Kirchfarth genandt; Sonata "CuCu," Vogelgesang/Sonata violino solo representativa,* and so on. Even whole collections exhibit similar formats, instrumentation and sacred/secular designations: Schmelzer's *Sonatae Unarum Fidium* and Biber's *Sonatae Violino Solo* are two of the milestones of the German violin school; while Schmelzer's two collections of instrumental ensemble music, the *Sacro-Profanus Concentus Musicus* and *Duodenum Selectarum Sonatarum, tam Foro, quam honesto Choro,* resemble Biber's *Fidicinium Sacro-Profanum, tam Choro, quam Foro* and his *Sonatae, tam Aris, quam Aulis servientes.*[36] Although there are no known connections between the two men during Biber's Salzburg years, Biber played before the Emperor in 1677, a time when Schmelzer must surely have been present; the appearance of Biber's "Crucifixion" sonata in Vienna under Schmelzer's name might therefore indicate a continuing exchange of some kind.

The main point of all this is not the assembling of evidence for Biber's having studied with Schmelzer, although that traditional view is now, perhaps, more likely than ever, but the origin of the individualistic nature of much seventeenth-century Austrian music in popular musical currents that extended quite far afield from the mainstream of Italian influence. In fact, the Vienna manuscript informs us that many of the characteristics of the German violin school—scordatura, virtuoso writing, folk and program elements—were more widespread than is generally known, and by no means confined to the greatest virtuosi. Biber's early years were spent largely in the company of musicians whose work, judged from a three-hundred-year perspective, must be deemed provincial. But that he drew much of what is strongest and most enduring even in his later work from this upbringing is a fact. The influence of forms of popular piety on Austrian church music of this time (and, indeed, of the other arts as well) has often been remarked. When Biber includes sonatas of very rustic character among publications designated for both church and court, when he produces a hybrid type of programmatic suite for solo violin and associates it with the mysteries of the rosary, or an ensemble sonata entitled *Sonata à 6 die pauern-Kirchfarth genandt,* that depicts a peasants' litany procession, and so on, it is not merely the influence of his background that is significant but perhaps the artist's conscious effort to broaden the musical language with the incorporation of elements that suggest a cutting across the barriers of class and national style as well as the sacred/secular dichotomy. Much of the widespread and deep-rooted nature of the Austrian love for folk life and art at all social levels arose in the period we are considering and had its earliest musical manifestation in the works of composers such as Biber and Schmelzer. Nothing could be more static, formal and hierarchical than the setup of the Salzburg court where Biber spent the greater part of his creative life; and yet both Biber and Schmelzer, born in the humblest of circumstances, died as members of the nobility and can be considered to represent an emergent national consciousness that created a *rapprochement* between German folk elements and the dominant Italian styles. Their situations in fact encouraged the particular synthesis of style elements that remains an animating force in their music and without which the nature, if not the depth of the achievements of later composers, such as Haydn, would be unthinkable.

Kroměříž (1668–1670)

Although the Kroměříž chapel existed since the fourteenth century, and reached a high point in the latter half of the sixteenth century under Kapellmeister Jakob Handl-Gallus, the tenure of Bishop Karl Liechtenstein-Kastelkorn has given the archive its present historical importance. The most significant part of the musical holdings is unquestionably that now called the Liechtenstein collection, after the bishop under whose rule (1664–95) and patronage most of the music was collected and performed.[37] Exactly when Biber entered the bishop's service is uncertain. Nettl suggests that Biber might have been in Kroměříž as early as 1666 and posits the definite date as 1668. Sehnal has more recently proclaimed that Biber was there no longer than two years—from 1668 to the end of summer 1670–and, indeed, there is no evidence that he was.[38] Apart from the *Salve Regina* of 1663, his earliest works in the archive are dated 1668. The only official position he is known to have held is that of chamber servant, the duties of which are not perfectly clear and may have been nominal.[39]

The bishop himself took an unusually lively interest in musical performances, and the surviving correspondence between him and various persons at the Vienna court (including Schmelzer for a decade) is illuminating, an exchange that, coincidentally or not, begins the year of Biber's arrival at Kroměříž.[40] The bishop was constantly in search of new music at first, asking for dance suites (*"Arien* ... new Allemandes, Gigues, Courantes, Sarabandes and the like") from Vienna and Schmelzer in particular. He also shows interest in "Muteten auf die Clarin, Trombon und Geigen," and states that he can provide "six or seven clarini, ten to twelve strings ('geigen') and seven, eight or more trombones."[41] Always Schmelzer is mentioned: five times in 1668, four in 1669. In early 1669 the references to Schmelzer's *Fechtschuele, Pastorella,* and *Vogelgesang* and a more detailed report of the last of these works gives a hint of one of the bishop's special musical leanings, towards what Schmelzer acutely called "pizaren Sachen."[42] When the following year Schmelzer himself wrote the bishop for the first time, in response to Biber's departure and the bishop's seeking replacement musicians, it appears that the bishop must have specified some of the qualities he was in search of, for Schmelzer mentioned "des Bibers qualiten" when recommending Prinner for the position. Bishop Liechtenstein-Kastelkorn had in fact stated in a letter to Schmelzer that Biber played "Violin Bass" (i.e., cello) and viola da gamba and composed with considerable ability ("noch zimblicher gestalt auch etwas componirt"); he did not mention the obvious—that Biber played solo violin as well.[43] But it is clear that Schmelzer understood what the bishop wanted, for in his first letter he referred twice to the ability of certain musicians to play alone, once linking this to the "pizaren Sachen" that had obviously been sought out by the bishop. After a while the bishop must have found someone who could play pieces of this kind, for in 1673 he sought specifically works for *scordatura* violins and was especially pleased to receive the above-mentioned *Ciaconna* for unaccompanied violin of Schmelzer along with Schmelzer's promise to obtain more "pizaria" from Vienna for the bishop.[44] It is difficult to know from this distance whether the bishop's taste for such pieces was developed before Biber came to Kroměříž, even whether the bishop might not have had a hand in Biber's musical education. After a few years, and a perhaps futile attempt to develop the abilities of another of his violinists in the area of solo playing and *scordatura,* the bishop ceased to look for *scordatura* works, an occurrence suggesting that his musical taste had been strongly influenced by the striking musical individualism he had encountered for two years.[45]

Besides Biber, the musician at Kroměříž who must have done most to influence the bishop's musical leanings, was Pavel Vejvanovský, the chapel's leader and most prolific composer. Vejvanovský was, in addition, the greatest trumpet virtuoso of the region and an indefatigable copyist and collector of music for the bishop (more than half of the Liechtenstein collection and numerous title pages and single parts are in his hand).[46] As teacher of Bishop Karl's trumpeters, Vejvanovský brought trumpet playing at Kroměříž to a very high level; the bishop's boast of providing six or seven clarini was no idle one. Apart from numerous difficult clarino parts in Vejvanovský's works, our best evidence of the quality of the Kroměříž trumpeters and their impact on Biber is the *Sonata à 7* (1668) for six trumpets, kettledrums and organ in which all six instruments play to the top of the clarino register. Even the wonderful *Sonata S. Polycarpi* for eight trumpets (six of them clarini) that Biber wrote five years later in Salzburg (and sent to Kroměříž) is not as technically demanding, and probably owes something of its conception to the Kroměříž trumpeters. Several of the sonatas for one or two trumpets and strings of the *Sonatae, tam Aris, quam Aulis servientes* (Salzburg 1676) were written at Kroměříž and perhaps also the twelve trumpet bicinia that conclude the publication.[47]

Although Vejvanovský was musical leader of the chapel, it seems likely that Biber attained a position of some influence over the bishop in musical matters. While he was at Kroměříž the bishop made an agreement to purchase several string instruments from the celebrated Tyrolean violin maker, Jakob Stainer. The correspondence relating to this transaction reveals that by early 1670 Stainer had delivered two violins, two *viole da braccio* and one viola da gamba to the bishop, while two *viole da braccio,* one "Postviolin" (*Passviolin?* i.e., cello?) and one violone ("octavViolin") were still to be manufactured. This set of nine instruments corresponds very closely to the ensemble required for the largest sonatas Biber wrote at Kroměříž; the relatively large number of violas is especially characteristic. In a letter Stainer spoke of the beauty and quality of his viola da gamba, the worth of which the excellent virtuoso Biber would undoubtedly recognize.[48] From this statement Sehnal concludes that at that time Biber was already an outstanding gambist and personally known to Stainer.[49] The 1663 *Salve Regina* has an agile and idiomatic gamba part, as do certain other anonymous works from the time and compositions signed "H. B." that are perhaps works of Biber; and the bishop did say that Biber played gamba at Kroměříž. But that Biber was an outstanding gambist does not necessarily follow from Stainer's letter; Biber need not have been a virtuoso to recognize the quality of the instrument. Stainer's phrase, "der vortreffliche virtuos" surely refers to Biber the violinist. Sehnal's conclusion that Biber knew Stainer personally by 1670 is convincing. Stainer's biographer, Walter Senn, suggests that the violin maker visited Kroměříž between 1668 and 1670;[50] if so, he must have met Biber and heard him play. Biber certainly was acquainted with Stainer later and owned one of his violins. One of the earliest documents concerning Biber's new position in Salzburg mentions that Biber himself had ordered a violin from Stainer and sent another, a "Cremoneser," to be repaired; from this letter one can assume, as did its author, that the archbishop had resolved to build up a complete ensemble as soon as possible.[51] And, in fact, within Biber's first few years in Salzburg the court there bought three violins and a viola da gamba from Stainer.[52] The inescapable conclusion is that Biber knew Stainer's instruments, preferred to work with an entire ensemble of them and persuaded both his patrons to make such instruments available.

Ironically, the opportunity Biber took of abandoning Bishop Liechtenstein-Kastelkorn's service was the occasion of his being sent to pick up instruments from Stainer. We do not know the extent to which Biber might have planned this action, which Schmelzer called a "disgraceful abuse," but Schmelzer later reported to the bishop that Biber had written him in September in search of a violinist and lutenist, presumably as replacements.[53] A letter from J. F. Khuen von Auer to Bishop Karl's house steward informs us that Biber left the bishop's employ *insalutato hospite*—that is without first obtaining leave.[54] The events concerning Biber's transgression are explained by Nettl: In August or early September 1670, the bishop sent Biber and another musician to Absam, where they were to fetch instruments for the bishop from Stainer. After they had left, the bishop learned somehow that they intended to escape from his employ (suggesting that the action was indeed preplanned), and he requested J. F. Khuen von Auer, who lived near Absam, to hold the two musicians at Stainer's shop. Biber, however, never turned up at Absam, but entered the service of the prince-archbishop of Salzburg instead. Financial considerations must have played an important role in his decision. His salary, even in his early Salzburg years, was higher than that earned by Vejvanovský after thirty years of service at Kroměříž.[55] And Salzburg was unquestionably a much more active musical center than Kroměříž. Moreover, Biber might well have found Bishop Liechtenstein-Kastelkorn's musical taste, with its decided leaning towards external technical devices, too restrictive. If the bishop was angry with Biber for running away, he must nevertheless have resigned himself to the *fait accompli* fairly soon afterwards. The presence in the Kroměříž archive of works composed by Biber in his early Salzburg years indicates that relations were resumed. A letter from the bishop's chancellery to Biber suggests that these compositions were sent to Vejvanovský by Biber himself.[56]

The surviving compositions from Biber's two years in Kroměříž are:

1. *Sonata à 7,* 1668
2. *Sonatae Duae* (1668–70)
3. *3 Sonatae à 6* (1668–70)
4. *Sonata violino solo representativa* (1669)
5. *4 Sonatae* (1670)
6. *Balletti Lamentabili,* 1670
7. *Missa in Albis,* September 1668 (ascribed to "H. B."; Biber's authorship is doubtful)[57]

Example 1-3.   Biber, Final Movement of *Balletti Lamentabili* (1670)

And certain other, anonymous, Kroměříž works from these years, such as the programmatic string sonata called *Harmonia Romana* (1669) were perhaps also written by Biber.[58] The nine sonatas which make up numbers two, three and five in this list were published by Biber in the *Sonatae, tam Aris, quam Aulis servientes* (Salzburg 1676). In addition it is highly likely that some, perhaps most of the *Mystery Sonatas* were also written in Kroměříž; as we have seen, the bishop had a particular fondness for *scordatura* and programmatic devices and looked for these qualities when attempting to replace Biber, whereas in the list of Biber's known compositions for Kroměříž only the *Sonata violino solo representativa* falls into this category. In the seventeenth-century inventory of the Kroměříž collection there are, however, additional titles of lost works of Biber's of this type; one such, *Sonata seu Lyra Speculativa,* intriguingly invokes a hint of the experimental character of early seventeenth-century violin music. The *Balletti Lamentabili* perhaps bespeaks a more direct and personal relationship between programmatic content and the composer's circumstances. In October 1669 Biber apparently either became seriously ill or had an accident that brought him near death. Sehnal suggests that the composition of the *Balletti Lamentabili* might have related to this illness.[59] The work, among the last Biber wrote at Kroměříž, is a dance suite in E minor of a highly affective character, ending with a free and rhetorically conceived movement that sounds particularly indicative of new resolve at its final cadence (ex. 1-3).

Salzburg (1670–1704)

The earliest definite reference to Biber's entry into the archbishop of Salzburg's service is dated January 1671, and it is possible, though hardly likely, that a few months elapsed between his leaving Kroměříž and his finding a new position. If he did go to Salzburg at once, then he must have witnessed part of the extravagant festivities in honor of the Bavarian Elector Ferdinand Maria and his wife, who were guests of Archbishop Max Gandolph from August 24 to September 9. The main musical event was the performance of a comedy in music in sixteen scenes, *Corona laboriosa heroum virtuti imposita,* with music by Andreas Hofer.[60] Biber's name appears on the list of personnel (232 in all) who attended the archbishop on his return visit to Munich in 1671 under the category "Kammerdiener und geheimbe Kanzelistere."[61] As part of the Munich festivities the opera *L'Erinto* by Johann Caspar Kerll, written in 1661, was revived and elaborately staged; and the printed description of the archbishop's visit mentions other *divertissements.*[62] Biber might himself have played before the elector on either of these two occasions. From a biographical note written by Carl Biber for Mattheson's *Ehrenpforte* we learn that Biber was highly esteemed at the Bavarian court; both Ferdinand Maria and his successor Elector Maximilian Emmanuel presented him with a golden chain and medal in honor of his musical knowledge.[63]

Biber's official position at the archiepiscopal court in Salzburg was at first identical to the one he had held at Kroměříž: *cubicularius,* or chamber servant. In fact, in the payments records of the court he is always listed under the category of "Kammerdiener, Portier and Cammerhaizer," even after his knighthood and elevations to the ranks of Kapellmeister and Truchsess.[64] His salary in January of 1672 was eighteen florins per month; by May 1672 it had increased to twenty, perhaps because on May 30 of that year Biber married Maria Weiss, the daughter of the well-to-do Salzburg "Bürger und Handelsmann," Peter Weiss.[65] Weiss was the owner of property in Hallein as well as the "Schwabengruber'sche Behausung" in Salzburg (Judengasse 13) where Biber lived from 1672 to 1684. The marriage record makes an enigmatic reference to Biber as "Celsissimi principis cubicularius de Sachsen Somburg" (chamber servant of the most high prince [i.e., the archbishop] from "Sachsen Somburg"); if this is not completely an error it might indicate some prior service of Biber's in Saxony of which nothing further is known.[66]

During the first two years of his marriage Biber became involved in negotiations with the court concerning a piece of property with a mill in Hallein; his wife had inherited this property on the death of her father, around 1672. The Salzach overflowed that year, doing extensive damage to the property. The repairs made were not adequate to prevent further damage when the river overflowed again the following year. The series of documents relating to these events, from summer 1672 to September 1673, contains two letters by Biber and his wife, respectively, requesting the court to order the carrying out of the necessary repairs.[67] In this, as in several other instances throughout Biber's life of his dealings with the court over personal matters, we catch a glimpse of his close attention to all that was due to his position, and his straightforward ability to advance his situation in life. From humble home circumstances he had, by the early 1670s, secured a position of some influence in a well-appointed musical center, married into a prosperous family and, as the following years will show, begun to prepare his publications and to advertise his name and talents.

From Biber's first few years in Salzburg we possess a number of works whose variety and quality attest to his endeavor to demonstrate his ability both at the archbishop's court, where he probably took over musical leadership altogether, and at the cathedral, where, despite the presence of an established older composer in Andreas Hofer, he certainly made a powerful impact. Among the most outstanding works of these years are the following:[68]

1. *Serenada à 5*, 1673
2. *Arien à 4*, 1673
3. *Battalia* or *Sonata di Marche*, 1673
4. *Lux Perpetua* (1673)
5. *Sonata S. Polycarpi à 9* (1673)
6. *Sonata à 6 die pauern-Kirchfarth genandt* (1673)
7. *Trombet- und musicalischer Taffeldienst* (1673–74)
8. *Vesperae à 32*, 1674
9. *Missa Christi Resurgentis* (1674)
10. *Laetatus Sum à 7*, 1676
11. *Sonatae, tam Aris, quam Aulis servientes*, pub. 1676
12. *Mystery Sonatas*, compiled 1676(?)
13. *Sonata à 6* (after 1670)
14. *Sonata pro Tabula* (after 1670)

The styles of other undated works by Biber, the *Missa Quadragesimalis* and *Nisi Dominus*, for example, suggest that they too might have originated around this time.

The majority of Biber's programmatic pieces thus descend from his first decade in Salzburg. These years must be viewed, however, not as a time of his starting out on new paths, but as one in which Biber carried certain tendencies of his early style to their fullest development. And this is reflected in the fact that at least some of his works from the 1670s and later go back to earlier origins. Most of the *Sonatae, tam Aris* were written in Kroměříž; two of the sonatas from the *Sonatae Violino Solo* descend, as we have seen, from very early sonatas; and a movement of the *Battalia* goes back to the *Sonata violino solo representativa*. In the publications around the turn of the 1680s, on the other hand, we will find him moving away from *scordatura* and explicit programmatic devices and towards concentration on the more general technical and rhetorical features of violin playing as well as questions of style and form. The latter qualities are to be expected, of course, in published works, where the need for an immediate "entertainment" value is not present. And there were probably other reasons as well for the change in outlook. But the works from the 1670s have all the appeal of extravagance, exuberance, discovery and wonderment that is usually associated with the early seventeenth century. This quality in fact never fades in Biber's work; and it does not require *scordatura* or programmatic devices. But in the works of this decade—and again in the *Harmonia Artificiosa-Ariosa* of twenty years later—Biber the individualist stands forth more clearly than anywhere else.

The variety in the above list is striking, as is the composer's apparent desire to break free from the usual social categories in addition to those of genre and their sacred/secular functions and associations. The suites are particularly interesting in this respect. The *Serenada* includes as the fourth of an otherwise straightforward six-movement dance suite a "Ciacona" on the well-known ground-bass type of Monteverdi's madrigal "Zefiro torna"; Biber, too, used this ground in a number of pieces (including the *Missa Christi Resurgentis*), all with great effect, and perhaps with knowledge of one or another of Monteverdi's models.[69] The movement omits basso continuo and Biber instructs that the violins and violas be played pizzicato, "under the arm, like a lute"; a bass voice then enters in the middle with two verses of the Nightwatchman's song, and Biber includes a variation of the ground that bridges the gap between the chaconne and the first phrase of the song. The beginnings of the second and sixth movements, Allemande and Retirada, are derived from the chaconne bass. The *Sonata à 6 die pauern-Kirchfarth genandt* imitates a processional litany with dialogue chant-like writing in octaves for the string ensemble and includes a fervent imitation of "organo tremolante" and a rustic dance before returning to the courtly perspective for the final movement. One set of dances goes so far as to include an "Aria Barbaresca," while another contains a movement entitled "Der Werber Aria" (aria of the infantrymen), with the words "puff, puff" written in the lower parts to indicate shots. The *Battalia* is a virtual compendium of rustic, military, and purely rhetorical elements, all combined brilliantly and with the greatest technical finesse. This work is, of course, one of Biber's most famous pieces and perhaps needs no special commentary. Still, even in a quodlibet the simultaneous sounding of eight different tunes in several different keys is highly unusual for any period; this device, and the other programmatic features, such as the anticipation of the "Bartok" pizzicato to imitate cannon shots, *col legno,* and the placing of paper between the violone strings to suggest snare drums, should be viewed as an extension of traditions in seventeenth-century string playing that appear in a number of early Italian compositions, most notably in Carlo Farina's *Capriccio stravagante.*[70] Biber's immediate predecessor in this respect was, of course, Schmelzer, who produced quite a number of such pieces; his "Fechtschuel" sonata is, perhaps, closest to Biber's; and the dissonant quodlibet of Biber's *Battalia* quotes a song that appears in parallel octaves in another sonata of Schmelzer's, called "Polnische Sackpfeiffen," from the above-mentioned Rost manuscript. The *Sonata pro Tabula,* with its antiphonal choirs of recorders and strings, also contains conspicuous folk elements, now assimilated into a courtly sonata with suite-like elements; the finale in particular has much of the rustic dance character; even the *Sonata S. Polycarpi,* a majestic church sonata for eight trumpets divided antiphonally, has a very similar idea in its closing section.

These programmatic devices, and the frequent use of *scordatura* that also links Biber and Schmelzer, have an importance that goes beyond their immediate function, which even at the time was considered something of a curiosity. From the earliest history of the violin the instrument's capacity to imitate other instruments was commented on and developed, and the emergence of its own idioms was linked with this chameleon-like quality.[71] In the *Battalia* (and the *Sonata violino solo representativa* of 1668, in which an earlier form of one of the movements appears) the violin imitates the fife; in the *Trombet- und musicalischer Taffeldienst* the opening movement is entitled "Tromba luditur in violino solo"—that is, it is an intrada to be played on the violin rather than the trumpet.[72] The *Mystery Sonatas,* of course, are the apex of such violin writing, in which the fourteen different *scordature* enable the violin to imitate trumpet intradas, the wind of Pentecost, chorale singing in octaves, and other sounds. Along with the enhanced resonance of the instrument that is created by the many "harmonic" tunings, all this gives the unmistakable impression that sonority and immediate effectiveness are so prominent as to threaten to eclipse the more dynamic, intrinsically musical qualities. The obvious entertainment value of many pieces surrounds them with an aura of immediacy that is further attested to in Biber's written instructions for performing several works of the 1670s that he sent to Kroměříž from Salzburg.[73]

And these qualities are by no means confined to instrumental music. The *Vesperae à 32* and *Missa Christi Resurgentis* give great prominence to pictorial invention, incorporating also short polychoral "sonatas" as introductions and interludes; the *Laetatus Sum* and a perhaps later *Nisi Dominus,* have such sonatas for solo violin, the latter work in its elaborate violinistic techniques suggesting a merging of solo motet and violin sonata. The texts often seem to be interpreted first of all in terms of sheer sonority; countless combinations and permutations of the vocal-instrumental resources—an Et resurrexit for three basses and trumpets, equal-voice duets with changing instrumental choirs, *stile antico* movements with *colla parte* instruments, double chorus antiphony, fanfare sections, passages of chromatic coloration, brief flashes of violinistic exuberance, and so on, ad infinitum it seems—all these virtually submerge the larger sense of integration on which most later generations have placed such high value. Nothing could be more pointless than to search for thematic relationships or other hidden unifying devices between the successive sections; these may occur, of course, but their presence cannot be expected, and the sense of unity they create cannot be taken as an aesthetic yardstick. The conception of form is often additive and sectional, utilizing much immediate contrast between sections. And this is a quality that is attested to more often in reports of the early seventeenth century, which relate the listeners' astonishment at the kaleidoscopic shifting of sonorities as well as of the physical locations from which they emanated.[74] Clearly, all this was related to the emphasis on visualization that is characteristic of the counterreformation, the evoking of the spiritual by means of direct sensuality; it suggests an art that is directed toward the common man; in its attempt to elicit the immediate response of wonderment it runs the danger of shallowness when it is expected to speak to later generations. Now that it seems clear that Biber was the composer of the huge festival Mass and Hymn that were formerly attributed to Orazio Benevoli and dated 1628, this issue becomes all the more urgent.[75] The "Festmesse" was declared conservative by Bukofzer, who knew only the 1628 date, which is more than fifty years earlier than the actual date of composition.[76] His pronouncement that the elaborate instrumental surface of the work could not hide the simplicity of its underlying harmonies introduces a question of essence versus appearance that is legitimate and forces us to consider as deeply as possible the question of the historical versus the universal as it applies to Biber's work.

In this connection it is interesting to speculate that Biber was aware of these questions. In each and every one of his extant settings of the Mass Ordinary the extravagant polychoral and pictorial style is dropped for the Qui tollis, which is always set as a fugue doubled by *colla parte* instruments, and is intended to represent the *stile antico*. In most cases the sudden style change is underscored by a tonal shift, sometimes by chromaticism and a "pathetic" style for the Qui tollis as well; the ensuing Qui sedes often begins with a trumpet fanfare. The obvious sense of worldly versus spiritual that appears here in association with the words "thou that takest away the sins of the world" (and in the setting of the Sanctus in *stile antico* in several other Masses) can be considered to reflect the fact that in the Salzburg cathedral trumpets and polychoral sonority were emblems of the formal ecclesiastical hierarchy, reserved for persons of the highest authority; in addition, the participation of the court musicians was often decided on a purely monetary basis, a situation that could not fail, even in this age, to remind many of the dichotomy of the worldly and spiritual that was embodied in those who held titles such as "prince-archbishop." Biber seems here to treat the contrast of *stile antico* and *stile moderno* in a manner that recalls Ludovico Zacconi's division of the effects of music into the two categories of *effetti intrinsici* (the traditional polyphonic basis of renaissance music) and *effetti estrinsici* (the overlayering of polyphony with improvised ornamentation).[77] Like Zacconi, Biber makes no pejorative association with the extrinsic features of music's sonorous surface.

The works from Biber's Kroměříž years, and those from the first few years in Salzburg raise these issues most clearly. Their surface attractiveness is undeniable, the quality that Bishop Liechtenstein-Kastelkorn demanded first and foremost. But, in spite of Biber's association in many minds with violin technique, *scordatura,* program music, folk-influenced instrumental music, and now a sonority-oriented approach to sacred music, and in spite of the fact that Biber's style is relatively untouched by the more advanced Corellian harmonic style that leads into the late Baroque, the music speaks powerfully and without any dependence on its historical trappings. This statement is paradoxical, for until a sympathetic performance style was developed—and this took place rather recently under the somewhat doubtful aegis of the "historical" instrument revival—the majority of Biber's music had no audience at all. The appeal of the music thus appears to depend on its "historical" features in a way that is directly opposite to the more abstract, durable spirituality of the *Art of Fugue.* This view, however, is deceptive. It is not the use of historical instruments that has allowed the music to speak once more, certainly not strict adherence to the performance instructions Biber occasionally provided, but a new affinity for a music that moves in frequent changes of style that can sound arbitrary and capricious and sections that are sometimes mercilessly brief.

Biber's music from this period, like that of his contemporaries, is not concerned with the construction of elaborately integrated sound structures, or with the sustained musical projection of a single affection that subordinates all contradiction. Instead, the works often unfold a series of shifting moods that in the best works is expressive of the true "baroque" mentality of the seventeenth century. On the one hand, there was, of course, the uncertainty caused by the clash of old and new in many facets of the spiritual life. The new science and philosophy suggested a picture of a mankind less stable physically and subject to strong, almost pendular, emotional swings, who inhabited a world less certain than ever in its physical ordering, and now scarred by religious strife. On the other hand, we must remember that the greatest of these shocks had passed by the middle of the century, and a time of spiritual retrenchment existed on both the Protestant and Catholic sides, the one dominated by orthodoxy and the other by militant counterreformatory assertiveness. The mentality of the age, although dogmatic, nevertheless took a pluralistic attitude towards many facets of life; hermeneutics, science, and even the writing of music history have been so characterized.[78] The attitude toward life and death could swing between two extremes without, however, threatening spiritual destruction. In the 1690s it would be possible for Biber to write two Requiems of polarized external characteristics: the one in F minor, quintessential key of lamentation, and characterized almost entirely by a profound heavy melancholy; the other in A major, with clarini and tympani pitched in that key and a highly exceptional appearance of oboes—the expression now of worldly ecclesiastical grandeur tinged nevertheless with the fear of judgment. The individual autonomy that characterizes the eighteenth century is lacking, of course; and in keeping with the pervasive sense of social hierarchy of its time the music of the second half of the seventeenth century does not make such a display of rationalistic integrative resources as that of the eighteenth. As a result the methods of modern thematic-motivic analysis are less suited to deal with it, a situation that makes the drawing of aesthetic-evaluative conclusions more difficult. Much of what Walter Benjamin has said of the seventeenth-century tragic drama, the *Trauerspiel,* is applicable here; allegory, exhibited here in its most prominent musical form, is a corrective to the traditional aesthetic approach to art.[79] The standards of the eighteenth century cannot be applied to this music.

Pausing now to form a picture of Biber's life in his first few years in Salzburg, we are impressed with the notion of his energy and industry (not such a pejorative, anti-artistic quality as it later became). He had obviously taken over direction of the court music; there is not a single extant instrumental work by his colleague, Andreas Hofer, or even any indication that Hofer wrote instrumental music. Although Biber stood behind Hofer in line for the positions of Kapellmeister and Inspector of the Choirboys Institute, his monthly salary of twenty florins was only one florin less than that of Hofer.[80] In addition, Biber's activity was by no means limited to the court music. And, since he was asked, apparently on very short notice, to write the magnificent *Sonata S. Polycarpi* for eight trumpets for the installation of the archbishop's nephew Polykarp von Khuenburg as provost of the cathedral in 1674, we might conclude that he was a favorite of Max Gandolph's.[81] The *Vesperae à 32* and *Missa Christi Resurgentis* might also have been produced for services of special importance to the archbishop and his family that were instituted that year.[82] The *Mystery Sonatas* were certainly compiled as a personal offering to Max Gandolph. Perhaps as a result of Biber's influence, in 1677 Max Gandolph reorganized the Choirboys Institute and had its house rebuilt. Biber was appointed teacher of figural music, but a lesser violinist taught the choirboys that instrument.[83] When we consider these facts along with the court's purchase of string instruments from Stainer and the increase in the number of court musicians during Biber's Salzburg years, it appears an inevitable conclusion that Biber actively spurred on the archbishop's interest in music.[84]

Then, in either this or the following year, Max Gandolph took another important step for the Salzburg court music when he hired another of the greatest musicians in Europe, the Alsatian organist, Georg Muffat, a cosmopolitan musician who had studied with Lully in Paris, and who provided a fascinatingly complementary figure to Biber.[85] Apparently Muffat came to Salzburg by way of Prague; a Kroměříž violin sonata of his bears at the end the perhaps autograph remark, "G. Muffat. Pragae 2 Julii 1677."[86] This work makes an interesting starting point for our understanding of the markedly different outlooks of the two men, as well as a deeper affinity that makes us regret our lack of any information concerning either their musical or personal relationship in Salzburg. Muffat's sonata is, despite striking differences from Biber's solos, an equally individualistic work, but one that betrays in its extravagant tonal devices the keyboard player more than the violinist. There are no double stops, even in the fugal second section; and, although the lengthy middle part of the work is conceived as a fantasy, just as are many of the sections of Biber's *Sonatae Violino Solo,* the violin writing never pushes the player to the limits that many of the Biber sonatas do. But if this is a lack, it is made up for by the extraordinary enharmonic modulations that are unique in the violin literature of the seventeenth century. Only a few years later Andreas Werckmeister would characterize such devices, pejoratively, as "grosse Metamorphoses in der Harmonie."[87] Muffat achieves in this work a fusion of the toccata-like elements and the ideas of the suite and sonata; apart from the daring middle section, free improvisatory passages lead into and out of the canzona-like second movement and the gigue-like fourth; the same adagio sonata movement begins and ends the work. Despite their differences, there is a great affinity between Muffat's sonata and the solos of Biber's *Sonatae Violino Solo* in their manifest dualism of strict and free elements. Years later Muffat would fuse these elements in the organ toccatas of his *Apparatus musico-organisticus* (1690) in terms of French and Italian styles; and, of course, he is famous for his claim of having been the first to introduce the Lullyian ballet style into Germany and his anticipation of the "gemischter Geschmack" of the eighteenth century through the joining of the Lullyian and Corellian elements of his style.[88] This cosmopolitan, forward-looking element in Muffat's work, has little parallel in Biber's. The coordination of strict and free sonata and suite elements in the *Sonatae Violino Solo* is remarkable, but it does not involve the invocation of outside influences. Herein, perhaps, lies the greatest difference between the two men, and the one that, no doubt, prompted Archbishop Max Gandolph to send Muffat rather than Biber to Rome to absorb the newer Italian styles under Bernardo Pasquini and Corelli. There is a pronounced—and one is tempted to say Germanic—conservatism in Biber's work that coexists with the extraordinary advances in violin technique and is in no way to be considered a denigratory feature.

Presumably the personal and professional interaction between Biber and Muffat at the Salzburg court was fruitful for both men. Biber's intensive activity in the publication of instrumental music in the early 1680s might be a sign of a certain rivalry in that area. Muffat had little to do with the church music other than as organist; no church works of his are known, and his name does not appear in the cathedral protocol books. We have no information about Biber's and Muffat's playing together, and almost none regarding Muffat's presumed introduction of the ballet and concerto styles at the court; there is very little sign in Biber's music of an influence from either of those quarters, although the general impact of Muffat's presence might be considered a factor in his apparent turning away from *scordatura* and program music in the works of the early 1680s. Biber's ensemble sonatas and suites are in any case far closer than Muffat's to older seventeenth-century types. Biber published very little instrumental music after this period, and none until after Muffat had left Salzburg—which may be indicative of changes in his duties that took place with his promotion to Kapellmeister in 1684. The attitude of the two men toward program music is strikingly different. Muffat's titles, such as "Patientia," "Bona Nova," "Convalescentia," "Quis hic?" and "Deliciae Regum," do not refer to the imitation of anything extra-musical by means of musico-allegorical devices; rather, they seem to point even beyond the baroque age in their fanciful subjective character. And Muffat was completely uninterested in folk music. At a somewhat later date Muffat spoke in one of his prefaces about the "immoderate runs" and "ill-sounding" leaps of German violinists, a remark that reveals a fundamental antagonism between French and German music of the time; still later Muffat qualified his statement in a manner that suggests closer familiarity with the virtues of the German players; one might imagine that he had Biber in mind.[89] Certainly, in terms of the basic rift that was often seen between French and Italian music (and art), the one closer to being classical in spirit and the other baroque, the Germans in general were far nearer to the Italians in the seventeenth century; and in the area of violin playing they were more baroque even than the Italians. We might perhaps say that while Muffat drew strength from the interaction of French and Italian styles, Biber concerned himself more with the uniting of folk (German) and more elevated, international (Italian) elements. Salzburg had, of course, profound and long-standing leanings towards Italy, and it was perhaps this that led Max Gandolph to send Muffat to Rome, just as it must have been a certain turning away from Italy to things German and an anti-French spirit later in the century that caused Muffat to leave Salzburg.[90]

According to a 1681 letter by Biber, he performed some of his sonatas before the Emperor Leopold at Laxenburg (near Vienna) in 1677.[91] He was rewarded by Leopold with a golden chain and a "Gnaden Bildnus" (i.e., a medal bearing the emperor's likeness). He is shown wearing this decoration in the engraving that prefaces his *Sonatae Violino Solo,* 1681. On January 12, 1679, Biber became Vice-Kapellmeister, with a "rank and position immediately after [the archbishop's] superintendents and court judges in Chiembsee, St. Peter and Nonnberg, who are not councillors."[92] This detailed spelling-out of rank can be observed in more detail in a formal court document of 1684, entitled *Praecedenz-Ordnung,* "according to which our court servants, high as well as low, and also other persons, have from henceforth to conduct and order themselves."[93] In a rigidly hierarchical scheme of thirty-one numbered degrees, Biber's old position of chamber servant was number twenty-nine; his new position, not named in the document, moved him immediately below number twenty-six, while his future positions of *Kapellmeister* in 1684 and *Truchsess* (Lord High Steward) in 1692 would move him to levels eighteen and eleven, respectively.

In the early 1680s Biber published three collections of instrumental music. The *Mensa Sonora* (1680) comprises table music for the Salzburg court, while the *Sonatae Violino Solo* (1681) represents one of the highest peaks of seventeenth-century violin music. His *Fidicinium Sacro-Profanum* (1682 or 1683) contains twelve string ensemble sonatas designated, like the *Sonatae, tam Aris, quam Aulis servientes,* explicitly for both court and church use; in the preface Biber refers to this publication as his fourth opus. The print contains a Latin dedicatory poem from the Nuremberg music lovers ("Philomusici Noribergenses"), an indication, presumably, of his renown. In addition, new editions of the *Mensa Sonora* and *Sonatae, tam Aris, quam Aulis servientes* appeared in 1681 and the *Sonatae Violino Solo* were reprinted in 1684.[94] There are differences now between the works of the early 1680s and those of the preceding decade. The *Sonatae Violino Solo* make far less use of *scordatura* than the *Mystery Sonatas,* and they are considerably more advanced in the area of violin technique as well as formal conception; the suites of the *Mensa Sonora* and the sonatas of the *Fidicinium Sacro-Profanum* are both much less involved with programmatic devices than the earlier manuscript suites and sonatas; and there is less emphasis on elaborate violinistic writing than there is in even the *Sonatae, tam Aris.* Biber is presumably attempting to reach a wider audience. Between the years 1680 and 1683 Biber received gifts of money from the Benedictine monastery at Kremsmünster, some of which was given in return for a copy of the *Sonatae Violino Solo* which Biber sent there.[95] In 1684 the payments cease, perhaps, as Altmann Kellner suggests, because Biber was promoted to Kapellmeister in that year, or because he had stopped publishing instrumental music. However, Biber continued to send manuscripts of instrumental music to the monastery; an inventory of music copied there in the year 1686 lists sonatas and *balletti,* all of which are lost today. Kellner also suggests that Biber might have supplied music for the Kremsmünster theatre.[96]

Clearly Biber was promoting his name and talents around the turn of the 1680s. On the strength of his renown and a second presentation of some of his works before Emperor Leopold, very likely in February or March of 1681, Biber petitioned the emperor for knighthood in May 1681. Leopold was, of course, a great lover of music and a talented composer; he was known to reward musicians with knighthoods, and Biber would probably have known this, for Schmelzer was one of those so honored.[97] In his letter, which survives, Biber reminds the emperor of the performances at Laxenburg in 1677, and refers to recent presentations of his *Sonatae Violino Solo* and other compositions for Leopold at Linz and Lambach.[98] Nettl suggests the dates 1673 and 1683 for Biber's second performance before the emperor.[99] Both dates are impossible in light of Biber's letter. I have proposed February or March 1681, because at that time Kaiser Leopold was in Linz on return from Prague. In March he travelled to Altötting, Bavaria, where he met Elector Max Emmanuel.[100] Quite possibly he travelled by way of Lambach and stayed for a while at the convent there. Biber could have travelled with the emperor's party and played for Leopold at the monastery; Lambach is directly on the route from Linz to Salzburg. It could not have been much before 1681 that the performances at Linz and Lambach took place. Biber's words "anizo auch wiederumb" ("and now once again") suggest that the event was recent. In any case, it must definitely have occurred after 1677, and the "Violino Solo ins Kupfer gegeben" that Biber says he played can only have been one of the *Sonatae Violino Solo* of 1681. Biber's petition was denied.

The year 1682 marks one of the greatest celebrations in the history of Salzburg: the 1100th anniversary of the founding of the archdiocese by St. Rupert.[101] From the seventeenth to the twenty-sixth of October numerous special services were held throughout the city's several churches; and the court musicians played in other churches as the archbishop held services outside the cathedral.[102] The occasion prompted the dedication of at least two, and probably three printed collections of music to Max Gandolph.[103] For the celebration Georg Muffat returned to Salzburg from Rome where he had been sent by the archbishop to study the newer musical styles.[104] Carl Biber's reference, almost sixty years later, to the "Jubeljahr" 1682 in a biographical note on his father reveals that the magnificence of the festivities was long remembered in Salzburg.[105] Although Carl Biber did not detail the role played by music, or his father's part in the celebrations, we know that several services were held every day in the city's four main churches, and many of these services featured musical performances. In the Fransciscan church, for example, at four o'clock in the afternoon of the seventeenth the court musicians performed a litany for all saints. On the twenty-sixth the anniversary ended with a sermon and high Mass "solemnessime gehalten" (celebrated very festively), an expression used frequently in descriptions of lavish musical events in the cathedral.[106] The central performances, however, were those of a high Mass and a *Te Deum*, the former before and the latter after a huge procession that took place on Sunday the eighteenth. It now appears very likely that Biber produced the fifty-three-part Mass, now known as the *Missa Salisburgensis*, and the identically scored Hymn to St. Rupert, *Plaudite Tympana*, that were formerly attributed to Orazio Benevoli, for these 1682 festivities.[107] An engraving by Melchior Küsel of a polychoral performance in the cathedral with the court musicians has survived from the "Jubeljahr."[108] The performance represented matches up closely with much that is known of the performing resources and cathedral appointments (see chapter 2). But the scale of the work shown is that of Biber's *Missa Christi Resurgentis*, *Vesperae à 32*, *Missa Alleluia*, and a number of others, including works by Andreas Hofer; the *Missa Salisburgensis* approximately doubles these resources. We must presume that the engraving was prepared well ahead of time (in order to be ready for publication in 1682) and represents an idealized version of the normal scale of polychoral performances in the cathedral, not a record of exactly what occurred in 1682 (although, of course, it is likely that performances with the normal polychoral arrangement also took place).[109]

On March 6, 1684, after the death of Hofer, Biber was made Kapellmeister, "in consideration of his good qualities and also diligent services carried out to date to our satisfaction and still hoped from him"; he now occupied the official position "after the rural deans and sacred doctors."[110] In the same year he also became Inspector of the Choirboys Institute and lived in the *Capellhaus*.[111] With the death of Hofer and Biber's becoming Kapellmeister his duties increased in the area of the cathedral music, not only in terms of composition and performance but also in administrative responsibility. Before this time matters relating to church music were referred generally to Hofer, and Biber's name hardly appeared in the official *Prothocollum capitulare* books. But now, in 1685, we find, for example, the record of a notice to Biber concerning the music for a particular anniversary service at the cathedral. Biber is informed that the music will no longer be performed below in the choir (as it formerly was) but instead will be more ornate, making use of organ and court musicians.[112] This marked change in Biber's musical duties is, no doubt, part of the reason for his ceasing to publish instrumental music between the early 1680s and the year 1696. There are also far fewer manuscript instrumental works extant that can be definitely dated to the 1680s in comparison with the number from the preceding decade. And, apart from the *Missa Salisburgensis* and *Plaudite Tympana,* only one Mass, the *Missa Catholica* (which has survived in incomplete form) can be placed in the 1680s, whereas after 1690 Biber's intense activity in the area of church music is amply documented with surviving compositions. The *Missa Catholica,* moreover, is both shorter and less extravagantly scored than Biber's other concerted Masses, a characteristic of the *Vesperae Longiores ac Breviores* (Salzburg 1693) as well, some of which were surely produced in the 1680s.

These facts have given rise to the notion, sometimes encountered in early literature on Biber, that his creative activity declined in the 1680s.[113] But this view is inaccurate, for it fails to take account of another very significant change in Biber's compositional activity around that time: the year 1684 marks the beginning of his music-dramatic composition, which would from henceforth demand a great part of his creative activity. During the next fifteen years he wrote music for at least two operas, *Alesandro in Pietra* (1689) and *Chi la dura la vince* (1690–92), a three-act cantata (*Tratenimento musicale,* 1698) and thirteen schooldramas, some of which were on the scale of operas; the operas and cantata were performed at the court by court singers, while the schooldramas took place at the university.[114] A presentation copy of the score of *Chi la dura la vince* has survived, along with the texts of the *Tratenimento musicale* and *Alesandro in Pietra* and various operas and schooldramas by Biber, Hofer and Muffat.[115] Otherwise, not a single note of Salzburg's dramatic music from the seventeenth century is extant. *Chi la dura la vince* is a drama on the story of the German hero of Roman times, Arminius, with intermingled comic scenes after the seventeenth-century Venetian model. The work moves within the basic framework of alternating secco recitative and short strophic arias accompanied by basso continuo only, but with instrumental ritornelli that are usually thematically related to the arias, yet almost always separated from the vocal sections by means of full cadences with pauses. The arias exhibit a variety of types and styles, with a heavy preponderance of the so-called "Devisen-aria" type.[116] There is a remarkable attention to key structure, however; in a general way the first and third acts, both in C major, favor modulations to the flat key areas, while the second act, in G major, modulates more extensively to the sharp keys. The limits are those of the late seventeenth and early eighteenth centuries generally, F minor and E major.[117] The virtuoso element familiar from Biber's violin music is generally not in evidence, although there is one military aria for tenor with trumpets and timpani that is conspicuously elaborate and difficult. We must recognize, in light of the occasional appearance of aria-like solos in Biber's later church music and his closer attention in those works to key structure and extension, that the experience of opera made a lasting impact on his style.

Archbishop Max Gandolph died in 1687, three months after becoming cardinal. Biber might have written a Requiem for his funeral services, which were accompanied by the court musicians; however, the two surviving Requiems by him were copied, and presumably composed, after 1690. The archbishop's death divides Biber's years in Salzburg into two periods of seventeen years each. While his creative life cannot be split so simply into two style periods, the change from Max Gandolph to Johann Ernst, Graf von Thun, had considerable influence on Biber's work. From the beginning of Johann Ernst's tenure, Biber's years of regular production of chamber music for the court were over. Under his new patron Biber published only one collection of instrumental music, whereas under Archbishop Max Gandolph he had compiled five. The last record concerning the copying of Biber's instrumental works at Kremsmünster is dated 1687, and the *Balletti à 6* is the only extant manuscript instrumental work composed by Biber after 1687. During the rule of the unmusical archbishop, Johann Ernst, musicians played in the church services but chamber music at the court must have been far less cultivated.[118] Yet it is also clear that the numbers of court musicians rose significantly in the last years of the seventeenth century, presumably in connection with opera and church performances rather than chamber music. The branches of Biber's creative activity that were least affected by the accession of Johann Ernst were church music and schooldramas. We cannot know Biber's feelings about the change of emphasis in his compositional duties, but it is entirely plausible that the new situation was agreeable to him and that he welcomed the challenge to abilities that he had not hitherto developed. Unlike Georg Muffat, who left Salzburg in 1690, Biber apparently continued on the best of terms with his new master.

During the *sedes vacans* Biber and two other court employees petitioned for financial aid in recognition of their faithful services. They were all remembered when 5000 florins were divided among the "faithful members of the court and archiepiscopate." Biber's share of 35 florins was the smallest on the list, most of the recipients being high court officials and members of the nobility.[119] Another petition of Biber's around the same time concerns his duty as Inspector of the Choirboys Institute. This duty had apparently been withdrawn from him. Biber reminded the chapter that the "inspection" belonged to his office, and requested that it be entrusted to him. He assured the chapter that both court and cathedral music would be better provided for in the future by means of the selection of qualified choirboys. The petition was granted for the duration of the *sedes vacans*.[120]

In 1690 Biber petitioned Emperor Leopold a second time for knighthood, apparently with greater expectation of success this time, for he included the design for his coat of arms. In his letter he reminds the emperor of the chain and medal of honor bestowed on him in 1677, and says, "I have also come so far, by means of my slight application in music, that my name is known at many great courts...."[121] Even with our limited knowledge of Biber's travels, the preceding statement appears to be no exaggeration.[122] Biber's second petition was granted. In a formal decree, the emperor acknowledges the qualifications Biber mentioned in his application and observes Biber's "good breeding, honesty, noble good sense, virtue and intelligence" as well as his "agreeable, loyal, obedient and willing service."[123] A letter of Biber's is preserved, in which he notifies the archbishop of his knighthood and asks that the fact be published.[124] It was made public in Salzburg on December 5, 1690.[125]

Two years later Biber's status at the archiepiscopal court was elevated yet again. On November 3, 1692 (not 1684 or 1690), he was made *Truchsess* (Latin "dapifer") or Lord High Steward.[126] Presumably, a raise in salary accompanied each of his promotions, but payments records have not survived for the years between 1674, when his monthly salary was twenty florins, and 1694, by which time it had risen to sixty.[127] The Salzburg "Personenbeschreibung" book informs us that in 1692 Biber's household numbered nine persons.[128] In view of the size of his family, it is likely that at this time he received some or all of the additional material benefits that supplemented his salary in 1700.[129] In 1693 Biber published his largest collection by far, the *Vesperae Longiores ac Breviores,* consisting of twenty-nine psalms and a set of *Litaniae Lauretanae.* He now used his new title, "dapifer ac Capellae Magister." His coat of arms is reproduced along with a Latin congratulatory poem headed "In Nobile ac Gentilitium Insigne Nobilis Domini Authoris" and signed "Musici Archi-Episcopales Salisburgensis." The same year Biber honored the Abbot of Mondsee with a "neue Vesper," presumably a copy of the print, and received accordingly a gift of six florins from the Abbot."[130]

By this time Biber was a famous man. He was listed by Printz (*Historische Beschreibung,* 1690) among the "newer and more famous composers and musicians of the century," and Daniel Merck (*Compendium Musicae Instrumentalis Chelicae,* 1695) referred to him as a renowned violinist along with Walther and Westhoff. Along with the considerable material benefits he enjoyed and his increased social status by the early 1690s, Biber must have desired more time for himself and the musical upbringing of his children. The departure of Georg Muffat from Salzburg in 1690 might have added to Biber's compositional duties. The need to lighten his official burden is no doubt reflected in his giving up the position of Inspector of the Choirboys Institute in that year. [131] By the mid 1690s at least three of Biber's children were in their teens. They all exhibited considerable musical ability, and three of them later held musical positions in Salzburg. [132] A strain of string playing continues through several generations of the Biber family and no doubt can be traced back to Biber's expert instruction of his children. We are fortunate in possessing a manual prepared by Biber in 1694 for his seventeen-year-old daughter, Maria Anna Magdalena. [133] This little booklet was intended as an aid in teaching rudiments and singing; from the fact that the twelve melodies "per cantar à battuta" that end the book appear to be single parts in a duet texture, we can conclude that Biber perhaps compiled a similar notebook for one of his other children. [134]

Biber's advancement to knighthood in 1690 had a very important consequence for his children, and one that he must have foreseen. His daughters were now eligible to enter convents reserved for daughters of the nobility; and one such was in Salzburg: *Stift Nonnberg,* the oldest Benedictine *Frauenstift* in the German-speaking lands (founded about 700 by St. Rupert for his niece St. Erentraud). Nonnberg, moreover, played a very important role in the musical life of the city. The brief records of events at the convent, which cover all of Biber's Salzburg years, make regular mention of musical performances (usually every few days, or at least every few weeks). [135] And these records are more interesting than those of the cathedral, which are inevitably formal and impersonal; the Nonnberg records sometimes mention the titles of works performed, the composers, the instrumentation, and other details, such as how the music was enjoyed and the rewards given to the musicians. The nuns themselves were capable of performing elaborate figural music, even without outside assistance, which was nevertheless also made use of regularly; and they were justly proud of the fact that only exceptional circumstances forced them to sing "choraliter" (plainchant), such as when, on one occasion, the musicians arrived late (even then the Mass was "musiziert" from the "Credo" on), or on another the musicians could not be placed in time, or on a third no antiphon for the particular feast was available in figural style; on yet another occasion, when the organist was away, the nuns sang figural music with violone accompaniment. [136] The norm was that Mass and Vespers were often "musiziert"; trumpet "Aufzügen" (Intradas) and "Larmae" (presumably fanfares) were played at beginnings and endings of services and for the entrance of important persons; and "Mezzopunte" (short, presumably ritornello-like instrumental pieces) were played, either with the Intradas or *as* Intradas; even, at times, the sermon was broken by the insertion of "Mezzopunte" as interludes. [137] Sonatas were played and motets sung for the offertory, elevation, communion, and at the beginnings and endings of services. Biber, of course, knew of the active musical life at Nonnberg, for the court musicians sometimes accompanied the archbishop to the convent for special services. From his earliest years in the city we read, for example, that on the feast of St. Matthew a Mass and "Veni Creator" were provided by Max Gandolph and the court musicians, or that, a few years later, for the feast of Saints Simon and Judas, Max Gandolph read Mass, while the court musicians performed "schöne Muteten" as well as the hymn "Veni Creator" and at the end the "Te Deum." [138] Usually for visits of the archbishop the court musicians were in attendance; but for Corpus Christi 1691 Johann Ernst sent Biber to inquire if the nuns wished to perform the music themselves at Mass; upon Biber's interpreting this request as the archbishop's real desire, the nuns were proud to perform the whole service themselves. [139]

Biber's daughter Maria Anna Magdalena entered the convent at the age of nineteen as a novice in 1695 and took orders there the following year as M. Rosa Henrica.[140] The Sunday before this latter occasion was the feast day of St. Henry (July 15), who was emperor in the early eleventh century and was especially revered at Nonnberg as the "second founder" of the convent.[141] He was also, of course, Biber's name saint. And it appears certain that this concurrence of events was carefully planned, for on the fifteenth the Prior of St. Peter sang the Mass of St. Henry at Nonnberg, and the court musicians performed music written for the occasion by Biber.[142] The work in question is, of course, the *Missa S. Henrici,* now preserved at Kremsmünster in a copy dated 1701; the work can now be dated 1696, and its departure from the more common eight-part double chorus arrangment of most of his other Masses is no doubt owing to its having been written for performance at Nonnberg.[143] It is interesting in this connection to note that another of Biber's daughters, Maria Zäzilia, (called after the patron saint of music), who was three years older than Anna Magdalena, entered the Clarissen convent of Sancta Clara at Meran; we know from a seventeenth-century inventory of works now lost that were in the library of Stift Michaelbeueren that Biber also wrote a *Missa Sanctae Clarae,* undoubtedly for his daughter's taking the veil there;[144] St. Claire's feast day, August 12, was Biber's birthday. Over and again in counterreformation Germany we encounter the sense of an almost mysterious power in the name as a link to perpetuity; and Salzburg was no exception. Biber had written a *Sonata S. Polycarpi* for the name day of the archbishop's nephew; his lost *Missa Praecursoris Domini,* also listed at Michaelbeurn, would have been written for the name saint of Archbishop Johann Ernst (John the Baptist, whose feast day was always especially celebrated by the archbishop); and Archbishop Max Gandolph, among many others, had instituted name-day services (called *Anniversaria* or *Jahrtage*) for his family at the cathedral, for which the court musicians played; the *Mystery Sonatas* have a preface by Biber explaining the significance of the letter "M"—"Sic Maria Maximilianum condecoravit"—as joining the mysteries of the Virgin Mary to the name Maximilian. The Passacaglia for unaccompanied violin from this collection that Biber associated with the guardian angel expresses this desire for an almost physical nearness, a symbolic link to the other world. The attempt to make a link between the spiritual world and that of the senses was, as suggested above, a strong impulse behind much Counterreformation art, an impulse that was given a personal tone in the celebration of name saints. By this time Biber was able to arrange similar occasions for himself and provide his own music.

Biber's connections to Nonnberg, however, go back earlier than his daughter's entry there, and might have paved the way for his contriving a festive Mass for the feast of his own name saint. On the day following Trinity Sunday 1692 (for which the court musicians had celebrated Mass "auf das schönist"), a "schöne Taffelmusic" was held, after which "Herr Biber" and two other musicians played "auf den lieblichen Instrumenten [i.e., harpsichord] mit 2 Geigen Viol: d'Amor genant eine grosse Zeit."[145] We have, in Biber's *Harmonia Artificiosa-Ariosa* (1696) a long suite for two viole d'amore, that could have been played at this occasion. The instrument in question, which is mentioned from time to time in the Nonnberg records and for which several solo motet-like pieces have survived at Nonnberg, was a six-stringed viola d'amore based on a "normal" tuning entirely in fifths from the top string of the violin downward, a tuning that appears never to have been used, since all surviving pieces from the Salzburg repertory are in *scordatura.*[146] Several exemplars of the instrument have survived in the Salzburg Museum.[147] In its incorporating the tuning of the violin and viola on its upper five strings the instrument was obviously suited to easy substitution by available violin players. Biber might, in fact, have been largely responsible for the popularity of the instrument in

Salzburg; his daughter Anna Magdalena also played it; and it is possible that one or another of the anonymous pieces in the Nonnberg archive are by Biber or one of his children. Apart from the above-mentioned suite, all we know of Biber's for this instrument is a lost composition entitled "Aria de Passione Domini: Wer gibt meinen Augen. Alt. Sol., 2 Viola di amor, 2 Flauten, 3 Instr. [continuo?]" from the Michaelbeuern inventory. [148]

Throughout the 1690s there are fairly frequent references to performances at Nonnberg at which the court musicians participated; and for some occasions, such as the funeral services in 1693 for the abbess, there are extant works of Biber's that might have been performed. [149] Then, on the night of August 27, 1703, for two hours, as part of the festivities for a noble wedding the archbishop had a "stately Serenade" performed by the court musicians "with trumpets, violin, lutes and all kinds of other instruments." Any nuns wishing to hear were given permission to do so by the abbess. The record notes that from the convent no one from outside was honored except the Kapellmeister, who received "4. Viertel Wein. Man hat die Music gar schen herauf gehört." [150] Less than two weeks after this, on September 8, a relative of the archbishop's, Countess Maria Madgalena Antonia von Thun was married at Nonnberg, and a detailed description of the ceremonies was recorded. Mass at the cathedral was held an hour earlier than usual, so that the court musicians could attend at Nonnberg. The great convent bell was rung until the archbishop arrived, then all the convent bells sounded at once until he entered the "Oratorium" and the trumpets played a fanfare (*Larma*) as he entered the church. Another fanfare was played as the bride threw the bridal wreath, after which the nuns performed a "Veni Sancte" by one Egglmayr with the organ. The archbishop himself celebrated Mass, which was performed by the court musicians with trumpets and timpani; the record notes that it had to be short, as a result of the bride's prior entreaty to the Kapellmeister, since she had to kneel for the whole Mass; among the other music mentioned was a "Veni Creator" played by the court musicians. At the end all the bells rang again and two castrati sang the "Regnum Mundi." This last piece was perhaps also by Biber, since later in the same month, at the end of a "Profession" or vows-taking service a "Regnum Mundi" of "herrn Piber" for organ, two sopranos and two violins was played. [151] A few days after the above-mentioned wedding it is noted in the record that the abbess invited to Nonnberg as guests of the father confessor several employees of the court who had served the convent especially well at the wedding; four of these—"herrn Kuchelmaister, herrn CapelMaister, herrn Controlor, herrn ConfectMaister"— all went away "very well satisfied." [152] Plenty of further references to music at Nonnberg perhaps involve compositions of Biber's, such as on September 10, 1704, a few months after Biber's death, when we read that the court musicians performed "ein Völlige Sonata" at the beginning of a service, later a motet with two altos and two gambas, and at the end another "Völlige Sonata"; [153] but the next specific reference to him will be that of his death, which is, characteristically, entered in a much more personal tone than it is in the court and cathedral records.

In the last decade of his life Biber sought to avoid hindrances in his compositional (and teaching?) activity. In 1695 he petitioned the court for the construction of a summer house in a garden near the Loretto Convent. He had, according to Schneider and Nettl, fought almost two decades for a peaceful place to work, and had already been allotted a piece of property in the early 1680s. He wanted, so the petition reads, a "little garden so that [he] have a little distraction, also a diversion at [his] *studio musicistico*. Biber's petition was finally granted and he reported that he had planted a little garden, cultivated wine and had a small wooden house built for 100 florins. [154] In this same year Biber entered his name as the first in a new book donated by Johann Ernst to the Holy Cross Brotherhood at the "Bürgerspitalskirche," a brotherhood founded in 1683 by Max Gandolph that later numbered W. A. Mozart among its members. The brotherhood was founded to enable those who were accustomed to attend Mass daily to make special devotions, feasts and meditations on the Passion of Christ, in particular the finding of the cross (May 3) and the exaltation of the cross (September 14).[155]

In the years just before and after the turn of the eighteenth century some of the kinds of administrative situations arose in connection with the *Choralisten,* or lay singers, and the Choirboys Institute that Biber had probably needed relief from. In 1698 Archbishop Johann Ernst quarreled with the cathedral chapter over the traditional right of the dean to choose the members of the choir, particularly the *Choralisten.* This right had encouraged the use of incompetent persons in the church music. Finally, in 1701 the archbishop decreed that at the admission of clerical and lay choir members (*Chorvikarien* and *Choralisten*) he would, in the presence of both choir directors (*Chorregenten*) and the Kapellmeister, arrange a "Concurs" with the competitors.[156] This problem was probably part of a larger one, since in 1699 two choirboys were dismissed from the *Capellhaus* and a third, who was *"in cantu* almost the best," petitioned to be released from the institute. That same year the *Capellhaus* was without an instructor for four months, until finally the order to find a replacement was communicated to the Kapellmeister; a *Praeceptor* was also hired.[157] These incidents, although not nearly so hotly contested by the parties involved, call to mind J. S. Bach's difficulties in Leipzig. Peregrinus believed that Biber used his influence with Johann Ernst to effect these reforms, crediting improvements in the court and church music as well as in the musicians' material conditions to the Kapellmeister's efforts.[158]

From February 6–10, 1699, the archbishop was visited by Emperor Leopold's son, Joseph, King of Rome and Hungary, later himself Emperor Joseph I, and his bride Wilhelmina Amalia, Duchess of Braunschweig-Lüneburg. The festivities were the most elaborate since 1682, and were commemorated in a substantial published booklet detailing the service at table, the celebration of Masses in the cathedral, the royal procession, the various triumphal arches erected in the city and their allegorical significance, the flowing of red and white Tyrolian and Austrian wine from four pipes of a public city fountain, the casting of coins from the residence for the people, and so on. For one *Tafelmusik* in the residence the duchess took part in the music and at another the prince of Liechtenstein played the lute.[159] The descriptions of the High Masses do not refer to the music; possibly the very long and festive Mass from this period formerly thought to be of Benevoli and published as the *Missa Bruxellensis* was heard on one of these occasions; it is copied in the same hand and score format as the *Missa Salisburgensis,* and was perhaps kept as a commemorative score. It is in all probability a work of Biber's.[160] On this occasion Biber's *Tratenimento Musicale,* a three-act drama with music for soloists, instrumentalists, large chorus and dancers was performed; the text of this highly allegorical work—with the characters of Homage, Love, Fame and Gaiety— was printed, along with engravings of the "Trabantensaal" in the residence, where a stage was erected; but the music has not survived.[161] The brief description of the performance of this *Serenada* refers to over one hundred musicians all costumed for the entertainment; trumpets and drums played for Joseph's entrance, and after he had taken his place under a "Baldachin," a sign was given and fifty cannon shots were fired, upon which the performance began with full chorus accompanied by trumpets and drums. After the *Tratenimento,* as well as during each of the intermissions between the acts (designated *Cantata prima, seconda, terza*), fifty more cannon shots were fired. This was Biber's last stage work.

By this time Biber enjoyed the peak of his success and fame. His income, as reported in the court records for the year 1700, was as follows:[162]

"Herr Franz Hainrich von Bibern
Capellmaister" monthly 60:
Annually .... florins 720:—:
2/4 Austrian wine from the court cellar
and 2 pairs of rolls daily .... florins 116:10:
12 cords of spruce-wood from the court chest .... florins   16:—:
Also free accommodation in the "Maudthaus"
                                                                    _____
                                                       Annually: florins: 852:10:

This amount may be compared with the 180 gulden annually that Vejvanovský received at the peak of his career at Kroměříž, and the 2000 florins which was the annual salary of the Vienna court Kapellmeister.[163]

The last works of Biber's that have survived are the following:[164]

1. *Balletti à 6,* around 1690
2. *Requiem à 15,* after 1690
3. *Requiem ex F con terza min:,* after 1692
4. *Vesperae Longiores ac Breviores,* 1693
5. *Harmonia Artificiosa-Ariosa,* 1696 (new edition 1712)
6. *Missa S. Henrici,* 1696
7. *Missa Alleluia,* after 1690
8. *Missa ex B,* around 1695–1704?
9. *Stabat Mater,* after 1690
10. *Muttetum Natale* (1690s?)
11. *Litania de S. Josepho à 20,* after 1692
12. *Offertorium de S: Michaele,* after 1690
13. *Offertorium pro festo 7 Dolorum à 8,* after 1690
14. *Huc Poenitentes,* after 1696
15. *Missa Bruxellensis,* after 1696
16. *Chi la dura la vince* (1690–92?)

This list is heavily dominated by church music, which, along with stage works, filled Biber's later years. It is to be presumed, of course, that still other church works that are now lost, including some of a more intimate character such as the *Regnum Mundi* produced at Nonnberg, were composed during these years. Further compositions may even survive at Nonnberg, where a large part of the holdings from the seventeenth century consists of anonymous works.[165] It is a wonder, in light of the large number of church works from this period—and the *Vesperae Longiores ac Breviores* alone comprises thirty works—that Biber was able to produce any instrumental music at all. But the one collection we have from him, the *Harmonia Artificiosa-Ariosa,* is highly interesting; for in it Biber returns to the *scordatura* tunings he had perhaps largely abandoned after the 1670s. Once again we hear the shimmering resonance of chordal tunings; the A major suite for two violins and the large final suite for two viole d'amore are the most interesting in this respect, with their extended chordal preludes over sustained pedal tones. The A major suite concludes with a chaconne for two violins in canon at the unison over the "Zefiro torna" ground bass that Biber had used several times in the 1670s; here the effect is of a wonderful exuberance in the elaborate violin writing, a kind of last flowering of the spirit of the seventeenth century. These pieces, like virtually all the others from the list, exhibit another quality that belongs more markedly to Biber's later years: their length. The extension of sections and individual movements stands as a move away from the canzona-like sections of the early chamber music and church works and toward the style of the eighteenth century. There is in evidence now a new seriousness of approach to the problems of musical composition, an attitude that must have been intensified by Biber's operatic experience, possibly also by teaching and study. While the virtuosity and extravertedness of the earlier compositions are still present, we now encounter a higher incidence of the planned as opposed to the improvised, a tighter control of the intellectual over the sensuous.

The Masses from this period, for example, attain almost unheard-of lengths when compared with the seventeenth-century average, and these lengths reflect the expansion of what would formerly be called sections into what must now be called movements. The *Missa ex B* for six-part chorus and organ, for example, has an obviously planned overall structure. Twelve of its twenty-two movements are in *stile antico,* in quadruple meter headed *alla breve,* while the remainder, all in triple meter, manifest varieties of the *stile moderno* for chorus; the two styles alternate regularly throughout the Mass. Most of the works exhibit carefully planned key structures; even the twelve-movement *Balletti à 6,* the opera, and the *Vesperae Longiores ac Breviores* fit this pattern.[166] The increased dimensions of the works are sometimes reflected in contemporary documents, such as in a remark of the Nonnberg archivist after the festivities at which the *Missa S. Henrici* was performed, which notes that vespers that day did not start until three in the afternoon because the meal that followed the Mass began so late; perhaps it was an anticipation of such a lengthy duration that caused the · archbishop's niece to beg the composer for a short performance.[167] It is tempting to link the increased sense of monumentality in certain of these works to the founding of lavishly funded Anniversary services and the love of baroque festivities at this time, not to mention Johann Ernst's architectural plans for the city.[168] We are all familiar with the restrictions in length that Mozart had to face when composing a Mass for the cathedral; in fact, the generation immediately after Biber already, perhaps, had to restrict the length of the Mass, a situation that is evident in the fact that numerous manuscripts of the cathedral archive from the early eighteenth century have timings on the title pages. But it is interesting to note that although Biber's late works move in the direction of the eighteenth century in terms of the extension of sections, the means by which such expansion is attained are not based on the late baroque, post-Corellian harmonic devices; Biber's work remains very much of the seventeenth century in spirit, right to the end.

Very little is known concerning the very last years of Biber's life; as we have seen, he seems to have been closer to the convent at Nonnberg during those years as a result of his daughter's entry there. A new organ was built in the cathedral in 1702-3, and Biber's name appears in the contract as a witness; he may also, as Hermann Spies suggests, have written the original music for the Salzburg Glockenspiel, built in the last years of his life.[169] Archbishop Johann Ernst was busily engaged in giving the city a monumental, baroque character; the great architect Fischer von Erlach built some of his most important early works in Salzburg during the last decade of Biber's life. The War of the Spanish Succession, which took place in the last few years of Biber's life, had an adverse effect on many public activities in the city. Although Archbishop Johann Ernst remained faithful to the city's traditional policy of neutrality, Salzburg feared the consequences of an attack on Bavaria, since it stood directly between the warring Austrian and Bavarian forces. The city's fortifications were strengthened, provisions were laid up in case of seige, and sharpshooters were billeted out in private houses; all dances and masked balls were forbidden.[170] It is no wonder, therefore, that we hear little outside of Nonnberg concerning Biber's activity in the few years before his death. The attack on Salzburg never took place, and with the victory of Prince Eugene in August 1704, all danger to the city was over. During the night of May 2–3 of that year, however, Biber died; once again, the only reaction of a personal nature is to be found at Nonnberg:

On the holy cross day [i.e., the feast of the *Inventionis Sanctae Crucis,* that was especially observed by the Holy Cross Brotherhood of which Biber was a member], in the night between twelve and one o'clock, after four days of outstanding illness, Sister M. Rosa's father, who was Kapellmeister, after receiving the holy sacraments, and with the most beautiful resignation, fell gently asleep in God's will. God give him the eternal rest.[171]

Biber was buried on May 4 at St. Peter's; his grave has not been found.[172] The last record from his lifetime is the *Approbatio* he wrote shortly before his death for J. B. Samber's *Manuductio ad Organum* (Salzburg, 1704).

We have the names of eleven of Biber's children:[173]

Arnold	b. Feb. 1, 1673; d. Apr. 18, 1673
M. Zäzilia	b. Feb. 3, 1674; d. ?
Josef Rupert	b. Mar. 27, 1675; d. ?
A. Katharina	b. June 30, 1676; d. ?
Maria Anna Magdalena	b. July 23, 1677; d. Jan. 17, 1742
Anton Heinrich	b. May 4, 1679; d. Tittmoning, March 18, 1742
M._____(?)	b. July 19, 1680; d. Oct. 6, 1680
Carl Heinrich	b. Sept. 4, 1681; d. Nov. 19, 1749
Franz Heinrich	b. Oct. 23, 1682; d. Oct. 10, 1683
M. Theresia	b. Dec. 17, 1683; d. ?
Franz Josef	b. June 5, 1685; d. Sept. 27, 1685

At least three children were musically gifted. Anton Heinrich was music master to the municipal council in Brno for half a year. A few years after his father's death he applied for a position in Salzburg, mentioning his father's thirty-four years of faithful service.[174] He was a court musician in Salzburg from 1710 to 1727. Carl Heinrich was the most celebrated and talented of Biber's children. One year after his father's death we read in the Nonnberg records that "on this occasion our lady musicians also held a *Taffel Music* and Herr Carl Biber [then twenty-four years old] helped them out with the violin."[175] Like his father, he became chamber servant, Vice-Kapellmeister in 1714, teacher in the Choirboys Institute from 1726 to 1744, Kapellmeister in 1743, and finally also *Truchsess* in 1746, in Salzburg.[176] A great many of Carl Biber's compositions are preserved today in the Salzburg cathedral archives. Maria Anna Magdalena Biber, as we know, took orders at Nonnberg in 1696; she held the positions of choir director and "Kapell-Meisterin" for thirteen years, was a good alto singer, and played violin, viola d'amore and kettledrums.[177] Of Maria Zäzilia nothing is known beyond her entering the convent of Sancta Clara at Meran; among three copies of the *Sonatae Violino Solo* preserved at Nonnberg today, one is inscribed as belonging to Sister "M: Caecilia: a Bibern: o: S: C: Meran"; presumably her copy came back to her sister at Nonnberg on her death.[178] Some of Biber's more remote descendants possessed musical ability and were active in Salzburg in and beyond the time of W. A. Mozart.[179] While Biber's offspring cannot be said to have attained his level of musicianship, it is nevertheless true that a strain of considerable musical competence, if not genius, runs throughout several generations and perhaps bears witness to a high level of musical instruction within the family circle. The surviving documents emphasize singing and string playing. Carl Biber's proclivity for strict contrapuntal writing has been taken as evidence of the good schooling he received at the hands of his father, a view that is certainly confirmed in his *Missa in Contrapuncto* (see chapter 3).

Apart from his teaching florid counterpoint at the Choirboys Institute, we have very little information concerning Biber's teaching outside the family circle. No violin students are known; Biber did not teach violin at the Choirboys Institute, which would undoubtedly have been too elementary and within the capabilities of one of his pupils; Georg Muffat did not teach organ there, probably for the same reason.[180] It has often been said that Biber was the founder of a Salzburg violin school that culminated in Leopold Mozart's *Violinschule* of 1756. This may be so, but Biber's name is not mentioned in Mozart's treatise and his direct pupils are unknown; Leopold Mozart, however, served under Kapellmeister Carl Biber in the last years of the latter's life. And copies of the *Sonatae Violino Solo* circulated widely; J. J. Quantz reports in his autobiography that he studied them as a student.[181] According to Schneider, Matthias Gugl, a mid-eighteenth-century organist at the Salzburg cathedral and the author of a thoroughbass method, was a pupil of Biber and Muffat.[182] It seems likely that Romanus Weichlein (1652–1706), who was a student at the Salzburg Benedictine University in the 1670s, must at the very least have had close contact with Biber. Helene Wessely points out that his *Encaenia Musices* (1695) bears many points of comparison with Biber's style. Like the *Sonatae, tam Aris* the collection comprises twelve string sonatas, some with the addition of two clarini; and like Biber's collection it contains a group of trumpet duos at the end (twenty-four as opposed to Biber's twelve).[183] Weichlein went from Salzburg to Lambach and was there when Biber played before Emperor Leopold in 1681. He returned to Salzburg a few years before 1690, lived in the immediate vicinity of Biber and Muffat and took up a position at Nonnberg as chaplain and musical instructor of the nuns until 1691; there are a number of references in the convent records to performances of his works there.[184] Another possible pupil of Biber's was Andreas Christophorus Clamer. He was a *chori vicarius* and choir director at the cathedral, teacher at the Choirboys Institute, and "ceremonius et presentarius" at the court. Two years after the appearance of Biber's *Mensa Sonora* he published his *Mensa Harmonica* in Salzburg.[185] Clamer's collection, like Biber's, contains a set of instrumental suites. If not a pupil, Clamer was certainly a close associate of Biber's. Johann Baptist Samber, for whose treatise Biber wrote an *Approbatio* was apparently a pupil of Muffat's, rather than Biber's; and younger colleagues at the court such as Matthias Sigismund Biechteler, who became Kapellmeister between Biber father and son, are not known definitely to have studied with Biber.[186]

Example 1-4.   Biber, Themes from the *Missa S. Henrici,* Kyrie and Agnus Dei

About all we can say further at this point is that Biber's descendants constituted a definite musical presence in Salzburg, and that Biber's impact on later musical traditions was much stronger than that of earlier Kapellmeister. The appearance of themes from Biber's *Missa S. Henrici* (ex. 1-4) in the "Credo" Mass, "Jupiter" Symphony, and *The Magic Flute* of Mozart may indicate a tradition that was not forgotten while Mozart was growing up in Salzburg.[187] That the direct influence of Biber's music extended to Mozart, however, is hardly likely. Biber's music was virtually unknown to the catalogers of the cathedral archive in the late eighteenth century.[188] Until the eighteenth-century repertory from the archive has been studied we do not know much about the continuance of musical traditions beyond those of the musical institutions and cathedral appointments (see the following chapter); that the latter remained basically unchanging throughout two or more centuries, however, is a fact that is significant in the area of church music. But essentially Biber's music had to be rediscovered by modern scholarship after the lapse of almost two centuries; convincing performances were even slower in coming. Now he is no longer a "forgotten musician," or merely a chapter in the history of the violin, but perhaps the most individualistic voice in the Austrian baroque style.

2

The Performance of Music in the Salzburg Cathedral

The Archbishops and the Cathedral

As the Salzburg historian Franz Martin has shown, the history of the Salzburg archiepiscopate from the sixteenth to the eighteenth centuries can be divided into periods of approximately sixty years' duration, each corresponding roughly to an era in the history of ideas.[1] For example, the archbishops of what might be called the early baroque period, Wolf Dietrich (1587–1612), Marcus Sitticus (1612–19) and Paris Lodron (1619–53), form a group that is in many respects unified in outlook; so, likewise, do those of the middle or high baroque period, Guidobald von Thun (1654–68), Max Gandolph von Khuenburg (1668–87) and Johann Ernst von Thun (1687–1709). Although we cannot say that abrupt changes in the practice of music at the cathedral occurred with the succession of one archbishop or group of archbishops by another, it is convenient to use Martin's divisions as a guide in outlining the history of musical styles in Salzburg. For instance, the years 1653–54 mark not only the death of Paris Lodron and the accession of Guidobald von Thun, but also the departure from Salzburg of Kapellmeister Abraham Megerle and the arrival of Andreas Hofer. These last two events were very important in the musical history of the cathedral, for Hofer's tenure clearly coincides with a new stage in the development of baroque music. This period, roughly the second half of the seventeenth century, was a vitally important one for the empire as a whole, corresponding to the reign of Leopold I (1657–1705), who was not only a great lover of the arts and music in particular, but also the emperor under whom the Turks were decisively defeated in 1683 and under whose reign a strong upswing in national consciousness took place. The outward signs of this new upsurge of Austrian nationalistic spirit became more and more visible in Salzburg toward the end of the century and the beginning of the next—in the elaborate baroque festivities and anniversaries, the architecture of Fischer von Erlach and the many monuments erected under Johann Ernst, and not least at the time, the later works of Biber.[2] If the first group of archbishops, with their conspicuously Italian outlook, brought Salzburg to the point that one Italian visitor at the consecration of the new cathedral in 1628 called it a "little Rome," the second group confirmed the view of another in 1670, that it was the "German Rome."[3]

The thirty-year period of Hofer's employ in Salzburg (1654–84) spans most of the tenure of the two archbishops Guidobald von Thun and Max Gandolph von Khuenburg, while Biber's thirty-four years of archiepiscopal service (1670–1704) extend from two years after the accession of Max Gandolph to five years before the death of Johann Ernst. In view of striking general similarities between the church music styles of Hofer and Biber, and the fact that these two musicians worked together for fourteen years, the period 1654–1704 can be considered a unified one in the history of performance practice at the cathedral. The stylistic differences between the church music of Biber and of Hofer do not warrant Constantin Schneider's grouping of Hofer and Megerle together under the rubric "early Baroque."[4] Hofer's music, of which some few examples have now been published, although conservative, has more in common with Biber's than it does with Megerle's. Many musical advances were made under the patronage of Max Gandolph, of course (not the least were the hirings of Biber and Muffat); but these do not affect the larger unity of the fifty-year period. The profoundest effects of Max Gandolph's musical interest were felt in the realm of court music, whereas the church music was, as we will see, more closely bound to tradition. And it was, as we have seen, in the area of the court music that the accession of Johann Ernst made its impact—in Biber's turn from instrumental music to church music and operas, in the departure of Muffat from Salzburg, and the like.

From the foregoing remarks it is perhaps apparent that, while the court music was to some extent subject to the archbishop's personal likes and dislikes, the same was not at all true of the cathedral. In fact, many of the performance traditions and institutions of the period under consideration—and those that follow up to and beyond the time of Mozart—have their roots in the time of Archbishop Wolf Dietrich. Wolf Dietrich was the first in a series of Italian-oriented archbishops, who looked to Rome for a model when reforming the liturgy, planning the city's architecture and providing for music at the cathedral. One of the first signs of Salzburg's leaning toward things Italian was the introduction of the Roman rite very soon after the election of Wolf Dietrich in 1587. Finding that the cathedral music had sunk to a deplorably low level under his immediate predecessors, Wolf Dietrich made provisions for the choir; his aim was to raise it to the level of the choir of the Collegium Germanicum in Rome, where he had studied.[5] His official "reformation of the choir and foundation of the archbishop's choral music at the cathedral" in the year 1591 led to the setting of fixed numbers for the choir and the raising of its standard.[6] Once established, the size of the choir remained the same until beyond the age of the Mozarts and Michael Haydn. Court music also flourished from the time of Wolf Dietrich on, and Italian influences increased markedly under him and his successor.

The mention of baroque music in Salzburg brings into many minds the name of Orazio Benevoli and the huge Mass, now known as the *Missa Salisburgensis,* that was formerly, and erroneously, believed to have been heard at the consecration of the new cathedral in 1628.[7] Although this extravagant, even extreme work belongs, as we now know, to the baroque festival- and monument-oriented mentality of the second half of the century, it represents a tradition in performance at the cathedral that goes back to Wolf Dietrich. Just as the existence of the present cathedral is a tribute to the archbishop's decision to rebuild on a huge scale after the fire of 1598, so too was the presentation of Steffano Bernardi's twelve-chorus *Te Deum* (the work that was actually heard at the consecration services) made possible by Wolf Dietrich's ideals and actions, above all the above-mentioned reformation of the choir. The consecration was by no means the first occasion at which polychoral music was heard in Salzburg. We know that renaissance-style music for double chorus had been performed regularly in the old romanesque cathedral. The description of the performance of a Mass in the year 1613 (when the cathedral services had to be held in the Franciscan church) mentions concerted music ("Concerten") in which the court musicians participated; the works were polychoral and included trumpets, strings, cornetti, trombones, lutes and theorbos.[8] The instrumentation is virtually identical to that of several of Biber's and Hofer's polychoral works. Thus, we see that the polychoral tradition in Salzburg remained, as elsewhere, basically conservative. It did not differ in principle from Venetian music of Gabrieli's time, and its appearance as a baroque phenomenon in Salzburg parallels the situation in Germany described so thoroughly by Praetorius and put into practice in works such as Heinrich Schütz's *Psalmen Davids* (1619).

As the result of an almost official acceptance of this kind of music for the most important and ostentatious services, the new Salzburg cathedral was equipped with everything necessary to accommodate traditional polychoral practices. A decision of the greatest importance for the cathedral was probably made when the plans for the building were drawn up in the time of Marcus Sitticus: to furnish the cathedral with several organs and balconies designed to facilitate the performance of polychoral works. When the cathedral was consecrated it had "two organs, nicely decorated and beautifully painted" that were situated on the front right and left piers of the crossing (that is, the two piers that are nearer the altar).[9] At some time after this two further organs were installed on the remaining piers. But, since there has been some confusion in the literature concerning when these two instruments were added, we must consider this question briefly.

The third and fourth organs (situated with musicians' balconies under the dome) as well as the fifth (a positive located below in the choir) are also shown in various engravings of the cathedral from the seventeenth century, of which the best known is that of Melchior Küsel from 1682.[10] But most of the literature has maintained that they were added in 1668, 1670 or 1675, none of which dates is accurate.[11] There is no record of the organs between 1628 and 1668. But in the latter year Kapellmeister Andreas Hofer wrote a *Memorial* to the chapter in which he mentioned that *all four organs* under the dome, as well as three positive organs, one in the cathedral, one in the "Kaisersaal," and one in the "Instrumentenstube," were very seriously in need of repair, and to some extent unusable, and reminded the chapter that he had recommended their renovation six years earlier (i.e., in 1662).[12]

Later errors concerning the dating of the organs can all be traced back to the late eighteenth-century chronicle of Judas Thaddäus Zauner, who stated that Max Gandolph had had the remaining organs installed in 1675.[13] It can now be ascertained, however, that Zauner's statement is based on his misunderstanding of a passage in Lorenz Hübner's *Beschreibung der Stadt Salzburg* written four years earlier, in 1792. Hübner states that in 1675, under Max Gandolph, the two smaller organs were *completed*.[14] He also gives us the correct information that "all five organs are from the time of Archbishop Paris." Unfortunately, Hübner complicates matters by confusing the fifth of these organs (the positive in the choir) with the sixth organ, built in 1703.[15] Hübner knew, however, that the sixth organ was built not in the time of Paris Lodron, but in 1703, for in the next paragraph he names the builder of this organ correctly as J. Christoph Egedacher. Hübner undoubtedly made a slip, probably in quoting an older source now lost or unknown; his statement, along with Hofer's 1668 reminder, must be taken as confirmation that the cathedral possessed five organs from the time of Paris Lodron (archbishop from 1619–53), the four under the dome and the positive in the choir, just as are shown in the later engravings. The organs must have been built well before 1662 to have needed such extensive repairs at that time. The "completion" of the two smaller organs that took place under Max Gandolph might well have been the renovations requested by Hofer in 1668. No records of such repairs have survived from that year or from 1675, but in 1677 one of the 1628 organs was renovated and somewhat enlarged.[16]

All five of the cathedral organs were modest in size, even by seventeenth-century standards. The principal instrument, the 1628 organ on the Epistle side—known as the "Hauptorgel" until the sixth organ was built in 1703-4—had fourteen registers, and its companion on the Gospel side had thirteen; both had two manuals and pedals.[17] These two organs normally accompanied figural music for soloists and instruments in the balconies as well as the chorus, which was situated on both sides of the choir below. The two smaller organs and the positive in the choir had only five stops each; the former pair appears to have been used primarily to accompany the trumpet choir, with or without vocal soloists, while the positive accompanied the chorus only. Nevertheless, the sensitivity to registration that was so characteristic of South Germany was an ostensible feature of organ playing in Salzburg. Muffat's toccatas, published the year he left Salzburg (1690), fall clearly into the category of the south German type: frequent extended pedal points with otherwise very little activity in the pedals and many changes of style, often featuring French dance-like sections. Muffat's pupil and successor as principal organist at the cathedral, Johann Baptist Samber informs us in detail about the registration used for various musical textures, styles and liturgical functions within the services.[18]

During the last years of Biber's life the sixth and by far the largest of the cathedral organs was built on the balcony directly over the entrance. This new instrument was located at a considerable distance from the organs under the dome, too far away to accompany the chorus. Thus concerted music continued to be performed, as it always had been, in the choir and the balconies under the dome, while the new organ was used exclusively for organ solos. In fact, vocal music continued to be performed in this manner throughout the eighteenth century.[19] The reason for this was primarily acoustical. The cathedral is too large to permit use of the nave as a performing area. The musicians' balconies attached to the piers of the crossing as shown in the old engravings presumably did much to make a relatively self-contained acoustical space out of the dome and choir; but when several locations were used simultaneously, which was often, the problems of ensemble must have been considerable, even with the aid of the various organs; Küsel's engraving, to be studied in detail below, pictures several conductors both above and below, coordinating a polychoral work. These musicians' balconies were not the ones in the choir, transepts and nave that are well known today. Some of the latter might have been intended originally for such a use, perhaps used for Steffano Bernardi's 1628 *Te Deum*; but they are much higher and, no doubt, acoustically inferior to the ones used in the seventeenth century. After 1800 interest in polychoral music was all but dead, and in 1859 the four organs under the dome of the cathedral were removed and disseminated to various parish churches, the balconies disappeared, and, as a further anti-baroque gesture the walls of the church were colored grey.[20] "Authentic" performances of polychoral church music by seventeenth- and eighteenth-century Salzburg composers (and even Mozart must be included here) have not been possible in the cathedral for over one hundred years.

Musicians and Musical Institutions

Perhaps the most important musical legacy bequeathed to Salzburg by Archbishop Wolf Dietrich was the continuance of securely established groups of musicians at both court and cathedral. The various musical institutions available for performance at the cathedral in the period immediately following his 1591 reform remained basically the same for two centuries. The archbishop expanded and improved each of the traditional divisions of the existing princely musical establishment, whose separation into two parts, the cathedral choir and the court musicians, reminds us that the prince-archbishop was at the same time the spiritual and worldly leader of Salzburg: archbishop and prince of the empire. Both court and cathedral required music that would enhance special celebrations. In addition, plainchant had to be sung at daily services. In the first half of the century opera had not been introduced, but music was nevertheless performed regularly at court. The several divisions of Salzburg's court and cathedral musicians reflected these various needs; there were basically four categories within the cathedral music:

1. the *vicarii chori* (also called *Chorvikaren,* or *Chorpriester*)
2. the *Choralisten*
3. the *Corporey Knaben* (also called *Corporaler* or *Pueri de Cantu Chorali*)
4. the *Kapell Knaben*

The *vicarii chori* were priests chosen on the basis of their musical ability; singing in the choir formed their chief function in the services. Following Wolf Dietrich's reform the *vicarii chori* increased in number and improved in quality. By the year 1608 their ranks numbered twenty, a total that remained fixed for the next two hundred years.[21] The *vicarii chori* were mostly tenors and basses, although some might have sung falsetto. Two of the most qualified and experienced members were choir directors (*regentes chori,* or *Chor Regenten*) with the responsibility of leading performances in the absence of the Kapellmeister; they are presumably the sub-conductors shown in Küsel's engraving. The role of *regenschori* could be held even by the Kapellmeister, as Andreas Hofer did (Hofer was also a priest). Usually several of the *vicarii chori* sang solo parts and took part in court performances as well. In Biber's time two or three *vicarii chori* appear regularly in the payments lists as court musicians. Some of the vicars also taught the choirboys singing and instrumental playing. Two such teachers in the late seventeenth century were Andreas Christophorus Clamer and J. M. Canata, both *regentes chori* as well. Clamer was, as we know, a composer of considerable ability; his above-mentioned *Mensa Harmonica,* a collection of suites used for table music at court, reveals a personality quite at home with secular styles. Canata was a bass who sang roles in the Salzburg schooldramas.[22] Not all the *vicarii chori* could sing solo parts, however. In 1668 the cathedral chapter reminded the newly elected archbishop that "the worship of God in the service consisted, among other things, of well-executed music" and hoped "that the archbishop would not only supply music using the same four reliable, excellent voices along with the other necessary musicians (*"musicis,"* i.e., court musicians), but would also give money weekly to any of the *vicarii chori* who were present and took part in the music." And, in fact, the payments lists for the court musicians always record weekly *Praesenzgeld* set aside for this purpose.[23]

The *Choralisten* were lay members of the choir. Their number (eight) remained just as standard in the seventeenth and eighteenth centuries as that of the *vicarii chori.* They, too, comprised chiefly tenors and basses; their duties related more closely to the regular singing of plainchant than to figural music. Very rarely do any of the *Choralisten* appear in the payments lists for the court musicians. And their salaries were much lower than those of the *vicarii chori.* One notable exception, Franz Kolberer, whose name headed the list for over thirty years, earned a salary almost three times as great as that of his colleagues.[24] Presumably he sang solo parts and led the *Choralisten.*

The remainder of the cathedral choir consisted of choirboys, who sang the upper parts. In the early seventeenth century especially, a distinction was drawn between the *Corporey Knaben* and the *Kapell Knaben.* The former were younger boys who sang plainchant but not figural music; the latter, older and more experienced boys, sang contrapuntal music as well as concerted solo parts. All the choirboys were fed, housed, educated and clothed at the expense of the court. It is likely, however, that, as their name suggests, only the *Kapell Knaben* (court choirboys) participated in court performances. Several lists from the seventeenth century provide us with the information that the usual number of choirboys was sixteen (eight *Corporey Knaben* and eight *Kapell Knaben*). In 1677 Archbishop Max Gandolph reformed the Choirboys Institute (*Institutum Puerorum ex Capella*); he had a new house built for them (the *Capellhaus*) in which their teachers (including Biber for a while) lived as well, and ensured that they received a thorough musical education.[25] Several court musicians, including Hofer, Biber, and organist and a violinist, were responsible for teaching the choirboys plainchant, figural music and instrumental playing. Max Gandolph's provision was for eight *Corporey Knaben* and a minimum of four boys "who are superior and more perfect, both of voice and in the art of singing."[26] The former took their places in front of the eight *Choralisten,* while the latter were exempt from plainchant duties and performed only in figural music for Mass and Vespers on Sundays and feast days in the cathedral. With his reforms Max Gandolph ensured the continuance of traditions that had existed since at least Wolf Dietrich's reform eighty years earlier and that had perhaps become subject to abuse now and again. Since the records of the Choirboys Institute from the seventeenth century have not survived, we do not know whether or not the number of boys exceeded the minimum of twelve after 1677. On the basis of earlier lists we can probably say with some degree of confidence that the number of from twelve to sixteen was standard at that time.

Salzburg's court musicians in the seventeenth and eighteenth centuries fell into two basic categories: the court musicians proper (*musici*, or *Musicanten*) and the court and field trumpeters. The former comprised solo singers and instrumentalists. As might be expected, the state of the court music owed much to the reforms of Wolf Dietrich in the 1590s. This archbishop had also reorganized the chapel from the ground up, after discharging fifteen *musici* and three trumpeters in 1592.[27] We are fortunate in possessing lists of the court musicians from the late sixteenth century and the first quarter of the seventeenth.[28] During this period the "Hochfürstliche Trumetterey" consisted of ten trumpeters and one timpanist.[29] This branch of the musical establishment had, of course, a more than purely musical function, and therefore its numbers could not be drastically reduced. The trumpeters were an emblem of the archbishop's nobility and were required for official ceremonies. From 1595 to 1599 the *musici* at the court numbered from fourteen to sixteen:[30]

	1595	1598	1599
Kapellmeister	1	1	1
Organists	1	2	2
Cornettists	2	3	3
Altos	4	2	3
Tenors	2	1	–
Basses	3	3	6
Bellows	1	1	1
Other	–	1*	–
Totals	14	14	16

*singer (*vicarius chori*)

During the latter part of Wolf Dietrich's rule and the tenure of his successor, Marcus Sitticus, the number of court musicians rose significantly:[31]

	1608	1611	1612	1613
Kapellmeister	1	1	1	2
Organists	1	2	–	2
Falsettist	1	1	1	1
Discantists	–	–	1	2
Altos	4	3	3	4
Tenors	4	4	4	2
Basses	6	3	4	3
Lutenist	1	1	1	–
Violinist	–	–	1	1

Cornettists	2	2	2	1
Trombones	1	2	1	1
Instrumentalist (harpsichord)	–	–	–	1
Organ maker	–	–	1	1
Lute maker	–	1	1	1
Capelldiener	–	–	–	1
Bellows	1	1	1	1
	22	21	22	24

In the following years, under Marcus Sitticus (who was half Italian), the number of Italian musicians, both singers and instrumentalists, at the court increased. Not all of these men remained in Salzburg, but half of the *musici* during this period came from south of the Alps. Most of the Italians, including the falsettist Vincenzo Barone and several discantists, presumably castrati, were singers. Their influence at the court must have been considerable. The German bass, Matthäus Frueauf, for example, sang "in the Italian manner" and Kapellmeister Peter Gutfreund Italianized his name to Bonamico.[32] In total, almost eighty musicians were available:

CATHEDRAL CHOIR:

Vicarii chori	20
Choralisten	8
Corporey Knaben	8
Kapell Knaben	8

COURT MUSICIANS:

Musici	ca. 21–24
Trumpeters and *timpani*	11
	ca. 76–79

These numbers were, as nearly as can be determined from contemporary documents, close to an average for the century. Although seventeenth-century records contain complaints from time to time about the music at the cathedral, and the number of choirboys appears sometimes to have fallen below sixteen, there are grounds for the belief that from seventy to eighty musicians were normally available.

The payment list of 1624 includes a still greater number of *musici*, possibly an indication that preparations for the consecration were already under way:[33]

Kapellmeister	1
Organists	2
Falsettist	1
Alto	1
Tenors	2
Basses	4
Cornettists	2
Instrumentalists (harpsichord)	2

Organ maker	1
Lute maker	1
Alumnus and *musicus*	2
Vicarii chori	2
Bellows	1
Unspecified	6
	——
	28

Listed in the procession that took place before the consecration service in 1628 were eighteen choirboys dressed as angels who sang a hymn for two choirs, in addition to ten trumpeters and timpanists, the *Chorknaben,* the *Choralisten,* the *vicarii chori* and the *Hoch-fürstl. Music.* [34] A mid-century inventory (1654) lists seventy-one musicians: "17 Chorherren Vicari, 8 Choralisten, 8 Corporeyknaben, 8 Kapellknaben, 30 Musicanten (presumably including the trumpeters)." [35]

Further important advances in Salzburg's court and cathedral music were also made in the last third of the century, above all through the efforts of Archbishop Max Gandolph who, like Wolf Dietrich, had a keen awareness of the necessity of maintaining musical institutions. Much more than either his predecessor or successor, Max Gandolph showed great interest in all aspects of music. When a contemporary chronicler wished to praise the archbishop's daily attendance at Mass in the Franciscan church, he wrote that "the prince...loved the Franciscans' plainchant more than the court music," a statement that reveals a veiled recognition of Max Gandolph's love of court music. [36] Another seventeenth-century writer spoke of Max Gandolph's enjoyment of celebrations in church when all the court singers and instrumentalists participated. [37] While Archbishops Guidobald and Johann Ernst together were the dedicatees of three musical collections, Max Gandolph alone garnered eight, most of which praise him extravagantly as a patron of music. [38] Today Max Gandolph is justly remembered for the rise of secular music (especially instrumental) in Salzburg. His considerable role in the development of the cathedral music was, apart from the hiring of more able musicians than Salzburg had seen in a long time, largely that of restoration; into this category falls his reformation of the Choirboys Institute just as much as the long-awaited repairs and improvements to the organs.

While the numbers of the *vicarii chori, Choralisten,* and *Corporey Knaben* remained the same throughout the second half of the century, a comparison of the payment lists of the court musicians from the early 1670s with those from earlier and later in the century reveals a drastic reduction in numbers during Biber's early years in Salzburg. [39] In the early 1670s the *musici* included one organist, the bellows blower, the alto Godefridus Haager, the violinist Johann Rögginger, and one other musician. The number of trumpeters remained the same as always. Even making allowance for the possibility that other musicians, who do not appear in the lists, were available, the court music must have been greatly understaffed during those years. Either this situation or perhaps a certain lack of dynamic quality in Andreas Hofer might have been the reason that problems arose with regard to the participation of the court musicians in an anniversary service in 1671. In 1672 the chapter minutes make reference to the music performed the preceding year at a service endowed by Archbishop Paris Lodron in 1654. [40] As the entry states, Paris had ordained the sum of twelve florins for the court musicians "in order that his *Jahrtag* be held in a stately manner." At the 1671 observance of this service the court musicians did not perform either the sung vigil or the Requiem; only the *vicarii chori* were present. This circumstance prompted the chapter to notify the Vice-Kapellmeister (Hofer) that if he did not fulfil his obligation in this regard, in the future the money would not be paid. It is quite possible that, like the court and cathedral organs, the musicians themselves deteriorated in quality and number under Archbishop Guidobald, causing the chapter to make the above-quoted recommendation to the new archbishop that he not depend on a few reliable musicians but give weekly *Praesenzgeld* for participation in the cathedral music. We do not know whether the number of *musici* declined in the early 1670s simply through neglect or whether, because of a reform of Max Gandolph's, musicians were discharged, as they had been in the time of Wolf Dietrich, in an effort to rebuild the chapel. We may remember the conclusion of Johann Khuen von Auer that the hiring of Biber and the purchase of instruments from Stainer represented the archbishop's resolve to build a complete ensemble as soon as possible.[41] Besides these actions, the reform of the Choirboys Institute, the hiring of Georg Muffat, and the repair of the organs, Max Gandolph had twelve silver trumpets with gold decoration made for special festivities, he increased the number of operatic performances in Salzburg and established an anniversary service to be held in memory of his family, for which a large amount was to be paid to the court musicians.[42] Under these circumstances some of the most exuberant and festive of Biber's works, such as the *Sonata S. Polycarpi* (1673), the *Missa Christi Resurgentis* (1674) and *Vesperae à 32* (1674) were produced, all a tribute to Max Gandolph's energy in the building up of his chapel. Since the payment lists for the court musicians do not survive between early 1674 and 1694, we do not know exactly when the chapel was again in full swing; but the Biber works suggest the latter part of 1674.[43] In any case a poem written and set to music in Salzburg by Father Romanus Müller in 1673 reflects—perhaps not altogether coincidentally—what was perceived at the time as the necessary complement of musicians to play together *ad pulpitum* (i.e., on the musicians' balconies).[44] In twenty-six strophes the author sings the praises of the violists, cornettists, composers, flautists (i.e., recorder players), gambists, harpists, lutenists, organists, trombonists, trumpeters and tromba marinists, violinists and double bass players. Deleting the tromba marina (which reflects the fact that the poem was written at Nonnberg), adding oboes and substituting theorbo for harp, the list represents almost exactly the Biber instrumentarium as we know it.

The payment lists from the last decade of Biber's life confirm that the number of court musicians was stable and comparable to that in the earlier part of the century. From this period we can supplement the information derived from the payment lists with data gleaned from the membership register of the Holy Cross Brotherhood as well as from records of the university schooldrama and court opera productions.[45] On the basis of these sources the following is a partial reconstruction of the court chapel for a sample year (1697):

Kapellmeister	1	
Vice-Kapellmeister	1	
Organists	2–3	
Organmaker	1	
Altos	2	
Basses	3	
Violinist (and violin teacher)	1	
Gambist	1	
Trumpeters	12	(one listed as "violinist and trumpeter," one as "Leibquardtier Trompether")
Timpanists	2	
Bellows blowers	2	
Undetermined	4	(one listed as "Portier und musico")

32–33

In addition to these musicians at least seven *vicarii chori* (two tenors, two basses and three undetermined) are known from their names to have participated regularly in the court music; in a somewhat fuller list from the year 1700 we find that of the twenty *vicarii chori* sixteen were paid extra money "wegen der Music"—that is, for participating in the court music, and all twenty were given weekly *Praesenzgeld* for participating in the cathedral music. One vicar was prefect of the *Capellhaus* and instructed the *Capellknaben* (violin and keyboard are mentioned; but it is known that the boys were taught singing and figural counterpoint also).[46] Of the eight *Choralisten* two were paid extra for participating in both the court and cathedral music; one of these earned a higher salary for teaching the *Corporeyknaben* and "Aufsuchung der Musicalien" as well. And of the twelve trumpeters two were paid *Praesenzgeld* for the cathedral music. Right through Biber's years in Salzburg the monthly payments for "unsalaried musicians who are used in the cathedral music" continue. At least six of the known number of vocalists, including both altos, frequently took solo parts, for their names crop up in connection with opera and schooldrama performances. These numbers remain the norm through the end of Biber's life, creating the impression that figural music must have been performed weekly in the cathedral.

The operas and schooldramas usually required about a dozen vocal soloists. In Muffat's *Plutone* (1688–89), for example, ten roles were sung by nine court soloists—three sopranos (male), two altos (male), two tenors and two basses, while Biber's *Chi la dura la vince* (ca. 1690–92) calls for three sopranos, one alto, five tenors and three basses. Singing roles in the schooldramas were taken by university students as well; thus the total numbers of singing parts frequently exceeded those of the operas. According to Schneider, nineteen court singers and nine students participated in a performance of Biber's *Corvinus* in 1688; and in a single chorus of fourteen "Bassistae," nine court singers and five students performed;[47] presumably a number of *vicarii chori* are included among the court singers. The names of some sopranos who do not appear in the lists of the court musicians are known from the opera performances. The fact that they were German, not Italian, suggests that *castrati* were not employed and that student falsettists or choirboys (who do not appear in the court lists) sang the female roles as well as the soprano parts in the church music.

In summary, the court and cathedral musicians together numbered about seventy-five to eighty in the mid 1690s and, indeed, throughout most of the century; besides the Kapellmeister there were two or three organists, about sixteen "Vocal Musici und Instrumentisten," fourteen trumpeters and timpanists, two bellows blowers, eight *Choralisten,* twenty *vicarii chori,* and twelve to sixteen choirboys. Of these it seems that about fifty were capable of performing regularly in concerted music. Even with these substantial figures we do not have a complete picture of the available performance resources. There is no mention of the cornettists and trombonists who were always used in the church music, nor of the occasional flautists and oboists; these were, no doubt, drawn from the town musicians and paid out of the fund for unsalaried musicians. We must also conclude that in the seventeenth century, as in Mozart's day, nearly all the court instrumentalists played more than one instrument; in 1757 four of the *Choralisten* played double bass and all the trumpeters and timpanists played stringed instruments; most of the string players doubled on winds and vice-versa.[48] It is probably safe to assume that this was the practice in Biber's time as well.

The Disposition of Musicians in the Cathedral

The information given above takes on far greater meaning when it is considered in conjunction with the actual music performed in the Salzburg cathedral and all that we know of the physical disposition of the musicians in the church. Of great value to us today in this regard is the above-mentioned engraving of Melchior Küsel from the year 1682, which shows a musical performance that appears to be either in progress or about to begin (Plate II). What Küsel has provided is in all probability a generalized depiction of the normal performance conditions for polychoral music; the "occasion" intended is one of the festivities of the *Jubeljahr* 1682. Although Küsel's engraving has been published in facsimile several times, it has never been carefully examined in conjunction with either the extant music from seventeenth-century Salzburg or knowledge of performance practice at the cathedral; several descriptions of the actual content of the engraving are, therefore, highly questionable.[49] As in many of his works, Küsel took pains to represent the scene with meticulous attention to detail, and we can be sure that accuracy was foremost in his mind. Since even the best reproductions are not as clear as the engraving itself, we may begin with an analysis of what can be observed in the original. An account by the contemporary historian, Joseph Mezger, tells us which persons had nothing to do with the musical performance.[50] The figures he describes are easily identified as those seated behind the long tables at the extreme left and right sides of the choir. We recognize the few other ecclesiastical personages depicted by Küsel from their clothing. The remaining individuals—vocalists, instrumentalists and conductors—are situated as shown in figure 2-1.

The musical performance shown in the engraving must have produced as luxuriant a sound as any of the extravagant works heard in Salzburg during the second half of the century. Its scoring, probably for two vocal choirs (SATB), strings, cornetti and trombones, trumpets and kettledrums, closely matches that of several works by Hofer and Biber: e.g., Hofer's *Missa Archiepiscopalis* and *Te Deum à 23*; Biber's *Vesperae à 32, Missa Christi Resurgentis, Missa Alleluia, Litania de S. Josepho à 20, Missa Bruxellensis,* and so on. A considerable number of the surviving works of Biber and Hofer are based on an eight-part double chorus. And the cathedral archive contains several works of Bertali and eight motets of Cazzati for eight-part double chorus, which remained the norm in the first half of the eighteenth century as well. The instrumental complements to the double chorus vary considerably in the works of Biber and Hofer, and we find the designations à 8, 13, 14, 15, 17, 20, 21, 22, 23, 24, 26, 32 and 36, referring to works whose numbers of real parts are much the same as one another. Titles such as *Missa Alleluia 8 voc.* (from an inventory of lost manuscripts) and *Missa à 8 Voci Reali* (the manuscript title of the *Missa Bruxellensis*) for two of the most fully scored works of the repertoire show that the vocal parts still greatly determined the conception of a work in the seventeenth century.[51] Almost any of the instrumental parts belonging to the most fully scored pieces might not appear in the smaller ones. As one might expect, however, the trumpets— emblem of the archbishop's nobility and office—are most often absent, while the ripieno instruments—violas and trombones—are usually retained.

The trumpet choir in the manuscripts of Biber's and Hofer's church music may comprise as few instruments as two clarini or as many as six or eight trumpets with timpani (either in vocal works or independent sonatas). Whether small or large, however, the trumpet choir appears always to have been divided so as to augment the antiphony between the vocal choirs.[52] In passages of double-chorus antiphony the first clarino plays with chorus I; the second, with chorus II. These two instruments, the foundation of the trumpet choir, often sound without the lower trumpets and timpani, not only when choral antiphony is employed, but also in instrumental movements. The *Praesenzgeld* paid to two of the twelve court trumpeters presumably reflects their greater indispensability.[53] To the other trumpets (with kettledrums) was relegated the role of playing the lower tones of the harmonic series. Thus restricted to tonic and dominant harmonies, they could scarcely be used outside of cadential points and a few other passages where extra force and much triadic sonority were required. Consequently, their parts often do not appear in the manuscripts. This does not mean, of course, that they were not and could not be used. The number of instruments in the trumpet choir of any particular work did not necessarily conform to that contained in the parts or specified in the title. The trumpets were the most flexible of baroque instrumental choirs. We know from Praetorius that the lower parts were often not written down; instead, the players, familiar with the style, found the notes themselves.[54] Thus Biber's *Missa Alleluia* can be performed with four trumpets and timpani, or with just two clarini, instead of the six trumpets and kettledrums specified in the manuscript. Similarly, low trumpet and timpani parts can easily be added at certain points in the *Missa Christi Resurgentis* and Hofer's *Missa Archiepiscopalis,* both of which contain parts for only two clarini.[55] The title page of Biber's *Missa S. Henrici* reveals that not only the lower trumpets and timpani, but also the ripieno doubling instruments (in this case trombones) are optional. Therefore, although in Küsel's engraving we see four trumpeters in the balconies (and one in the choir) the work being performed might just as easily have been Hofer's *Missa Archiepiscopalis* (two clarini) as Biber's *Vesperae à 32* (four trumpets and timpani).

In figure 2-1 the groups of performers in the right and left sides of the choir have been designated chorus I and II, respectively. That these two small bodies of musicians make up the vocal choirs cannot be doubted. The parts written for the fifth organ, located in the choir, contain only the figured bass of the ripieno passages, since this instrument sounded only with the chorus.[56] In the seventeenth- and eighteenth-century sources this organ was referred to as the "Chororgel," "Organo [pro] Ripieno" and "Organo in Capella." The organ parts of Biber's *Requiem in F minor,* for example, include indications concerning the use of the positive organ for tutti passages: "Con organo in capella," "senza organo in capella," "organo in concerto," "organo in concerto e in capella."[57] The positioning of vocal soloists cannot, however, be determined with certainty from Küsel's engraving. We do not know whether the eight solo singers sat with the rest of the choir or were situated in the musicians' balconies. The placing of the soloists of chorus I with the strings and those of chorus II near the cornetti and trombones would permit a close proximity between the singers and the organs, and is therefore a likely arrangement. Varied mixtures of vocal soloists and obbligato instrumental parts in the polychoral works overrule hasty conclusions concerning the spacing. Some of the more common combinations, such as altos with trombones, and basses with strings or trumpets, are favored for reasons of color, or the matching of high and low sonorities, not of spacing. Most of the works contain equal-voiced duets which combine or alternate with one or more instrumental choirs. Asymmetrical spacings occur frequently. Mid-eighteenth-century descriptions reveal the normal spacing of the musicians in the cathedral at that time.[58] For the highest feasts all five organs were used, the "Chororgel" with the ripieno singers and a violone player, both situated in the choir. The sixth organ, built in 1703–4 over the entrance to the church, was restricted to organ solos. During performances of vocal music the "court organ" on the southeast pier of the crossing (i.e., the Epistle side, nearest the altar) sounded continuously. The solo singers (six court singers and two court choirboys) and several instrumentalists, mostly continuo players, were situated on the balcony with this organ. Eleven string players stood near the organ on the opposite side of the church. Two choirs of trumpets and kettledrums were located on the remaining balconies further west. The late seventeenth-century performance recorded in Küsel's engraving agrees with the mid-eighteenth-century descriptions in some ways while differing in others. By Leopold Mozart's time cornetti were practically obsolete; oboes and flutes were more frequently used, and the string players had shifted from the right side of the choir to the left, presumably so that the vocal soloists could more easily be accommodated with the court organ.[59] In the polychoral works of Biber and Hofer strings almost always double chorus I, the cornetti and trombones chorus II; clarino I usually plays with the first choir and clarino II with the second, while the lower trumpets do not clearly divide, since they normally play at cadential points only. The strings were probably situated regularly as they are shown by Küsel (on the balcony with the court organ), since the best of the five smaller organs was located there. The payment lists in Biber's time make a distinction between the court and cathedral organists, the former being paid over twice as much. This disparity probably does not reflect the difference between sacred and secular music, but rather which organ was played in church and the quality of the organist: i.e., the court organist played the court organ, the instrument that played continuously in both solo and ripieno sections, while the "Dom-organist" played either the positive in the choir or the instrument across from the court organ. A third organist is sometimes specifically mentioned in the lists, presumably for playing the 1628 organ on the Gospel side or the positive; the organists who accompanied the trumpet choirs from the remaining two balconies are not listed, although there are often five organ parts.

The performance of solo sections must have presented great difficulty, especially in an interior as large as that of the Salzburg cathedral. In passages requiring rapid alternation from side to side and the accompaniment of a solo voice by instruments situated on the other side of the building, the problems of coordination are considerable. For instance, in a nine-bar excerpt from Hofer's *Magnificat à 17* two basses from different choruses alternate, with some overlapping, a dozen times. Starting in the fourth measure of this passage, the vocal/instrumental combinations reverse, so that each bass, at first accompanied by a pair of instruments on the same side of the church, is now accompanied by two on the opposite side. The problem of synchronizing widely separated soloists was alleviated, however, by the fact that there were several organs to keep the pitch accurate and by the presence of the *chori regentes,* who, as it appears in Küsel's engraving, took the *tactus* from the Kapellmeister and transmitted it to the soloists.

We may note that the term "solo," when used in connection with concerted church music by Biber and Hofer, means a single vocal soloist (or instrumentalist) and never "a single voice range," that might be filled by all the sopranos, tenors, or violins, and the like.[60] The music was not intended to be entirely choral or orchestral. In some manuscripts (that of Biber's *Missa Christi Resurgentis,* for example) the word "solo" is lacking in the vocal parts and there are no separate ripieno parts. However, "solo" and "ripieno" indications can usually be found in the organ or M. D. C. (Maestro di Cappella) part. Failing that, musical style and the presence or absence of instrumental doubling generally provide adequate bases for judgment. Since we know, for instance, that elsewhere in Hofer's music choral basses never sing alone with an obbligato string choir, the passage "Te gloriosus..." in his *Te Deum* is obviously for solo bass.[61] In the preface to his *Ver sacrum* (1677) Hofer explained his use of solo/ripieno designations as follows: "The letter S characterizes single, or concertizing voices, in contrast to which, R designates a fuller vocal choir, if there is a sufficiently large number of musicians to permit this; anyone who suffers from a lack of singers must do without it."[62] This statement means that a concerted church work can be performed entirely soloistically if the number of singers necessary for solo/tutti contrast is not available; it does not indicate that solo parts may be performed by a chorus. Nor does it suggest that any situation other than "suffering" from lack of singers would prompt solo performance of tutti sections.

If we total up the number of singers pictured in Küsel's engraving, and assume that there are a few more soloists hidden from view in the boxes on the piers of the crossing, we arrive at a figure of twenty-six or twenty-seven vocalists.[63] The following scheme represents a possible disposition of the singers:

Figure 2-1.   Engraving by Melchior Küsel Showing a Musical Performance in the
Salzburg Cathedral, 1682
(Salzburg, Museum Carolino Augusteum)

Figure 2-2. Disposition of Musicians in Küsel's Engraving *(facing)*

CHOIR: LEFT (Chorus 2)
(8 musicians)

Six singers (seated). From
left to right: 1 & 2 share a
book, 3 & 4 each have a sheet,
5 & 6 share a book.
Singer (standing) in front
with book (soloist?)
Conductor? standing in foremost position, with manuscript
open in left hand and right
hand slightly elevated (Kapellmeister?)

BALCONY: LEFT FRONT
(at least 8 musicians)

Left to right:
One singer (?) holding book
One singer (?) with book on box
One figure (head only visible)
Two trombones (or trumpets; one
player with crook in left hand)
Organ (built 1628)
Cornetto
Conductor with rolled paper in
left hand (elevated) and manu-
script open in right hand

BALCONY: LEFT REAR
(at least 5 musicians)

One singer or *conductor*
with open manuscript
One figure facing forward
Two trumpets
Organ (built under Paris
Lodron, rebuilt 1675)

CHOIR: RIGHT (Chorus 1)
(16 musicians)

Seven singers (seated) with
Leader or *soloist* (standing)
Two singers (standing in front)
Cornetto
Violone
Regal and bellows blower (calcant)
Trumpet (or trombone?) player with
Two singers (?) on his right
and left, each singer holding
an open book

BALCONY: RIGHT FRONT
(at least 7 musicians)

Right to left:
Two string players
One figure (head only visible)
Organ (built 1628, enlarged 1677)
One string player
One figure (head only visible)
Conductor with rolled paper in
left hand (elevated) and manu-
script open across box

BALCONY: RIGHT REAR
(at least 7 musicians)

Two figures (heads only visible)
Two figures facing forward, one
with rolled manuscript (conductor?)
Two trumpets
Organ (built under Paris Lodron,
rebuilt 1675)

CHORUS II	CHORUS I
Left Choir	*Right Choir*
3 sopranos	4 sopranos
1 alto	2 altos
1 tenor	2 tenors
2 basses	3 or 4 basses
Left Balcony	*Right Balcony*
soprano 2 solo	soprano 1 solo
alto 2 solo	alto 1 solo
tenor 2 solo	tenor 1 solo
bass 2 solo	bass 1 solo
(cornetti and trombones)	(strings)

(e.g., nine *Kapellknaben*; six court singers—2A, 2T, 2B; eleven *vicarii chori*—3A, 3T, 5B)

The number of singers in the two choirs (nineteen) may seem too small for a work as large as Biber's *Missa Alleluia* or the *Missa Bruxellensis*; but three facts should be considered: first, the solo singers sang with their respective choirs; second, for a great part of Biber's double-chorus works the two choirs sing together; third, the singers are doubled by winds and strings and accompanied by three organs as well as several bass instruments. Moreover, the total number of singers in both choirs is larger than the ideal of sixteen suggested by J. S. Bach in his memorandum to the Leipzig town council, and the number in the first choir alone is not much smaller.[64] Chorus I (on the right) is noticeably larger than chorus II. Also the positive organ and violone are situated on this side of the choir, and the nearest balcony contained the largest and best of the four organs. The scores of the Salzburg polychoral works reveal the reason for this disproportion: in antiphonal passages chorus I always begins and chorus II answers. It was probably felt to be more effective (and secure) if the first entry was stronger and that of the answering choir weaker, like an echo. Two facts suggest that the soprano parts of the choirs were strongest in number: first, the boys had weaker voices and less experience than the court singers; second, in Biber's double-chorus music we frequently find five-part choral writing with two different soprano parts, while the lower parts of both choirs are the same; the ripieno parts are quite often doubled only for the lower parts. To maintain balance, therefore, the chorus requires an augmented soprano section.

The number of instruments shown in Küsel's engraving accords with the relatively modest vocal forces. Quite possibly none of the instrumental parts was doubled, except, perhaps, the violins and, of course, the continuo. From Georg Muffat's writings we learn that the contrast between solo and ripieno strings was exploited in the Salzburg instrumental works, so the doubling of string parts, in ripieno sections only, is therefore valid in the performance of a late seventeenth-century church work. Doubling was naturally limited by the amount of space in the organ balconies, each of which could hold some eighteen musicians, including organist and conductor.[65]

One more detail in Küsel's engraving remains to be considered; the artist has pictured a small group of performers near the regal on the right side of the choir—one cornettist and one trumpet player with a figure (apparently a singer) on his right, another on his left. This particular detail was undoubtedly recorded during a specific performance, and tells us that we cannot be inflexible about matters of spacing in a concerted work. The only musicians in the engraving who appear to be performing at the "instant" depicted are those in the small group just mentioned, as well as one cornettist and one trombonist in the left balcony. Such a combination of vocal and instrumental parts suggests the vocal duets with cornetti and trombones commonly found in Biber's and Hofer's polychoral works. Quite possible the trumpet shown in the choir is an inaccurate representation of a trombone: Küsel does not render the "trombones" in the left balcony with perfect knowledge of the instrument, since the bells clearly extend beyond the crooks. The moment Küsel attempts to catch represents the performance of a solo section. The conductors in the balconies are standing with their arms raised, as if about to bring in a tutti.

It is possible to gather further information about performance practice from the music manuscripts of the Salzburg cathedral archive; these were used as performance material and therefore assume considerable importance. All late seventeenth-century copies of concerted music in the archive contain multiple continuo parts, seldom less than three of which are figured. Several works also include second copies of the ripieno vocal parts. The title page of the "Triumphate sidera la Madonna à 18" of Johann Caspar Kerll, for example, lists ripieno choral parts "in duplo," and, in addition to two organ parts, fully figured, and an "organo ripieno" part, there are parts for organ or viola, organ or bassoon, organ or theorbo (all figured) and two violone parts. From these manuscripts we confirm the fact that in performances of concerted church works (whether scored for double chorus or not) the musicians were antiphonally spaced. Let us consider, for example, Biber's offertorium *Quo abiit dilectus tuus,* a relatively modestly scored composition (four-part chorus with soloists, four violas, and continuo). The manuscript of "Quo abiit" includes five organ parts, four of which contain the figured bass of the entire work, while the fifth ("Organo pro Rippieno") lacks the bass of the solo passages. The offertory consists of a series of vocal solos and duets followed by a choral, rather strict, fugal Amen. Obviously, the choir was situated in its usual place—right and left sides of the choir, below—while the soloists probably stood in the musicians' balconies. The performers were most probably arranged so that the strings occupied one of the east balconies, the solo singers the other. Two of the organ parts were no doubt used by the conductors who coordinated the ensemble. This spacing emphasizes the sharp contrast in style between the solo and ripieno portions of the setting.

The Salzburg manuscripts of Biber's church works contain second copies of some or all of the chorus parts. Although in some cases extra ripieno parts may be lost, the total at that time, which is sometimes enumerated on the title page of the folder that contains them, usually did not exceed two per vocal register. Not once in the seventeenth-century repertory have more than two been preserved. The manuscript of Biber's *Requiem in F minor,* for example, includes two ripieno parts for each voice (besides the solo parts), and the number agrees with that on the original title page. These facts indicate that only a choir of small numbers could have been used. They indicate, as well, that there was a clear distinction between solo and ripieno sections, that the works were not performed "one to a part." One set of vocal parts must have belonged to each of the two choruses; and, since it is unlikely that more than two or three persons shared a part, the maximum number of singers in one four-part choir would have been twelve, and the more likely number eight. The two choirs would often have sung together, however, making the sound of sixteen voices normal for choral writing in four real parts. A large choir (by modern standards) is not needed in light of the extensive amount of doubling that took place in ripieno sections; and the acoustic properties of the cathedral render a small choir more successful. In Küsel's engraving we can see that two pairs of singers in the left choir share parts, while two others have parts to themselves; as we know, the number of singers on the right (their parts cannot be seen) does not exceed twelve. The large size, stiff paper, sewn sheets of parts when several pages are involved and large clear notes of the parts suggest that they were prepared with use by more than one person in mind.

Divided choirs, multiple organ parts, and spacing of solo singers and instrumentalists were all characteristic of concerted works performed in the cathedral during the late seventeenth century, whether or not antiphonal choral writing was employed. The favored choral settings in the works of Biber and Hofer are those of four (SATB), five (SSATB), six (SSATBB; Hofer also uses SSATTB while Biber does not), and eight (two SATB choirs) parts. Most likely all the larger concerted works, whether scored for four-, five-, six- or eight-part chorus, involved about the same number of choir members and the same spacing (half the chorus on the left, half on the right). Four- and five-part vocal writing occurs most often, even in double-chorus music, while choral antiphony is reserved chiefly for special effects at key places. The manuscript of Biber's *Offertorium de S. Michaele,* like those of a number of other similarly scored works, contains doubled ripieno parts for alto, tenor and bass, but only a single copy for each of the two soprano parts of the chorus, a circumstance that suggests that the piece was performed with the following spacing of the choir:[66]

S2	S1
A	A
T	T
B	B

The five-part chorus of the *Missa S. Henrici* could well have been distributed in the same way, although it was performed at Nonnberg, not at the cathedral; the arrangement is effective, for the two soprano parts frequently alternate over the more or less constant lower voices. However, Biber's *Requiem in F minor* must have been performed with a five-part choir on each side of the cathedral since two copies of each of the five chorus parts exist. Two types of spacing, both of which approximate double-chorus writing, are possible for six-part SSATBB choruses:

S2	S1		S2	S1
A	A	or	T	A
T	T		B2	B1
B2	B1			

Some works suggest the first distribution, others the second.[67] The division of soprano and bass parts reflects not only the baroque love for a texture emphasizing melody and bass, but also the fact that two institutions in Salzburg, the *vicarii chori* and the Choirboys Institute, provided trained basses and sopranos. The existence of this style (i.e., division of only one or two parts of the chorus) plus the fact that Biber used antiphonal choral writing rather sparingly and less in the later than in the earlier works, leads to a conclusion that seems almost obvious in view of the layout of the cathedral: for the listener in the nave of the church, antiphony between the right and left sides of the choir was not perfectly clear. The length of the nave is too great in relation to the width of the choir for the effect to be wholly successful. And the revival of the *Missa Salisburgensis* for the twelve-hundredth anniversary of the archdiocese in 1974—without, of course, the performance conditions available in the seventeenth century—certainly made these problems only too obvious.[68] In his *Missa Alleluia* Biber used choral antiphony only twice (both times briefly on the word "gloria"); the two sides are not perfectly differentiated, and Biber departs from the normal doubling of one chorus by winds, the other by strings. On the other hand, in the *Vesperae à 32* of about twenty years earlier the traditional doubling holds, and Biber assumes that the antiphony will be perceived, for he employs it for descriptive purposes (e.g., "dispersit," "Dominus a dextris tuis"—to paint the word "dextris" Biber employs the normal beginning of the antiphony from the right-hand side). The spatial illusion was unquestionably augmented by the coupling of each chorus with the instruments of one family and by the fact that the instrumental choirs in the balconies were considerably more widely spaced than the vocal choruses in the choir below.

There is no reason to believe that there was any essential difference between the performances of purely soloistic and ripieno church music in Salzburg and those of similarly scored sections within polychoral works. Biber's *Laetatus Sum à 7*, for two basses and strings, and his *Nisi Dominus à 2*, for bass and solo violin, which are comparable in style to the "deposuit" of the *Vesperae à 32* and the "et vitam" of the *Missa Christi Resurgentis*, must have been executed from one of the musicians' balconies. This was presumably true of the church sonatas as well: the *Sonata S. Polycarpi* was, as Biber's performance instructions tell us, antiphonally spaced as the trumpets always were. For the performance of Biber's *stile antico* works and strict fugal movements in the concerted music, the vocal parts were usually doubled by either strings (violas and *violettae* rather than violins) or trombones (with cornetto on the soprano part). It is also possible that they were accompanied only by continuo (without other instruments), or doubled by strings as well as winds; both of these settings are found in the concerted works, although the favored disposition is to double the chorus by a single instrumental choir. Although in one late work, the *Requiem à 15*, Biber chose to substitute oboes for cornetti (probably to create a "special" sonority, since they are "ad libitum" and *colla parte* throughout), the listeners of Biber's time did not identify cornetti and trombones with old-fashioned music so closely as did those of a generation or more later. J. S. Bach, for example, reserved these instruments for strict, motet-like or *stile antico* movements, such as his arrangement of Palestrina's *Missa brevis* and certain movements from the cantatas. Although Biber still used cornetti as obbligato instruments and even gave them demanding solo parts from time to time, they were clearly less indispensable than in former times in that role; as far as we know Biber, unlike Schmelzer, wrote no independent sonata parts for cornetto, and he probably considered the instrument more appropriate in its traditional role of doubling the voice in choral movements (a work of Kerll's in the cathedral archive has, for example, parts designated for "cornetti ripieni").[69] Likewise, violas and *violettae* (a designation for instruments playing viola parts written in soprano clef) were preferred to violins as *colla parte* instruments because of their more restrained, archaic sound. The first violin part of Biber's *Missa Catholica* is notated in soprano rather than treble clef at those places where it doubles the soprano part in strict style (the Christe and Qui tollis). The change of clef might have cautioned the violinist to moderate his tone, or even, perhaps, to change instruments.

Guido Adler's belief that *stile antico* works such as Biber's *Missa Quadragesimalis* should be performed "a cappella" in the modern sense (without continuo) is based on a misunderstanding of the use of the word "cappella" at that time. In his edition of Biber's *Missa S. Henrici*, Adler omits the words "da cappella" that appear in the manuscript organ part of the *stile antico* "Christe."[70] Since the vocal parts of this movement are doubled by strings and trombones, the modern usage of the term obviously does not apply. According to seventeenth-century terminology, "da cappella" designates ripieno settings (usually fugal, motet-like movements associated with the *stile antico*) in which the chorus might or (less often) might not be doubled by instruments; omission of the basso continuo is never indicated. In the fugal Crucifixus of Hofer's *Missa Archiepiscopalis* the vocal parts bear the heading "da cappella," and the *colla parte* trombones are designated "4 in cappella." Over the first violin part of the fugal Christe in Biber's *Missa Catholica* the word "capp[ella]" appears. The Seitenstetten manuscript copy of Biber's *Missa Quadragesimalis* is entitled *Missa alla Cappella,* and contains parts for one *violetta,* three trombones and basso continuo. Biber and Hofer, in conformity with contemporary practice, usually head strict fugal movements "alla breve." This term was commonly used for strict or *stile antico* movements written in long note values, a visual association with tradition. Such movements were performed at twice the normal tempo, as if they had been notated with the note values halved. The tempo markings "allegro" or "presto" that often appear in the parts of these fugal sections were either intended as a substitute for the "alla breve" designation, or served as a reminder that the tempo should be faster than the long note values would suggest.

Many characteristics of Salzburg's musical performances were by no means unique to that city, as we know from works written for other centers. Instrumentation varied as the practice differed from place to place, but certain features were common to all or most areas. Of course, few churches could offer performing conditions as ideally suited to polychoral music as those of the Salzburg cathedral, which was built at the very time when polychoral music was coming into its own in Italy; and the greatly varied musical settings for such works often reflect the limitations imposed by gothic structures.

Johann Caspar Kerll's *Missa à 3 cori,* written for performance at St. Stephen's cathedral in Vienna, and Martin Meuer's *Jubilate à 37 ô 44* (1675), performed at the church of St. Mary Magdalen in Breslau, bear comparison with the polychoral music of Hofer and Biber written in Salzburg.[71] Kerll's Mass is scored for three four-part vocal choirs with soloists, one choir each of strings, cornetti and trombones, and trumpets with timpani (there were three organs in the Vienna cathedral at the time).[72] The *Missa à 3 cori* falls very much within the same tradition as Biber's works. Soloistic passages alternate regularly with triple-chorus antiphony, and the Crucifixus, which is scored for three solo basses and trombones, recalls the Crucifixus for four basses and trombones in the *Missa Salisburgensis.* We are exceedingly fortunate in the case of Meuer's *Jubilate* in knowing the exact number of musicians who participated:[73]

CHORUS I

These thirteen persons are all on the "Singechore"		
	1)	The cantor
	2)	Ten vocalists (those who sing solo parts receive more than those who only sing in the chorus)
	3)	The positive organ player
	4)	A large bass violin [violone]

CHORUS II

These eleven persons sit on the side by the "Dresskammer"		
	5)	Six violins
	6)	One "Quintfagott"
	7)	Four violas

CHORUS III

These ten persons sit on the other side by the "Kretschmer" and "Schneider" chapel		
	8)	Four *viole da gamba*
	9)	A little bass violin [cello]
	10)	Four flutes
	11)	A little "Stort" in place of the bass flute

CHORUS IV

These seven persons are at the
organ by the "Singechor"

12) The organist
13) Four trombonists
14) Two cornettists

DOUBLE CHORUS V

These nine persons are on the
"Bürgerchor"

15) Two clarini
16) One principal
17) One "Ducade"
18) A pair of kettledrums
19) Two clarini
20) One principal
21) One "Ducade"

Similarities to polychoral performances in the Salzburg cathedral are immediately apparent. We note the divided trumpet choirs, the choirs of strings and of cornetti with trombones, the situation of the latter instrumental choir nearest the chorus, the small number of singers (a total of ten for a setting of SSATBB chorus and soloists), the accompaniment of the chorus by a positive organ and violone, the location of the cantor with the choir, and so on. Obviously the violins were doubled but not the other instruments. Excerpts quoted from this work by Schneider disclose techniques comparable to those employed in Biber's polychoral music. Also Meuer's *Jubilate* was composed for an anniversary service, just as, presumably, were some of Biber's more lavish compositions. In principle, therefore, the performance practice of polychoral music in Salzburg was entirely representative of its age. Concerted antiphonal music reached its peak there as elsewhere during the second half of the seventeenth century. In fact, because of Salzburg's ideal performance conditions and resources, as well as the survival of a considerable part of the musical repertoire, practice at the cathedral occupies a central position in our understanding of south German and Austrian Catholic church music of the baroque period.

Church Music in Seventeenth-Century Salzburg

Although the performances resources and institutions at the Salzburg cathedral remained fundamentally unchanged for about two hundred years, throughout that time, of course, a great range of musical styles succeeded one another, and even coexisted, within the basic polychoral framework. On one end of the time scale was late renaissance music; and on the other, the majority of Mozart's Salzburg church works and even later compositions were produced, all under similar outward circumstances. The great disparity of styles and musical value of the works produced throughout the period as a whole suggests a kind of dialectic relationship between the "static" institutions, their hierarchical conditions and restrictions on the one hand, and the composers' individuality on the other. This quality is perhaps more fascinating in Biber's music than in that of any other composer, at least of the seventeenth century; and several of his works—the *Missa Salisburgensis* above all—raise the issue of convention versus expression in a manner that cannot be ignored, for it touches on the very question of musical value. As a background to the cultural and aesthetic issues that surround Biber's sacred music, we must understand something of the tradition that faced the young, but still relatively inexperienced virtuoso upon his arrival in Salzburg, and that, as the years went on, drew him more and more away from the instrumental music that was certainly the root of his genius and into the sphere of church music.

Although we will summarize the general character of musical events at the cathedral through the seventeenth century, we may observe at the outset that within the series of seventeenth-century Kapellmeister Biber occupies a unique position as the musician whose background in instrumental music and inclination toward unusual sonorities, folk and program music stood in the sharpest contrast with the traditional training and practice of German Kapellmeister of the time. This does not mean, of course, that Biber did not receive thorough training in the traditional arts of counterpoint; his expertise in this area is amply documented in his *stile antico* movements, in works such as the *Missa ex B, Stabat Mater,* and *Missa Quadragesimalis* as well as the many "Gegenfugen" in his work. There is a certain tension, nevertheless, between the contrapuntal and the pictorial, instrumentally conceived elements of his work, a tension that can already be seen in the early violin sonatas of the Vienna manuscript. There the expressive and skillful fugal *lamento* that would later be used, virtually unaltered, as the introduction to the sixth of the *Sonatae Violino Solo* appears in conjunction with an ostinato movement that reveals more than a little of the youthful composer's difficulties with musical extension; likewise, the *Fantasia* from the same manuscript contains a fugal continuation—deleted from the final version—in which the strange crossing of the bass line with the violin in the upper register, the extraordinarily long figural sequences of the bass, and the weakening of the contrapuntal intent with the incongruous introduction of rustic elements all betray an exuberance that is not yet under control. Something of the same quality exists in the more mature *Missa Quadragesimalis,* a work in *stile antico* that makes many departures from the seventeenth-century norm for such Masses, departures that are often to be considered the source of its originality and strength, although there is sometimes a certain unmistakable crudeness in style. When Biber does learn how to effectively harness these extravagant tendencies, however, the result is a very impressive synthesis that retains a certain "extreme" character that is connected to the idea of baroque extragavance. The fourteen *scordatura* tunings and pictorialisms of the *Mystery Sonatas,* the scoring of the *Missa Salisburgensis* and the dissonant quodlibet of the *Battalia* obviously reveal this extreme aspect in their different ways; but so do many other relatively unknown features of Biber's church works: the range of the cornetti in the *Missa Alleluia,* the size of the viola choir in the *Litania de S. Josepho,* the length of the *Missa Bruxellensis,* the use of trumpets pitched in low A in the *Requiem à 15,* the virtuoso violin writing that merges motet and sonata in the *Nisi Dominus,* the elaborate trumpet parts of the *Sonata S. Polycarpi,* and so on. It is unquestionably the interaction between the daring character of his instrumental music and the restrictions of the conventions in church music at the Salzburg cathedral that gives Biber's sacred music its unusual vitality.

Music at the Cathedral before 1650

Relatively little is known today about the church music heard in Salzburg during the thirty-year period between the burning of the old romanesque cathedral in 1598 and the consecration of the new building, a time during which the cathedral services were held in the Franciscan church. The most important musicians of that era in Salzburg were Jakob Flory (1596?–99), Johann Stadlmayr (1603–7), Peter Gutfreund or Bonamico (1608–ca. 25) and Steffano Bernardi (1627–3?). As the very names suggest, this period was characterized by a move away from the Netherlands polyphonic styles of the sixteenth century, increasing Italianization of the chapel, and growing absorption of Italian styles.

Although we know from payment lists and the occasional description of sacred festivities that large numbers of instrumentalists took part in church music in early seventeenth-century Salzburg, the surviving scores and parts usually give little or no indication of this practice; in most cases the instrumental parts are not included. A title such as *Cantiones sacrae quinque vocum* "tum omnivario instrumentorum concentui accomodae" (Jakob Flory) is by no means unusual for the turn of the seventeenth century. The texture of vocal parts doubled by instruments—sometimes with instruments substituting for voices on one or more parts—was standard in church music of this time. The most common instruments were those indicated in the early inventories at Salzburg: strings, cornetti, trombones and trumpets. The latter, however, sounded only on the highest occasions, such as the installation of the new archbishop in 1613. In eight-part double chorus works each vocal choir was reinforced by a "choir" of instruments, either strings, or cornetti and trombones. The two instrumental choirs were completely interchangeable in many church works: Stadlmayr's concerted Masses, for example, contain the designations "cornetto ô violino," "viole ô tromboni" and "cantate e sonate."[1]

This situation explains why specific instrumental parts are seldom prescribed. If a score of the music performed for Marcus Sitticus in 1613 had survived, it would in all probability give us no hint of a performance such as that described in the contemporary report. In any case, the work might be presented entirely differently on another occasion. The director could choose to execute one section of an eight-part vocal work with or without *colla parte* instruments; he could, for example, at another place have trombones play the lower vocal parts as accompaniment to a soprano solo; and, if appropriate to the occasion, he could insert an introduction and interludes for trumpets and kettledrums. The practices described in such detail by Praetorius indicate just how flexible the question of scoring was.[2] The range of possibilities was indeed large, but by no means left entirely to the Kapellmeister's personal choice. Certain services required particular settings, and even the location of the musicians was ordered according to ecclesiastical hierarchy. Decrees dated 1729 and 1746 tell us that for the highest feasts (*festi Pallii, Praepositi, Decani* and *Canonici,* as well as the third Sunday of the month) the music was performed from the balconies ("oberen Chor") by the court musicians; full scoring involving the four balconies was utilized for the "festi Pallii" (feasts of the archbishop), the same scoring minus trumpets and drums (i.e., two balconies) for the "festi Praepositi et Decani" (provost and dean), and five violinists with three trombones and bassoon on the "Principal-Chor" alone for the "festi Canonici."[3] It is evident, therefore, that the scoring of large church works was often quite standardized and dependent upon tradition. In matters of style and instrumental detail the composer naturally had more freedom, and it is within these elements that we observe major changes from one generation to another.

In the concerted works of Stadlmayr we encounter an intermediate stage between a complete lack of instrumental designations and the absolute precision of scorings and idioms in the late seventeenth and eighteenth centuries.[4] In choral movements Stadlmayr sometimes added an extra cornetto or violin part that often resembles an untexted vocal line in everything but range; Stadlmayr also included short instrumental interludes from time to time. In addition we sometimes find in his works *concertato* sections for vocal soloist(s) with instruments; despite indications such as "cornetto ô violino," which imply a disregard for individual instrumental styles, such sections represent a more "advanced" mode of writing than those based entirely upon the substitution of instruments for voices in a balanced polyphonic texture.

Conservative as this mode of writing appears from the perspective of the late seventeenth century, it nevertheless persisted throughout much of the age. In Antonio Draghi's *Missa Assumptionis* (1684), for example, the only stylistic distinction that can be made between a bass solo with two cornetti and a bass solo with two sopranos is the slightly wider range of the instrumental parts.[5] Andreas Hofer used indications such as "2 violini ô cornetti, 3 violae ô tromboni."[6] Biber is more discriminating in this regard, but his early church works retain conservative features, such as independent introductory "sonatas" and interludes that are unrelated motivically to the remainder of the works. These instrumental passages do not appear to be essential to the music and could probably be omitted at will, whereas in the later works all instrumental sections are thematically bound to the vocal parts and inseparable from them. In one early "sonata" introduction, from the *Lux Perpetua* of 1673, a work that still preserves traits of the inexperienced composer, the viola and trombone parts are identical; this practice is not followed anywhere else in Biber's instrumental music.

Another important aspect of Salzburg's church music in the seventeenth and eighteenth centuries was the cultivation of sixteenth-century polyphony side by side with *concertato* practices. Music of renaissance composers, especially by Victoria, was copied up to the middle of the century, and the older contrapuntal style continued in newly composed works, such as Steffano Bernardi's parody Mass based on Arcadelt's *Il bianco e dolce cigno,* and later, Biber's *Missa Quadragesimalis;*[7] still within this tradition are some severely archaic Masses by Michael Haydn, written in the late eighteenth century.[8] In all such works, as in the countless *Missae* "in cappella" and "in contrapuncto" and the *Gradus ad Parnassum* of Fux the sense is preserved of a vocal basis behind all that is musically "intrinsic." Even the physical location of the manuscripts of the cathedral archive reflected this stylistic dualism.[9] The work that most exemplifies this dualism, however, is one without obbligato instruments, Biber's *Missa ex B,* in which the composer took on the task of writing in both "strict" (*stile antico*) and "free" (*concertato*) choral styles in regular, systematic alternation.

A high point for the earliest phase of concerted music in Salzburg was the consecration of the present cathedral in September 1628, one of the greatest celebrations in the history of the city. At a time when all of Central Europe underwent the prolonged misery of the Thirty Years' War, Archbishop Paris Lodron's neutral policy rendered Salzburg an oasis of peace. Its citizens could enjoy festivities that had been months, if not years, in preparation.

The music performed at the consecration service has aroused much interest since the discovery, about one hundred years ago, of the score of the fifty-three-part Mass presumed until quite recently to have been composed for this occasion by Orazio Benevoli, and now known as the *Missa Salisburgensis*. [10] For numerous reasons, however, it is certain that this work had nothing to do with the 1628 occasion and does not even date from the period in question. [11] But a large number of erroneous statements about the work and its performance persist in the literature, statements that can usually be traced back (though seldom directly) to four surviving contemporaneous documents referring to the music at the consecration service. [12] We know the following facts: the music was executed at Mass under the direction of Kapellmeister Steffano Bernardi; all kinds of musical instruments, including trumpets and organs, were used along with the voices; the performers were divided into twelve choirs situated on twelve of the marble balconies that protrude from the cathedral walls, and were thus visible to all; among the pieces presented Bernardi's *Te Deum* made the greatest impression; the service lasted from seven in the morning until two in the afternoon.

The attempt to reconcile the 1628 reports of music divided into twelve choirs with the score of the *Missa Salisburgensis* and its nineteenth-century inscription naming it as the consecration Mass, has led to many unfortunate pronouncements, both historical and aesthetic, concerning the *Missa Salisburgensis* and its performance, as well as an ill-considered introduction of the term "colossal baroque" to Salzburg's seventeenth-century church music. Although the score of the *Missa Salisburgensis* indicates only six "cori" and two trumpet choirs, headed "loco 1" and "loco 2" respectively, we find Hermann Spiess, who knew the score, suggesting that four hundred singers sang in the work, a complete departure from the performance practice in Salzburg that Spies himself did much to document. [13] Later literature, not based directly on the contemporary documents, has wandered even further from the truth, Rolf Damann suggesting, for example, that there was *even* a twelve-chorus version of the work—that is, another version for twelve vocal choirs. [14] The chief error in reports such as these (and there are others) consists of a confusion between the modern and seventeenth-century uses of the word "choir." In the score of the Mass the word refers clearly to both vocal and instrumental groups, and indeed the term was used in this manner throughout the seventeenth and eighteenth centuries. In the 1628 reports of the consecration the word "choir" designates the balconies upon which the musicians stood. [15]

While the *Missa Salisburgensis* belongs to the latter part of the century, the work is a kind of symbol for all the issues surrounding polychoral music throughout the century. If the work had been written in 1628 it would represent an exceptionally advanced piece of church music for the time. Nevertheless there is significance in the fact that it was mistaken for a work of the early seventeenth century for so long. This significance is, however, not so much in the external performance characteristics of the work, much as we have said to point out the sense of continuity in this respect in Salzburg, as it is in a deeper affinity between Biber's style and that of the spirit of the early seventeenth century, Monteverdi in particular. What the Mass shares with Bernardi's *Te Deum,* apart from general aspects of performance practice, is the baroque aim of heightening the meaning of the text by creating an overwhelming impact on the listener, even by astonishing him. To this end the extensive deployment of vocal and instrumental resources is not primarily so much a function of sheer size and monumentality as of the successive sensuous impressions created by continually shifting sonority. The changes of scoring in the *Magnificat* for seven voices and six instruments in Monteverdi's 1610 Vespers provide a case in point, just as much as Domenico Mazzochi's placing of an echo choir in the cupola of the dome of St. Peter's in Rome (Adler used the term "acoustic perspective" to characterize this aspect of baroque art).[16] In this music the architectural element plays a decisive role, one that would be developed to the scale of the entire church as late baroque "Gesamtkunstwerk" in southern Germany in the eighteenth century. Seventeenth-century polychoral music may be considered the first manifestation of this impulse in Germany and Austria, and Salzburg was unquestionably a center in the interrelatedness of architecture and music. As Bukofzer states, "Rarely again have music and architecture been as closely associated as in the baroque period, where space as such became an essential component of musical structure."[17] Such music shares the aesthetic aims of sacred baroque art in general. The example par excellence in the visual arts is Bernini's *Ecstasy of St. Theresa* (1645–52) in the Cornaro chapel in Rome. Bernini enhances the reality of an intensely emotional moment, surprising and arousing wonder in the viewer with a hitherto unimagined variety of means: white marble, colored marble, gilt wood, painting, stucco, and sunlight passing through a hidden colored-glass window. All this is contained within an almost theatrical architectural frame comprising the reactions of the Cornaro family, represented as privileged witnesses whose presence invites the modern viewer's participation as well. Thus the viewer is related both to the mystical experience of the saint and to the response of pious modern-day individuals.

Misguided pronouncements about the *Missa Salisburgensis* and its performance have led to both curious lapses of historical perspective and aesthetic misjudgments of the work—usually pronouncing it "simple" on the basis of its diatonic, often purely triadic sonority. Bukofzer, for example, has the following to say:

> Benevoli's polychoral Mass for 53 parts, comissioned for the inauguration of the Salzburg cathedral, bears witness to the stupendous facility of spatial dispositions, and, at the same time, the inflation of essentially modest music to mammoth dimensions...the Mass is held together by a master continuo which readily discloses how simple the underlying chord progressions actually are.[18]

The aesthetic judgment passed in the words "inflation of essentially modest music" has broader implications than those concerning the scoring and harmonic style of the *Missa Salisburgensis* alone. Behind it lies an attitude toward certain features of baroque art, especially its extravagance and sensuousness, that prompted, for example, the coloring of the walls of the Salzburg cathedral "stone grey" in the nineteenth century. A moral judgment is often involved in such aesthetic stances, and one that is sufficiently deep-rooted to become itself a subject matter for artistic treatment, in, for example, Charlotte Brontë's remarks (in *Villette*) on baroque art of the Catholic, Italian variety (Rubens, in particular). Through the views of her heroine, Lucy Snowe, Brontë reveals a fundamental attitude toward baroque art that remains with us, even if its force has lessened.[19] Such art does indeed deal with worldliness, the transience of wealth and, in music, of fleeting sensory impressions. While appearing to glorify the monumental, or the mammoth, as Bukofzer puts it, it makes all too clear the role of the monument in commemorating the dead. That is, it seems to have nothing left for posterity except its monumental, historical aspect. And this emblematic quality, this continual pointing to symbols of transience, as Walter Benjamin has shown for the seventeenth-century tragic drama, is a part of what makes this art, in its almost anti-aesthetic stance, a "corrective to art itself."[20] Of course, the indicating of its own transience, or "historical" character, was not directly the aim of works such as the *Missa Salisburgensis,* whose elaborate instrumentation was probably intended, like Bernardi's *Te Deum* to invoke images of transcendence. But, although there was never such a suspicion of the senses in Catholic as there was in Lutheran art of the seventeenth century, the awareness of the inadequacy of the senses was still fundamental to religion; and the virtual flaunting of the sensuous character of art was not taken to be its entire, or chief value. If it had been we would have had no Missae "in contrapuncto" and no sense, from Fux and others, that the root of greatness in music lay in traditional contrapuntal values. Instead, the amplifying of the sensuous aspect of art made all the clearer the distinction between the historical—conceived as the sensuous, the fleeting and momentary—and the "universal." It is clear then, that we cannot judge baroque art—either positively or negatively—by its external features, of which "simple harmonies" may be one, any more than we judge Charlotte Brontë by the view from *Villette* referred to above. And statements about the "simple" harmonies of the Mass often fall wide of the mark on purely historical grounds because they fail to take account of the aim of the work and the performance conditions for which it was composed. The number and wide spacing of the musicians, as well as the exceptionally long reverberation time of the cathedral dictated a measure of harmonic restraint that is not in any sense a weakness of either the style or the composer.

We must not believe too readily that the performance resources demanded by works such as the *Missa Salisburgensis* can be dispensed with on the grounds that such compositions would make an equally good impression with more modest means (even though such reductions were permitted at the time). A principle basic to the "architectural" character of much baroque art is the building of a complex form of expression out of a subject that in the Renaissance would have been treated in another way. There is no doubt that much of the expressiveness of the *Ecstasy of St. Theresa* could be conveyed in a painting, without the extravagant and complex setting Bernini gave the sculptural group; its value is not confined to its scale and drama. To judge the work from that viewpoint, however, would be to deny a masterpiece of baroque art one of its most characteristic qualities: the arousal of wonder in the viewer by means of all the visual means at the artist's command. The *Missa Salisburgensis* would be damaged about as much as Bernini's work by any diminishing of its "illusionistic" devices. Reduction of scoring and simplification of spacing would be an easy matter in many places in the score. For example, the twenty-eight vocal and instrumental parts of the *Christe* can be reduced to eleven: six voices, four instruments, and continuo, perhaps even less. If this were done, however, the movement, would become lifeless and almost intolerably repetitious in places. The work was conceived with elaboration in mind and should be judged on that basis. Unless we are willing, and able, to eliminate from music all allegorical and even rhetorical devices—echo effects, dynamic contrasts, orchestration, to name a very small number—we stand on shaky ground in using external criteria as a yardstick for artistic value. Criticism, on the other hand, has the task of recognizing the role played by the dialectic of intrinsic and extrinsic features of art in our analysis, perception and evaluation of the works.

The presence of such a dialectic is no guarantee of musical quality, of course; and in the seventeenth century Salzburg did not enjoy the presence of a first-rate composer before the time of Biber and Muffat. The Kapellmeister between Steffano Bernardi and Andreas Hofer was Abraham Megerle, a very unusual personality. Megerle, a pupil of Stadlmayr, copied works by renaissance composers, including Clemens non Papa and Victoria. He continued Netherlandish polyphonic traditions, even to the extent of composing highly intricate, if dull, canons. Of over two thousand works Megerle professed to have written, very little has survived, and his claim may be doubted in view of the indifference with which he included works by other composers in his manuscript collections.[21] Nevertheless, one very large set of church music by Megerle was published in Salzburg in 1647; this *Ara musica* (over one hundred compositions for the entire church year) contains concerted church music for vocal and instrumental combinations ranging from one solo voice with basso continuo to huge polychoral works. The scorings, which are extremely varied, reflect early seventeenth-century principles as we know them from the music and writings of Praetorius, Schütz and Banchieri. In the preface to the *Ara musica* Megerle, like Hofer, allows reductions in the scoring of large works when sufficient numbers of performers are not available, stating, for instance, that one voice and three trombones may be substituted for a four-part chorus.[22] Most of Megerle's titles indicate that great latitude in scoring was permissible:

1. *Alleluja. Hic est Sacerdos* (à 2, C[anto] B[asso], et à 4, con 2 V[iolini] et 1 Viola si plac. et absque Alleluja.)
2. *Festiva haec Solemnitas* (à 4, CC et 2 Vi, sed melius à 9 alias à 10, CC & Vio.)
3. *Confitebuntur coeli* (Temp. Pasch. 6 Voc. tantum alias 12 Vo. 6 Inst. & 4 Trombette con 4 Rip.)
4. *Justus ut palma* (à 8 Vo. 1 Corn. 1 Trombet, alias à 22. 12. Vo. 5 Inst. 1 corn. 4 tromb. et 5 Trombettae, 1 Clar. con 4 Rip.)[23]

Many of the works have "Alleluia" refrains, as well as optional instrumental movements with varied scorings (introductions or ritornelli) that are designated "Sinfonia" or "Sonata." The conductor's "score" of the *Ara Musica* is more detailed than the usual M. D. C. (Maestro di Cappella) or "Battuta" score that is often found in Salzburg church works, in that it contains as many as six systems, each with the bass line of a choir.[24] Megerle's *Ara Musica* is our chief witness to the fact that polychoral music continued to be cultivated at the cathedral during the tenure of Archbishop Paris Lodron.

Church Music during the Second Half of the Century

With Megerle's successor, Andreas Hofer (1629–84), we enter a period that has been studied in more detail than the preceding one, even though few sacred works from that time have been published. This period has been called the "first flowering of the high Baroque" in Salzburg.[25] Schneider's statement most accurately describes those years during which Max Gandolph and Johann Ernst were archbishops. Unquestionably, Biber and Muffat were two of the greatest German composers of the age. From the second half of the century we possess the first body of music in Salzburg's history that covers the full range of contemporary styles. Furthermore, one can perceive a sense of the newly flourishing Austrian national consciousness in much of the music written at this time in Salzburg. The texts of the schooldramas deal frequently with German subjects, and the story of a German hero, Arminius, forms the basis for Biber's opera *Chi la dura la vince.* The title *Missa Catholica* reflects the spirit of militant Catholicism that accompanied the rise in national feeling, while the *Missa St. Henrici* honors the feast day of a saint who had been emperor as well. The hymn to St. Rupert that accompanies the *Missa Salisburgensis,* and Biber's *Litania de S. Josepho,* written in honor of Salzburg's *Landespatron,* all affirm the patriotic character that was coming to the fore in the late seventeenth century.

In addition to the 1682 *Rupertusfest,* at which, perhaps, the *Missa Salisburgensis* and hymn to St. Rupert, *Plaudite Tympana* were heard, documents relating to events at the cathedral often provide us with information regarding special occasions at which concerted church music was presented; apart from the frequent and generalized references to trumpet music and the singing of a festive *Te Deum,* however, there is never any mention of the actual music performed. For instance, the court musicians, trumpeters and drummers executed a *Te Deum* when Paris Lodron left to take part in the Peace of Westphalia in 1648, and when the *pallium* was brought for Archbishop Guidobald in 1654. On the latter occasion the trumpets and timpani also sounded alone with the organs.[26] Similar performances took place on the following occasions: a service held while the remains of the Abbot of St. Peter's were transferred to the cathedral in 1661, a service in honor of the visit of Emperor Leopold in 1664, a service held in honor of the visit of Elector Ferdinand Maria and his wife in 1670, a festive celebration of the defeat of the Turks in 1683, the elevation of Archbishop Max Gandolph to cardinal in 1684.[27] In a contemporary description we read that during the *pallium* service in 1687 the whole church resounded with bells; while Johann Ernst accepted the *pallium,* trumpets, drums and the four organs sounded simultaneously; after Mass, trumpets and drums accompanied a procession from the sacristry to the high altar.[28] Although only those descriptions of the more remarkable contemporary celebrations at the cathedral make reference to performances, and then only occasionally, it goes without saying that music played an important role at many other festive services. For example, Archbishop Max Gandolph's nephew, Polykarp von Khuenburg, was installed as provost of the cathedral in January 1673. He was elected to the office on January 13, just thirteen days before the feast day of his name saint, St. Polycarp.[29] The records of this occasion yield no information concerning the music performed during the celebration (other than the customary *Te Deum*), but it seems obvious that Biber's *Sonata S. Polycarpi à 9,* written in 1673, must have been heard on January 26 in honor of the new provost (and was presumably written in the thirteen days between Polykarp's elction and installation).[30]

Perhaps the most interesting type of occasion for which concerted church works were commissioned in Salzburg was the *anniversarium* or *Jahrtag,* a commemorative service instituted by someone of wealth and high standing—frequently the archbishop himself or a member of the chapter—and intended to be observed *in perpetuum.* One or two days were set aside for the annual celebration in the cathedral, usually in remembrance of the founder of the service or his family. The yearly interest from the capital investment provided by the founder paid for the various Masses celebrated, the participation of priests and other clergy, the music, and so on. The anniversary was commonly celebrated with a vigil followed by a High Mass the next day. Underlying these services was the conception of *splendor familiae* so important to a baroque ruler during the baroque era, as well as the desire to leave something lasting behind, the major impetus for the erection of churches and monuments.

Records have survived relating to the institution of several *anniversaria* at the cathedral during the years when Biber and Hofer were Kapellmeister. Unfortunately they give us virtually no facts concerning musical performances or works, but we can draw inferences from the amounts paid to the musicians. Information about such services usually exists only when the anniversary is founded or altered in some way, such as the expansion of a *Jahrtag* with the participation of the court musicians in 1685, or when, as in 1671, the musical observance of the *Jahrtag* did not conform to the requirements.[31]

In November 1674 Archbishop Max Gandolph donated the sum of 160 gulden, part of which was to provide for musical performances at the cathedral. An already-existing *anniversarium* held in memory of two of Max Gandolph's ancestors who had also been archbishops of Salzburg was expanded by the provision of twelve gulden for the court musicians (among other things). In addition, the archbishop decreed that a second *Jahrtag* in honor of all members of the Khuenburg family, living or dead, be established. The payments list for the new service contains the following amounts for the musicians:[32]

	Florins	Schillings	Kreuzer
20 *vicarii chori*	2:	5:	10:
The 8 *Choralisten*		4:	8:
8 *Corporey Knaben*		2:	4:
For the court musicians 8 gulden altogether			

Each of these services, including a sung vigil and high Mass, lasted two days (November 15–16 and 17–18). Max Gandolph made it clear in his decree that the new conditions applied for the 1674 celebrations. From the relatively high amount paid to the court musicians (more than twice that allotted to the cathedral choir) we can conclude that the performances required vocal soloists and instrumentalists. We do not know whether Hofer or Biber composed the music. No extant work of Hofer's is dated 1674. However, two polychoral works by Biber—the *Vesperae à 32* and *Missa Christi Resurgentis*—were composed in that year and could have been intended for Max Gandolph's *anniversarium.*

During the last few years of the century several *Jahrtage* were endowed by the archbishop and prominent members of the chapter. Johann Ernst founded three in 1695, the first for himself, the second in memory of his family, the third to honor the "faithful ministers and officials of the archdiocese of Salzburg."[33] For these services he gave the unusually large amount of ten thousand florins, which yielded five hundred florins in interest per year as payment for the celebrations. Similar, if somewhat more modestly endowed *anniversaria* were established in 1697 (by the bishop of Chiemsee), in 1699 (Wilhelm, Freiherr von Fürstenberg, dean) and in 1700 (for the family of Count J. Königsegg, senior member of the chapter).[34] In all of these anniversaries provisions were made for musical performances requiring both the cathedral choir and the court musicians. The substantial amounts given to the latter suggest that concerted works were heard. No reference to the music itself appears. The dates when these services were established, however, correspond closely to the dates of some of Biber's largest surviving church compositions, for example, 1674 (*Vesperae à 32*), and 1695–1700 (*Missa Alleluia, Missa Bruxellensis*); one of Biber's two Requiems (both after 1690) might have been written for the funeral of Dean Fürstenberg, who died in 1699 leaving the specifications for his anniversary service in his will.[35]

Whether or not concerted church music was performed at an *anniversarium* depended upon the amount of money donated. More than once the founder increased the original sum in order to pay for the participation of court musicians. In 1696 the prince-bishop of Vienna endowed a *Jahrtag* in Salzburg with three hundred gulden, an amount yielding only fifteen gulden in interest per year.[36] The interest sufficed to pay the *Choralisten* and *Corporey Knaben,* but not the *vicarii chori* or court musicians. We may therefore conclude that plainchant only was sung as the prince-bishop's service. We cannot be certain how strictly these annual memorial services were observed in seventeenth-century Salzburg. That a large number were in existence by that time is beyond doubt. A. J. Hammerle reports that an *anniversarium* founded in 1530 was still being celebrated in the late nineteenth century.[37] By the year 1775, however, so many *Jahrtage* had been established that strict observance of them all was no longer possible and a drastic reduction took place.[38] It is clear, nevertheless, that a number of important ones were still observed in the latter part of the seventeenth century, and thus provided occasions for the composition and performance of concerted church music.

The surviving church music performed at the cathedral in the latter part of the seventeenth century is made up almost entirely of the works of Biber and Hofer, with a few compositions by Johann Caspar Kerll, Antonio Bertali and Maurizio Cazzati.[39] In the area of instrumental music for the service it is quite possible that some of the sonatas of Georg Muffat's *Armonico tributo* (1682) and the toccatas of his *Apparatus musico-organisticus* (1690) were heard in the context of church services. Otherwise, the compositions of the two Kapellmeister must have dominated the cathedral music. Hofer's surviving output is not large—a little over sixty compositions—although we know the titles of a substantial number of lost works; there are no known independent instrumental works at all. Two published collections of church music of his are extant. The first, *Salmi con una voce, e doi violini, e motetti con, e senza violini,* of 1654, contains fifteen compositions, mostly in trio texture—either solo voice and two violins or three solo voices—above the basso continuo. The second, *Ver sacrum seu flores Musici,* of 1677, contains eighteen offertories, all but one—a composition for eight voices and three instruments—for five-part chorus (mostly CCATB) with two violins and either violas or trombones).[40] In addition, a number of manuscript works by Hofer have survived, mostly at Kroměříž: a set of six *Psalmi Breves* for small vocal and instrumental resources, five separate psalms (including a "Dixit Dominus" for eight-part double chorus with instruments), two *Magnificats* (one for CCATB chorus with instruments and one for eight-part double chorus with instruments), two *Te Deum* settings with eight-part double chorus and instruments, ten offertories (one for CCATB chorus and instruments, four for CCATTB chorus and instruments, five for eight-part double chorus and instruments), and three Masses (two for CCATB chorus and instruments; one for eight-part double chorus and instruments).[41] The disposition of the chorus is identical with the majority of Biber's church works, except that Biber's six-part chorus favors the disposition with two basses rather than two tenors. As might be expected the most fully scored compositions with the eight-part double chorus have been dubbed examples of the "colossal baroque";[42] they are the most obviously polychoral of Hofer's works, the ones in which all or most of the organs would have been used, and in which the antiphonal trumpet choir sometimes appears.

Biber's extant church music includes ten Masses, thirty-three compositions for Vespers, two litanies, nine miscellaneous church works (offertoria, hymns and motets) and between fifty and sixty sonatas that could have been used in church services; a considerable number of church works is known to have been lost.[43] Both men wrote operas and schooldramas; but the influence of these dramatic genres on their church music was strikingly different. The operatic experience in Biber's case was probably of influence on the expanded scale of individual movements (especially in the case of some aria-like solos in the later works) and the greater attention to overall planning and key structure exhibited by the multi-movement works in general. Hofer's works—especially some of the *Ver sacrum*—sometimes contain designations such as *stylo rec. . . . ariose, aria,* and the like, whereas Biber's never do; Hofer's designations of this kind in the *Ver sacrum* seem to be part of a larger concern for projection of style that comes through in the remarks concerning tempi in both of his collections, as well as in the detailed dynamic, tempo and solo/ripieno indications in the 1677 collection.[44] Biber's works, on the other hand, rely far more on everything that relates to instrumental and pictorial characters. Both instrumental idioms and the sense of instrumental sonority are far more developed in his music. This is particularly true, of course, in the case of the string writing. Hofer's music seldom reveals any sense that the composer thought of the violin as a voice of individualistic character. It represents a stage that is more idiomatic, of course, than the works from earlier in the century in that it is no longer derived so extensively from vocal idioms and devices; it may even carry most of the lively motivic material of a piece. But works such as Biber's Dresden *Nisi*

Dominus and Kroměříž *Laetatus Sum* are completely beyond the scope of Hofer's vision of the instrument, and so to a lesser extent are the violin parts of all Biber's church works; the range of the instrument is greater, its general level of activity and the color it adds to the ensemble are more imaginative. Among Biber's lost works were some for viole d'amore, with and without other instruments, such as recorders; these, too, were compositions of a kind that we do not have from Hofer.

Externally—that is from the standpoint of instrumentation, disposition of vocal and instrumental parts, and even in terms of the planning of individual movements—much of Hofer's church music, especially the polychoral pieces, resembles Biber's. It is for this reason that the performance shown in Melchior Küsel's 1682 engraving could have been of a composition by either man. And in terms of watermarks, handwriting and general vocal and instrumental features, the *Missa Salisburgensis* and hymn *Plaudite Tympana* might be considered as works possibly by Hofer (although even on these grounds his authorship is less likely than Biber's). But as soon as we examine these two pieces and the *Missa Bruxellensis* (the score of which dates from after Hofer's death) in conjunction with Biber's and Hofer's works, striking stylistic differences emerge that make it overwhelmingly more likely that Biber, not Hofer, was their author. We may now consider the *Missa Salisburgensis* with a view not only toward the issue of its authorship—a question that has been gone into adequately from the side of the "objective" evidence—but toward a delineation of those musical features that make the piece one of the most representative compositions of its time. On that account we may point more clearly to Biber than to anyone else; for usually those composers whom history judges as reflecting the ideals and aspirations of an age—that is, both Bach and Telemann, for example (since the question of universal genius is not the main one)—are those whose work stands forth as highly individualistic in some respects; and this is true of Biber, but not of Hofer.

On the evidence of watermarks and handwriting Ernst Hintermaier has shown that the scores of the *Missa Salisburgensis* and *Plaudite Tympana* date between 1652 and 1696, and that of the *Missa Bruxellensis,* from after 1696, probably around 1700.[45] And since these dates are confirmed by everything in the styles of the works, the question of Benevoli's authorship can no longer be considered seriously. The pieces bear no resemblance at all to Benevoli's known Masses. Since the same erroneous ascription was made in the case of both scores, however, it is likely that the two Masses were written by the same composer. And in order for that composer to have been Hofer rather than Biber, we would have to believe that the score of the *Missa Bruxellensis* was copied more than a decade after his death, which is very unlikely. These facts and the close association of the copyist of both Masses with Heinrich Biber's works makes a compelling case for Biber's authorship. The characteristics of style that will emerge in the following discussion and throughout this study as a whole make it a virtual certainty.

Preserved along with the *Missa Bruxellensis* as part of the *Nachlass* of François Fétis is a score of the *Missa Salisburgensis* copied in the late eighteenth or early nineteenth century by a German from the Salzburg score of the work. This manuscript—entitled *Missa à quatuor Coris in Sexdecim Vocibus cum aliis Instrumentis Autore Horatio Benevoli*—actually comprises two separate scores of the *Missa Salisburgensis*. The first has voice and violin parts only, in twenty-one staves, with some cues in the violin parts for other instruments; the second is a nine-staff supplementary score with parts for two oboes, two recorders, two violas, two clarini, and kettledrums. Together, both halves of this Brussels copy contain thirty of the fifty-three parts of the Salzburg score.[46] The late eighteenth- or early nineteenth-century copyist attempted to bring the work more in line with the practice of his own day by omitting most of the trumpets and inner viola parts, the trombones, and the cornetti, all of which were obsolete by then. When necessary, he incorporated the cornetto parts into the violin lines. The anonymous arranger thus tried to present in his scores what he felt were the essential parts of the enormous work. The designation "a quatuor Coris...cum aliis Instrumentis" resembles the title page of the *Missa Bruxellensis*: *Missa à 8 Voci Reali, a piu stromenti Del Sig.ʳ Orazio Benevoli,* and points out, along with the reduction of the instruments, that the core of the *Missa Salisburgensis* is a doubling of the normal scale of the works for eight-part double chorus with various instrumental choirs that were often performed in the cathedral. Thus, instead of one eight-part double chorus (or two SATB choirs) the *Missa Salisburgensis* has two (or four SATB choirs); instead of one string choir and one of woodwinds, the *Missa Salisburgensis* has two of each (but only one of cornetti and trombones, while the other is made up of oboes and recorders); instead of one trumpet choir, the Mass has two (although the number of balconies used remains the same, since the usual trumpet choir was divided in the cathedral).

The scoring of the *Missa Salisburgensis* reads in the score from top to bottom as follows:

CHORO I	8 Voci in Concerto [SS, AA, TT, BB]
	Organo
CHORO II	2 Violini
	4 Viole
CHORO III	2 Hautbois
	4 Flauti
	2 Clarini
CHORO IV	2 Cornetti
	2 Tromboni
CHORO V	8 Voci in Concerto [SS, AA, TT, BB]
CHORO VI	2 Violini
	4 Viole
LOCO I	4 Trombe
	Tympani
LOCO II	4 Trombe
	Tympani
	Organo
	Basso continuo

At a number of places in the *Missa Salisburgensis* where the two eight-part choruses (I and V) are treated antiphonally (Kyries I and II, Agnus Dei, "pacem"), we can form an idea of the ideal spacing of the instrumental choirs: vocal chorus I is accompanied by a string choir (II), the choir of flutes, oboes and two clarini (III) and the cornetti and trombones (IV); the second vocal choir (V) is accompanied by the other string body (VI). The first trumpet choir (Loco I) is usually heard with vocal chorus I, the second (Loco II) with vocal chorus II. Each of the two organ parts plays with one of these two major divisions of the work, while the basso continuo plays throughout the entire work. The organs and the greater dimensions of the first choir in relation to the second fit with aspects of the normal practice at the cathedral that have been presented above. This level of subdivision of the performing resources must represent right/left antiphony. At several other points in the score ("bonae voluntatis," the Amen of the

Gloria, "descendit," "et resurrexit," "et iterum," "judicare" and "gloria tua") the two eight-part choruses subdivide internally along with their doubling instruments: that is, the first SATB of chorus I couples with the first SATB of chorus V in antiphonal alternation with the second SATB of both choruses. The appearance of both types of antiphony suggests that a cornerwise spacing of the four SATB choirs was used; in certain sections of the Mass antiphony would then occur between the two sides of the church, while in others alternation between front and back would be heard. The front/back antiphony, which occurs more often, is balanced in sonority, while the right/left is not. But the right/left antiphony represents the primary division into choruses (i.e., in terms of location) and was presumably more distinctly heard as such.

Apart from these complex-sounding antiphonal details the *Missa Salisburgensis* presents a truly kaleidoscopic shifting of sonorities and locations in the sixteen solo sections. A favored pattern that represents an amplification of practices in the eight-part double-chorus works, is that of changing equal-voice duets (sometimes two pairs alternating between the choirs) against an accompanimental background of frequently shifting instrumental choirs (see, for example, the ground-bass Gratias). Another is the contrast of high and low sonorities from one movement to another: the Et incarnatus is set for alternating vocal trios of two sopranos and alto plus solo violin from the two choirs, while the Crucifixus is for the four solo basses with trombones. Echo effects (written into the music rather than specified by means of dynamic markings) abound throughout the majority of movements. And the reverse effect of climactic increase in sonority, usually leading from solo to tutti is just as regular (see the Christe to Kyrie II, and the Quoniam/cum sancto Spiritu); in four movements (Kyrie I, Et vitam/Amen, Osanna/Benedictus and Agnus Dei/dona nobis/pacem) one or more themes of lively character are introduced among the soloists, then combined with a ripieno theme in fugal style. Only once, however, in the Qui tollis, does a full ripieno fugue with the entire roster of *colla parte* instruments appear. Finally, a number of sections—including several of the major antiphonal ones—are composed throughout in fanfare style, with very slow harmonic change and restricted chordal range, often little more than tonic and dominant in alternation (Kyrie II, Cum sancto Spiritu, Amen [Gloria], Et resurrexit, Et unam Sanctam, and several shorter passages). In such cases the melodic content is highly static, sometimes virtually a single note (the quintessential instance is Et unam Sanctam), while the bass becomes more animated. This last type is the style of most of the *Plaudite Tympana,* which, as its name suggests, is a form of festive choral fanfare.

It is obvious in such a work that discussion of "simple harmonies" is pointless. At the same time, it is not the sense of "inflation" that is most impressive, although it is present of course. The *Missa Salisburgensis* owes its unusual length to the number of short sections and the enormous variety of vocal and instrumental sonorities that are created; echo effects and solo/ripieno combinations prolong many of the movements, rather than harmonic-tonal means of extension, which might not be nearly as effective.

In some of these respects the *Missa Salisburgensis* is comparable to the *Missa Christi Resurgentis* and *Vesperae à 32* of the 1670s and the *Missa Alleluia* (probably of the 1690s) more than to any other Masses of the time. The extravagant scoring of the *Missa Salisburgensis* is, of course, unique. But of all the possible composers of the time and region Biber gives us the greatest number of comparably elaborate settings. The Mass contains ten trumpet parts: two choirs each of four instruments (two clarini and two lower parts with timpani), plus two extra clarini situated with the woodwind choir. Biber's *Sonata à 7* (1668) also contains six clarino parts, all of which play to c''' (as do five of the six clarini of the *Missa Salisburgensis*); his *Sonata S. Polycarpi* (1673) requires two choirs of four trumpets each, six of which are clarini; and the *Missa Alleluia* contains the largest trumpet ensemble of any other Mass from seventeenth-century Salzburg (six trumpets and timpani). The two string bodies of the *Missa Salisburgensis* are also unusually large: six parts each, with four violas, to which we may compare the five-part setting with three violas of the *Missa Alleluia* and several sonatas, as well as the seven-part ensemble with five violas in Biber's *Litania de S. Josepho à 20*; the latter is the largest string choir in a Salzburg choral work of the time. Judging from the surviving manuscripts, woodwinds were not commonly employed by seventeenth-century Salzburg composers; apart from the choir of two oboes and four recorders in the *Missa Salisburgensis,* only Biber supplies us with examples: two oboes as *colla parte* instruments in his *Requiem à 15,* two oboes and two recorders in his *Muttetum Natale,* a choir of four recorders in his opera *Chi la dura la vince,* one of five recorders in his *Sonata pro Tabula.* Also, a few of his lost compositions, both sacred and secular, specified recorder parts.

The *Missa Salisburgensis* and *Missa Bruxellensis* are outstanding in one other respect: their lengths of circa 920 and 1275 bars respectively. South German and Austrian Mass settings of this time are always considerably shorter, the longest being usually somewhere between five and six hundred measures. Of the more than one hundred seventeenth-century Austrian Masses studied by Guido Adler, Biber's *Missa S. Henrici* was the longest (ca. 910 bars).[47] It is, however, not the most extended of Biber's Masses: apart from the two works under discussion the *Missa ex B* contains 975 bars. In fact, these four works stand apart within the seventeenth-century Austrian Mass repertoire because of the degree to which they reveal desire for extension, large-scale formal planning and differentiation of individual movements, all traits that became prominent in Biber's late works generally. The *Missa S. Henrici* has been singled out by several writers in this respect. As a result of the expansion of sections, ground-bass settings appear in these lengthy works as self-contained movements, sometimes with a tonal plan for the keys of the various statements of the ostinato. The Gratias of the *Missa Salisburgensis* provides one of the most notable examples. Biber's *Missa ex B* and *Requiem in F minor* also contain ground-bass movements, and the *Missa S. Henrici* and *Missa Bruxellensis* have pronounced quasi-ostinato bass sections. Also, several other church works by Biber contain ground-bass sections as relatively self-contained single movements within multi-movement frameworks.[48] Yet this feature was otherwise very uncommon in seventeenth-century Austrian Mass settings; Adler reports in his study that he found no ostinato basses in the Mass repertoire.[49]

A further illustration of Biber's concern with formal considerations in his Masses reveals a strong link between the *Missa Salisburgensis* and *Missa Bruxellensis* and what are probably his three last settings of the Ordinary (*Missa S. Henrici, Missa Alleluia* and *Missa ex B*). In the latter three works Biber follows a particular scheme for the Et incarnatus and Crucifixus: he always sets the former as a light "bassetgen" trio in the relative minor, and the latter as a grave and sombre-colored movement in the subdominant.[50] A triadic Et resurrexit in the tonic then follows. This pattern appears virtually exactly in the *Missa Salisburgensis,* the only variation on the pattern is the use of *two* "bassetgen" trios, one from each choir, and the addition of two violins. In the *Missa Bruxellensis* the Et incarnatus adheres to the above-mentioned pattern, but the Crucifixus is in the relative minor instead. These details characterize Biber's late Masses and those of no other composer of the time or region, just as does the use of *stile antico* for the Qui tollis in all Biber's Masses (including the *Missa Salisburgensis* and *Missa Bruxellensis*). Many more details of style could be produced in support of the ascription of the two Masses to Biber. But deeper knowledge of the music ultimately removes the last doubts without the necessity of further argument.

Virtually all that has been said up to now has concerned polychoral works, or at least works with large scorings. These are the only compositions whose performance is at all reflected in the minutes of the cathedral chapter and the various court and cathedral records, and there only as an almost incidental part of the ecclesiastical occasions. But among Biber's *oeuvre* there are works of smaller instrumentation, not necessarily less ambitious on that account of course—witness the extraordinarily virtuosic violin part of the *Nisi Dominus*—but not so obviously linked to circumstances that necessitated a ripple on the official records. Such a work is the charming *Muttetum Natale* for two sopranos, two recorders and two oboes as well as the *Laetatus Sum* (1676) and the above-mentioned *Nisi Dominus*. The titles of a few other soloistically conceived compositions are known from old inventories—e.g., the *Regnum Mundi* for two sopranos and two violins that was performed at Nonnberg, the *Aria de Nativitatis Christi Domini* for alto and two recorders and *Aria de Passione Domini: "Wer gibt meinen Augen"* for alto solo, two viole d'amore, and two recorders that were in the library of Stift Michaelbeuern in the seventeenth century, for example.[51] And other pieces, such as a motet with two altos and two gambas that was played at Nonnberg by the court musicians in 1704, might have been by Biber also.[52] The list is disappointingly small, and there are no works of this type at all among the seventeenth-century holding of the cathedral archive, a situation that might well have been the result of a weeding-out of works no longer considered of use in the eighteenth century.[53] Another explanation is possible, however: such pieces might have been performed elsewhere than in the cathedral—in the Franciscan church, for example, or within the archbishop's residence; the acoustics of the cathedral might have made performance in more intimate circumstances preferable.

In fact, not only the records but also the musical holdings at Nonnberg suggest that the performance of smaller-scale compositions was a regular feature of musical life in less "official" surroundings. At Nonnberg there is frequent reference to the performance of sonatas and motets (among which are included solo pieces) both within the service and afterwards— i.e., for purely musical and spiritual recreation (headings such as "Recreation Gesang" and "Zu einer Geistl: Recreation" appear).[54] The repertoire of sacred (and secular) arias—short, often strophic compositions for one or more voices with ritornelli for strings—indicates that music was cultivated extensively even outside the liturgy. There was, of course, no dividing line between daily life and spiritual observances at Nonnberg, and the records of musical performances mix the genres of aria, motet, sonata, Intrada, and the like, in connection with both liturgical and festive "secular" occasions in a manner that indicates the extensive degree of overlap that was possible. Music and musical recreation were entirely linked to spiritual devotions. Not infrequently we read of motets and sonatas being performed *after* Vespers, and of motets performed as table music. Sonatas were, of course, played regularly in the service, often at the beginning and end, but also for the communion, whereas motets were more often sung for the Offertory and Elevation. Sometimes there is even an impression that the service was given a sense of structure by the performance of music. Thus, for the visit of "Herr Romano Prelaeten" in 1668, the *Te Deum* was sung with organ, trumpets and drums as he entered the church, later three motets and at the end a "Canzon" were performed.[55] On another occasion the service began with bells and a short "Larma" (fanfare), followed by "quite a beautiful Mass with trumpets and drums" by Romanus Weichlein, and at the end "the beautiful long *Aufzug* (trumpet intrada)"; the day before the nuns had performed a Dixit and Magnificat with trumpets and drums of Weichlein preceded by a *Veni Sancte*.[56] Another service began with a sonata, after which a motet "Venite" with trumpets and drums, then a "Gesangl, 'Emitte'" and at the end another sonata; another began and ended with sonatas and featured a "Voce sola" with "2 Discant."[57] A familiar pattern was to begin with a sonata, perform motets for the offertory and elevation, then to end with another sonata.[58] On other occasions "Völlige Mutteten" or litanies were performed after Vespers or Mass, so that the service seemed to end by leading into a sacred concert, so to speak.[59] Sometimes the descriptions are a little more specific: for a visit of the archbishop the court musicians performed a "Völlige Sonata" at the beginning of the service, then a motet with two altos and two gambas and another full sonata at the end; the trumpeters played a "Larma" followed by an "Aufzug" as the archbishop went to the table; then motets and a sonata were played for table music.[60] On various occasions throughout the year the chief relic of the convent, the head of St. Erentraud, niece of St. Rupert, was viewed by the archbishop or other important visitors, and often for these occasions music was played; once for such a visit the motet "Qui sperat pascitur" with two sopranos and bass by Johann Caspar Kerll was performed.[61] For a province-wide festivity held by Johann Ernst in 1704 we are told that St. Erentraud was decorated just as for the "grossen Festivitet Anno 1682"; then the motets of the holy mother that had been performed at the 1682 festivity were heard again with two trumpets but "much shortened."[62] For particular feasts such as the Assumption and the Presentation of the Virgin (August 15 and November 21), music was performed at several services throughout the day; in 1670 the Magnificat was "musiciert" at first Vespers, then Mass and the Tenebre were "musiciert"; after Vespers a litany was "musiciert" with organ then several motets and a *Salve Regina*. As mentioned earlier, for the Feast of the Assumption in 1695 sonatas with trumpets and drums were played at the beginning and end of the sermon to enhance the sense of the "Eingang der Selligisten Jungfrau in das Himmlische Jerusalem"; during the sermon itself two "Mezopunct" (presumably pauses for instrumental music) were made; and in 1698 for this feast the *Te Deum* with trumpets and drums of Romanus Weichlein was performed in the night "für ein Prob," and a few days later Weichlein's "long Magnificat" with two sopranos and a litany to the Virgin were played.[63] On yet another occasion early Mass was "musiciert," then a *Te Deum*; later Mass was spoken and "beautiful motets" "musiciert" as well as the hymn "Veni Creator" and the *Te Deum*, all by the court musicians.[64] These and many other such descriptions bear witness to the richness of the union of musical and spiritual life at Nonnberg.

Just how much of the music, if any, might have been composed by Biber is uncertain, although one would think that the presence there of a highly skilled musician in his daughter must have led to more performances of his works there than we know of. The convent contains a substantial number of anonymous pieces of the kind just described; ascriptions were in fact very casually made and more often than not unconcernedly omitted; once the indication "Vom Herrn Kapellmaister" makes Biber's authorship possible, although the piece in question is a very simple "aria" in several strophes with ritornelli that a much lesser musician could have produced. This is, in fact, the case with the majority of such pieces. The text "Wer gibt meinen Augen" exists in an aria setting at Nonnberg that does not match up with the description of Biber's lost solo; likewise, the convent preserves several solos with *scordature* viole d'amore parts and various anonymous *Regnum Mundi* settings, all of the general type of piece Biber is known to have composed; some of these works certainly date from the late seventeenth century.[65] In the nineteenth century Sigismund Keller claimed to have seen in the upper sacristy of the cathedral a printed collection of Biber's entitled *Hymni Sacri* and dated 1684.[66] No other reference to such a collection has ever come forth; but if Keller's statement is not an error, Biber might have written more of the kind of piece that was widely heard at Nonnberg. The convent archive contains an anonymous (and regrettably incomplete) manuscript collection of hymns from the seventeenth century: twenty-five pieces in all, nineteen for the proper of the saints, six for the common.[67] And in the case of these pieces the almost inevitable gap in quality that exists between Biber's work and that of his lesser Salzburg colleagues— Clamer, Weichlein, and others, even Hofer—is not in evidence. The hymns are very attractive compositions in several strophes with ritornelli, often featuring a considerable degree of florid vocal writing and extended fugal Amens that help them stand out among the Nonnberg works;

they might seriously be considered as a possible Biber compilation. But in general the attempt to make positive ascriptions on the basis of watermarks, copyists, and texts cannot be confirmed by musical criteria, for the hallmarks of Biber's style hardly emerge in these compositions. Either they are not by him or, what is quite conceivable, the performance circumstances at Nonnberg dictated the composition of a different, and much less elaborate, kind of piece than that performed by the professional court musicians. Although it is unlikely that there are musical masterpieces from the seventeenth century to be discovered at Nonnberg, the performances there give us a glimpse into the role of music in religious life of the time in a manner that is rarely encountered.

4

The Masses

The surviving corpus of Biber's Masses includes ten compositions: two vocal settings of the ordinary (one entirely and one partially in *stile antico*), six concerted settings of the ordinary and two Requiem Masses. In addition, the titles of several lost works, representing all three categories, are known.[1] Not all the ascriptions of the extant Masses are clear, however: the *Missa Salisburgensis* and *Missa Bruxellensis* are certainly Biber's for reasons given earlier; while the *Missa in Albis,* ascribed to "H. B." at Kroměříž is much more likely to be a composition of Heinrich Brückner's than Biber's; and the *Missa in Contrapuncto,* preserved in a nineteenth-century copy under Biber's name, is probably, on the evidence of an old catalog that ascribes it to Carl Biber, a work of Biber's son.[2] Taking these facts into account, the six concerted settings of the ordinary, in their most probable chronological order, are the following: *Missa Christi Resurgentis* (1674), *Missa Catholica* (1680s?), *Missa Salisburgensis* (1682?), *Missa Alleluia* (1690s), *Missa S. Henrici* (1696), *Missa Bruxellensis* (ca. 1700?).[3] On the basis of the way Biber's name appears on their title pages, the two Requiems were written after 1690 and 1692, respectively; and these dates are confirmed by their styles. Finally, the two vocal Masses, the *Missa Quadragesimalis* and *Missa ex B,* are undated; but their styles suggest a date in the 1670s, perhaps even earlier, for the former work, making it Biber's earliest surviving Mass, and one in the 1690s or later for the latter.[4]

Vocal Masses

Although the *Missa in Contrapuncto* was, in all likelihood, written by Carl Biber, it makes a fruitful work to discuss in comparison with the *Missa Quadragesimalis,* since it represents more closely the "normal" *stile antico* Mass of the late seventeenth and early eighteenth centuries; and, if it was not written by Biber himself, it certainly reveals the considerable influence of Heinrich Biber's teaching on his son's work in a number of ways. Comparison of the two pieces reveals immediately that the *Missa in Contrapuncto* is in most respects the more polished, if less adventuresome, work, while the *Missa Quadragesimalis* reveals a sometimes crude vigor that seems to run contrary to the ideal of contrapuntal serenity we associate with the *stile antico.* These qualities, however, have little or nothing to do with the relative values of the two pieces.

Formally, the two compositions follow traditional divisions of the Mass very closely. Both Kyries are in three-sectional da capo form, while each of the Sanctus settings exhibits the normal five-movement division: Sanctus, Pleni sunt caeli, Hosanna, Benedictus, Hosanna da capo. Likewise, the two Agnus Dei settings follow familiar patterns:

	Missa Quadragesimalis	*Missa in Contrapuncto*
Agnus Dei...	A (a + b)	a
miserere nobis		b
Agnus Dei...	A (a + b)	a
miserere nobis		b
Agnus Dei...	B (c + d)	a
dona nobis pacem		c

Because of their long, nonrepeating texts, the Gloria and Credo are less formally standardized than the Kyrie, Sanctus and Agnus Dei. In both Masses these movements follow the common practice of beginning virtually every phrase of the text with a new motive (usually treated imitatively), thereby creating a form consisting of a large number of short sections. These are then organized into several larger groupings on the basis of the more decisive cadences (that is, those with longer note values and other features, such as rests, pauses or double bars). In both works the major cadential points in the Gloria and Credo—especially those at Qui tollis and Crucifixus—mark traditional textual subdivisions.

Both Masses utilize the repetition of music for certain movements. The Qui tollis and Qui sedes are the same in both pieces. In the *Missa Quadragesimalis* the Qui tollis is then repeated when the words "qui tollis peccata mundi: miserere nobis" reappear in Agnus Dei I and II. In this work Kyrie I and II also serve as the Benedictus. Other reiterations of musical material in the *Missa in Contrapuncto* (with slight modifications to accomodate the new texts and occasional alteration of the key of the cadence) are Domine Deus / Domine Fili as Dona nobis pacem, and Et in unum Dominus as Et ex Patre. In these works the repetition of sections (which is far less common in the concerted Masses) is, in fact, a facet of the desire for musical interrelatedness that is prominent in both works, although realized differently. In the *Missa Quadragesimalis* Biber makes extensive use of melodic and harmonic patterns that move from tonic to dominant emphasizing both the raised and lowered leading tone and the Phrygian cadence (ex. 4-1). These patterns, which are sometimes expanded to the level of variation-like points of imitation, are placed at key structural divisions (frequently the beginnings of movements and sections) giving the Mass as a whole a prominent Phrygian harmonic character at such points.[5] A few other repeated motives and figures in the *Missa Quadragesimalis* increase the sense of interrelatedness somewhat, but none is used systematically for this purpose.

Example 4-1.   Biber, Themes from *Missa Quadragesimalis*

Example 4-2. Carl or Heinrich Biber, *Missa in Contrapuncto*

(a) Beginning of Christe

(b) Beginning of Domine Deus

The *Missa in Contrapuncto,* on the other hand, is practically a variation work, so extensively are its major themes and even contrapuntal points of imitation interrelated. Behind many of the themes is the minor-key form of the four-note motive made famous by Mozart in the finale of the "Jupiter" Symphony, and used by him in the "Credo" Mass and *The Magic Flute.*[6] This theme occurs in no fewer than six of Biber's vocal works: Cum Sancto Spiritu of the *Missa Catholica* (in Phrygian rather than major form), Agnus Dei of the *Requiem à 15,* as the ground bass of a movement of the *Litania de S. Josephi* (those petitions addressed to St. Joseph as priest), the Agnus Dei of the *Missa S. Henrici,* where it appears in almost emblematic fashion, the aria with recorders that ends the second act of *Chi la dura la vince* and the Et unam Sanctam of the *Missa ex B* (where it appears in inversion as well). The *Missa in Contrapuncto* uses the minor-key form in the Christe. In addition, variants of the motive (two resemble its retrograde inversion) appear as themes in certain sections that are basically harmonic and contrapuntal variations of the first five bars of the Christe (ex. 4-2). In the Credo three successive movements—Crucifixus, Et resurrexit, and Et iterum—present varied forms of this theme: first in augmented note values, second in its most usual form, and finally, in simultaneous combination with its inversion (ex. 4-3); the Crucifixus is also a variant of the beginning of the Christe and Domine Deus, its theme elongated, the contour altered and the tonality modified after the entry of the third voice. Apart from such often intricate relationships involving this theme, a second motive, based on the descending triad, and varied in equally subtle ways, forms the thematic basis of several other movements; this is also a familiar theme type of Heinrich Biber's. A form of it that appears in the *Requiem in F minor* and *Missa ex B* underlies the Qui tollis of the *Missa in Contrapuncto.* In all three works descending triads are presented throughout the parts in close (syncopated) imitation over harmonies that move according to the circle of fifths. The beginning of the Sanctus of the *Missa in Contrapuncto* seems almost to have been taken over (in minor) from the *Missa S. Henrici* (ex. 4-4). In the *Missa in Contrapuncto* the influence from Biber's late works seems particularly direct and palpable, and it may be the case that the work was actually written by the elder Biber.

Example 4-3. *Missa in Contrapuncto*

(a) Crucifixus, Beginning

(b) Et resurrexit, Beginning

(c) Et iterum, Beginning

Example 4-4. Similarities of Theme Types in Biber's Music

(a) *Missa S. Henrici,* Sanctus, Beginning

Example 4-4 (continued)

(b) *Missa in Contrapuncto,* Sanctus, Beginning

The *Missa in Contrapuncto* is also very carefully planned in the alternation of its texture between polyphony and homophony, as the following scheme of the Credo reveals:

POLYPHONY

1) Patrem . . . terrae
3) Et in unum dominum
5) Et ex Patre
7) Genitum . . . Patri
9) Qui propter . . . salutem
10) Descendit de coelis
12) Crucifixus . . . Pilato
14) Et resurrexit . . . scripturas
16) Et iterum . . . est
18) Et in Spiritum
20) Et unam sanctam
22) Et exspecto
24) Amen

HOMOPHONY

2) visibilium . . . invisibilium
4) Jesum . . . unigenitum
6) ante . . . vero
8) per quem omnia facta sunt

11) Et incarnatus
13) Passus et sepultus est
15) Et ascendit . . . Patris
17) Cum gloria . . . finis
19) Qui ex Patre
21) Confiteor
23) Et vitam venturi saeculi

Such careful planning is characteristic of Biber's late works, and was no doubt transmitted to his son; works such as the *Missa St. Henrici* and *Missa ex B* exhibit this feature to a pronounced degree, whereas Biber's earlier works (those before the 1680s, at least) do so to a far lesser extent.

The *Missa Quadragesimalis,* however, lacks such a pronounced sense of overall planning of themes and textures. Whereas in the *Missa in Contrapuncto* (as in most *stile antico* Masses of the time) the polyphonic writing is fugal, following the pattern of four entries, two on the tonic, two on the dominant, in the *Missa Quadragesimalis* we find a great deal of very free imitation, and even nonimitative counterpoint. In fact, points of imitation where the theme remains unaltered throughout four successive entries are exceptional in this work. Often the successive voices enter with different textual and musical phrases, such as the alto with "Et in Spiritum," the soprano with "Et vivificantem," tenor and bass with "Qui ex Patre." Even when Biber retains the theme more or less in its original form, the pitches of the entries often deny the standard tonal scheme and seem to reflect an underlying harmonic rationale rather than abstract contrapuntal logic: for instance, at "Et in unum" the four voices enter on F, C, B-natural, and F (above harmonies of D minor, A minor, E minor and D minor), while at "Sub Pontio" seven entries outline a series of rising fifths: F, C, G, D, A, A, E.

Although the *Missa Quadragesimalis* evinces a less normal set of contrapuntal, textural

Example 4-5. *Missa Quadragesimalis,* Cadences

(a)   Christe, mm. 6–7

(b)   Kyrie, mm. 23–24

and tonal observances than the *Missa in Contrapuncto,* in addition to the fact that its melodic lines are occasionally angular, and some parallel fifths occur, it is not an inherently inferior work on these accounts; in fact, it succeeds admirably as a piece of music. Some of the harmonic devices elevate the desire for striking effect above that of contrapuntal correctness. For example, in quite a number of the characteristic Phrygian cadence endings the progression from the G-minor six-chord to the A-major dominant involves one part leaping a diminished fifth from B-flat to E (to avoid parallel octaves with the bass); then, in a few movements, when the principal theme enters on the note D simultaneously with the sounding of the G-minor chord, then moves to the tone F as the harmony changes to A-major, we hear either the clash of the E and F in the second chord, or else the A chord becomes an augmented triad that later "resolves" to A major; both of these cadences occur several times in the work (ex. 4-5).

And whereas, as we saw, the *Missa in Contrapuncto* utilized contrapuntal and variational means to create a sense of progressive intensification through the sequence Crucifixus, Et resurrexit, Et iterum (the Et incarnatus, following traditional usage, is homophonic in both works), the *Missa Quadragesimalis* makes much more extensive use of harmonic and pictorial devices. In the latter work the Crucifixus consists of a succession of three themes, the first ("Crucifixus") energetically leaping up through the fifth to the octave above, only to fall a

Example 4-6. *Missa Quadragesimalis,* Final Cadence

seventh to cadence where it began ("nobis"); the character of the upward surging suggests both the elevation of the cross and the idea of redemption; the fall downwards, man's unworthiness. This idea gives way to a lively motive ("sub Pontio Pilato") that enters at ascending fifths in the successive voices (F, C, G, D, A, E); it will be heard again in varied form at "Et unam Sanctam." Finally, the Crucifixus ends with a sudden slowing of the rhythm as alto and bass, then soprano and tenor, drag out the word "passus" with descending scale patterns. The Et resurrexit begins on an A-major chord, then moves to cadence in F major and back to a full close (V–I) on A major (Tierce de Picardie). The sudden harmonic shifts in purely homophonic style create a sense of wonder,[7] while at the same time the juxtaposition of F-major and A-major harmonies underscores the Phrygian harmonic character we have mentioned. The movement closes in D minor, and the Et iterum picks up on the pitch D in the bass with a repeated-note theme in which the rhythm of the text becomes an intrada-like idea, while the upper voices sing "judicare vivos et mortuos" in parallel thirds, the whole suggestive of fear. This musical idea moves first to cadence in G minor, then in the flattest key of the Mass, C minor ("mortuos"). The "cujus regni," repeats the words "non, non" in SAT chords over a bass line moving in circle-of-fifths harmonies. From all this we conclude that the motive force behind the *Missa Quadragesimalis,* unlike that of the *Missa in Contrapuncto,* is harmonic and pictorial in origin, not contrapuntal. The work is, of course, a contrapuntal Mass (in one manuscript [Kroměříž] it is called *Missa in Contrapuncto,* in another [Seitenstetten] *Missa alla Cappella*), but it relies extensively on an underlying dramatic-pictorial sense far more than most works of its type. The *Missa in Contrapuncto* is also a very satisfactory piece of music, but one in which the emphasis on traditional contrapuntal devices looms, we might say, too large on the horizon. It bears, in fact, a much stronger relationship to Biber's later church works, in some of which contrapuntal devices are more in the foreground, than it does to the *Missa Quadragesimalis.* The latter is probably, as we suggested, a relatively early work of Biber's, one in which the enthusiastic spirit of the seventeenth century, manifested in the vividness of counterreformation sensuality, seems to have encroached on the territory of the *stile antico;* the Monteverdi-like dissonances that end the Mass should have the last word (ex. 4-6).

The *Missa ex B* (Mass in B-flat), for SSATBB chorus and organ, is perhaps a unique example among the vocal Masses of the seventeenth century in the manner in which the composer, throughout a sequence of twenty-two separate "movements," none of which is repeated, exploits the contrasts between both triple and duple meters (*alla breve*) and the stricter and freer polyphonic styles (fig. 4-1). In no fewer than twelve movements the same type of theme is used: a rising fourth from tonic to subdominant, usually in slow scalar patterns, that then (usually) returns to the tonic. At "Et unam Sanctam" it becomes the "Mozart" theme

Figure 4-1. Scheme of the *Missa ex B*

	Movement	Meter	Tempo	Measures	Key	Number of Real Parts	Form, Style, Texture
1	Kyrie/Christe/ Kyrie	¢	alla breve	80	B-flat	6	ABA¹. Fugal, quasi-ostinato "walking" bass.
2	Et in terra	¢	alla breve	38	B-flat	6	Freely homophonic. Quasi-ostinato "walking" bass.
3	Gratias	3/2		26	B-flat	5: SSATB	Imitative
4	Domine Deus	¢	alla breve	48	G minor	5: SSATB	A,A¹. Fugal.
5	Qui Tollis	3/2	[allegro], adagio	28	B-flat to D minor	4: SATB	Fugal, then homophonic
6	Quoniam	¢	alla breve	26	B-flat	5: SSATB	Freely homophonic. Voices paired in parallel thirds.
7	Cum Sancto Spiritu	3/4		22	B-flat	6	Fugal
8	Amen	¢	alla breve	39	B-flat	5-6: SSATB(B)	Fugal
9	Patrem	3/2		34	B-flat	5-7: SSATB(B)	Quasi-ostinato bass and harmony
10	Et in unum	¢	alla breve	57	B-flat	4: SATB	A,A¹. Fugal.
11	Qui propter	3/2	adagio	25	G minor	6	Freely homophonic, then freely imitative at "descendit"
12	Et incarnatus	3/4		27	G minor	3: SSA	Fugal. Bassetgen.
13	Crucifixus	¢	alla breve	55	E-flat	4: SATB	Fugal
14	Et resurrexit	3/2	[presto], adagio, presto	63	B-flat	5-6: SSATB(B)	ABA¹. Quasi-ostinato, "walking" bass in "A" sections.
15	Et in Spiritum	¢	alla breve	54	G minor to B-flat	4: SATB	A (fugal, G minor), B (chordal, D minor) C (fugal, B-flat)
16	Confiteor	3/2		25	E-flat	6	Freely homophonic
17	Et vitam/Amen	¢	alla breve	56	B-flat	5: SSATB	Double fugue
18	Sanctus	¢	alla breve	46	B-flat	6	Fugal
19	Pleni	3/4		44	G minor	5: SSATB	Quasi-fugal
20	Hosanna/Benedictus	¢	alla breve	70	B-flat	5-6: SSATB(B)	Fugal (two themes)
21	Agnus Dei	3/2	adagio	66	B-flat	5-6: SSATB(B)	AAB. Fugal.
22	Dona nobis	¢	alla breve	46	B-flat	6	Fugal

again, now presented in conjunction with its inversion, which was heard in two preceding movements. The degree of independence and extension of the movements of the *Missa ex B* is comparable to that of the *Missa S. Henrici* (1696); and the scheme of triple meter "bassetgen" trio in the relative minor for the Et incarnatus, and subdominant for the Crucifixus, suggests a further link between this Mass and the *Missa Alleluia, Missa Salisburgensis* and *Missa S. Henrici.*[8] A number of other characteristics—ground-bass movements, double fugues with contrast themes, and the like—are widely found in Biber's later Masses as well, while the general level of overall planning is one of their most interesting newer developments.

Whereas in the two vocal Masses just discussed the organ seldom departs from the role of *basso seguente,* and never sounds alone, in the *Missa ex B* it assumes greater independence. Biber assigns the instrument short introductions to seven sections, two of which it also closes. Just before the conclusion of the Mass the organ plays alone the closing bars of the "dona nobis pacem" theme, rendering more effective the concluding plagal cadence of the chorus on the final word "pacem." The organ also adopts a unifying role in the four movements with quasi-ostinato basses; the continuo patterns determine not only the melodic content of the vocal parts and the structures of these movements, but in some cases even the sonorities, which in several places—most notably the Patrem and Et resurrexit—are as exuberantly triadic in character as parts of the *Missa Salisburgensis* (ex. 4-7).

The treatment of the two vocal basses, and to a lesser extent the two sopranos, as alternating partners in several movements of the *Missa ex B* (Kyrie, Gloria, Sanctus, Benedictus/Osanna, Dona nobis pacem), suggests that at least the basses were antiphonally spaced. And of the two surviving gatherings of parts for the Mass, one contains parts for organ, sopranos 1 and 2, alto, tenor and "Basso 1mo concert[ato]" and "Basso 2do conc[ertato]" (all in two copies), while the other consists of extra copies of the two soprano and bass parts (the latter still designated with the word "concertato"). There are no solo/ripieno indications in any of the parts; but the solo designation for the basses, along with the fact that a number of movements begin with two basses and obbligato organ, invites performance with small divided forces, in which the alternation of the basses will be audible:

S2	S1		S2	S1
A	A	or	T	A
T	T		B2	B1
B2	B1			

In sum, the *Missa ex B* represents a kind of meeting ground for the *stile antico* and *stile moderno* different from that in the *Missa Quadragesimalis*. Here the two styles are differentiated and juxtaposed systematically, used as the basis for a larger structure, whereas in the earlier work they merge into one another, their distinctions blurred. Biber's work, in fact, moved in the direction of sharper distinctions of this kind, the grammar, so to speak, of seventeenth-century styles. The tendency toward extension of individual movements necessitated such distinctions, which are more pronounced in the concerted works. While Biber's earlier works, such as the *Missa Quadragesimalis,* have a lingering echo of the early baroque harmonic style, later ones, such as the *Missa ex B,* move into another sphere: that of seventeenth-century rationalism and systematization. Bukofzer, perhaps, put his finger on the historical position of these works when he said of Biber, "His music is equally far removed from the experimental harmonies of the early baroque and the fully developed tonality of the late baroque style."[9] Works such as the *Missa ex B* and *Missa S. Henrici* can be said to justify the use of the term "middle baroque" in music history.

Concerted Settings of the Mass Ordinary

The *Missa in Albis* survives at Kroměříž in a manuscript that gives only the initials "H. B." as a clue to the identity of its composer. Nettl ascribed the work without question to Biber because the copy is dated September 1668, when Biber was almost certainly at Kroměříž. Breitenbacher and Sehnal raise the possibility of Heinrich Brückner's authorship.[10] Unfortunately, the title *Missa in Albis* is known from no other collection or inventory that might help in identifying its author; in the original Kroměříž inventory of 1695, however, the work is preceded and followed by works of Brückner, a situation that supports Brückner's authorship.[11] And there are other reasons to suggest here that the Mass was not composed by Heinrich Biber at Kroměříž in 1668. For example, the manuscript parts of the *Missa in Albis*

Example 4-7. *Missa ex B*, Credo, Beginning

contain an unusually large number of copyist's errors, far too many for the work to be successfully performed from that copy. It is difficult to believe that such errors could have remained uncorrected if the composer had written the work at Kroměříž with the intention of immediate performance and therefore supervised the copyist. The large number of errors suggests the hypothesis that if the work was composed by Biber, it dates from an earlier period in his life and was simply copied in 1668 for the Kroměříž collection. This is possible; the *Missa in Albis* was entered in the collection in September, whereas the *Domenica in Albis* (Quasimodo Sunday) for which it was written is the first Sunday after Easter. Although at present style criticism alone is insufficient to definitively settle the question, since Brückner's work is almost completely unknown, it does suggest that Biber was not the author of this piece; considering the question of his authorship will help as well to sharpen our sense of all that separates him from the countless lesser composers of the time and region.

Turning, then, to the work itself, we find more repetition of musical sections in it than in any Mass known to be by Biber. The *Missa in Albis,* if by Biber, is also the only work of his in which a movement is reiterated in a different meter and with modified rhythm. This traditional variation technique stemmed from renaissance notation, in which the time signature determined rhythm as well as meter. In the early seventeenth century this procedure was frequently employed in instrumental music; a vestigial use appears in the refrain of the first sonata from Biber's *Fidicinium Sacro-Profanum.* We commonly find it in church music from the second half of the century, such as the *Missa Angeli Custodis* of Emperor Leopold and the *Requiem* of Johann Caspar Kerll.[12] The technique passed out of general use in the late seventeenth century, along with outmoded notational practices such as flagged half notes and stemless black whole notes.[13] In the *Missa in Albis* a single movement serves, with slight alterations, as Kyrie I and II, Dona nobis pacem (all in quadruple meter), and both Amen and Osanna settings (in triple meter) (ex. 4-8). Also, the music of the short Qui tollis section is heard three times in succession within the Gloria: 1) Qui tollis...miserere nobis; 2) Qui tollis...nostrum; 2) Qui sedes...nobis. The scoring of the vocal parts varies with each restatement, and the final miserere builds up to a tutti. The music of 1) and 2) then reappears, with very slight modifications, for the Qui tollis of Agnus Dei I and II.

Repetition of music in the *Missa in Albis* undoubtedly increases the sense of musical interrelatedness and overall structure: not only does the Mass open and conclude with the same movement, but all five sections close with it as well. The gains in the sense of unified structure, however, are dearly paid for, and the work sounds monotonous at times. The internal form of the Kyrie is A, A^1, the second section only slightly differentiated from the first. Later in the Mass this form expands to A, A^1, A^1. since the movement appears seven times, we hear the fairly short, unmemorable "A" section a total of nineteen times. Other movements of the Mass are likewise built upon short, reiterated passages that are too often dull and unimaginative. The Domine Deus, for example, consists of little more than a few chords, that quickly cadence. Each of the three statements passes from a solo trio to a tutti setting. Like many other passages in the *Missa in Albis,* this section is completely homophonic, harmonically simple, apt to cadence too frequently, and overly reliant upon restatement. The very simplicity of the instrumental opening of the Sanctus (ex. 4-9) leads us to expect considerably more from the movement than we actually get—a reiteration (with varied scoring) of the same music. One is tempted to conclude that by varying the instrumentation the composer has attempted to compensate for a serious lack of musical substance.

Superficial resemblances to Biber's style can be found in a few sections of the *Missa in Albis.* The scoring of the Benedictus, for example (two solo basses with strings and continuo), recalls the *Laetatus Sum* (1676) and movements such as the Et vitam of the *Missa Christi*

Example 4-8. "H. B.," *Missa in Albis*

(a) Kyrie, Beginning

(b) Amen, Beginning (Identical in Gloria and Credo)

Resurgentis (1674). There are, however, striking differences. When Biber uses this texture he emphasizes the highest and lowest parts, an ornate solo violin and the two bass voices. The short phrases of the basses in the *Laetatus Sum* imitate each other, and the parts frequently cross. In the Benedictus of the *Missa in Albis,* on the other hand, the violin parts are technically rudimentary, and the string parts in general are confined to a block-chordal style. Following the usual procedure, the bass soloists sing separately at first, then combine on the concluding phrase. Although it expands into florid phrases, the motive assigned to the basses is overly patterned; its treatment in parallel thirds toward the end of the movement is suspiciously unlike Biber's work.

At first glance, the fugal writing for chorus (headed "cappella") with *colla parte* instruments in the Crucifixus appears to be consistent with Biber's style. The introduction of two new themes (the first at "sub Pontio Pilato," the second at "passus") arouses our expectation of a double fugue, a favorite device of Biber's. However, at this point the author of the *Missa in Albis* continues to avoid all but the most elementary counterpoint. He abandons each of the three themes after its entry in all voices, does not venture a single note of nonthematic material, and seldom essays more than two-part writing. Repetition again serves as the basis of extension: the form is A, A^1 (in the dominant), B, C, B, C.

Example 4-9. *Missa in Albis,* Sanctus, Beginning

Because of their rhythmic and figurational simplicity, and because the accompanying instruments often play in the same rhythm as the vocal parts, the soloistic passages in the *Missa in Albis* are difficult to reconcile with Biber's style. The inclusion of recitative-like melodic style is also uncharacteristic of Biber's church music. In short, it is very difficult to believe that Biber could have written the *Missa in Albis* at any point in his career. Everything we know of Biber's early works opposes the ascription of this work to him. In comparison with the music Biber wrote at Kroměříž between 1668 and 1670, this Mass lacks imagination as well as technical mastery. Even if we assume that the work was written several years before 1668, its style remains incompatible with Biber's development. Biber's early works, such as the newly discovered violin pieces at Vienna and the Kroměříž *Salve Regina* are by no means so devoid of substance. For the most part they reveal a dynamic musical personality, enthusiastic and full of ideas, but lacking experience and maturity. The occasional crudeness in the style of the *Missa Quadragesimalis* seems to result from the composer's difficulty with the *stile antico.* One senses in that work the conflict between earlier musical experiences and the limitations imposed by the style. On the other hand, the *Missa in Albis* appears to be the creation of a more experienced, but far less gifted composer than Biber. It is far more likely that another Kroměříž church work signed with the initials "H. B.," *Congregamini Omnes Populi* (dated

1663 by Sehnal), was written by Biber early in his career.[14] If Biber produced the *Congregamini Omnes Populi* in 1663, he could not have written the *Missa in Albis* in 1668.

The *Missa Christi Resurgentis* (1674), perhaps the first Mass Biber wrote for Salzburg, is a far more attractive work than the *Missa in Albis.* Its confidence and festive exuberance are qualities very rarely so directly and convincingly projected in Masses of this period. As its title reveals, the *Missa Christi Resurgentis* was written for Easter. At Easter 1674 Archbishop Max Gandolph's nephew, Polykarp, for whose election as provost of the cathedral the previous year Biber had produced the *Sonata S. Polycarpi,* was consecrated Bishop of Gurk.[15] Although services might have been held at the romanesque cathedral in Gurk, which probably could not accommodate a performance of the *Missa Christi Resurgentis,* the event would certainly have been acclaimed in Salzburg, the center of the archdiocese. Polykarp's position as provost of the Salzburg cathedral (which he retained after being made bishop) ensured this. One might expect in any case that Easter celebrations in the cathedral would be of particular splendor, since the iconographical scheme represented in the frescoes and paintings deals largely with the triumphal events in the life of Christ, culminating in a huge painting of the resurrection at the high altar.

The *Missa Christi Resurgentis* typifies the scoring and spatial disposition of the musicians described in chapter 3: eight-part double chorus, the first choir doubled by strings and the second by winds, with the two clarini dividing with the choirs in antiphonal passages. To augment the splendor of several solo sections Biber increased the number of vocal soloists to nine by including a third solo bass part (which doubles the bass of Chorus I in ripieno passages). This addition allowed him to introduce the sonority of a bass trio at several chosen places in the work, most notably those passages that relate to Christ and the resurrection and therefore underscore the function and title of the Mass. Extended bass trios serve as the Christe and Et resurrexit (the latter in fanfare style with two clarini); shorter trios appear at "Patrem" and Agnus Dei II.

In fact, the *Missa Christi Resurgentis* seems almost to have been laid out with a spectrum of variegated scorings and styles in mind; many of the other solo combinations are also particularly interesting (fig. 4-2) As we found in the *Missa Salisburgensis,* Biber creates kaleidoscopic effects of shifting sonorities by means of the juxtaposition of sections in widely disparate settings. The fugal Qui tollis is preceded by a series of solos with instrumental interludes (no. 2 in fig. 4-2) and followed by a "sonata" for two clarini in the style of the trumpet duos in the *Sonatae, tam Aris, quam Aulis servientes.* The contrast between the Crucifixus and Et resurrexit is strikingly drawn: the former, a fugal five-part choral movement in the relative minor concludes with the descending scalar motive traditionally used to depict the word "passus"; it is succeeded by the brilliant trio for basses and trumpets (ex. 4-10). At one point in the *Missa Christi Resurgentis* there is a manifest connection to the two "pseudo-Benevoli" Masses (as well as Biber's *Missa ex B*): the beginning of the Gloria with a bass duet in antiphonal imitation between the choirs (Et in terra pax). The idea behind this passage is just the same in the *Missa Christi Resurgentis* and *Missa Salisburgensis*: a tutti enters on the word "pax," repeating it several times with dramatic rests, before making a full sectional cadence at "bonae voluntatis."

Although the emphasis on solo writing and sonorous combinations is striking in the *Missa Christi Resurgentis,* the sectional divisions of the work nevertheless reflect traditional usage very similar to that of the vocal Masses. The ABC form of the Kyrie/Christe/Kyrie complex employed here is slightly less common for the time than the da capo; Biber's three earlier concerted Masses utilize it, while the three later ones—and both vocal Masses—have various forms of da capo Kyries.[16] Here Biber observes the normal procedure of framing the

Figure 4-2. Solo Textures in the *Missa Christi Resurgentis*
The continuo is always present.

1) A, T1, B1 vs. A2, T2, B2   "Laudamus . . . glorificamus te."
                                       Antiphonal.

2) S1, S2 + cornetti & trombones   "Domine Deus rex . . . omnipotens."

    A1, T1, A2 + strings   "Domine fili . . . Jesu Christe."

    T1, T2, B2 + strings   "Domine Deus agnus . . . Patris."

3) A1   "Quoniam . . . Christe."

4) S1, A1, S2 vs. T1, A2, T2   "Et in unam . . . facta sunt." The two
                                       groups alternate on successive phrases
                                       over a quasi-ostinato "walking" bass.

5) S1, S2 + cornetti & trombones   "Et in spiritum . . . prophetas."

6) S1, A1, S2   "Et exspecto . . . mortuorum."

    B1, B2 + strings   "Et vitam . . . Amen."

7) S1, A1, T1, B1 + clarini,   "Sanctus . . . Sabaoth."
    then cornetti & trombones

8) A1 + strings   Benedictus

9) T1, T2, B1   Agnus Dei III

soloistic Christe with two similar Kyries; as in the *Missa Salisburgensis* and *Missa Bruxellensis,* the Kyries feature double-chorus antiphony. There is no attempt to unify the whole Mass motivically; and the only instances of repeated material are the reappearance of Kyrie II as dona nobis pacem and the Amen of the Gloria as that of the Credo (by this device four of the five major sections of the Mass end with movements featuring double chorus antiphony, as do three of those in the *Missa Salisburgensis*). Fewer sections of the *Missa Christi Resurgentis* extend to the dimensions of self-contained movements than in Biber's later works. Nevertheless, in this Mass Biber goes further than his older contemporaries (Kerll, Hofer, Schmelzer, Draghi, Bertali), in that several sections are sufficiently long and integrated (in scoring, key, meter and thematic material) to be labelled "movements." They correspond basically to those sections that were traditionally set apart by means of cadences and the like: Domine Deus, Qui tollis, and Amen in the Gloria, Qui propter, Crucifixus, Et resurrexit, Et in Spiritum and Amen in the Credo. The Qui tollis/Qui sedes complex in the Gloria and the Crucifixus in the Credo are set as motet-like pieces evocative of the *stile antico*; the former comprises a large A, B, A^1 form:

A: Qui tollis   (SATB fugue without *colla parte* instruments)
B: Suscipe   (a homophonic tutti)
A^1: Qui sedes   (the Qui tollis fugue, now doubled by cornetti and trombones)

Example 4-10. *Missa Christi Resurgentis*, Et resurrexit

In the *Missa Christi Resurgentis* we encounter for the first time a series of techniques that reappear in Biber's other polychoral works, many of which were not only traditional in Salzburg, but inherited from polychoral practices of the early years of the century. Among the latter is the presence of independent instrumental movements, both introductions and interludes, often entitled Sonata; the *Missa Christi Resurgentis* begins with such a movement, canzona-like and evocative in its blend of majestic and lively qualities of the polychoral sonatas of Gabrieli. The movement—which features alternation of the three instrumental choirs—is thematically unrelated to the Kyrie that follows and could have served just as easily in another work. And all of Biber's known church works from the 1670s have such sonatas: *Lux Perpetua* (1673: for strings and trombones); *Vesperae à 32* (1674: virtually identical in layout, length and scoring to that of the *Missa Christi Resurgentis*); *Laetatus Sum* (solo violin and violin with string accompaniment). The Dresden *Nisi Dominus,* perhaps also from this period, opens with a sonata for violin and basso continuo. The Agnus Dei of the *Missa Christi Resurgentis* has a similarly laid-out interlude following the trio for basses that opens the movement; and another sonata, designated as such, for two clarini and basso continuo, appears after the Qui tollis/Qui sedes complex, ushering in a solo section (Quoniam), as if dividing the Gloria at that point. Polychoral instrumental sections remain in Biber's later works; but beginning with those from the 1680s their thematic material is always shared with the vocal parts.

Other features of the *Missa Christi Resurgentis* that will remain with Biber are the *stile antico* conception of the Qui tollis and (a little less consistently) the Crucifixus, the ornate violin writing that appears in three solo sections, a type of solo section that features all eight vocalists separately and in various combinations, and another that features one or several equal voice duets with changing instrumental choirs. But one that has not appeared as yet will become a favorite means of extension and climax in Biber's later works: the fugue with slow-moving grave subject and ornate and lively counter-subject. The *Missa Christi Resurgentis* still exhibits more concern for sonority per se than for larger formal concerns. The vigor and inventiveness of the work, however, exude a kind of youthful assurance, a positive tone that characterizes most of the music Biber wrote at this time, and links it spiritually to the early baroque period. Biber is heir to Monteverdi in more than one aspect of this Mass as well as the *Vesperae à 32* of the same year and the *Laetatus Sum* of 1676. One particularly striking instance stands out: in the Credo Biber underscores the opposition of the words "mortuorum" and "vitam" with exactly the same means employed by Monteverdi to contrast "piange" and "ride" in his "Canzonetta morale," "Spontavi il di," and the words "piango" and "canto" in the famous madrigal "Zefiro torna e di soavi accenti."[17] Biber gives the section "Et exspecto resurrectionem mortuorum" an affective, suspension-laden *bassetgen* trio texture; then, at "Et vitam" the bass soloists of the two choirs burst forth with four antiphonal statements of the famous syncopated chaconne bass, that seems just as characteristic of Biber as of Monteverdi, leading joyfully into the double-chorus Amen.[18] But here, as in most other recollections of early seventeenth-century style in Biber's music, the composer adds a dimension in sound: in this case, two vivacious solo violin parts above an accompaniment of sustained viola chords (ex. 4-11). It is, in fact, the continuation of the spirit of early baroque music, with the incorporation of more up-to-date details such as obbligato instrumental writing, that makes much of Biber's church music so compelling. The exuberance and textural diversity of polychoral music from the early years of the century live on in many of Biber's sacred works, just as the daring, improvisatory qualities of the earliest idiomatic violin music (that of Marini, Farina and others) reach a peak in his solo sonatas.

The *Missa Catholica* survives at Kroměříž in sadly incomplete form: none of the four vocal parts is extant; nor are the first clarino and basso continuo parts; from the surviving

Example 4-11.   *Missa Christi Resurgentis,* Et expecto and Et vitam, Leading into Amen

Example 4-12.   *Missa Catholica,* Sanctus, Beginning (Only String and Clarino 2 Parts Survive)

second clarino, violin and viola parts, however, it is possible not only to discern much of the formal design of the work, but to calculate the scoring in many places.[19] The Mass has been dated in the 1680s by Sehnal, a date that fits with the high degree of motivic integration between the instrumental and vocal parts; the *Missa Salisburgensis* is otherwise the earliest of Salzburg's polychoral church works to exhibit this feature. The *Missa Catholica* was no doubt composed for a service evincing the spirit of militant Catholicism, such as that held in Salzburg in celebration of the defeat of the Turks in 1683; it might have been linked to Max Gandolph's forceful assertion of the faith against the rising tide of Protestantism in Salzburg at that time.[20] Just as the title of the *Missa Christi Resurgentis* seems to be illustrated in the brilliant Et resurrexit, that of the *Missa Catholica* almost certainly relates to the lengthy section that stretches from "Et in unum sanctam catholicam" to "peccatorum." This portion of the text, the article of belief in the Catholic Church and the necessity of baptism in the Church, is not singled out for such extended treatment in any other of Biber's Masses. Since of the extant parts only the second clarino and third viola play throughout this section, almost all we can deduce (apart from the way the rhythm of the text is represented from time to time) is that it was triumphant in tone and scored for one or more vocal soloists with trumpets.

In form the *Missa Catholica* reveals little that is out of the ordinary. The two Amen sections are almost identical, and the Qui tollis reappears in Agnus Dei II. The Kyrie/Christe complex constitutes an ABC form in which the two Kyries are concerted movements with similarly triadic main themes, while the Christe consists of a choral fugue with *colla parte* strings. The Gloria and Credo are more loosely sectional with fewer extended movements than in the *Missa Christi Resurgentis.* The principal sections, Qui tollis/Qui sedes and Crucifixus, compare in form and style to the earlier Masses. The former constitutes a complex of two ripieno fugues in motet style framing the suscipe in more concerted style. We can deduce from the single surviving part of the Crucifixus, the third (bass) viola, that the movement must have been a fugue without *colla parte* instruments; the movement is unique for Biber in that it is set in the tonic minor (with some chromaticism in the theme).

The character of the *Missa Catholica* ranges mostly from majesty (Kyrie I) to jubilation (Et resurrexit), even gaiety (Osanna, Kyrie II). We can frequently trace the imaginative treatment of the various triadic themes to Biber's instrumental music; this quality may be owing to the fact that the Mass is, apart from the clarini, not really polychoral, but reliant on the string body, which has survived. The manner in which the themes are combined in Kyrie II, for instance, recalls the opening movement of the first of the *Sonatae, tam Aris.* The Osanna is gigue-like (ex. 4-12). After an introduction for strings in the Et resurrexit, the entering vocal parts form a fanfare motive over a tonic pedal; a similar effect occurs at "Et exspecto." At "Et iterum" a descending trumpet arpeggio symbolizes the Second Coming and Last Judgment.

Example 4-13. *Missa Catholica,* Duo for Clarini (Beginning of Agnus Dei)
First clarino part supplied by the author.

Passages with more prominent obbligato instrumental writing are, however, fewer in number and generally shorter than those in the *Missa Christi Resurgentis.* A twenty-seven-bar antiphonal trumpet duo opens the Agnus Dei; we can deduce the missing clarino 1 part fairly confidently from the echo pattern of the bass; this movement appears to have been a hangover from the independent "sonata" movements of the earlier works, for, as mentioned above, the instrumental parts are not generally independent in this work (ex. 4-13).

One kind of movement, familiar from the later works, that makes a more conspicuous appearance here than before, is the vocal solo with two violins. Judging from the relationship between the parts in similar movements in Biber's works, the missing voice in the Benedictus was most likely a bass. My reconstruction, which begins as follows (ex. 4-14), has points in common with the beginning of the Domine Deus of the *Missa S. Henrici.* The chief characteristics of this movement type are a thirty-two-bar length, $\frac{3}{2}$ meter, relative-minor tonality, and an echoing in the strings of the opening motive of the vocal part.[21] The motivic imitation at the beginning recalls the repeated-motto opening of the seventeenth-century "Devisen" aria type, which appears in abundance in Biber's opera; and it is perhaps significant that a movement such as this should first occur in Biber's church music in the 1680s, the time that Biber embarked on his career as composer for the Salzburg opera and schooldrama productions.

The *Missa Salisburgensis* has been discussed independently of the chronological sequence of Biber's Masses for several reasons: its date of composition, although probably 1682, is not certain; the particular set of compositional problems associated with its scoring are not shared

Example 4-14.   *Missa Catholica,* Benedictus
Bass part reconstructed.

by any other Masses produced in Salzburg at the time; and, above all, as an extreme manifestation of the polychoral ideal, the *Missa Salisburgensis* embodies all the aesthetic issues that surround this kind of music more clearly than any other work of the time. Nevertheless, the *Missa Salisburgensis* was no isolated phenomenon, as the next of Biber's Masses, the *Missa Alleluia à 36.* illustrates. This work, probably to be dated in the 1690s, is, apart from the *Missa Salisburgensis* the Mass with the largest scoring to survive from seventeenth-century Salzburg: eight-part double chorus and soloists, six trumpets and kettledrums, two cornetti and three trombones, and a string body comprising two violins and three violas; the continuo specifies theorbo as well as organ.[22] The handling of the instrumental doubling in ripieno passages differs somewhat from that of the earlier works, and explains the extra viola. Only on the alto, tenor and bass parts has Biber followed the usual arrangement of doubling one chorus by winds, the other by strings;[23] now soprano 1 is doubled by both cornetto 1 and violin 2, and soprano 2 by cornetto 2 and viola 1 (the extra part, in soprano clef). This disposition allows greater reinforcement of the soprano parts; and because of the extra viola Biber can retain the obbligato first violin that is a characteristic element in his tutti sonority. The spacing of the string and wind choirs, however, must have been the usual one, for at several points in the Mass we have the familiar polychoral introductions and interludes; these are now fully integrated with the vocal parts and in one case, the fugal Amen of the Credo, in which the main theme is inverted, the separate choirs echo both forms of the theme. The Sanctus illustrates this kind of beginning[24] (ex. 4-15).

This modification of the normal arrangement of *colla parte* instruments indicates that Biber was more interested here in the balance of vocal and instrumental sonority in ripieno passages than in absolute clarity of double-chorus antiphony. In fact, antiphonal writing between the two choruses occurs only twice in this Mass, both times when the word "gloria" appears: at "propter magnam gloriam tuam" in the Gloria and "gloria tua" in the Sanctus. In the remaining tutti passages Biber concerns himself less than usual with the regular doubling of the alto and (especially) tenor parts: sometimes one of these will be played by both a stringed and a wind instrument, the other left undoubled. In addition, the three lower parts of one

Example 4-15.   *Missa Alleluia,* Sanctus, Polychoral Beginning

Example 4-15 (continued)

chorus often duplicate those of the other, although seldom consistently. The soprano parts, however, always remain independent and consistently doubled.

It is possible that these details reflect increased concern for formal considerations as opposed to the enormous focus on sonority that dominates the *Missa Christi Resurgentis*; in any case, the *Missa Alleluia* stands clearly between the earlier work and the later Masses in this respect. The Kyrie provides a good illustration. For the first time known to us Biber chooses to use the integrated ABA' form that is so impressive in the *Missa ex B* and *Missa Bruxellensis* rather than either the ABC or straight da capo (ABA) types. The complex comprises, after some introductory tutti chords, a statement of the Kyrie (23 measures), followed by the Christe (17 measures), a section in which the thematic material of the Kyrie and Christe combine (9 measures) and finally a compressed reiteration of the Kyrie (12 measures). This fairly short movement reveals a logically unified and economical, yet diversified treatment of the solo/tutti resources and contrasting themes. Following the ripieno fugue-like Kyrie, the Christe introduces its static, repeated-half-note theme in brief duets (for two tenors, two altos and two basses in succession, accompanied by strings) in which the entry of the second part is always delayed a quarter note; this takes place above slow-moving harmonies that fall first to the subdominant (F), then by thirds through D minor and B-flat, the whole creating an unmistakable sense of supplication. The Christe continues, now in eight-part ripieno choral scoring without instruments, so that the syncopated entries of the single-note theme create almost arythmic, slowly moving harmonies. Against this the Kyrie gradually reenters, moving to the dominant as the Christe theme moves up to its highest register for the first and only time. This beautiful climax is resolved by the drop of the Christe theme to the tonic for its last appearance; and, after a shortened form of the Kyrie, the movement ends as it began with largely homophonic tutti sonorities.

In the movement just described the question of musical value arises in conjunction with the use of extensive vocal and instrumental resources, on the one hand, and simple harmonies, on the other. In his later works Biber used and reused this type of *Gegenfuge* many times, sometimes in motet-like *stile antico* form (the Christe of the *Missa S. Henrici*), and sometimes with enormous resources (the Osanna of the *Missa Salisburgensis* is probably one of the earliest instances). Already in the *Missa Salisburgensis* a magnificent, but gentle climax occurs as the slowly moving Benedictus theme moves to its highest register in combination with the ornate Osanna. These tremendously affective moments are often enhanced by the scoring, which underscores the contrast between the themes with solo/ripieno contrasts; but they are never dependent on the scoring. Rather, they make their effect by means of a highly successful pacing of the harmonic, thematic and registral motion. The means are unquestionably simple from the standpoint of harmonic chord analysis; but the genius that is apparent in such places makes this use of the word "simple" meaningless. The falling-third harmonies that appear in the Christe have a wider significance both in the *Missa Alleluia* and Biber's work as a whole. Several passages in the *Missa Alleluia* (notably the antiphonal Propter magnam Gloriam tuam and most of the Crucifixus) as well as the *Missa Bruxellensis* are conspicuously built over falling third harmonies; and this idea expands here and elsewhere, as we will see, to the keys of successive movements.

Like the *Missa Christi Resurgentis,* the *Missa Alleluia* conveys a high degree of magnificence and splendor; this was practically the only conception of the Mass in seventeenth-century Salzburg. The Gloria is organized, much like the earlier work, by means of the presentation of soloistic sections around a *stile antico* Qui tollis and a climactic final Amen (fig. 4-3). The vividness of some of the style contrasts is remarkable. For example, Biber leads the Qui tollis to a "pathetic" cadence in E minor, then calls for a blaze of C major from the trumpets (ex. 4-16): The soloistic beginning of the Gloria, with its initial leap in the voices (for "terra") and florid writing at "glorificamus te" strikes a sensuous keynote (ex. 4-17).

The Credo is longer and organized in more loosely sectional fashion, although with several extended movements that make up a kind of structural core. It contains three well-spaced fugal sections: Qui propter/descendit, Et ascendit and Amen, the first and last of which build to impressive climaxes by means of motivic combination and increase in instrumentation in their closing bars. Most of the remainder of the Credo is conceived in soloistic terms, with the Et incarnatus and Crucifixus as a kind of centerpiece. These two movements illustrate something of how Biber uses harmonic *catabasis* to add a significant structural and affective dimension to a large form. The Et incarnatus is the familiar triple-meter *bassetgen* trio (here for two sopranos and tenor) in the relative minor that Biber developed for this movement (and occasionally the Benedictus as well). The Crucifixus is also scored for three soloists (now two altos and bass) with a continuous harmonic background of three trombones, and two clarini that play at the uppermost level of the pitch range; quadruple meter returns and the movement is set in the subdominant. Tonally, the subdominant in Biber's Masses is reserved for the

Figure 4-3. Gloria of the *Missa Alleluia*

	Movement	Measures	Scoring	Key	Solo/Ripieno
1	Et in terra	17	8 voices & continuo	C	Solo
2	Gratias	38	Tutti, with double chorus antiphony at "propter . . . tuam"	C	Ripieno
3	Domine Deus rex	7	Soprano duet with violins & violas	A minor	Solo
	Domine fili	10	Alto duet with cornetti & trombones	A minor	Solo
	Domine Deus agnus	7	Bass duet with 2 clarini	C	Solo
4	Qui tollis	31	5-part chorus doubled by strings. Fugal.	C to E minor	Ripieno
5	Qui sedes	10	Bass duet with 6 trumpets & timpani	C	Solo
	Quoniam	7	Tenor duet	C	Solo
6	Cum sancto/Amen	39		C	Ripieno, solo, ripieno

Crucifixus, where it is usually linked to a subdued, passive, downward-moving quality; it does not paint the agony and pain of the crucifixion so much as the death and burial, the grave rather than the cross. In the *Missa Alleluia,* therefore, the word "Crucifixus" is uttered only once, and in the opening four bars the soloists present the entire first phrase (to "Pilato") almost summarily in homophonic, syllabic style. The remainder of the movement (twenty-five bars) is devoted to the words "Passus et sepultus est," which Biber treats melismatically. The tonality passes by falling thirds away from the F-major tonic through D minor (a very low bass cadence) and B-flat, while in the final bars Biber introduces the tonic minor (F minor) before closing in F. Altogether the keys moved downward by thirds from the C major of the Descendit and the A-minor Et incarnatus to this strong emphasis on the subdominant (flat) region, all of which lends a striking "drooping" effect that is increased by the descending chains of suspensions in the voice and clarino parts. This sensitivity to tonal direction is an idea that will reappear more and more as we become familiar with Biber's work; the range of keys is never large (except in the case of his opera), but the consistency and sureness of application are remarkable.

Although the *Missa Alleluia* is in some respects a forward-looking work in Biber's output, it retains, in the solo sections of the Credo above all, much of the sonority-oriented approach to text setting that tends to weaken the sense of overall structure by breaking it into many contrasted subsections. Thus, the sections from "sedet" to "finis" (ripieno) and "Et in Spiritum" to "saeculi" (solo) are rather too diverse in style to function well as unified wholes. Biber faithfully and often imaginatively observes the spirit of each phrase of the text—witness the sudden changes in tempo and the introduction of chromatic, minor-key harmonies for the two four-bar passages "Sedet ad dexteram Patris" and "judicare vivos et mortuos"—but chooses not to give an extended setting to any one. Possibly he was not entirely satisfied with this procedure, for one of the most impressive features of the *Missa S. Henrici* is his solution to this problem.

The *Missa S. Henrici* is arguably Biber's most "advanced" piece of church music, a feature that may be related to its composition for an occasion of personal significance as well as to the fact that it departs from the double-chorus idiom: it is scored for CCATB chorus with obbligato strings and clarini, plus *colla parte* trombones. Although generally conservative in

Example 4-16.   *Missa Alleluia,* Ending of Qui tollis and Beginning of Qui sedes

harmonic idiom, it surpasses the *Missa Alleluia* in the development and stylistic differentiation of the individual movements. It is also one of the longest and most carefully planned Masses from this period, comprising eighteen separate movements that average about fifty bars in length (only four have fewer than thirty bars). Division of the Mass into autonomous units emerges as one of the most forward-looking characteristics of the *Missa S. Henrici* and the *Missa ex B.* Whereas in broad terms seventeenth-century composers developed for the first time an extensive and systematically ordered awareness and cultivation of many different musical styles, composers of the eighteenth century became concerned with the extension and dimensions of individual movements, a development that made it possible for a single style or affection to have far greater duration than before. This desire for extension is very much in

Example 4-17. *Missa Alleluia,* Et in terra pax

Example 4-18.   *Missa S. Henrici,* Christe, mm. 1–34

evidence in the *Missa S. Henrici,* although the common methods and means of the eighteenth century do not appear. The energetic concerto-derived style, with its highly developed modulatory tonal structure and seemingly endless capacity for the spinning out of motives is not a basic element of Biber's technique. Biber more often extends his movements with contrapuntal and textural means, such as the combining of themes previously heard in succession, solo/ripieno contrasts, and fluctuation in instrumentation. Also, contrary to Adler's assertion that there were no ostinato basses in the late seventeenth-century Masses he studied, Biber does employ ground-bass movements in his larger church pieces. [25] Although the *Missa S. Henrici* still antedates the confident and more powerful breadth of the late baroque style, it represents a point well removed from the tonal insecurity of the early seventeenth century, a style in which the tonal sense is always stable, though without the modulatory and chordal range of the following generation.

We have seen that one of the most vital of seventeenth-century style distinctions, that between *stile antico* and *stile moderno,* fugures prominently in Biber's Masses and can even control the organization of an entire work (*Missa ex B*). Within Biber's concerted Masses any of the following four movements may be a ripieno fugue in a more or less strict style, with *colla parte* instruments: Christe (*Missa in Albis, Missa Catholica, Missa S. Henrici*), Qui tollis (all Masses), Crucifixus (*Missa in Albis, Missa Christi Resurgentis, Missa Catholica, Missa S. Henrici*), Sanctus (*Missa Alleluia, Missa S. Henrici, Missa Bruxellensis*). Only in the *Missa S. Henrici* does Biber choose this setting for all four. Themes in long note values and tied notes give the Christe and Qui tollis an arhythmic, unaccented quality, while the secondary contrasting themes introduce a sense of pulse. The Christe is an outstanding illustration of this idea, which was realized differently in the *Missa Alleluia* (ex. 4-18). The opening of the Sanctus in this Mass has been compared with that in the *Missa in Contrapuncto* (see ex. 4-4 above). Nevertheless, in the *Missa S. Henrici* the stylistic distinction between fugal movements in *stile antico* and *stile moderno* is sometimes not as forcefully drawn as in the *Missa ex B.* Movements such as the Kyrie and Agnus Dei, for example, might just as readily be taken for the former were it not for the presence of obbligato instrumental parts and solo/ripieno contrasts. Harmonically and contrapuntally these movements are hardly more forward-looking than the Sanctus. One of the reasons for this lies in Biber's frequent use of traditional themes in his church music. Those of the Kyrie and Agnus Dei of the *Missa S. Henrici* were widely disseminated in the seventeenth and eighteenth centuries, and one or both can be found in a

Figure 4-4. Scheme of *Missa S. Henrici*, Gloria and Credo

Movement	Measures	Meter	Key	Instrumentation and Style
				Gloria
1 Et in terra	23	¢	C to A minor	2 solo sopranos, strings
2 Gratias	14	$\frac{4}{4}$	C	Ripieno chorus & trumpets; 2 bars of homophonic chords; 12 bars fugal
3 Domine Deus	32	$\frac{3}{2}$	A minor	Bass solo & 2 solo violins, imitative
4 Qui tollis	53	¢ alla breve	A minor	Five-part ripieno chorus doubled by strings and trombones. Chromaticism in theme.
5 Qui sedes to end	123	$\frac{3}{2}$	C	Finale: composed of several sections with same thematic material. Scoring varies from soloistic to full orchestration.
				Credo
Patrem	10	¢	C	Introductory. Full scoring. Homophonic and chordal.
1 Et in unum	29	$\frac{4}{4}$	A minor	Florid soloistic writing with strings. Ground bass elements.
2 Qui propter	18	$\frac{4}{4}$	C	Ripieno chorus & trumpets; 6 bars of homophonic chords; 12 bars fugal.
3 Et incarnatus	32	$\frac{3}{2}$	A minor	Soprano solo (bassetgen) and 2 solo violins. Imitative.
4 Crucifixus	22	¢	F	Four-part ripieno chorus doubled by strings & trombones. Chromaticism in theme.
5 Et resurrexit	47	$\frac{3}{2}$	C	Full orchestration. Homophonic block-chord style in vocal parts.
6 Et in spiritum to end	69	$\frac{4}{4}$	C	Finale: composed of several sections with same thematic material. Scoring varies from soloistic to full orchestration.

great variety of works. Fux was especially fond of traditional themes and, like Biber, used that found in the Agnus Dei of the *Missa S. Henrici* many times. Some of these themes appear to have been derived from Gregorian chant and probably carried ecclesiastical associations.[26]

The Gloria and Credo present the most impressive achievements in form within the *Missa S. Henrici*. In their extension Biber departs sharply from the Masses of his predecessors. The Gloria would be remarkable in any case, if for no other reason that that it exceeds the Credo in length. In concerted Masses of this period (e.g., Kerll's Masses, Schmelzer's *Missa Nuptialis*) the Gloria is usually considerably shorter than the Credo. Now the problem of reconciling the textual variety of the Gloria and Credo with the demands of musical coherence led Biber to follow similar plans for the structures of the two sections (fig. 4-4). The most outstanding features are the large closing complexes consisting of several sub-sections bound together thematically (in the Gloria: Qui sedes, Quoniam, Cum sancto Spirito, Amen; in the Credo: Et in Spiritum, Et vitam, Amen). These finales occupy sizeable portions of the Gloria (123 of 244 measures) and Credo (69 of 227 measures) and create purposeful, climactic endings. Of the two, that of the Gloria is longer, occupying fully half the movement, and makes the greater impact. The more consistent imagery and tone of the Gloria text, especially from the word "Quoniam" to the end, suggests a longer treatment, whereas the diversity of the Credo text does not permit the composer to draw as many sections into the finale. But although the motivically unified finale of the Credo is shorter than that of the Gloria, the structural parallel between them becomes more apparent if we consider that the Et resurrexit belongs to some extent with the succeeding section. It shares with the finale its tonality, instrumentation and exultant quality (but not its thematic material). If we view the Et resurrexit in this light, we perceive that the ending of the Credo occupies 117 out of 227 measures, or slightly more than

Example 4-19.   *Missa S. Henrici,* Themes from "Finale" of Gloria

half the movement, as in the Gloria. Biber has now solved the problems of unity and direction which still encumbered him in the *Missa Alleluia.*

The finales of the Gloria and Credo warrant closer attention because the techniques of constructing climactic endings employed here assume greater importance during the course of the eighteenth century. We can see some of the same principles at work in the Gloria and Credo of Bach's *B-minor Mass* and even (making allowance for obvious differences) in the eighteenth-century operatic finale. The combination of themes previously heard separately and the accumulation of vocal and instrumental parts are major techniques. In the finale of Biber's Gloria, after an initial tutti statement of the main theme ("Qui sedes" to "miserere nobis"), which appears in several slightly different versions (ex. 4-19), the texture reduces (at "Quoniam") to two solo voices. At "Cum sancto spiritu" the number of soloists increases to three before the second theme enters ("in Gloria Dei Patris"). In the following Amen, sonority accumulates as follows: two to four solo voices (themes stated separately); ripieno chorus with obbligato violin and *colla parte* instruments (the themes are combined from this point on); the same scoring with the addition of two clarini; finally, full orchestration for the last seventeen bars. The ending of the Credo reveals a similar construction but the texture expands in a less continuous manner. The main theme first appears as a quasi-ostinato bass motive accompanying solo voices (Et in spiritum); Et vitam is devoted to the second theme, and in the Amen the two combine.

Quite a number of correspondences can be found between other sections of the Gloria and Credo as well. The setting of Et in terra from the Gloria resembles Et in unum from the Credo in length, meter, scoring, and general style. Gratias (Gloria) and Qui propter (Credo) are approximately the same length and parallel each other in key and meter; each begins with a brief, fully scored syllabic phrase ("Gratias agimus tibi" and "Qui propter" to "salutem," respectively) then continues in imitative style.

Far closer parallels, however, exist between the ensuing sections of the two movements, Domine Deus and Et incarnatus. Both are solo arias (the first for bass, the second for soprano), thirty-two bars in length, in the relative minor key and $\frac{3}{2}$ meter, with two solo violin parts which imitate the vocal phrases. The soprano solo exemplifies the *bassetgen* texture more fully than in any other Biber vocal work, although the Et incarnatus settings of the *Missa Salisburgensis* and *Missa Bruxellensis,* as well as those of Biber's *Missa ex B, Missa Alleluia* and *Missa S.*

Henrici all belong to the same category. Other notable examples from the seventeenth century are the *Sinfonia alta* and *Coro in cielo* which picture the realm of Jove as opposed to that of Neptune (the latter represented by a *Coro marittimo* of low voices) in Monteverdi's *Il Ritorno d'Ulisse in patria.* A particularly beautiful *bassetgen* aria is Night's solo from Purcell's *The Fairy Queen.* Probably the best-known of all such pieces is the aria "Aus Liebe will mein Heiland sterben" from Bach's *St. Matthew Passion*; in order to create an affect of innocence Bach replaces the low bass by a pair of oboes da caccia, which accompany two high melodic parts. The Et incarnatus setting of Biber's *Missa S. Henrici* aims to depict the gentleness and purity of the Virgin Mary as well as the wonder of the Incarnation. In the Et incarnatus the soprano part, doubled entirely by the *bassetgen* continuo line, functions as the "fundament" to the same extent as the bass part of the Domine Deus. Also, the two movements resemble each other closely in structure. Internal cadences at approximately the quarter and halfway points clarify their forms. In addition, each movement begins with a conspicuous motive that appears freely inverted in the second half (ex. 4-20).

The Qui tollis and Crucifixus also resemble each other. Although set in different keys (relative minor and subdominant, respectively), the two pieces are based on melodies that stress the chromatic descent C, B, B-flat, and A. Both are ripieno movements scored for chorus with *colla parte* strings and trombones. Since the Qui tollis must be performed alla breve and the Crucifixus adagio, we do not perceive the seeming disparity in length between the two (53 and 22 measures, respectively). The two sections share a general similarity of mood which is a very characteristic one for Biber (ex. 4-21). Their chromatic themes occasion frequent changes from major to minor. Downward motion creates a feeling of melancholy: humility is expressed in the Qui tollis by means of falling sequences at "miserere nobis" and "deprecationem"; in the Crucifixus the melodic line steadily descends, and at the conclusion all vocal parts fall in pitch level (the bass reaches a sepulchral C). In both cases affective harmonies delay the final cadences, and in the Crucifixus the tonic minor is introduced just before the end. The tutti reiterations of C major at Qui sedes and Et resurrexit create sharp, dramatic contrasts enhanced by the very sparing use of the trumpet choir in the preceding sections of the Gloria and Credo.

The foregoing commentary on the Gloria and Credo illustrates the concern with large-scale planning that, as we have already indicated, characterizes the late works. This trait is by no means confined to Biber's church music, but figures in other of his late works as well. The opera *Chi la dura la vince* (ca. 1690-92) affords the best example. Its first and third acts are centered around C major (as the tonic) and modulate mainly to the flat side of the key. On the other hand, the second act is primarily in G major and most of the secondary key areas occur on the sharp side. Working on a large scale in opera undoubtedly stimulated Biber's interest in tonal relationships. In another late work of large dimensions, the *Balletti à 6,* Biber departs from the usual practice of setting all movements of a suite in the same key (fig. 4-5). As in the Gloria and Credo of the *Missa S. Henrici,* the sequence of separate movements creates a series of contrasting styles, secondary key areas occur in pockets, and the tonic, C major, returns regularly, reinforced by the sound of trumpets.

The *Missa Bruxellensis,* on the basis of its watermark and style, is probably Biber's last Mass (1700-1704?).[27] In it we have the last of the works for eight-part double chorus, strings and winds, the identical scoring in this case to the *Vesperae à 32* of 1674. But now, despite some obvious similarities between it and the works from the 1670s, there are enormous differences. The *Missa Bruxellensis* is considerably longer than any comparable work of Biber's; and this fact reflects a marked change in outlook. We have spoken several times of a manifest desire for extension of the musical dimensions that runs fascinatingly parallel to both the rise of baroque

Example 4-20.   *Missa S. Henrici*

(a), (b), (c) Domine Deus, Excerpts

architecture and of Austrian imperialism in the years just before and after 1700. The *Missa Bruxellensis* exhibits this quality more than any other work of the time; at the same time the work is still not as forward-looking as the *Missa S. Henrici* because the means of extension are so closely attached to the polychoral idiom. In fact, the *Missa Bruxellensis* is in many respects remarkably like the *Missa Salisburgensis,* a fact that relates not to the question of authorship, which we take to be settled, but to the fact that both Masses at times exaggerate the fanfare effect that obviously belonged to occasions of the greatest pomp and display; this quality is connected to the means by which the works are extended, on the one hand, and probably, on the other, to the fact that carefully prepared scores of just these two Masses were preserved.[28]

Apart from the *Missa Salisburgensis* and hymn *Plaudite Tympana* the clearest antecedents for the *Missa Bruxellensis* in Biber's work are to be found in the *Sonata S. Polycarpi*; and it is conceivable that, as in the sonata, this fanfare quality was especially created in the Mass for an event of particular significance to the archbishop, perhaps the celebration of his *anniversarium,* established in 1695, or the festivities for one of the various institutions, such as the order of the knights of St. Rupert, founded by Johann Ernst.[29] The principal fanfare movements of the *Missa Bruxellensis* are the Glorificamus te and the Quoniam, in both of which the harmonies are virtually limited to tonic and dominant (with some key changes), just

Example 4-20 (continued)

(d), (e), (f)   Et incarnatus, Excerpts

as are several sections of the *Sonata S. Polycarpi*; but certain other movements—the Kyrie, Et in terra, Cuius regni, Patrem, and a few more—contain a great deal of the effect as well. For example, in the *Sonata S. Polycarpi* the bass often becomes active, moving in brisk eighth notes, when the harmonies are particularly static; and this procedure is used in both the *Missa Salisburgensis* (Glorificamus te, Amen, Et resurrexit, Et unam sanctam, and Pleni sunt coeli, plus two sections of the *Plaudite Tympana*) and *Missa Bruxellensis* (parts of the Kyrie, Et in terra, Glorificamus te, Patrem, and Osanna). There is a particular resemblance between the melodic style of the Patrem in the *Missa Bruxellensis* and one such section from the sonata, even though the Patrem is for solo voice (ex. 4-22). It is obvious that in such music extension is not a problem; repetition, echo effects, and the like are part and parcel of the style, and the *Missa Bruxellensis* revels in them, building whole sections on the smallest amount of text. In addition several movements begin with lengthy trumpet solos (Cum Sancto, Et resurrexit and Et exspecto) while others (the Osanna, for example) have interludes for trumpets. As a result,

Example 4-21.   *Missa S. Henrici*

(a)   Qui tollis, mm. 1–35

(b)   Crucifixus

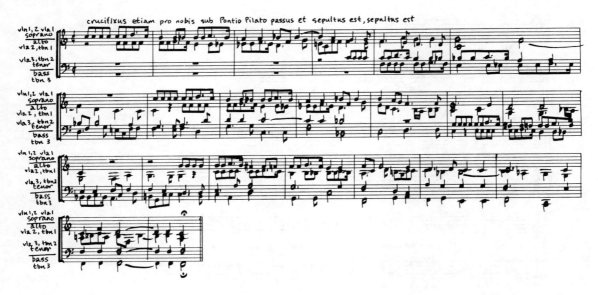

the character of the thematic material in this Mass is based to a greater extent than that of any other on repeated phrases and motives, sometimes in sequence, but often at the same pitch. And a certain energetic, even motoric quality emerges from the patterned rhythmic elaboration of the harmonies that is not unlike the slow harmonic rhythm and *Fortspinnung* of the eighteenth-century concerto at times. The fanfare style has opened a window to the breadth of eighteenth century style, and the *Missa Bruxellensis* is at one and the same time conservative and forward-looking.

The *Missa Bruxellensis* also reveals influences from another quarter of Biber's *oeuvre*— opera. There are more solo passages for single voice in this than in any other of his Masses. And some, most notably the Gratias, are constructed in a manner that recalls the prevailing aria styles and forms of *Chi la dura la vince*. As in several others of Biber's works where the operatic influence is clearest—the Dixit Dominus from the *Vesperae longiores*, the offertory *Quo abiit dilectus tuus*, the Domine Deus and Et incarnatus of the *Missa S. Henrici*—we find

Figure 4-5. *Balletti à 6*
　　　Scoring: 1 violin, 2 violas, 2 clarini, basso continuo

1	Sonata	C major, strings & clarini
2	Allemande	C major, strings
3	Amener	C major, strings
4	Aria	C major, strings & clarini
5	Balletto	G major, strings
6	Trezza	G major, strings
7	Gavotte	E minor, strings
8	Canario	C major, strings & clarini
9	Amoresca	A minor, strings
10	Sarabanda	A minor, strings
11	Gagliarda	F major, strings
12	Ciacona	C major, strings & clarini

solos that reveal structures of balanced phrases and modulations rather than deriving their impetus primarily from the representation of individual words by means of vocal melismas, and the like. Of course the older type appears abundantly in the *Missa Bruxellensis*; but there is now a significant number of the more modern type as well; and several movements—the Gratias, Patrem and Osanna in particular—begin with solos for individual voices that give way, not to the accumulation of solo voices, such as the sections for eight soloists in the *Missa Alleluia,* but to similar solos for other single voices. The newer procedure is by no means successful all the time; the listener may tire of hearing the same material several times in succession, despite its attractiveness and overall modulatory scheme. But there is no doubt that it adds a significant dimension of breadth to the music. The beginning of the Osanna for the four soloists of the first choir is a case in point. The opening phrase, for alto and continuo, is a familiar Biber theme type featuring one of his favorite beginnings—the repeated descending triad—and moving to a long melisma on "excelsis" before cadencing in the sixth bar on the dominant. The tenor then picks up this theme on the dominant, abbreviating it by one bar, and confirming the dominant with another decisive cadence. The soprano, beginning on the dominant, parallels the initial phrase and ends on V of V, while the bass parallels the tenor phrase, beginning on V of V but cadencing in the mediant instead. Finally, the soloists of the second choir sing basically the same phrase in duets, the first pair cadencing on the mediant once more, and the second moving back to the tonic for the entrance of a tutti. The whole occupies twenty-eight bars, a typical length for a Biber aria, and makes a satisfying, well-rounded form, but one in which the same phrase is restated, with slight modifications, six

Example 4-22.   Similar Melodic Styles in Works by Biber

(a)   *Missa Bruxellensis,* Credo, Beginning

(b)   *Sonata S. Polycarpi,* mm. 115–129

times. One cannot help feeling that the Domine Deus and Et incarnatus "arias" from the *Missa S. Henrici* are more successful, or even similarly constructed solos for different voices that do not repeat the thematic material at all from voice to voice (the above-mentioned Dixit from the *Psalmi Longiores*). Here the splendor of the polychoral idiom encumbers the more modern solo style.

Another probable instance of operatic influence in combination with polychoral style is more successful because it draws the expressive solo element into the sacred style. Biber set the text from "laudamus te" through "glorificamus te" as an alternation of three short passages in double-chorus antiphony ("laudamus te, benedicimus te") with three short alto solos with a homophonic string accompaniment ("adoramus te, glorificamus te"); this section immediately precedes the "fanfare" glorificamus te section mentioned above. The alto solos, each suddenly adagio following the energetic choral passages, produce an effect of similar intent for the word "adoramus" to that used by J. S. Bach at the same place (and also three times) in the A major *Missa Brevis,* BWV 234.[30] The first of the solos completes a move to the dominant with an inflection from the dominant minor; the second moves at once, via chromatic motion in the bass, to the mediant—now the diminished seventh and Neapolitan sixth (used by Biber in his opera and a small number of late church works) add an affective dimension; the third solo introduces another diminished seventh to suggest the supertonic and returns to the tonic with the minor third in the melody before the cadence. The harmonic devices—especially the Neapolitan sixth and diminished seventh that are more familiar from Biber's operatic style— add a dramatic element to the *Missa Bruxellensis* at this point.

The polychoral element in the Mass is, of course, basically conservative. But some alteration in the pattern of doubling hints, more than in the *Missa Alleluia,* for example, at a newer orchestral style. First of all the doubling, like that of the *Missa Alleluia,* departs somewhat from the usual reinforcing of one choir by strings the other by winds. As in that work, each of the sopranos is doubled by both a violin and a cornetto; but now there are some new textures that suggest a degree of experimentation within the polychoral idiom: 1) ripieno passages (in the Kyrie, for example) where the orchestra, independent of the voices, is used to dramatically punctuate the chorus; 2) places where the doubling in antiphonal passages involves composite lines for violin and cornetto formed out of the upper parts of both choirs; 3) a similar non-antiphonal doubling of the lower parts of both choirs, while the sopranos are doubled by antiphonal cornetti and the two violins are freed to alternate with the choirs; 4) the doubling of the sopranos an octave below; 5) the presence of slightly different lines for voices and doubling instruments. All these occurences are slight and for the most part overshadowed by the more traditional usage; but they do indicate a measure of separation of the orchestral and vocal textures that is a sign of eighteenth-century techniques of orchestration.

There is also, of course, much in the *Missa Bruxellensis* that is traditional, as well as much that is particular to Biber. The fugal settings of the Qui tollis, Crucifixus and Sanctus are features of many of his Masses; but even here there are interesting differences: the Qui tollis is repeated to create a da capo form around a "miserere nobis" in block-chord homophony with strings in the *tremulante* style (the latter then reappearing after a completely contrasted Qui sedes); the Sanctus is augmented by the addition of an obbligato violin line, albeit in exactly the same style as the vocal parts; and the Crucifixus is set for four solo voices rather than chorus doubled by *colla parte* instruments (its theme and countertheme closely resemble the two secondary themes of the fugal beginning of the sixth of the *Sonatae Violino Solo*). The *bassetgen* Et incarnatus has already been mentioned; and, like several of Biber's other Masses, the Benedictus is a solo movement in the relative minor, now for two sopranos and continuo over a walking bass that almost, if not quite, evokes Corelli's style. The ripieno treatment of the triadic Osanna theme recalls quite a number of similar passages in Biber's work, including the Osanna of the *Requiem in F minor.* And the appearance of a bass solo with strings at "genitum non factum" recalls a similar setting at the same point of the *Missa Alleluia.* Finally, the Dona nobis pacem must be mentioned; Biber has constructed the movement almost entirely upon series of descending-third sequences—C, a, F, d—that move back to the tonic to begin again in quasi-ostinato fashion. The contrapuntal idea that fills out the sequence is of striking simplicity—parallel thirds against a scalar bass in contrary motion—and similar to a number of Amen themes from the *Vesperae Longiores ac Breviores.*

In the *Missa Bruxellensis* a mixture of techniques, both traditional and forward-looking, come together to produce one of the longest and most ostentatious compositions of the age. As a whole, the Mass is not one of Biber's best; the conflict between the polychoral idiom with its omnipresent demands for ecclesiastical splendor, and the composer's innate desire to experiment with sonority, in combination with the pull from other musical directions such as opera, give the work its moments of great expressivity, to be sure; but the youthful exuberance that animates the *Missa Christi Resurgentis* is missing. Much of the work seems artificially extended. At times it sounds empty in comparison with the instrumental music and the two Requiems that Biber also produced in his later years.

The Requiem Masses

The Masses of the preceding section were all composed for services of marked festivity and splendor in Salzburg. Regardless of the ceremony—whether an *anniversarium,* consecration, commemoration, royal visit or taking of the veil—the music had to enhance a measure of external solemnity and display. All such occasions were to varying degree joyful and always imposing. As a result, all Biber's concerted settings of the Mass ordinary include prominent trumpet parts and are in the "trumpet key" of C major. Reflection on the natures of these works tends to bring to mind the more ostentatious movements—the Gloria and Credo endings of the *Missa S. Henrici,* the Et resurrexit and instrumental movements of the *Missa Christi Resurgentis,* and the like. Although not the most profound passages, they represent most directly the spirit of baroque exuberance in which the works as a whole were conceived.

On the other hand, the death of an archbishop requires music that, externally, matches his stature and suggests the magnitude of the loss to the living, while at a more universal level projecting hopes of eternity and, inevitably, fear and awe at the prospect of death. In the age that produced the German *Trauerspiel* death was an event that received an enormous attention, both private and public. If the deceased, an eminent personage, had been especially pious, relics might be taken from the body, countless Masses were sung and spoken, mourners in mourning clothes who kept vigil beside the corpse were paid for, several services elaborately furnished in terms of music as well as the rest would often be held, money might be given to the poor, and a funeral monument (*castrum doloris*) might be erected for an extended period of time.[31] The constant reminders of death and transience in baroque art—flowers at their peak, beginning to decay, timepieces, rotting fruit, skulls and skeletons—constitute a vital and omnipresent countertheme to the celebration of life in the churches of Catholic Germany. The vision of heaven that opened above for the congregation in many churches, the theatrical representation of miracles and scenes of transfiguration, often with their own special "transcendent" lighting, made clear, despite their emphasis on sensuous immediacy, the very illusory quality of human life. In some churches, particularly those of the earlier phase of German baroque architecture (around the turn of the eighteenth century), dramatic contrast in lighting between the realm of the congregation and that of the "vision" was emphasized.[32] Triumph was, of course, the Catholic church's favored expressive sphere in the counterreformation. The attitude toward death that is more familiar to musicians today from the Bach cantatas—the longing for release from a life in which human works and achievements, even reason itself, had been devalued, a life in which man lived under the cross, so to speak—is not at all identical with the Catholic viewpoint, which celebrated and memorialized works and achievements. The images of transience have a far less prominent place in the churches than those of transcendence; but their presence is nonetheless inevitable and their power compelling. The Catholic attitude towards death allows grief, awe, fear, hope, and triumph all to emerge in varied degrees; and the Requiem Mass offers, despite the often-cited fear induced by the Dies irae, an exceptionally rich and contrasted textual source for musical settings.

In this light we are very fortunate in possessing two Requiem Masses by Biber, not only written at the peak of his maturity as a church composer, but also disclosing obvious differences in outlook. The title pages reveal the important variance in their scorings:

Requiem à: 15. in Concerto.	*Requiem ex F con terza min:*
2 Canti	a 5 Voci e 5 Viole in Concerto
1 Alto	5 Voci in Capella

1 Tenore	3 Tromboni ad libitum
2 Bassi	Authore
4 Viole di Brazzio	Henrico Francisco de Bibern
2 Trombe Basse	dapifero ac Capellae Magistro
3 Tromboni	Partes 29
2 Piffari ad libitum	
6 Voci in Capella	
Authore	
Henrico I: Franc: a Bibern	

From the forms of Biber's name used on the manuscripts we assume that the *terminus post quem* for the *Requiem à 15* is 1690, that for the *Requiem in F minor*, 1692. Both the five- and six-part choral settings of these works (CCATB; CCATBB) were common in the seventeenth century; Biber and his Salzburg contemporaries used both as alternatives to the eight-part double chorus, whose absence from both Requiems is probably a significant fact. The scoring of the *Requiem in F minor* is by no means unusual. That of the *Requiem à 15,* however, arrests attention on several counts. First of all, the use of oboes (*piffari*) instead of the more normal cornetti to double the soprano parts of the chorus is unique in Biber's output; perhaps he wished to distinguish the tone of the work from his settings of the ordinary by so varying the choral sonority. The composition of the string body—violins replaced by soprano-clef violas (*violettae*), plus the standard instruments in alto and tenor clefs—also marks a departure from the brighter sound of the obbligato violins that in other works Biber made an effort to have. By far the most extraordinary aspect of the instrumentation of the *Requiem à 15,* however, is the inclusion of two "Trombe Basse" (called "tiefe Trompeten" in the parts) pitched in A, a minor third below the usual instruments in C; the key of the piece is therefore A major, a very rare key for Masses at this time and probably unique for a Requiem. No other instance of trumpets pitched in low A is known in seventeenth-century music. The "Trombe Basse" are in fact clarino parts, notated in C and reaching as high as the sixteenth partial, written c''', but sounding a minor third lower than written.

The use of clarini coupled with the choice of a major key strongly suggests that Biber intended in the *Requiem à 15* to bring out a positive, hopeful view of death. While the transposition of the normal pitch level of the Mass down a third, as well as the departures from the usual string and wind sonorities, enabled the composer to create a more subdued overall sound that certainly comes forth in the various places where low-pitched choral sonorities and soft dynamic markings are present, the presence of clarini reflects another side of the work altogether. In fact, Biber exploits two quite different associations of the instrument: in a number of places (Requiem, Kyrie, Recordare, Domine Jesu, Sanctus, Osanna, and Lux aeterna) a brilliant, florid clarino sound indicates optimism and majesty, just as in the triumphant movements of Biber's concerted settings of the ordinary, while at other points (most notably the beginning of the work, much of the Dies irae, rex tremendae, lacrimosa— where many repeated-note melodic patterns occur) a lower, more sombre trumpet sound reminds us that the instrument represents fear as well as glory, is the emblem both of majesty and the "last trump." Biber's use of two clarini in the Crucifixus of the *Missa Alleluia* prepares us for this disparity. And in the *Requiem à 15* the trombones are not restricted to the ad libitum *colla parte* role that they are in the *Requiem in F minor*; instead they vary both the accompanimental sonority in both choral and solo passages and even combine at selected points with the clarini to provide a brass choir for antiphonal effects with the strings (this combination returns in the *Litania de S. Josepho*).

The keys of the two Requiems could hardly be further apart—one in a sharp major and the other in the deepest flat minor key in use at the time. And this is undoubtedly a highly significant detail in light of the theoretical background for baroque key associations at the time and the attention to tonal patterns that emerges in Biber's later work. Even as late as the time of J. S. Bach the keys of E major and F minor—the sharpest and flattest keys used by Biber— constitute limits that are practically never exceeded as the keys of vocal movements. [33] A long and solid tradition lay behind the association of the sharp keys with the old *cantus durus* and the flats with *cantus mollis,* terms with obvious affective associations that carried over into many of the more modern keys and even, to some extent, into the circle of keys that became the conceptual and practical model for key relationships in the generation after Biber. [34] In these terms A major is usually considered a bright, optimistic key ("affecting and brilliant" but also "inclined to complaining, sad passions" according to Mattheson), while the association of F minor was universally linked to lamentation. [35] In Biber's music the key of F minor is unmistakably associated with lamentation (e.g., the final bars of the Crucifixus settings of the *Missa Alleluia* and *Missa S. Henrici*); and in choosing this key for his Requiem Biber confirms the predeliction we find in his other works for representing lachrymose affections in flat minor keys: e.g., the *De profundis* of the published vespers (C minor), the *Huc Poenitentes* (C minor), an "aria lamentevole" from *Chi la dura la vince* (F minor), the Crucifixus of the *Missa Catholica* (C minor), the "Crucifixion" and "Mount of Olives" from the *Mystery Sonatas* (G minor and C minor, respectively, the latter entitled "Lamento" in the autograph) and the sixth of the *Sonatae Violino Solo* (C minor). These remarks should by no means be taken to indicate that such associations were universally accepted, that we can learn from them to "read" the affect of a piece, or that Biber's two Requiems are polarized in the affective spheres they represent. One of the most fascinating aspects of the two works, in fact, is the extent to which they resemble each other. But there are, nevertheless, important differences between them that are suggested in the orchestral and tonal disparities, and these qualities help us to focus upon the composer's musico-allegorical intent.

Both Requiems comprise those portions of the text most commonly set to music in the seventeenth century:

1. Introit: Requiem; Te decet; Requiem
2. Kyrie/Christe/Kyrie
3. Sequence: Dies irae
4. Offertorium: Domine Jesu Christe
5. Sanctus
6. Agnus Dei
7. Communion: Lux aeterna

Biber generally follows the textual form of the Mass quite closely, so that the two settings reveal similar structures. All seven divisions are clearly distinguished in the two works; but by musical means larger-scale groupings of some sections that are adjacent to one another in the service can be discerned. Thus, the *Requiem à 15* can be divided into six or seven major sections, depending on whether one groups the Agnus Dei and Communion together; the former ends with a long, drawn-out cadence in E that can be interpreted as dominant of the movement to follow. The *Requiem in F minor* should probably be grouped into five major divisions, with the Introit and Kyrie, and the Agnus Dei and Communion taken as larger complexes. In the *Requiem à 15* the Introit forms a large Requiem (ripieno)/Te decet (solo)/Requiem *ut supra* complex, while the Kyrie is a separate ABA movement, a fugue with

Example 4-23. *Requiem à 15,* Kyrie and Christe Themes

a contrast Christe theme as countersubject. The Kyrie theme is a form of the four-note "Mozart" theme again, in major mode (ex. 4-23); it has an inevitably "emblematic" character to anyone who has encountered it over and again in Biber's music; in style this movement as a whole could have served in any of the concerted settings of the ordinary just as readily as here. Although also a fugue of comparable dimensions to that of the *Requiem à 15,* the Kyrie of the *Requiem in F minor* belongs to a greater extent with the Introit for two reasons: first, the Introit of this work is not an imposing closed structure as is that of the *Requiem à 15*: no musical sections are repeated and the Requiem aeternam reappears at the end in a new, shorter setting that ends on the dominant; second, the theme and countersubject of the Kyrie unmistakably refer back to the short fugal passage for soloists at "ad te omnis caro veniet." By virtue of its weight and tonality, therefore, the Kyrie fugue rounds off a larger Introit/Kyrie complex.

In each work the Dies irae comprises a long multi-sectional grouping that offers a large number of solo/tutti alternations ending with a fugal Amen that is relatively short (no doubt because of the length of the Dies irae as a whole). Persistent eighth-note rhythms and melodies based on repeated tones, sometimes in combination with static harmonies and resembling a kind of musical recitation, are derived rather obviously from the meter of the sequence in both Requiems. At the same time a kind of homophonic recitational character with much use of syncopation, hemiola, the juxtaposition via tied notes of duple and triple patterns, second-beat accentuation in triple meter, and the like, pervade both the solo and ripieno sections of the Dies irae in the two Requiems (ex. 4-24). These characteristics extend to a few other places as well: in the *Requiem à 15* the Introit in particular features long static melodies in the character of intonations as part of the contrapuntal fabric, while the Hostias utilizes a similar melodic character in block-chord homophony; in both pieces chordal homophony is used, usually with static harmonies, for places such as the final "Requiem aeternam" and "quia pius est." But it is in the Dies irae that such devices appear most frequently, especially in the *Requiem in F minor.* While, as we will see, the *Requiem in F minor* utilizes extensive variation techniques to link many sections of the Mass to one another, especially in the Dies irae, in that work Biber makes no actual reuse of music for sections with different texts. The *Requiem à 15,* however, reuses two sections within the Dies irae. The hypnotic metric and strophic character of the sequence encouraged the use of the same music for the Dies irae and Rex tremendae, while in the long solo section between these two places the Quantus tremor repeats as Mors stupebit. This occurence reflects a somewhat different approach to musical structure in this work when compared with its counterpart. The *Requiem à 15* makes much use of structural symmetry—in the Introit, the Kyrie, here in the Dies irae, the endings of the Offertorium, Sanctus, and Communion—all of which, in combination with the greater length of the work, as well as the use of trumpets and major key, gives the work a rather more monumental character than the *Requiem in F minor.*

The foregoing point may be illustrated by the differences between the endings of the two Dies irae movements. In the *Requiem à 15* the Amen is set in motet style similar to the *stile*

Example 4-24.   Comparison of Themes from Two Dies irae Movements by Biber

(a)   *Requiem à 15,* Themes from Dies irae

(b)   **Requiem in F minor,** Themes from Dies irae

antico movements of the concerted Masses; its theme belongs to the melodic type that reappears many times in the *Missa ex B,* and others of Biber's church works. The movement has what we might call a general ecclesiastical character similar to that of the Kyrie, making use of the instruments in *colla parte* fashion; toward the end the trumpets enter with the vocal theme. In the *Requiem in F minor,* however, the Amen is shorter and structurally less imposing; the primary structural weight near the ending of this Dies irae is the wonderful fugal Lacrimosa with counter theme "cum resurget ex favilla" (this movement, as we will see, can in fact be called the spiritual center of the Dies irae, even of this Requiem as a whole). Following the Lacrimosa, a three-bar tenor solo, "Huic ergo parce Deus. Pie Jesu Domine," enters with a remarkably moving phrase of supplication, bridging two blocks of ripieno writing and suggesting the "pathetic" character of the Amen theme that is derived from it (ex. 4-25). Although enhanced by its setting, the affective power of this phrase comes chiefly from within, especially from the lengthening of the flat sixth degree (D flat) on the word "pie" and the subsequent fall of the melody. In these details the ending of the Dies irae in the *Requiem in F minor* projects a personal character that contrasts with the more general ecclesiastical character of the corresponding place in the *Requiem à 15.*

In both Requiems the Offertorium consists of five sections: Domine Jesu Christe, Libera eas, Quam olim Abrahae, Hostias, and Quam olim Abrahae. In the *Requiem in F minor* the

Example 4-25.   *Requiem in F minor,* Huic ergo

Example 4-26.   Quam olim Themes

(a)   *Requiem à 15*

(b)   *Requiem in F minor*

Offertorium occupies a central position in the five-division plan and Biber therefore sets it in the dominant, C minor. Both offertories begin with a splendid representation of the words "Domine Jesu Christe, Rex gloriae": in the *Requiem à 15* a duet for two basses with antiphonal contrast between the trumpets and trombones (with Basso 1) and the strings (with Basso 2); and in the *Requiem in F minor* a bass solo with some ornate writing for the two violins. And in both Requiems the Offertorium ends with an impressive, climactic Quam olim/Hostias/ Quam olim complex, the fugal Quam olim framing a movement of lesser weight in both cases. Also in both Requiems the principal theme, "Quam olim Abrahae promisisti," is of grave, serious character, while the contrast theme, "et semini ejus," is joyful and lively, the dualism suggesting the combination of serious and playful moods in baroque sculptural groups, exemplified by *putti* frolicking at the feet of the church fathers (ex. 4-26).

Whereas in Biber's settings of the Mass Ordinary the Sanctus usually contains five divisions, in the two Requiems it comprises only four: Sanctus, Osanna, Benedictus, Osanna (Pleni sunt caeli is not treated as a separate section). As a result the ABA Osanna/Benedictus/Osanna complex occupies a larger part of the Sanctus. And in general plan the Osannas parallel the Quam olim settings, but with somewhat less contrasted themes. The final movements of the two Requiems embrace an extended Agnus Dei, a shorter Lux aeterna, and a concluding Cum sanctis tuis/Requiem aeternam grouping, this last section a da capo in both cases. The relative weights of these sections are quite different, however. In the *Requiem in F minor* the Agnus Dei is a long integrated fugal movement based on another theme of traditional pedigree for the Agnus, and a countertheme derived from it and treated in inversion for the Dona eis requiem; the Cum sanctis tuis/requiem aeternam grouping is fairly short and entirely in homophonic style, the highly rhythmic, energetic and syncopated Cum sanctis sections juxtaposing the chorus with the strings and surrounding a requiem aeternam of quiet, static chords from the chorus. The *Requiem à 15,* however, gives most of the weight to the concluding Cum sanctis complex, which comprises a long imitative movement with a theme of very similar type to that of the *Requiem in F minor* juxtaposed and combined with a separate "quia pius es" theme; the entire lengthy section is repeated da capo after a very brief Requiem aeternam, marked *ppp*. The trumpets introduce the Lux aeterna and punctuate the Cum sanctis at selected points, details that add to the sense of festive solidity at the end. The

Example 4-27.   *Requiem à 15,* Sed signifer

conclusion of the *Requiem in F minor,* however, creates a different atmosphere, despite the thematic similarity: here the composer of dance music replaces the contrapuntist in order ostensibly to endow the Cum sanctis tuis with a sense of hope, although the minor key and relative brevity of the Cum sanctis music might well be considered to impart rather a character of struggle that overshadows the final, solemn "quia pius es."

Much of what these large-scale correspondences and differences between Biber's two Requiems represent can be characterized generally as a sense in both works of mingling doctrinal and personal attitudes toward death. Both works make much greater use of homophonic choral writing than the concerted Masses, especially in sections of prayer-like character. In some cases, such as the striking juxtaposition of major and minor modes in the Lacrimosa and Huic ergo of the *Requiem à 15,* these places take on a deeply affective character. In comparison to one another, however, the *Requiem à 15* projects a more festive, extraverted character, from which momentary flashes of the triumphant styles of the *Missa Salisburgensis* and *Missa Bruxellensis* are not excluded (ex. 4-27).

Since the *Requiem in F minor* has been available for many years in a modern edition, has been recorded admirably, and differs more than its companion from Biber's concerted Masses, it makes a good piece to examine more closely at the end of this treatment of the Masses.[36] As an achievement in textual expression alone, Biber's work stands out among compositions written in the same period and region. No other composer in south Germany or Austria at the time has left us such an astonishingly imaginative and intrinsically musical response to the Requiem text. At the same time, the stylistic restraint characteristic of Austrian seventeenth-century church music lends a dignity and universality to this Requiem, one of the most deeply moving of Biber's works. As in Bach's *Actus tragicus,* the *Requiem in F minor* conveys a sense of the lamenting side of death in combination with its counterfoil, the hope of resurrection; to some extent even their respective means of representing this dualism are similar.

More than in any other Mass Biber employs subtle variation technique in the *Requiem in F minor,* for the dual purposes of general musical integration and a consistency of tone that will underlie the multiplicity of varied sections that follow, on the surface, the changing images of the text, while suggesting on a deeper level the *scopus* as opposed to the *sensus* of the Requiem.[37] Several motives crop up more than once in the work, and one principal idea runs throughout the Requiem linking all five major sections. Occasionally the melodic and harmonic components of this idea appear separately. The melodic part outlines a rising and falling semitone followed by stepwise descent, while the harmonic element consists of a progression through the circle of fifths, usually from F to D-flat, but sometimes from C to A-flat. In the following places Biber combines both facets of the idea in a variety of rhythms: "Te decet hymnus," "Exaudi," "Requiem," "Dies irae," "Teste David," "Preces meae," "Domine

Example 4-28.   *Requiem in F Minor*, Recurrent Melodic Type with Circle-of-Fifths Harmonies

Example 4-29.   *Requiem in F minor*, Lacrimosa Theme and Derivation from Plainchant

Example 4-30.   *Requiem in F minor*, Dies irae, Ground Bass Pattern

Jesu," "Sed signifer," and "Cum sanctis tuis" (ex. 4-28). Only in the fugal Lacrimosa does the melody appear alone as a subject, at which point it is apparent that Biber derived his theme from the plainchant for this part of the Mass (ex. 4-29). This melodic type appears in countless lamenting pieces throughout music history of which only a few need be named as examples: Schütz's "Ist nicht Ephraim" (*Psalmen Davids,* 1619), Dowland's *Semper Dowland semper dolens,* Bach's *Actus tragicus,* of course, and from Biber's works the *Balletti Lamentabili* (1670), *"Crucifixion" Sonata* and *Stabat Mater* (on the words "O quam tristis et afflicta"). At several places in the *Requiem in F minor* (e.g., "Qui Mariam," and the final "Requiem aeternam") there are references to the melodic and harmonic elements of the theme that stop after alternation of the initial minor semitone and a single fifth progression (tonic/dominant). The full circle-of-fifths harmonic pattern alone predominates in several sections, especially at "Quantus tremor" and "Osanna," but also at "Oro supplex," "Libera eas," "Agnus Dei," and parts of "Et semini ejus." The Dies irae is, however, the focal point for this all-pervading idea; and the section from "Quantus tremor" to "judicetur" is built upon a tenfold repetition of a circle-of-fifths ground bass pattern (i.e., 1 plus 9, since the first statement is varied). Here it appears in a repeated eighth-note *tremulante* rhythm undoubtedly developed to represent the word "tremor," but in its wider usage relating closely to the rhythm that runs throughout the Requiem and might have been intended, as in the *Actus tragicus,* to convey a sense of the throbbing, painful character of life and perhaps also the measured passing of time (ex. 4-30). In

Example 4-31.   *Requiem in F minor,* Judex ergo

Example 4-32.   *Requiem in F minor,* Offertorium, Rex gloria Melody

this section of the Requiem the rhythm and melody of the bass pervade all the accompanying string parts; and at "Liber scriptus" (the eighth statement, now in A-flat) the ripieno chorus enters with an imitation of the ground bass. As if to counteract the eighth-note rhythm of this section, Biber wrote the following series of solo and tutti passages from "Judex ergo" to "fons pietatis" entirely in homophonic style, all parts at any given point conforming to the off-the-beat rhythm of quarter-half-quarter-half per bar (ex. 4-31). Nothing could convey so forcefully as these rhythmic and tonal aspects of the Requiem the inexorability of death and the grave, and the underlying character of mourning that pervades human life.

The pictorial qualities of this magnificent Requiem cannot be given justice in words alone. The Offertorium alone provides an abundance of instances. Near the outset the words "Rex gloriae" receive a flourish from the solo bass and two violins (ex. 4-32); "de poenis" elicits diminished-chord harmonies, and "inferni" follows immediately with a drop of a minor ninth in the soprano and a sharply dissonant ninth chord. At "de ora leonis" Biber takes the trouble

Example 4-33.   *Requiem in F minor,* Libera eas

Example 4-34.   *Requiem in F minor,* Fac eas Domine Melody

to depict the opening and closing of the lion's mouth (ex. 4-33); triadic descent throughout the vocal parts conveys falling ("ne cadant"), and at "in obscuram" hemiola obscures the meter. At "de morte transire ad vitam" Biber devised the following melody to portray the passing from death to life (ex. 4-34). Considering the amount of pictorialism in the Offertorium it is a wonder that the movement does not sound disjointed. Also, due to the structure and imagery of the Requiem text, the *Requiem in F minor* contains more short sections than any of Biber's late settings of the Mass Ordinary. In combination with the harmonically unifying circle of fifths, the varied succession of musical ideas that represent the shifting images of the text in a more determinedly graphic manner than in any other of Biber's works suggests just that obsessively allegorical quality that Walter Benjamin points to as most characteristic of the seventeenth-century German *Trauerspiel,* in which history and human events, the pomp and power of the ruler are subject to decline and death. Biber's work has an almost unrelieved quality of harmonic and melodic *catabasis,* and its hypnotic eighth-note rhythms and clinging to the F minor tonality come to suggest something of the nature of a human life emptied of its intrinsic significance and awaiting transformation into the eternal, in order to point at which it takes on an exaggeratedly allegorical character. The expressive realm of the *Requiem in F minor* is as far removed from the ostentatiously festive tone of the concerted Masses as possible; the "shadow" side of counterreformation art has rarely been so convincingly portrayed in music.

5

Music for Vespers

MANUSCRIPT WORKS

Biber's extant Vespers music consists of compositions contained in three sets of manuscript parts, two at Kroměříž and one in the Sächsische Landesbibliothek, Dresden, as well as the publication *Vesperae Longiores ac Breviores* (1693). The first of the Kroměříž manuscripts, entitled *AMDGBMV* [Ad maiorem Dei gloriam Beatissimae Mariae Virginae] *Assumptae H. Vesperae à 32* (1674), comprises a *Dixit Dominus* and *Magnificat*, both in C major. The second manuscript is a *Laetatus Sum* in D major (1676). The undated Dresden manuscript contains a *Nisi Dominus* in G major. Both Kroměříž manuscripts survive in autograph copies (a second copy of the *Vesperae à 32* exists at Kroměříž in another hand).[1]

Vesperae à 32 (1674)

The *Vesperae à 32* are scored for the familiar eight-part double chorus with choirs of strings, cornetti and trombones, and trumpets (4) with timpani, like a large number of other Salzburg works of the time. And quite a number of movement types heard in those other works crop up here also: independent introductory Sonatas and interludes; *stile antico* choruses with *colla parte* instruments; triple meter sections of double-chorus antiphony, the first chorus doubled by strings, the second by cornetti and trombones; solo sections for equal-voice duets with changing instrumental choirs; sections for eight vocal soloists; a bass solo with elaborate first violin; and, finally, the climactic Amens. The following scheme of the *Dixit Dominus* (fig. 5-1) might be compared with that of the Gloria of the *Missa Alleluia* (see fig. 4-3) in this connection. But the presence of these familiar styles, several of which are to be found in Hofer's works as well, still leaves a great deal of room for uniquely imaginative sonorities and pictorialisms, and the *Vesperae à 32* are very impressive in these respects. Even in these early Salzburg works Biber goes beyond what had been heard from Hofer. A large part of his achievement must be attributed to the role of two instruments in particular—violin and trumpet—in the orchestral palette, the ones for which he had written so successfully at Kroměříž. The violin emerges as a soloist in a number of places, ranging from the briefest painting of a single word, "splendoribus," in the *Dixit* (ex. 5-1) to an entire section with bass solo at "Deposuit" (ex. 5-2). Generally the violin is paired with the bass, so as to provide an emphasis on the top and bottom parts. Since solo basses and violin are so clearly the protagonists of both the *Laetatus Sum* and *Nisi Dominus* we will defer discussion of that style until we deal with those pieces. But Biber's use of the trumpets must be introduced now, for it is one of the major clues to his church music, bound up with the jubilant, festive style of the majority of the larger pieces as well as their tonal-structural plans.

Figure 5-1.   Scheme of *Dixit Dominus (Vesperae à 32)*
            All sections are in C major

Movement		Meter	Measures	Style and Instrumentation	Solo/Ripieno
1	Sonata	¢	24	2 trumpets, 2 cornetti, 3 trombones & strings	
2	Dixit...meo	¢	10	8 vocal soloists	Solo
	Sede...meis		23	Both choruses combined, <u>colla parte</u> cornetti & trombones. Presto. 4-part fugue.	Ripieno
3	Donec...tuorum		9	2 solo basses, with antiphonal trumpets, timpani, and double chorus	Solo/ripieno
	Virgam...tuorum		23	2 solo altos with cornetti & trombones	Solo
	Tecum...sanctorum		17	2 solo tenors with strings	Solo
	Juravit...Melchisedech		18	6 vocal soloists (S1, A1, T1, B1, T2, B2)	Solo
4	Dominus...reges	3/2 ¢	19	Full scoring. Double-chorus antiphony with instruments. Presto.	Ripieno
5	Judicabit...multorum	¢	16	4 vocal soloists (S1, S2, B1, B2) with trumpets & trombones. Full scoring at "conquassabit"	Solo/ripieno
6	De torrente...caput		11	4 vocal soloists (S1, A1, T1, A2)	Solo
7	Doxology		18	Full scoring. Double chorus with alternating instrumental choirs.	Ripieno
8	Amen		23	8 vocal soloists, then full scoring.	Solo/ripieno

Example 5-1.   *Vesperae à 32, Dixit Dominus,* Violin Writing at "in splendoribus sanctorum"

The lively fanfare style of the *Sonata S. Polycarpi* makes its presence known in the *Dixit Dominus* from the opening theme of the introductory Sonata to the echoing of brief motives of jubilation between the instrumental choirs at the end of this Sonata and the final Amen. There is even a thematic idea from the *Sonata S. Polycarpi* that appears here right from the start: the melodic rise from the third degree of the scale to the fifth, with the goal of this ascent—the sixth degree—sometimes deferred; when it arrives it is a point of melodic climax, falling to the second degree and from there to the tonic, often with much echoing of the final three–two–one scale degrees. This melodic idea runs through several sections of the *Dixit,* both vocal and

Example 5-2. *Vesperae à 32, Magnificat,* Deposuit

instrumental, while the entire passage of double-chorus antiphony from "Dominus" to "reges" (fig. 5-1, no. 4) is based on a nine-fold alternation of the cadential three–two–one pattern; a similar idea pervades the opening section of the *Sonata S. Polycarpi*. Numerous fanfares were produced in Salzburg during the late seventeenth and early eighteenth centuries, of course; and a number of Carl Biber's sonatas of this type and a repertoire of trumpet intradas from Nonnberg have been published.[2] But it can be argued, with works such as the *Sonata S. Polycarpi* and the *Vesperae à 32* as evidence, that no other composer of the time mastered so well the very difficult task of producing music of lasting quality within the obvious restrictions of this style. Certainly, no one integrated the fanfare style so successfully within vocal church pieces; and this fact, unlikely as it sounds (in view of the limitations of the harmonic style), is one of the strongest points of style in favor of Biber's authorship of the *Missa Salisburgensis*.

Two short sections from the *Dixit* may be considered in illustration of Biber's use of trumpets to suggest the omnipotence and even severity of the Old Testament God of the psalm. The section "Donec ponam inimicos tuos scabellum pedum tuorum" (while I make your enemies into your footstool) follows the motet-style fugue "Sede à dextris meis," with a contrast that immediately removes the picture of the Deity from any lingering sense of distance that the *stile antico* might have suggested (ex. 5-3). The section does not require extension to the dimensions of a movement, such as it would have received in the eighteenth century. Instead, the very extravagance of the use of double-chorus antiphony at tutti and solo levels in a mere nine-bar passage makes the point of God's intervention in human affairs in a manner that could hardly be achieved so successfully in a trumpet aria, for example. Such a piece exists in Biber's opera, the tenor ground-bass aria of Germanico, "All'armi," containing two strophes of what may well be the most virtuosic example of the military style for voice in the seventeenth century, both followed by ritornelli with the same trumpet scoring as the *Vesperae à 32*. But this piece can only serve effectively in the secular context; the vocal display would be ridiculous as a portrayal of the Deity, and the very degree of extension bespeaks a concern for projection of affect, that is something other, more analytical and less immediate, than the artistic ideal of the counterreformation. The second example, scored for two sopranos and two basses with trombones and trumpets, is the seven-bar passage that sets the text "Judicabit in nationibus" (The Lord will judge among the heathen) (ex. 5-4). This excerpt bridges the preceding section of tutti antiphony that never ceases to cadence in the tonic, C major, and the following military-sounding C-major tutti for "conquassabit capita." In example 5-4 the gap between the highest and lowest voices is filled in with a somber trombone chordal accompaniment, while the trumpets echo the pitch e' as symbol of divine justice; this pitch is the pivot between the alternating E-major and A-minor chords of "judicabit in nationibus" and the four C major trumpet chords that end all dispute over the key in an allegory of God's judgment. Here the trumpets invoke a sense of fear rather than majesty.

These two brief passages illustrate the ways that Biber's flair for the pictorial leads him to devise imaginative sonorities involving the trumpets for the purpose of creating a sense of God's wrathful presence. In fact the structure of the *Dixit* as a whole can be thought of in terms of the points of climactic re-entrance of the trumpets, which tend to affirm a sense of motion from the severe, fearful and military to the jubilant—on both small and large scales. The opening sonata suggests such a dynamic in its progression from the canzona-like opening to the tossing about of the motive ♩♪♪ among the separate choirs. Then the first solo complex has an introductory character leading into the strict "sede a dextris" fugue upon whose archaic atmosphere the "donec ponam inimicos" section breaks like a thunderbolt from above. The long section of duets with accompaniment from the wind and string choirs has a sensuous character that is similarly overwhelmed by the succeeding fanfare antiphony of the "Dominus à dextris tuis"; the "judicabit in nationibus" climaxes in a militant tutti at "conquassabit capita in terra multorum." And the final solo section, also of sensuous

Example 5-3.   *Vesperae à 32, Dixit Dominus,* Ending of "sede a dextris" Fugue and Beginning of "donec ponam"

Example 5-4.   *Vesperae à 32, Dixit Dominus,* Judicabit in nationibus

character, at "de torrente in via bibet," leads into the sumptuous, and wonderfully climactic Doxology and Amen. The Doxology begins with a three-fold antiphonal "Gloria" from the chorus, each followed by a short passage from one of the instrumental choirs in its most characteristic manner (ex. 5-5), while the Amen is a crescendo in sonority from a soloistic beginning to the tutti of the closing bars. More and more as the Amen proceeds a motive very similar to the one that pervaded the opening sonata infiltrates the parts, echoing back and forth among the instrumental choirs and totally dominating the closing bars.

The almost eschatological character that is imparted to the dynamic of the *Dixit* by the role of the trumpets above all is one of Biber's major successes in the sphere of church music. But there is no denying that pieces of this type, whether this effective or not, bring up a number of other issues that relate to the question of larger structural organization in seventeenth-century music generally. Along with the trumpets, the key of C major returns with a kind of hypnotic regularity in the *Vesperae à 32* and many other works of its type; no single section in the *Dixit* is set entirely in a contrasting key area. And the focus on sonority and pictorialism throughout a fairly lengthy psalm setting leads to a conception of composition that is built as a chain of separate sections—contrasted in many ways of course, and linked by the magnetic attraction of the tonic key, but seeming to derive their impetus and their dynamic qualities primarily from outside the work. It often appears as if the *scopus* of the text is represented in many instances in the festive orchestration and C-major tonality, while the structural details are given over entirely to the *sensus* of the succeeding images it presents. The composer has several known styles at his disposal, and the structure of the text is planned and its meaning represented with their aid, plus a few additional sections of more individual character. [3] Certain dynamic principles are at work, of course: the placing of sonatas, climactic fugues, and solos is done so as to achieve a plausible overall dynamic; and there may be in addition some thematic interrelationships that add further integration. But the motivic material of the work does not generate its own inner coherence, and the dynamic curve of the composition is made up of

Example 5-5.   *Vesperae à 32, Dixit Dominus,* Polychoral Beginning of Doxology

Example 5-5 (continued)

numerous stops and starts that scarcely permit the illusion of inner causality; rather the reverse: the sense of "cosmic inevitability" that Tovey praised in Beethoven's music would undoubtedly have been shunned, could it have been conceived of at all.

Taken in conjunction with the objective, rationalistic character of the baroque conception of style, it was inevitable that musical compositions produced under the far-reaching aesthetic connotations of "representational style" and "Oratio as mistress of the harmony"—i.e., the manifesto of heteronomous, allegorical music—would often exhibit sequences of changing styles and multi-sectional forms to match texts or more general extra-musical ideas. Just as inevitable for us is the fact that in terms of the idea of "unity" of form at a larger level the seventeenth-century sectional conception of form will often appear unsatisfactory in comparison with its successor. For, regardless of the textual motivation for shifting styles, any composition must be considered a reflection of the psychological dynamic of a single individual—the listener. Even though the successive events of a Mozart concerto, for example, might be perceived as equivalent to the interaction of several different characters and plot events—as the analagous themes, modulatory passages and structural events are often represented on the operatic stage—the unbroken musical continuum must still represent a plausible inner scenario. But our conception of what makes up a convincing dynamic has changed since the seventeenth century. Although what appears to be happening in the *Vesperae à 32,* and in the most pictorial works of the age such as Biber's *Mystery Sonatas* and Kuhnau's *Biblical Histories,* is the representation in music of a sequence of objective, external pictures as suggested by the imagic content of the text, no music succeeds wholly at such a level. And, in fact, such pieces—the successful ones, that is—do exhibit strong dynamic characters, but of a different nature from that of later music. In this sense, if in Mozart's time the affective character of music became psychologically complex, and in Bach's it was meditative or analytical, concerned with affect, in Biber's it might be described as discontinuous, momentary, or even metamorphic in the way it externalizes a series of quickly shifting affective states.[4] Seventeenth-century music, by virtue of its sense of pictorial, or allegorical justification, emphasizes the split between "sound" and "script" that Walter Benjamin introduced into criticism.[5] The dialectic is revealed above all in the way the "expressive" or "sound" aspect seems to be given over to conventional requirements of counterreformation art. The optimistic cast of this music is bound up with its religious intent in that, centered on pictorialism rather than the projection and extension of affect, it never suggests that the independent, self-determining spirit of man is a sufficient *raison d'être* for musical expression. The fragmented sequence of relatively independent images is something that the inner dynamic must adjust to, in whose terms it moves through existence. If we have difficulty with the sequential, additive character of the seventeenth-century allegorical conception of form, this— and not its failure to attain the "unity" that is considered the universal touchstone of artistic worth—is the reason. The highly developed sense of internal unity that characterizes music in the eighteenth and nineteenth centuries is of very questionable value in the understanding of much seventeenth-century music. And, although it sounds paradoxical, the dynamic qualities of this music are greatly reduced when performers attempt to superimpose a modern dynamic, a sense of direction, on the affective sequence of the works; for the latter is often alien to the music. The instrumental music of Biber, for example, began to speak to modern audiences when—largely along with the revival of "historical" instruments—a sense of the rhetorical meaning of small details, often pictorial in character, that would have been swept into the motion of the larger dynamic currents of eighteenth- and nineteenth-century music, was appreciated anew. We all know now, however, that the historical recreation of musical performances is of little or no value without the dynamic expressive element that the performer adds, even though this particular feature can never be "historical." What has allowed seventeenth-century music to speak again is something more than mere reconstruction: the sympathetic ability to take the music on its own terms, not as a rudimentary stage along the way to the monumentally integrated works of Bach, but a music that moves in short, often segmented series of styles, each of which must be grasped in its rhetorico-affective character in order for the overall dynamic to emerge.

Turning to the still longer and more sectional *Magnificat* we find that Biber has provided a sense of division in the work with a second sonata for trumpets and drums before the section "Suscepit Israel" (fig. 5-2). Between this point and the end of the work some types of movement—chorus with *colla parte* instruments, eight solo voices—appear a second time. And now some sections are set in keys other than the tonic. This last detail should not, however, be interpreted as the reflection of a desire for key structure, of the kind that emerges in the later works, but as a facet of the pictorial interpretation of the text. And, as such, it introduces the question of "tonal allegory" for works such as these.[6] The keys that appear in both the *Dixit* and *Magnificat,* either in terms of passing cadences or in more independent terms, are limited to the six that constitute the ambitus of C major (or A minor): C, d, e, F, G, and a (any of the minor keys can, and usually does, cadence with a Tierce de Picardie).[7] This

Figure 5-2. Scheme of *Magnificat (Vesperae à 32)*

	Movement	Meter	Measures	Style/Instrumentation	Key	Solo/Ripieno
1	[Sonata]	¢	10	4 trumpets & timpani	C	
	Magnificat...	¢	10	C1, A1, with trombones	C	Solo
	Quia respexit humilitatem		11	T1, A2, T2, B2	C-a	Solo
	Omnes generationes		7	Tutti	C	Ripieno
2	Quia fecit		25	Both choirs combined. <u>Colla parte</u> strings (with obbligato first violin from "et Sanctum"). 4 part fugue.	C	Ripieno
3	Et misericordia		17	A1, C2 plus trombones	a-e	Solo
4	Fecit potentiam	$\frac{3}{2}$	24	Tutti, double chorus antiphony	C	Ripieno
5	Deposuit	C	16	Bass and strings; ornate first violin part	C-F	Solo
	Esurientes		19	C1, T1, B2 + cornetti & trombones & tutti chorus near end. Chromaticism & instrumental interludes.	d-C-e-C	Solo/Ripieno
6	Sonata		12	4 trumpets & timpani	C	
	Suscepit Israel	$\frac{3}{2}$	20	B1, C2 & strings, then 8-part chorus & strings	C	Solo/Ripieno
7	Sicut locutus est	¢	14	Eight vocal soloists	C	Solo
8	Gloria Patri		16	Florid vocal solos leading into tutti	C	Solo/Ripieno
9	Et in saecula		17	Both choruses combined plus <u>colla parte</u> cornetti & trombones. Freely imitative texture.	C	Ripieno
10	Amen		22	Double fugue increasing instrumentation from solo to full orchestration	C	Solo/Ripieno

configuration descends, of course, from the early seventeenth-century concept of the system of modal finals grouped within one of the transpositional levels represented by the hexachords: *cantus durus, cantus mollis* and their extension by fifths in both directions.[8] In the earlier years of the seventeenth century the existence of various cadence degrees at a single transpositional level did not necessarily imply a tonal hierarchy around one of these as "tonic." The changeover from this concept to that of the eighteenth-century ambitus that forms a close analogy to our perception of key relationships, and the circle of keys that attempted a full-scale organization of all possible keys, by no means followed a straight line of development. Biber's earlier works represent a version—one of many possible at the time—of the role of secondary key areas within a single modal/tonal center.

And, while it may not be possible to draw up a scheme of tonal relationships on the basis of allegorical or purely musical usage, it is certainly possible to see intelligible patterns. The turn to the subdominant key in the bass solo "Deposuit," for example, is unmistakably a detail that relates to the word "humiles" in the twelfth bar of the solo (see ex. 5-2, above); and perhaps the dominant key of the first phrase ("Deposuit potentes de sede") represents the opposite affect with the *durus* now, rather than the *mollis* direction. As the text continues, the music unfolds more of the character of key change and tonal direction in this music. After the F-major cadence on "humiles," the music turns via a diminished third drop in the bass to D minor and B-flat for "esurientes" (hungry), while the cornetti and trombones continue on alone to paint the word with melodically ascending, but tonally descending chromaticism that works back to C major for a lively "implevit bonis" (he hath filled with good things). From here the word "divites" (the rich) prompts the jump to an E-major chord that becomes, three bars later, the Tierce de Picardie close of a modulation to E minor for "dimisit inanes" (he hath sent empty away) (ex. 5-6). In this sequence of textual and tonal events the move downward from the modulation to F at "humiles" through the D minor and suggestions of B-flat, G minor and C minor at "esurientes" projects a clear sense of tonal-harmonic *catabasis,* while the sudden

Example 5-6. *Vesperae à 32, Dixit Dominus,* Esurientes implevit bonis et divites dimisit inanes

move to the E-major chord suggests a contrary event (corresponding to the unexpected entrance of the chorus on "et divites"). Throughout this passage the key of F and its association with downward motion and that of E with its sense of surprise and opposition are polarized as primary cadences on either side of the C-major "implevit bonis." It is probable, therefore, that in such a passage these keys stand in some sense for the flattest and sharpest tonal areas—as well as the "fa" and "mi"—of the ambitus, just as the character of falling fifths and thirds is to some extent perceived as the opposite of rising thirds and fifths.

Certain modulations to A minor and E minor in both works, more than those to other keys, seem to have been placed so as to underscore particular ideas of the text. Although these cannot be completely systematized, the three E-minor cadences—at "non penetebit eum" of the *Dixit* and "timentibus eum" and "dimisit inanes" of the *Magnificat*—all evoke, like the alternation of E-major and A-minor chords at "judicabit," a sense of God's judgment; and three modulations to A minor—"ecce enim ex hoc beatam me dicent omnes generationes," "et miseracordia eius," "miseracordiae suae"—suggest, largely because of the sense of modulation downward from C, a more gentle connotation of mercy and blessedness.

But one feature of the modulatory style is inescapable: the total subordination of secondary keys to the tonic, C major: other keys are clearly to be thought of in relation to C at all times. Thus, in some movements a form of "bracketing" of these other keys occurs; the motet-like "et in saecula" of the *Magnificat,* for example, moves unmistakably to A minor towards the end; A minor was introduced as a strong tonal presence as early as the seventh bar of this seventeen-measure movement, and there are cadences in A minor in four of the last five bars, the last one particularly strong on the word "Amen." But Biber simply repeats the word with a C-major cadence to close the movement. Likewise, following the above-mentioned cadence to E minor for "dimisit inanes," Biber places a three-bar postlude for cornetti and trombones; the first cornetto begins with the melody of "dimisit inanes" in A minor, which is quickly transformed into the "implevit bonis" idea cadencing in C major. It is as if the "dimisit inanes" was too severe to be allowed to close the major division of the *Magnificat* that comes at this point; and the composer preferred to end in an optimistic manner even though the passage is followed by a C-major sonata for trumpets and drums. In these and other similar places we can see that the conception of key contrast was not basically a structural one. The ruling idea of the piece, like the tonic, was festive, and contradictory ideas were to be clearly heard within the prevailing context.

This, then, is a music that makes its effect largely by other means than tonal structure. We have emphasized the sense of immediacy and its relation to the visual, pictorial element. This quality is by no means placed in the service only of festive moods, and the entrance of the voice at the beginning of the *Magnificat* can be cited as an example of Biber's giving a brief, almost intimate picture of the Virgin that contrasts sharply with the triumphant, public character of the opening trumpet sonata (ex. 5-7). The sudden quickening of the rhythm on "anima," the hint of subdominant, and the lowering of the voice, set in relief against the somber trombone background, all depict in a few bars the combination of exultation and humility that characterize the Virgin's words. Biber was second to none at the time in this respect.

Laetatus Sum (1676)

Biber's *Laetatus Sum* and *Nisi Dominus* are among his most representative pieces of church music, as original and individual for the time as his violin works are in the realm of the solo sonata, and even more rarely encountered. In these two psalms we see the virtuoso violinist at work. Each boasts a truly advanced solo violin part such as could have been written by very few

Example 5-7. *Vesperae à 32, Magnificat,* Alto and Soprano Solos

seventeenth-century composers. In both cases the vigorous bass parts perfectly complement the exuberance and brilliance of the violin line.

In most seventeenth-century music the vocal bass remains very close to the basso continuo even in solo passages. Whereas the soprano, alto and tenor parts form independent melodic lines above the basso continuo, the bass is often accompanied by one or two melodic upper parts, either voices or instruments; this is a procedure followed by Biber as much as by other composers of the time, and we have seen the results in examples from the *Dixit* and *Magnificat.* The *Laetatus Sum,* however, presents a far richer texture than we normally encounter in soloistic motets and cantatas. The second bass part ensures that at least one of the voices is always independent of the basso continuo, and the artistic crossing of parts enhances the illusion of melodic independence still further. In fact, with a few exceptions, the strings are not accompanimental parts to the voices in this piece, but rather serve as an alternating body that provides instrumental preludes and postludes to the bass duets; these latter sections often feature a virtuosic solo violin part that provides a form of successive polarity with the basses. These points may be clarified by referring to the outline of the *Laetatus* (fig. 5-3).

The text of the *Laetatus Sum* (Psalm 121) is one of the most consistently joyful of the psalms, and Biber's setting achieves the necessary tone by means of the style of ensemble dance music in the strings, especially in the sections in $\frac{6}{4}$ meter. The buoyancy of the solo violin, spirited imitation and echoing of short phrases back and forth between the basses, and an abundance of triadic themes developed from the opening "Laetatus" motive all contribute to a festive tone that at times distinctly recalls the Monteverdi of the *Selva Morale.* Although Biber utilizes subtle variation devices to link the sections of the work, it is ultimately the relationship between the two contrasted sound bodies that determines the fact that the *Laetatus* is at one

Figure 5-3. Scheme of *Laetatus Sum* (1676)

	Section	Meter	Measures	Key	Form, Style, Texture
1	Laetatus sum	$\frac{6}{4}$	40	D	Bass duet framed by instrumental prelude and postlude
2	Stantes erant	₵	43	A	Instrumental interlude, vocal duets and instrumental postlude
3	Quia illuc	$\frac{6}{4}$	35	A/D	Duet and instrumental postlude
4	Fiat pax	₵	19	D	Basses with violas
5			16	A	Sonata. Solo violin, then full strings
6	Doxology/Amen		32	D	Full scoring from "et in saecula"

and the same time both consistent and integrated as well as "free" sounding. The work owes a great deal to Biber's instrumental music in this respect; and it is not difficult to point out connections between it and a number of the *Sonatae, tam Aris* that Biber published in the same year. As in some of those works, the violin part of the *Laetatus* includes several solo sections that contain changes of tempo and writing of highly rhetorical character, sometimes with specified bowings and articulations. Of these the Sonata that intervenes between the psalm proper and the Doxology is the most striking (ex. 5-8). But there are also several passages in which strings and voices join forces in styles that are very familiar from the seventeenth-century sonata literature; one such is the Adagio "organo tremulante" imitation in the strings at "Rogate quae ad pacem sunt Jerusalem" ("pray for the peace of Jerusalem"), a device Biber uses in the *Sonatae, tam Aris* and (with similar programatic intent) in the *Sonata à 6 die pauern-Kirchfarth genandt* (ex. 5-9); another is the virtuoso violin flourishes above static open fifths between the two basses at "stantes erant pedes nostri" (our feet stand [within thy gates, Jerusalem]). And at "et in saecula" the violin plays a *tremolo longo* (a long trill) while the remaining parts execute a $\frac{6}{8}$ rhythm contrary to the quadruple meter at that point (ex. 5-10). This latter device, which combines a sense of the two meters that alternate throughout the *Laetatus,* has such a striking character of eschatological immediacy that it can stand almost as a symbol for the intent of counterreformation art in general.

Nisi Dominus

The violin writing of Biber's *Nisi Dominus* is even more virtuosic than that of the *Laetatus Sum*; but, since the work lacks the second bass and violas of the *Laetatus,* it does not project either the same warmth or richness of sonority. And, owing to the different character of the text, the dance rhythms, too, are not present. The violin part, however, makes greater use of harmonic writing of various kinds: arpeggiando figuration, string crossing and multiple stops. As might be expected, the bass assumes greatest independence from the continuo when the violin is silent and least when the violin plays in an elaborate style. In general the two soloists interact to a greater extent than do the basses and violin in the *Laetatus*.

The text of the *Nisi Dominus* comprises six verses, with a marked change in tone between the third and fourth. Verses one to three dwell on the vanity of human activity (building a house, guarding a city, arising early or staying up late, even "eating the bread of grief") without God's presence, while the remaining three describe how the beloved of God, to whom He gives

Example 5-8. *Laetatus Sum à 7,* "Sonata" for Solo Violin and Strings

sleep, benefit from the blessing of offspring. Biber's setting exhibits a clear structure in which three movements—an introductory sonata for violin and continuo, the Doxology (a ground bass movement for bass, violin and continuo) and the Amen (a fugue for all three parts)—are relatively self-contained, while the text of the psalm proper forms a lengthy span in which the division into verses is clearly reflected (fig. 5-4). Following the tenor of the text, Biber places a major point of division between the third and fourth verses: a single measure in a free improvisatory style for the violin (m. 66) bridges the high tonic cadence that ends a violin solo meditating on the close of verse three and the low-pitched dominant with which an entirely new figuration enters for verse four.

The sonata introduces the violin in a harmonic style that features imitation and development of a basic thematic idea: a falling fourth followed by a rising second (ex. 5-11). The movement exhibits a great deal of concern for the voice-leading implications of the separate tones of the violin chords and the importance of satisfying resolution of any that are

Example 5-9. *Laetatus Sum à 7, Organo tremolante* String Writing at "Rogate"

Example 5-10. *Laetatus Sum à 7,* Excerpt from Doxology

Figure 5-4. Scheme of *Nisi Dominus*

	Section	Meter	Measures	Key	Form, Style, Texture
1	<u>Sonata</u>	𝄴	14	G	Solo violin and continuo
2	Nisi Dominus aedificaverit	𝄴	8	G	Verse 1: bass and continuo
	Nisi Dominus custoderit		7	G-D	Verse 2: bass, violin and continuo
			7	G-D	Solo violin and continuo
	Vanum est nobis		8	D-G	Verse 3a: bass and continuo
	Qui manducatis		7	e	Verse 3b: bass and continuo
			15	e-G	Solo violin & continuo, multiple stopping, postlude to "Qui manducatis," followed by one-bar transition to D
3	Cum dederit	𝄴	16	D	Verse 4: bass violin & continuo, violin arpeggiation
	Sicut sagittae		17	G-D	Verse 5: bass violin & continuo, violin passage work, high register
	Beatus vir		12	D-G	Verse 6: bass & continuo
4	Doxology	3/4	32	G	Eight statements of 4-bar ground bass; bass, violin & continuo; Allegro/Adagio
5	Amen	𝄴	32 (repeated)	G	Fugue: bass, violin, continuo

Example 5-11. *Nisi Dominus à 2,* Introductory "Sonata" for Solo Violin and Basso Continuo

left dangling: the move into the highest register (m. 7) and the subsequent fall to the d two octaves below (m. 8) illustrate how the harmonic violin style combines the suggestion of more parts than can be represented literally with melodic climax, rhetorical gesture, and shift of sonority from string to string. Then the final four measures telescope the full register used in the introduction into a motivically integrated descent over dominant and tonic pedals. The sonata belongs to the older type that is basically independent from the thematic material of the movement as a whole; but it perhaps represents a move towards integration in that its main thematic idea returns with the violin in verse two (m. 23), and later serves as the source of the "connecting" measure (m. 66, the fourth now expanded to an octave), and passages in verse six as well as the closing measures of the psalm.

The majority of the psalm verses in this setting end with either a postlude for violin or a climax for voice and violin together. The ending of verse three is outstanding in this respect. On the words "surgite postquam sederitis" the bass cadences in G with a recall of the music with which the voice had entered in verse one; the remainder of verse three, "qui manducatis panem doloris," is marked Adagio and turns to a suspension-laden *lamento* style in E minor; this may be compared with an arioso passage from Biber's opera (ex. 5-12). The violin, picking up the "qui manducatis" idea, now produces an extended postlude of meditative character that features double, triple and even quadruple stopping and leads the key back to G. Here the connecting bar sets up a section of arpeggiando figuration (for "somnum"?) that moves directly into the "sicut sagittae" (verse five), in which the "arrows" of the text are represented by rapidly ascending scales in thirty-second notes that lead naturally into a tremendously virtuosic passage in thirty-seconds reaching up to the fifth-position f'''-sharp at the magnificent cadential climax in the dominant (ex. 5-13). The dynamic of the work, with its increasing sense of virtuosity, leads to this point; in light of Biber's use of an elaborate violinistic style with solo bass at the "genitum non factum" of the *Missa Alleluia* and *Missa Bruxellensis,* we might almost conclude that this incredible association of violin display with fecundity embodies the idea of virtuosity as a gift with which one is born. The sixth verse, "Beatus vir," calms down and the violin drops out in preparation for the Doxology, a set of elaborate violin divisions above eight statements of a triple-meter ground with which the bass voice is joined. Finally, a monothematic fugue caps off the work with bass and violin on equal terms; although this movement is longer than many (32 measures), it is indicated to be repeated.

While Biber's *Laetatus Sum* is remarkable for its integration of vocal motet and ensemble sonata, the *Nisi Dominus* is certainly the most outstanding example of the merging of solo sonata and sacred cantata that the age produced. This type of piece was very rare and examples with violin have survived only from the great virtuosi; Nikolaus Bruhns' *Mein Herz ist bereit* may be classed with Biber's work in this respect.[9] In the eighteenth century such compositions were, of course, more widely composed within the framework of the aria; "Komm, süsses Kreuz" for bass and viola da gamba from J. S. Bach's *St. Matthew Passion* might be singled out as a work in which the character of the instrument stands forth with comparable prominence. In everything that concerns the development of the violin in the seventeenth century Biber naturally stands out; we are fortunate that his violinistic genius found scope in a few sacred pieces as well.

VESPERAE LONGIORES AC BREVIORES

Biber's penultimate publication is his largest by far in terms of the number of works it contains and the quantity of part books printed; apart from the fact that the print appeared in Salzburg in 1693, we have no information concerning the dates of composition of the pieces contained therein. Biber dedicated the collection to his patron, Archbishop Johann Ernst von Thun,

Example 5-12.   Comparison of *Chi la dura la vince* to *Nisi Dominus*

(a) *Chi la dura la vince*, Excerpt

(b) *Nisi Dominus à 2*, mm. 44–70

Example 5-12 (continued)

de- de-rit di-lec-tis su-is som-   num, di-lec-tis su-   is

Example 5-13. *Nisi Dominus à 2*, mm. 88–99

violin

bass
si-cut sa git-tæ   in ma-nu po-ten-   tis, si-cut   sa

basso
continuo

git-tæ   in ma-nu po-ten-

tis: i-ta fi-li-i,   i-ta fi-li-i

ex-cus-so-   rum,   fi-li-i

ex-cus-so-   rum

using his titles of Kapellmeister and *dapifer* as well as the name *von* Bibern and a reproduction of his coat of arms all for the first time in print. A prefatory Latin poem and dedication contain several puns on musical terms (pausa, chorda, corona, suspira, triplo, dura, tactu, altus, etc.).

The *Vesperae Longiores ac Breviores* comprises twenty-nine psalms and one *Litaniae Lauretanae,* all scored for four soloists (SATB), four-part ripieno chorus (doubled by one cornetto and three trombones whose parts exist in manuscript but were apparently not printed), two violins, two violas and organ continuo. The psalms fall into four groups: six *Psalmi Longiores* (nos. 1–6), six *Psalmi de B. M. Virgine* (nos. 7–12), ten *Psalmi Breviores* (nos. 13–22) and seven *Psalmi per Annum Necessarii* (nos. 23–29); the litany ends the collection. The first three groups form unified sets of Vespers in function and key, while the fourth, as its title indicates, consists of works for different feasts of the church year (arranged in the print in a logical sequence around the key of D minor). Following is the arrangement of the print:

Psalmi Longiores

1)	*Dixit Dominus*	D major
2)	*Confitebor*	B minor
3)	*Beatus Vir*	G major
4)	*Laudate Pueri*	D major
5)	*Laudate Dominum*	A major
6)	*Magnificat*	D major

Psalmi de B. M. Virgine

7)	*Dixit Dominus*	G minor
8)	*Laudate Pueri*	B-flat major
9)	*Laetatus Sum*	F major
10)	*Nisi Dominus*	D minor
11)	*Lauda Jerusalem*	B-flat major
12)	*Magnificat*	G minor

Psalmi Breviores

13)	*Dixit Dominus*	C major
14)	*Confitebor*	A minor
15)	*Beatus Vir*	E minor
16)	*Laudate Pueri*	C major
17)	*Laudate Dominum*	G major
18)	*Laudate Pueri*	A minor
19)	*Laetatus Sum*	E minor
20)	*Nisi Dominus*	C major
21)	*Lauda Jerusalem*	G major
22)	*Magnificat*	C major

Psalmi per Annum Necessarii

23)	*Credidi*	D minor
24)	*In Convertendo*	A minor
25)	*Domine Probasti Me*	F major

26)	*De Profundis*	C minor
27)	*Memento*	G minor
28)	*Beati Omnes*	B-flat major
29)	*In Exitu Israel*	D minor
30)	*Litaniae Lauretanae*	E minor

It is apparent that the *Psalmi Breviores* consist of music for not one, but two complete sets of Vespers psalms with titles corresponding to those of the *Psalmi Longiores* and *Psalmi de B. M. Virgine.* These two shorter Vespers share a common *Dixit Dominus* (no. 13) and *Magnificat* (no. 22), and their psalms follow exactly the same key sequence, C major, A minor, E minor, C major, G major and C major, which is very close to that of the *Vesperae Longiores* (transposed).

In addition to several copies of the printed edition, none of them perfectly complete, we possess eighteenth-century copies of the *Litaniae Lauretanae* and sixteen of the psalms (in seven manuscripts at the Benedictine monastery of Göttweig, Lower Austria).[10] They may have been copied from the print since no essential differences can be found. A number of the pieces have trombone parts instead of viola parts; these, however, are identical to the printed viola parts. Two works, the *Dixit Dominus* and *Magnificat* of the *Vesperae Breviores,* include manuscript clarino and timpani parts that were certainly not composed by Biber.[11] The Göttweig copies also have performance dates on the covers of some of the manuscripts, indicating that a number of Biber's psalms were heard at Göttweig until well into the second half of the eighteenth century.

To give a complete overall picture of the thirty quite varied works that make up the *Vesperae Longiores ac Breviores* is an impossible task. The disparity in length between the compositions in the various segments of the collection—an average of 127 measures for the *Psalmi Longiores,* 110 for the *Psalmi de B. M. Virgine,* 48 for the *Psalmi Breviores* and 79 for the *Psalmi per Annum Necessarii*—has a considerable impact on both the overall structures of the psalms and the styles of individual movements. One may, however, speak of salient formal and stylistic traits common to most of the pieces and identify the unique features of others. Most of the psalms consist of sections that are sometimes quite short, and generally separated from one another by meter changes, occasionally tempo designations as well. Contrasts of style and texture, particularly in the alternation between solo and ripieno, serve to delineate most of the psalms. None of the pieces is completely soloistic, and only one is ripieno throughout. We do not find psalm-tone usage, like that of Monteverdi's 1610 Vespers, for example; but occasionally a phrase made up of repeated tones, heard in one part or passed from part to part and combined with a contrast motive, creates the impression of plainchant. In example 5-14, such a motive depicts the words "non commoveatur." Three complete psalms, and part of a fourth owe their construction to ground basses; these pieces and a few others offer more integrated structures than most of the works in terms of musical interrelationships among sections. Biber uses literal repetition of music from one section to another, however, in only three psalms, mostly in connection with his utilizing the opening of the psalm to underscore the text "sicut erat in principio." A few psalms exhibit a relative clarity of structural planning by means of a smaller-than-average number of sections, each of which is expanded in length. Every one of the twenty-nine psalms ends with an extended and self-contained Amen; these sections assume greater structural importance in the *Psalmi Breviores* owing to their occupying a greater proportion of the settings. The Amen, which may include the Gloria Patri as well, is often fugal, frequently a double fugue built on either two contrasting "Amen" themes or a combination of "et in saecula" and "Amen" themes. In some cases the

Example 5-14. *Psalmi Longiores, Beatus Vir,* mm. 31–36.

Doxology forms a penultimate movement on its own. Occasionally the strings, used as a wholly obbligato choir, alternate with the vocal parts in the Gloria Patri or Amen; most of the time they are independent in solo sections and play *colla parte* in ripieno.

Psalmi Longiores

Owing to their greater length, the *Psalmi Longiores* are the most immediately attractive works in the set for the listener of today. The larger formal dimensions permit a wider range of contemporary styles including, occasionally, those of the opera aria and instrumental music. In the *Psalmi Longiores* the "et in saecula" and "Amen" combine more often into double fugues and the Doxology expands into an independent section. Biber was also freer to introduce sections in keys other than the tonic, to expand the setting of particularly descriptive words (i.e., "confregit" in the *Dixit*) and to balance the final Amen with a strong opening movement. The string parts of the *Psalmi Longiores* are relatively independent of the voices, sometimes playing short introductions and interludes, and even in one case (the final movement of the *Laudate Dominum*) opposing the vocal choir antiphonally.

The *Dixit Dominus, Confitebor* and *Laudate Dominum* illustrate three distinctive formal types, the first sectional, the second homogeneous, and the third a three-movement ripieno structure (ABC). The *Dixit* comprises six stylistically differentiated sections that alternate between solo and ripieno; most of the text is presented in the solo passages, the second of which forms an extended complex (fig. 5-5). The lengthy grouping of solos for all four voices in succession recalls the soloistic beginning of the Osanna of the *Missa Bruxellensis*, where a logical modulatory plan created a sense of larger ordering of the solos. Here the idea is more successful, owing to the greater variety of thematic material and the better suitability of the melodic style to such an arrangement (ex. 5-15). In fact, both melodic style and modulatory plan suggest influences from the operatic experience. In length, melodic style and overall structure the bass solo that concludes the first solo section of the *Dixit* belongs to a type we have encountered already in the Domine Deus and Et incarnatus of the *Missa S. Henrici*: the bass (or *bassetgen*) "aria" with two violins. In terms of this form, each of the soprano, alto and tenor solos is the equivalent of half an "aria." In fact, the soprano and alto solos together can be said to constitute one such "aria" that modulates to the dominant in the first half (the soprano solo), begins with a new idea in the second half and returns to the tonic (alto solo). In terms of the ordering of the entire complex, then, the tenor solo is an abbreviated "aria" in a contrast key area (B minor) between two "arias" in D major with their own internal modulations.

Since the viola parts constitute a harmonic filler, all four solos are variations of the trio texture for two melodic parts (voice and violin 2 in the SAT solos, two violins in the bass solo) and bass (which includes the vocal part in the bass solo). This means that the close relationship

Figure 5-5. Scheme of *Dixit Dominus (Psalmi Longiores)*

	Section	Measures	Meter	Key	Style/Instrumentation	Solo/Ripieno
1	Dixit Dominus...meis	9	₵	D	Introductory tutti; chordal homophony	Ripieno
2	a) Donec ponem	14	3/2	D-A	Soprano; violin 2 alternating with voice, 2 violas & basso continuo	Solo
	b) Virgam virtutis	18		D	Alto, same instrumental style as a)	
	c) Tecum principium	17		b	Tenor; same instrumental style as a) and b); bassetgen continuo part	
	d) Juravit Dominus	31		D	Bass; violins 1 & 2 plus basso continuo	
3	Dominus...reges	15	₵	D-A	Fugal "confregit" framed by homophonic tutti	Ripieno
4	Judicabit...caput	29		D	Vocal trios (SAB, then SAT)	Solo
5	Gloria...semper	7		D	Block-chord homophonic tutti	Ripieno
6	Et in saecula/Amen	26		D	Fugue (Amen) with countersubject (Et in saecula)	Solo/ripieno

Example 5-15. *Psalmi Longiores, Dixit Dominus,* Soprano, Alto and Tenor Solos

Example 5-15 (continued)

between voice and basso continuo that obtains in the opera arias—in which the voice usually announces a motive, then pauses while the continuo echoes it, before picking it up again and continuing—is taken over by voice and second violin, while the bass remains basically a slow-moving support line. In fact, a similar idea appears in one of the rare arias for bass and two violins in Biber's opera.[12] Allowing for this difference the phrase structures of these solos remain remarkably like those of many arias, as a comparison between the beginning of the soprano solo and the first aria of *Chi la dura la vince,* "Di gioia amabile," reveals (ex. 5-16). The following points are common to both examples: at the outset the motive alternates back and forth between vocal and instrumental parts; it appears a second time, in somewhat extended form, in the vocal part, which then pauses; a new sequential figure occurs twice ("la doglia e labile"; "scabellum") and then expands in its second appearance to lead to a cadence in a related key ("s'e fermo il cor"; "pedum tuorum"). Another characteristic of operatic style is the presentation of the beginning of the second phrase at the close of the first without a break, followed by a pause in the voice before the second phrase continues (alto, mm. 30–31; bass, mm. 64–65). The main differences from the aria style are the lack of ritornelli, of a pregnant motive that runs throughout an entire solo and of da capo structure.

Biber frames this solo section with two tutti passages, the first of decidedly introductory character (and perhaps an echo of the psalm tone in the soprano), the second vigorously contrapuntal. In the latter the word "confregit" is represented in the conflict between the quadruple meter and the natural accentuation of the word (con-fré-git: emphasized by the melodic contour in a pattern of three eighth notes) (ex. 5-17). The second solo section displays another favorite texture of Biber's: changing vocal trios; the first is set for soprano, alto and bass; the second, for soprano, alto, and a tenor *bassetgen* line. In the first trio canonic writing between alto and bass on "judicabit" accompanies a florid soprano line on "nationibus" (ex. 5-18). The Doxology is given entirely in block chords, while a vigorous fugue on a subject beginning with the famous four-note "Mozart" theme, and a contrasting "et in saecula" countersubject closes the piece.

Example 5-16.   *Chi la dura la vince,* Aria "Di gioia amabile"

The second of the *Psalmi Longiores, Confitebor tibi Domine,* can be considered unique within the collection as a whole since it has been totally unified without the aid of a ground bass. As in the *Dixit,* well-spaced tutti articulate a largely soloistic setting. But, owing to the consistent tone of praise throughout the psalm, one main idea dominates the melodic content of the piece. This idea, a gently flowing lyrical descent in triple meter, maintains a single tone (ex. 5-19). And for the most part the style and unfolding of sections are uncomplicated: vocal solos lead into refrains, either vocal trios or solos with strings, all based on the main idea; the modulation of this idea into closely related keys and its appearance near the beginning of the work for strings alone impart something of the character of ritornello structure to the piece. The melody of the refrain is sometimes inverted, and Biber combines the two forms for the "et in saecula" (inversion) and "Amen" (theme) combination of the final movement. Exact repetition of both solo and refrain occurs, however, only at "sicut erat in principio," where the music of the opening bars of the psalm returns. In contrast with practically every other setting in the collection, *Confitebor* offers neither stylistic contrasts nor the depiction of individual words by means of inventive musical figures. It is rather unusual to find in the seventeenth century a fairly lengthy composition that so concentrates on the representation of a single, predominating mood. In its aesthetic character, if not its style, this piece looks forward to the *Affektenbegriff* of the eighteenth century.

Laudate Dominum, the fifth of the *Psalmi Longiores,* and the only fully ripieno setting in the collection, presents a straightforward, three-movement structure. Of the 150 psalms *Laudate Dominum* has the shortest text: "Laudate Dominum omnes gentes: laudate eum omnes populi. Quoniam confirmata est super nos misericordia ejus: et veritas Domini manet in aeternum." Biber observes the customary division into two verses for the first two movements, while the third comprises the Doxology and Amen. All three movements are in triple meter,

Example 5-17. *Psalmi Longiores, Dixit Dominus,* Choral Writing at "confregit"

but stylistically quite dissimilar; the first (Presto) is triadic, lively and joyful, the second (Adagio), simple and chordal, the third (Presto), energetic and, above all, rhythmically compelling. Between the adagio and final presto Biber calls for an interval of silence (one bar's rest with a pause in all parts) in order to increase the effectiveness of the vigorous entrance of the strings in the Gloria (ex. 5-20). For, in the final movement the strings play as a separate choir entirely in the following rhythm: ♩♩♩♩ | ♩♩♩♩ . This configuration, accented against the barline, opposes at first the more regular metrical rhythm of the choir; but beginning with the word "Amen" the choir too adopts the off-the-beat rhythm. It seems as if the ecstatic pattern of the strings cannot rest until all the parts have been injected with its enthusiasm, for, whenever the choir sounds alone the strings insinuate their syncopated rhythm into the texture (a single violin enters first, followed by the whole body). The rhythmic contrasts and the eventual triumph of the syncopated rhythm bring about a sense of an almost uncontainable elation and expansiveness in this movement.[13]

The foregoing commentaries by no means exhaust the points of interest in the *Psalmi Longiores*. In is hoped that they convey something of Biber's careful attention to the creation of a variety of imaginative structures. The *Magnificat* in particular is a remarkable piece that

Example 5-18. *Psalmi Longiores, Dixit Dominus,* "judicabit in nationibus"

Example 5-19. *Psalmi Longiores, Confitebor,* mm. 31–52

might have been chosen instead of the *Dixit* to illustrate extended sectional form. In it the string body plays an even greater role in integrating the solo complexes: alto, soprano and tenor solos with full strings open the work; later the familiar bass solo with two elaborate violin parts and a "new" combination of alto and tenor solos with two violas are heard; in the Doxology (marked Grave) imitative duets in flowing parallel thirds are punctuated by an insistent rhythm in the strings corresponding to the words: "Gloria, gloria Patri." In *Beatus Vir,* on the other hand, a long series of solos for all four voices is accompanied by basso continuo alone; even the bass is independent.

Example 5-20.   *Psalmi Longiores, Laudate Dominum,* Ending of Adagio and Beginning of Presto

Psalmi de B. M. Virgine

These somewhat shorter psalms present a number of interesting features not found in the *Psalmi Longiores*. Three of the settings, *Laetatus Sum, Lauda Jerusalem* and the *Magnificat* are of the rather long, sectional type, while one, the *Dixit Dominus,* has a straightforward plan comprising four contrasted movements: 1) fugal prologue with chorus; 2) solos for all four voices; 3) triple-meter Doxology in block-chord homophony; 4) Amen fugue with countersubject. The remaining two settings, *Laudate Pueri* and *Nisi Dominus,* are built on ground basses, the second of which is in continual "walking" eighth notes. The solo sections in

Example 5-21.   Related Theme Types

(a)   *Magnificat* of *Psalmi de B. M. Virgine*

(b)   *Beatus Vir* of *Psalmi Breviores*

the *Psalmi de B. M. Virgine* share their principles of construction with those of the longer psalms; in fact, extended strings of solos are just as common here, and since the voices are often accompanied by basso continuo alone there is more interaction between these two parts than in the *Psalmi Longiores.* And the solo/tutti contrasts exhibit some new features, including several rapid changes from one to the other in a section of the *Magnificat,* the framing of a short chromatic solo by tutti blocks in *Lauda Jerusalem,* and the juxtaposition of soprano solo with alto, tenor and bass ripieno in the *Laetatus Sum.* Finally, the Amens of all six psalms have all, in some way or other, been planned to provide conclusions of special character, either in terms of contrapuntal devices (*Lauda Jerusalem,* and the two ground bass settings) or in their utilizing *Gegenfugen* whose main themes are versions of the "cuckoo" motive that was common in south German and Austrian instrumental music in the seventeenth century (the *Dixit Dominus* and *Laetatus Sum*). The Amen of the *Magnificat* uses a type of counterpoint that Biber favors in several other places within this collection: a short theme of static melodic and harmonic character is doubled at the third and imitated by two other voices a third apart at the distance of a half-measure, producing the illusion of activity on a single chord (ex. 5-21).

The *Psalmi de B. M. Virgine* exhibit features of calculated planning, as commentary on a few of the pieces makes clear. Of all the above-mentioned features the construction of entire settings on ostinato basses has by far the greatest influence on the styles and forms of the works in question. Thus the *Laudate Pueri* and *Nisi Dominus* resist division into sections, and the tonal organization of their basses does not invite grouping into larger patterns. The ground shifts to a related key after a few repetitions, while the changes in texture overlap rather than follow the modulations of the bass; in fact, they often overlap the individual statements of the ground as well (fig. 5-6). Consequently, the ostinati bind the works into long, continuous entities rather than articulating sectional divisions, so that there are sometimes unusually rapid fluctuations between solo and tutti; this is particularly true of the *Nisi Dominus,* where the walking bass supplies the sense of continual forward motion. The ripieno passages, therefore, lose some of their customary form-defining function and serve more closely the expression of the text. In addition, the bass pattern in both pieces has a profound effect on the melodic styles;

Figure 5-6. Plans of Two Ground Bass Psalms from the *Psalmi de B.M. Virgine*

Key	Ground Bass Statements		Solo/Ripieno
	Laudate Pueri		
	(B-flat)		
B-flat major	1-2	(soprano)	Solo
	3-4	(tenor)	
	5-6	(bass & strings)	
F major	7-8	(alto)	
B-flat major	9		Ripieno
F major	10		Solo/Ripieno
B-flat major	11		Solo/Ripieno
	12-13		Solo
F major	14-15		
B-flat major	16-17		
	18-19		Ripieno
F major	20-21		
B-flat major	22		
E-flat major	23		
	Nisi Dominus		
	(D minor)		
D minor	1-4		Solo
F major	5-6		
D minor	7-8		
	9		Ripieno
	10		Solo
A minor	11-13		
	14		Ripieno
D minor	15-16		
F major	17		
A minor	18		
D minor	19		
G minor	20		

Example 5-22.   *Psalmi de B. M. Virgine, Laetatus Sum,* Amen Beginnng

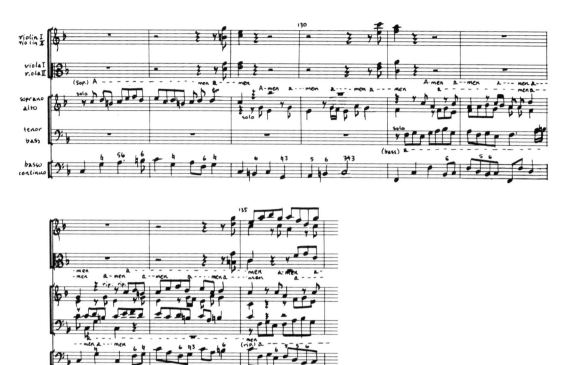

as in many of Biber's ground-bass pieces the bass motives pervade the textures of these two psalms, especially since their construction permits close imitation by the upper parts. The ostinato of *Laudate Pueri* allows four-part fugal imitation with alternating tonic and dominant entries above a single statement of the bass, while that of *Nisi Dominus* can be imitated by a second part at the distance of a quarter note. These devices are exploited to the full in the two Amen sections. Yet, although ground-bass techinque was perhaps somewhat old-fashioned in the late seventeenth century, in these two psalms it appears to serve something resembling a larger sense of unity of affect.

Two of the longer, more sectional psalms utilize other means of achieving consistency and integration. The *Laetatus Sum* is, of course, a wholly joyful text, and to convey this its opening section features a soprano solo comprising a balanced phrase structure moving mostly in four-measure units of simple major-key melodic character and sequential repetition of melodic units; the separate phrases are then answered by the three lower voices in ripieno, the whole producing an effect of a dance-like dialogue. This entire section is then repeated beginning with the words "sicut erat in principio," now preceded by a short solo for bass and strings set to the first phrase of the Gloria Patri text. Emphasis on the dominant throughout this latter passage creates a sense of expectancy that is resolved by the return of the opening music. And the "cuckoo" fugue that follows immediately seems to take its simple F-major character from this section; here the joy of the *Laetatus* is given almost a childlike character (ex. 5-22).

The *Lauda Jerusalem,* a five-section structure (fig. 5-7), also makes systematic use of contrasted sound bodies in its opening movement, this time trios for soprano, alto and tenor versus solos for bass and strings. The second section then frames a soprano solo of "pathetic" character ("He casts forth his ice like morsels: who can stand before His cold") by two brief ripieno blocks; the soprano solo ends with a drawn-out cadence on "quis sustenebit" that

Figure 5-7. Scheme of *Lauda Jerusalem* (*Psalmi de B. M. Virgine*)

	Section	Meter	Measures	Form, Style, Texture
1	Lauda Jerusalem	3/2	34	SAT trios vs. bass solo with violins
2	Qui dat nivem	C	13	Soprano solo framed by short tutti passages
3	Flabit spiritus eius	3/2	16	Choral homophony
4	Qui annuntiat	3/2	25	Alto and tenor solos
5	Doxology	3/2	17	Texture and style of bars 1-34. Bars 100-105 (Et in saecula) identical to bars 4-9.
6	Amen	C	20	Fugue with theme in inversion (Solo/Ripieno)

Example 5-23.　*Psalmi de B. M. Virgine, Lauda Jerusalem*, Alto Solo "qui annuntiat"

features the Neapolitan sixth chord, a device that appears in several places in the *Vesperae Longiores ac Breviores* and in the *Missa Bruxellensis* but is generally more a feature of Biber's operatic style. After the first fully ripieno section in the work, a pictorial representation of "he causes His wind to blow and the waters to flow," another extended section of solos begins, appropriately, on "qui annuntiat" ("He announces His word to Jacob"), which Biber represents with the "Devisen-aria" style of motto beginning (ex. 5-23). Continuing, this sequence of solos leads into the Doxology, which begins in a setting for bass and strings that is suggestive of the opening movement; at "sicut erat in principio" the soprano, alto, tenor trio style with which the psalm began returns, but Biber saves literal repetition of music for the text "et in saecula saeculorum" (mm. 4-9) of the psalm. The effectiveness of this stage-by-stage return to literal repetition is enhanced by its subtle move from E-flat and C minor to the dominant (F) that prepares the Amen (B-flat). This last movement is a schematic contrapuntal finale in which a favorite device of Biber's appears: the simultaneous combination of the theme with its mirror inversion, in which the entries are systematically presented:

Soprano	:			inver.		inver.		inver.	theme
Alto	:		inver.		inver.		inver.		inver.
Tenor	:	theme				theme		theme	inver.
Bass	:			theme	theme		theme		theme

Figure 5-8. Scheme of Text Overlap in Second *Laudate Pueri* Setting (*Psalmi Breviores*)

```
S:              Sit nomen Domini  benedictum,     ex hoc nunc et usque in saeculum.

A:                                                      Excelsus    super omnes

T:                           A    solis ortu usque  ad occasum,   laudabili

B:  Laudate Pueri Domi--num: laudate nomen  Domi--ni.

    _____

S:                                            et humilia       respecit in coelo

A:  gentes Dominus, et   super coe------los  glo----------ria e-------jus.

T:  nomen  Domini.

B:            Quis sicut Dominus Deus noster, qui in altis habitat et      humilia

    _____

S:       et in       ter------ra?

A:

T:

B:  respecit in coelo et in terra?
```

The *Lauda Jerusalem,* like most of the *Psalmi de B. M. Virgine,* reveals a strong sense of direction towards the end and the kind of careful overall planning that we have associated with Biber's later work.

Psalmi Breviores

Short psalm settings with titles such as *Psalmi Breves* (Hofer) and *Psalmi Brevissimae* (Schmelzer) were a ubiquitous feature of Vespers music in the seventeenth century; and they generally reflect a curtailment of many of the musical features we have been outlining. Their often extreme brevity—sometimes little more than a dozen bars for an entire psalm with doxology—places severe restrictions on the musical extension of any given idea. Thus, for the most part, in his set Biber confines ripieno treatment to chordal, syllabic passages in which large portions of the text can be very quickly presented. He greatly abbreviates the length of soloistic vocal passages, often presenting two, or even three phrases of the text simultaneously among the various parts, as in the following scheme of his second *Laudate Pueri* setting (fig. 5-8). The Amen sections form significant exceptions to this economical type of text treatment; nevertheless, the Amens of the *Psalmi Breviores* are generally shorter than those of the other psalms in the collection and contain neither the familiar *Gegenfugen* nor any solo/ripieno contrasts.

That shorter psalms such as these were useful to music directors well into the eighteenth century is revealed by performance dates for Biber's *Psalmi Breviores* on the Göttweig copies and a similar catalogue of dates on Schmelzer's *Vesperae Brevissimae.*[14] Comparison between these two collections reveals the nature of the shorter psalm setting in the seventeenth century, as well as some of the general similarities and differences between Biber's music and that of his supposed teacher in an area where their respective generations count less than in the instrumental music. Schmelzer's set, like Biber's, contains psalms for two Vespers services ("de beatissima Virgine" and "de Apostolis in 2ndis Vesp."). As in Biber's *Psalmi Breviores,* the *Dixit* and *Magnificat* serve double duty; but Schmelzer includes only one setting of *Laudate Pueri* (which is common to both services) while Biber's set has two. This fact is significant: since the *Laudate Pueri* occupies a different place in the two Vespers, the key scheme that Biber worked out for both sets of psalms required a second setting (it appears that Biber wanted the second psalm of both sets in the relative minor and the fourth in the tonic, a situation that obtains in the *Psalmi Longiores* as well). Schmelzer's collection reveals no such marked interest in key structure. Outside of the key signature limits of one sharp and one flat, we find no planned sequence of keys, either within each of the two sets or between the one set and the other. The most one can say is that the psalms are grouped loosely around A minor, or perhaps C major:

Dixit Dominus	A minor
Laudate Pueri	E minor
Laetatus Sum	C major
Nisi Dominus	G major
Lauda Jerusalem	D minor
Credidi	A minor
In Convertendo	F major
Domine Probasti Me	C major
Magnificat	G major

In Schmelzer's *Vesperae Brevissimae* regular alternation of solo and tutti textures is vital and was probably carefully laid out in advance of composition. In the longest psalm, *Domine Probasti Me,* for example, every fourth verse has a ripieno setting; only the necessity of concluding with a tutti alters the pattern at the very end. Schmelzer applies similar formal schemes to some of the shorter psalms as well, although not always so strictly. The solo sections of the psalms are generally two or three times as long as the tutti. But both textures treat the text almost completely syllabically, with rhythms derived from the words and only the occasional use of florid solo writing. The ripieno passages are invariably in block-chord style with two obbligato violins; cornetti and trombones double the vocal parts. The solo passages consist chiefly of short overlapping phrases presented by the soloists in turn. Two violins always accompany the bass solos, brief vocal duets and trios often appear, and the last few words of a vocal solo often expand into a trio. In three of the psalms obbligato trombones accompany brief solos at carefully chosen places in the texts. With the exception of the seven-bar, nonfugal Amen of the *Magnificat,* Schmelzer's psalms contain no extended Amen sections and no meter or tempo changes, or otherwise clearly marked sectional divisions apart from solo/ripieno alternation.

On the average Biber's *Psalmi Breviores* are about the same length as Schmelzer's *Vesperae Brevissimae* (48 and 52 measures, respectively). Yet, although similar in obvious ways, Biber's set shows far greater interest in maintaining as much as possible of the stylistic and formal variety of the longer pieces. The Amen always expands into a separate section that comprises a substantial part of the setting; it usually has an interesting basic idea that is primarily musical, and often appears in a different meter. In three of the psalms changes of meter mark divisions other than the Amen as well. Despite the fact that Biber's *Confitebor* is one of the longest psalms of the set, it does not contain a large number of sections, as did Schmelzer's *Domine Probasti Me;* instead, Biber takes the opportunity of enlarging the

Example 5-24. *Psalmi Breviores, Laudate Pueri*

(a) Beginning

(b) mm. 13–19

dimensions of the individual sections. The *Laetatus Sum* reveals a marked musical relationship between the melody of the opening solos and the theme of the Amen; this latter movement occupies almost half of the total setting. Although merely thirty-two measures in length, the second *Laudate Pueri* exhibits masterful constructive and expressive powers: its two parts consist of a twenty-bar ground-bass section comprising the psalm text and the Doxology, plus a twelve-bar Amen in contrasting meter. The first movement encompasses soloistic writing over four statements of the ground in A minor (eight bars), a syllabic tutti over two statements in C (four bars), and another soloistic passage accompanied by three and one-half statements in A minor (seven bars). At the beginning of this piece the soprano line consists of a reiterated e″ in rapid syllabic style suggestive of chanting, while the three lower parts present various other phrases of the text in overlap; when the ground moves to C major the choir sings in similar reciting style and the alto part, which has the repeated tones (now g′), is doubled an octave higher by the first violin. The solo soprano then returns with the recitational e″ and the Doxology text above a melismatic tenor solo (ex. 5-24); the e″ starts off the descent of the Amen fugue theme by fifths through the four voices and the soprano states the final entry at this pitch, while the first violin rises to play it in the final chord. The scale of this setting is extraordinarily small, but the sense of integration and variety are wonderful. Even the mercilessly short syllabic *Laudate Dominum* (18 measures) manages to generate a three-fold structure of vocal soloists in pairs (5 measures), Doxology in ripieno (7 measures) and Amen with contrast theme (Presto: 6 measures) that makes a sense of climax at the Amen through emphasis on the dominant throughout the preceding sections. Others of the *Psalmi Breviores* resemble Schmelzer's psalms more closely in structure, although the Amen section always marks an important difference. But generally, in terms of smaller expressive details, such as florid solo writing, use of obbligato strings, chromatic harmony (including the Neapolitan sixth), and numerous graphic depictions of individual words Biber's set is much more ambitious than Schmelzer's.

Psalmi per Annum Necessarii

On the basis of lengths ranging from 41 to 119 measures it appears that some of this last group of psalms might be classified as "psalmi breviores," others as "psalmi longiores." But such a procedure would be misleading if it failed to take into account that what differentiates the two types from one another is more a function of style than bar numbers. The lengths of the seven psalm texts, too, vary extensively, from seven to twenty-seven verses; and, as it happens, the two psalms with the shortest and longest texts (*Beati omnes* and *In Exitu Israel,* respectively) are also the shortest and longest in Biber's settings. But *In Exitu* is very much in the style of the *Psalmi Breviores* nevertheless; and it seems obvious that this was done *because* the text was so long. The same is true of the other long psalms, *Domine Probasti Me* and *Memento.* In these pieces Biber planned the placing of ripieno passages carefully so as to combine the formal consideration of regular spacing with textual content. Whereas Schmelzer had set every fourth verse of his *Domine Probasti Me* in ripieno, Biber sets every sixth in his, choosing verses dealing with the wonder of God's knowledge (six and seventeen) and the image of hiding in darkness (eleven). For *In Exitu* Biber sets the first three verses and thereafter every eighth in ripieno (e.g., verses 1–3; 9; 17; 26–7), selecting the well-known verse "non nobis Domine, non nobis, sed nomine tuam da gloriam" and the verse beginning "O Israel" (i.e., a call to trust in God) in ripieno, besides groupings of verses at the beginning and end. In *Memento* verses one, ten and fifteen are so chosen, the last one probably for structural reasons, and the other two because they refer to David, the tenth bringing in a reference to "Christi" as well.

Because of the brevity of the ripieno passages *Memento* delivers most of its text in the solo sections; by this means the setting is kept as short as possible; only the Amen is more expansive. But this kind of emphasis on solo writing is completely different from that in the psalms of the first two groups. In *Memento,* and in fact the majority of these pieces, there is much simultaneous sounding of different texts, just as in the *Psalmi Breviores*; and this procedure is probably the foremost characteristic of the "brevis" style. This does not mean, however, that the works are therefore inferior; rather the reverse in some cases. *In Exitu* has three extended solo sections that, despite much overlapping of solo lines, have sharply profiled musical characters and a relationship to the tutti sections that was carefully planned to increase the sense of formal continuity of the whole. This consists of the fact that the short punctuating tutti at "non nobis Domine" and "Domus Israel speravit" introduce changes of tone in the text, first from the narrative beginning of the psalm to the address to God (verse 9) then to an exhortation to Israel (verse 17). The solos that follow these block-chord passages continue with the textual content that has just been introduced; and their simultaneous singing of different texts has the effect of suggesting the spread of the "collective" prayer or exhortation to the larger group of individuals. But the solo sections begin with changes of meter from the tutti introductions, a device that seems to suggest that the tutti belong to the preceding rather

Example 5-25.   *Psalmi per Annum Necessarii, De Profundis,* Et in saecula/Amen Fugue Themes

than the following solo sections. In both cases, however, the tutti begin after full cadences from the soloists in F major: the first in D minor and the second with the dominant of G minor; they both end firmly with perfect cadences on an A major chord that serves as the dominant of the solo section that follows with the meter change. Thus, in terms of metrical and textural characteristics the sections of the work must be divided differently from those suggested by tonal and textual considerations. In fact the tutti are "preludes" to contrasted solo sections, the first of which has a tremendously lively triple-meter character, while the second is built entirely over a walking eighth-note bass line that ties together the many overlapping phrases. *In Exitu* is a remarkable instance of how the necessity of presenting a very long text as quickly as possible can be turned to musical advantage.

Certain other features of the "brevis" style seem almost to contradict the principles of text setting followed in the longer pieces. In several psalms, for example, the beginning of the Doxology—the place that receives the most splendid soloistic elaboration in all the manuscript works as well as the majority of the longer psalms of this collection—is overlapped with the closing phrases of the psalm text. In the *De Profundis* this procedure involves the entrance of the phrase "Gloria Patri et Filio" in the bass beneath a soprano line that moves at once to a Neapolitan sixth chord for the word "iniquitatibus"; the bass line rises a semitone to the flat sixth of the key (on "Gloria") in a manner usually associated with phrases of lamentation, and the two parts cadence together. From one standpoint it appears that the Doxology has been subordinated to the restrictions of length; but the manner in which it enters here, conforming to the "pathetic" character of the soprano line, suggests that Biber is more concerned with the overall tone of the *De Profundis,* which he sets in a key (C minor) having associations of lamentation throughout his work. The Et in saecula/Amen "Gegenfuge" that follows is, in fact, one of the more developed instances of this type in the collection (ex. 5-25).

On the other hand, *In Convertendo,* one of the shorter psalm texts, has a consistently joyful tone and is set wholly in triple meter; it is also the second longest of the seven settings that make up this part of the collection. *In Convertendo* departs more than any other of these psalms from the "psalmi breviores" style; while its vocal solos are not long, they overlap only at cadence points where the register changes. And Biber clearly intends to create a sense of climax

Example 5-26.   *Psalmi per Annum Necessarii, In Convertendo,* Amen Theme

at two points, the joyful "venientes autem venient cum exaltatione" section, which is allowed to expand well beyond the limits of the "brevis" style, and the Amen. The former of these two sections tosses a theme based on a falling fifth throughout the voices with a countertheme doubled at the third, the whole making a jubilant effect with its alternating tonic and dominant harmonies; the falling fifths at the outset represent the idea of an assembly as well, like a very similar idea from the *Congregamini Omnes Populi* that we will argue is a work of Biber's. [15] Anticipations of the "venientes" idea, however, are introduced into *In Convertendo* at two earlier points to form joyful answers to otherwise different phrases (e.g., the second half of verse six: "they that sow in tears shall reap in joy"). And the Amen is also built from a short cadential idea in tonic and dominant harmonies with doubling at the third (ex. 5-26). The Amen generates its joyful effect from constant change of key between the ten statements of this idea; at the outset it is transposed through five of the six keys of the A-minor ambitus before repeating a key: a, G, e, d, C.

Musical integration and the presence of a consistently joyful tone do not necessarily go hand in hand with extended length, however; the shortest psalm of the set, *Beati Omnes,* is constructed over twenty statements of a blatantly major-key ostinato that never once modulates. This piece is not one of the more successful of the collection; it is clearly in the "psalmi breviores" category, but now somewhat perfunctory and unvaried in tone. Like the other ground-bass psalm settings, its Amen section features fugal imitation at the fifth above the ground, now beginning at the almost erratically irregular time intervals of six quarter notes, two quarter notes and one eighth note (i.e., syncopated) after the previous entry.

Finally, a mixture of the "longiores" and "breviores" styles is possible within a single setting. *Credidi,* the first of these psalms, and also on one of the shorter texts, comprises a quasi-symmetrical structure formed of two "framing" fugues of fairly extended proportions and very much in the archaic motet style ("Credidi" and "Amen"), that surround a section of solos with overlapping texts. In the midst of the solo section, at virtually the exact center of the composition appears a four-bar, syllabic ripieno whose text was chosen for this place because in the psalm it introduces a turn to prayer.

Miscellaneous Church Compositions

This chapter will introduce eleven compositions in several different liturgical categories—one Marian antiphon, three hymns, two litanies, five offertories and one *Muttetum Natale*—and an array of musical styles and scorings ranging from the smallest to the largest in Biber's *oeuvre*. These pieces encompass a wide variety of styles that include the *stile antico* (*Stabat Mater*) as well as those exhibiting the influence of opera and instrumental music. Clearly Emperor Leopold's reference to Biber's "verschiedentlichen gethane künstliche compositiones" in the document that elevated him to knighthood was no empty panegyric; the emperor was more familiar with Biber's instrumental works, but the statement applies even to the sacred music alone.[1] In addition to their variety, the works in this chapter reach from the very earliest datable composition of Biber's (*Salve Regina*, 1663) to what may well be his last work (*Huc Poenitentes*, ca. 1700).[2]

1. *Salve Regina à 2* (1663)
2. *Congregamini Omnes Populi* (1663?)
3. *Lux Perpetua* (1673?)
4. *Plaudite Tympana* (1682?)
5. *Stabat Mater* (after 1690)
6. *Offertorium pro festo 7 Dolorum: Quo abiit dilectis tuus* (after 1690)
7. *Huc Poenitentes* (ca. 1700)
8. *Ne Cedite* (ca. 1700)
9. *Muttetum Natale* (after 1690?)
10. *Litaniae Lauretanae* (published 1693)
11. *Litania de S. Josepho à 20* (after 1692)

This tremendously variegated body of music cannot be perfectly arranged according to chronology; in most cases the above ordering assumes temporal proximity between the copying dates of the manuscripts and the composition of the works.[3] We will begin with what are probably Biber's first three extant vocal pieces; but a loosely ordered sequence that mingles chronology with liturgical category as much as possible allows us to complete the discussion of Biber's vocal church music with examples that represent in many respects an overview of his career as church composer.

Salve Regina à 2

This setting of the well-known Marian antiphon, copied at Kroměříž in 1663, and written when Biber was nineteen years of age or younger, is perhaps the earliest surviving work of Biber's. Although the soprano part has been lost, leaving only the organ continuo and obbligato viola

Figure 6-1. Outline of *Salve Regina* (1663)

	Section/Text	Measures	Scoring	Comments
1	Salve Regina, mater misericordiae, vita dulcedo, et spes nostra, salve	14	Soprano & continuo	Cadence on dominant in bar 9 and new bass motive in 10 (vita, dulcedo)
2		18	Gamba & continuo	
3	Ad te clamamur exsules, Filii Hevae	9	Soprano, gamba & continuo	Rests in gamba part indicate alternation of soloists; gamba rhythms match those of text
4		10	Gamba & continuo	
5	Ad te suspiramus, gementes et flentes in hoc lacrimarum valle	11	Soprano, gamba & continuo	Rests indicate alternation of soloists; lamento style in 57–62 suggests "ad te suspiramus"
6	Eia ergo, Advocata nostra, illos tuos misericordes oculos ad nos converte	8	Soprano & continuo	Organ rhythms match those of text
7	Et Jesum benedictum Fructum ventris tui, nobis post hoc exsilium ostende	6	Soprano, gamba & continuo	The words "Et Jesum" appear in gamba part
		4	Gamba & continuo	
8	O clemens: O pia: O dulcis Virgo Maria	10	Soprano, gamba & continuo	Descending triad motive suggests this text

da gamba parts, it is possible to reconstruct much of the layout of the work according to its scoring and the disposition of the text. From the division of the work into sections articulated by cadences, the sometimes ornate and obviously soloistic gamba part, a few details such as rests and text indications in the gamba part, and the presence of motives and rhythms matching certain words and passages of the text, we can determine changes of texture with a reasonable degree of confidence. Figure 6-1 is offered as an approximate outline.

The fairly large number of cadences, usually coinciding with changes of texture and motivic material, and the many varied motives in the viola da gamba part typify traits of the young composer not yet used to handling ideas on a broad scale. In comparison to the solo violin part of the Dresden *Nisi Dominus,* the gamba phrases are short-winded, sometimes abandoning a figurational pattern almost as soon as it is introduced, then proceding to do the same with the next one. The favored means of creating a larger sense of order in the work is its many persistent scale patterns in the bass, some of which recall Monteverdi, especially when the patterns appear in half- and quarter-note versions as well as variations in dotted rhythm (ex. 6-1). These traditional devices, which resemble the styles of gamba divisions described by Christopher Simpson, Thomas Mace and others, often utilize long sequences of first-inversion chords.[4] The figuration remains consistent for the duration of the bass pattern, and different sections close with the same cadential formula (ex. 6-2). Some of these traits also figure prominently in the *Fantasia* for violin preserved at the Minoriten convent in Vienna, and subsequently reworked by Biber into the fourth of the *Sonatae Violino Solo,* as well as several other anonymous pieces from the Vienna collection, and the *Sonata à 4 violis* of "H. B." (1663) that is preserved at Kroměříž in the same hand as that of the *Salve Regina* and on the same kind of paper.[5] If anything, the *Salve Regina* is better constructed than the *Fantasia,* which may be earlier still.

Example 6-1. *Salve Regina à 2* (1663)

(a) mm. 70–74

(b) mm. 83–90

Example 6-2. *Salve Regina à 2,* mm. 15–25

Although unmistakably immature in some respects, the *Salve Regina* points to directions familiar to us from Biber's later work. In particular, the conception of a piece with an agile instrumental part that takes a considerable role in the text interpretation is present here. The number of passages for solo gamba and those where (as far as can be determined) the two soloists would have concertized together suggest something of the various seventeenth-century sonatas for violin and viola da gamba. And indeed, some of the motives and instrumental figures of the gamba part have much in common with some sonatas from the Vienna manuscript, in which the second part appears to have been intended for gamba.[6] The descending triadic figure that combines with extended scalar bass patterns in the final section appears in them and in countless of Biber's later works.

Congregamini Omnes Populi à 15 (1663?)

SSATB chorus and soloists, three trombones, two violins, two violas, basso continuo. The Offertorium "de Martyribus," *Congregamini Omnes Populi,* is of uncertain authorship since the title page of the manuscript supplies only the composer's initials: "H. B." Sehnal dates the work 1663 on the basis of handwriting and paper type.[7] As in the case of the *Missa in Albis,* Heinrich Brückner's authorship also comes into question here. The text of the work is as follows:

> Congregamini omnes populi
> Concurrite gentes
> Concurrite omnes
> Et laudem dicite Domino
> Omnes qui timetis Dominum pusilli et magni
> Alleluia
> Quoniam adest nobis celebris Dies
> Quo Gloriosus Praesul et Martyr Sanctus Vincentius
> Eonum certamen certavit cursum consumavit
> Ideo reddidit illi Justus Judex
> Coronam iustitiae
> Ideo assumptus est cum Angelis
> Gaudet cum prophetis
> Laetatur cum Apostolis
> Triumphat cum Martyribus
> Exultat cum sessoribus
> Gaudeamus et exultemus et demus gloriam ei
> Alleluia

Offertoria for the feast of the martyr saints Vincent and Anastasius (January 22) are rare, and this one must surely have been composed for a patron whose name saint was Vincent; who it was has not been determined. Although the work calls for six-part chorus with strings and trombones, most of the choral writing is five-part (SSATB); the basses of the choir sing in unison in all but two short passages. At "Ideo reddidit" unison soprano parts result in four-part chorus writing; six soloists are used regularly.

Although *Congregamini Omnes Populi* is not a profound composition, it reveals considerable mastery in the area of vivid text expression. In the opening section the tenor solo, representing the leader of the congregation, exhorts the people to assemble in order to praise God (ex. 6-3). The congregation is ingeniously represented. First we hear the young and old of the gathering separately (mm. 5–12); then all members sound as a single body (unison tutti: mm. 14–15). The falling fifths and fourths from soprano to bass and the succeeding counterpoint in parallel thirds resemble, as mentioned earlier, the section "venientes autem veniunt" from Biber's *In convertendo* of some thirty years later. Five triple-meter choral sections of *Congregamini* ("omnes populi," "idei reddidit illi Justus Judex Coronam justitiae," "et demus gloriam" and the two "Alleluias") depict the assembly and maintain an exultant atmosphere, while vocal trios and a section with two basses and two lively violin parts suggest Biber's style (ex. 6-4). Yet, if we judge the work to be Biber's, it must be acknowledged that certain of its stylistic traits are not typical of his later work. For example, *Congregamini* has several examples of the so-called "Corelli clash," or simultaneous sounding of leading tone and tonic in the penultimate chord of a cadence, producing parallel seconds or sevenths between two parts. Although this type of cadence was used for decades after *Congregamini* was written, it appears very rarely in Biber's music. Weak harmonic progressions and long sequences characterize *Congregamini* as much as the *Sonata à 4 violis* of 1663 and the early Vienna

Example 6-3. "H. B.," *Congregamini Omnes Populi,* Beginning

sonatas, while several motives of the piece figure prominently in the gamba part of the *Salve Regina.*[8] In this piece there is generally more voice leading in parallel thirds than we normally find in Biber's music. But the piece is unquestionably better than the *Missa in Albis* and is consistent with the little that we do know of Biber's earliest works.

Lux Perpetua (1673)

Eight-part double chorus and soloists, two violins, two violas, three trombones, and basso continuo. The offertorium *Lux Perpetua,* dated 1673 by Sehnal, is the earliest extant vocal

Example 6-4. *Congregamini Omnes Populi,* Excerpt from Duet for Two Basses and Two Violins

work written by Biber during his Salzburg period, possibly even the earliest after 1663. The text appears in the manuscript as follows:

> Lux perpetua lucebit Sancto N. [Carolo]
> Et in perpetuas aeternitas vivet.
> Alleluia.
> Iste est qui ante Deum
> Magnas virtutes operatus est
> Et omnis terra Doctrina eius repleta est
> Ideo Elegit eum dominus sacerdote Sibi
> Ad sacrificandum ei hostiam laudis
> Iste est qui contempsit vitam mundi
> Et pervenit ad caelestia regna.
> Alleluia.

The first line of the text, which is repeated many times in Biber's setting and occurs in all vocal parts, always ends with the capital letter "N." This letter, an abbreviation for the word "nomen," indicates that the piece may be used on the feast day of any saint, whose name is inserted at that point. In a single part the word "Carolo" appears once in the hand of the original copyist (Biber?), with the letter "N" written above it. Biber undoubtedly wrote the work for Salzburg, perhaps as seems to be suggested in the text, for an anniversary service, and prepared this copy for Kroměříž. It is clear that, like Alessandro Poglietti's *Motetto de sancto Carolo, ô vero per ogni Sancto e Santa* (also preserved at Kroměříž), Biber's work might be performed on a great number of occasions. The presence at Kroměříž of many works of varied types in honor of St. Charles indicates that they were either written or adapted for Bishop Karl Liechtenstein-Kastelkorn and performed on the feast day of his name saint (November 4).

The scoring of *Lux Perpetua* deviates slightly from the practice of doubling one of the choirs by winds and the other by strings: in antiphonal passages the second violin joins the trombones in doubling the second choir, while the remaining strings support the first chorus. This arrangement, as well as antiphony between the two violin/solo bass pairs at *Ideo elegit,*

Figure 6-2. Scheme of *Lux Perpetua*

	Section	Meter	Measures	Form, Style, Texture
1	Sonata	C	15	
2	Lux perpetua	C	16	Successive vocal duets (SS, BB, TT)
3	Lucebit		17	Ripieno double chorus antiphony
4	Alleluia		12	Ripieno, florid style
5	Iste...laudis		19	Duets (AA, then BB with violins)
6	Iste...regna	$\frac{3}{2}$	24	Ripieno
7	Alleluia	$\frac{4}{4}$	12	Ripieno, florid style

hint that the violins were separated. The absence of cornetti necessitated that the first violin serve as a *colla parte* instrument in tutti passages, as a result of which the usual high first violin part is lacking, except for the antiphonal "lucebit" section, where Biber has the instrument double the first soprano at the octave above. In the introductory sonata the two violins are set against a slow-moving background of trombones doubling the lower strings, also a unique texture for Biber.

The *Lux Perpetua* displays a measure of formal clarity in its double solo/ripieno/refrain sequence (fig. 6-2). In this respect it compares with the later offertoria (see below). Conservative means of extension are employed in the solo sections. Biber organizes the bass duet with two violins, "Ideo elegit," over scale patterns in the basso continuo that are not far removed from passages of the *Salve Regina* (ex. 6-5). The vocal duets at "Lux perpetua" rely on strict, quasi-canonic imitation at the unison: two sopranos (in G), two tenors (in D) and two basses (in G) present basically the same material (ex. 6-6).

Plaudite Tympana

Little regarding this work needs to be added to what was said about the *Missa Salisburgensis* in chapter 4. The scoring of the hymn is identical to that of the Mass, and the style is just as ostentatious. The ending of the main section (the piece is in da capo form), "applaude patria, Rupertum celebra," extends what is essentially a delayed cadential three–two–one pattern antiphonally over an animated quasi-ostinato bass pattern; there is no basic difference, beyond that of scoring, between such passages and the fanfares of the *Sonata S. Polycarpi*. More than the varied and imaginative *Missa Salisburgensis*, this piece suggests an intent to overwhelm with sheer sonority, and therefore can be identified with the "colossal" ethic.

Stabat Mater à 4

SATB chorus and organ. Biber's *Stabat Mater* comprises four of the twenty verses of the medieval hymn (Nos. 1, "Stabat Mater," 3, "O quam tristis," 11, "Sancta Mater," and 20, "Quando corpus morietur" with Amen). It is preserved in score in the so-called "Wachskammer" collection of the Salzburg cathedral in a large volume entitled *Hymnus Buch* that preserves a total of six compositions, including three by Matthias Sigismund Biechteler

Example 6-5. *Lux Perpetua,* Ideo Elegit for Two Basses and Two Violins

and two anonymous works, all in score.[9] Biber's is the last piece in the book. Another copy, in parts, including organ continuo (not specified in the "Wachskammer" score) made in the eighteenth century, and with no essential differences, is preserved in the archive of St. Peter's in Salzburg.[10]

The *Stabat Mater* is a *stile antico* piece, comparable in style to the *Missa in Contrapuncto* and *Missa Quadragesimalis,* and sections of the *Missa ex B.* As in the Masses the meter is *alla breve* with fairly long note values (mostly quarter and half notes), breves and/or longs appearing at all four sectional cadences. The four sections are approximately equal in length (13, 16, 14, and 17 measures, respectively); and from their exaggerated note values at the cadences and the omission of the remaining verses we must conclude that these four verses were separated by verses sung in plainchant. And there appears to be some influence from the plainchant on a few of the themes, manifested chiefly in their contours, since the modes are different. It is more probable, however, that these slight resemblances can be attributed to the fact that this category of composition makes extensive use of traditional theme types that may appear in a wide range of church music in archaic as well as more modern styles. Virtually every theme in Biber's *Stabat Mater* falls under this heading. The "crucifixi fige plagat" melody, for example, combines characteristics of two familiar motives; one emphasizes a

Example 6-6. *Lux Perpetua,* Quasicanonic Duets

rising minor sixth and falling semitone, while the other is a well-known "crucifixus" theme of the time, embodied here, in the pitches E, D-sharp, G, F-sharp and presented, as it often was, in syncopated rhythm. The same four pitches underlie the "Stabat Mater" theme as well. On the other hand, the "O quam tristis" theme, whose main idea is the rising and falling semitone followed by a scalar descent, belongs to the same type as that of the Lacrimosa of the *Requiem in F minor* and the *Balletti Lamentabili,* as well as an "aria lamentevole" from *Chi la dura la vince* and the next piece in our discussion, the offertory *Quo abiit dilectus tuus* (also for the feast of the Seven Sorrows), to name but a few of a great number of compositions by Biber and others (ex. 6-7). At "corde meo" we find a subject of a "drooping" character frequently associated with the word "miserere"; Biber intensifies its affect by incorporating a syncopated rhythm and diminished-fourth interval.

Whereas the D minor tonality of the *Missa in Contrapuncto* and *Missa Quadragesimalis* descends from the most widely used church mode—the first (Dorian)—the E minor of the *Stabat Mater* has its roots in the Phrygian, by this time very closely associated with compositions of threnodic character. E minor is the key of the *Balletti Lamentabili,* as well as of the above-mentioned "aria lamentevole" and of *Quo abiit dilectus tuus.* Connections to the Phrygian mode, whose chief characteristic is, of course the semitone above the final, are by now confined to Phrygian cadences, which are too generally found in all modes and types of music to be given any special weight.

Example 6-7. *Stabat Mater à 4,* Themes

Offertorium: *Quo abiit dilectus tuus*

Four violas, four-part choir and soloists, basso continuo. The text of Biber's offertory for the feast of the Seven Sorrows of the Virgin is in part an adaptation of portions of the Song of Solomon such as were used as antiphons for the above-mentioned feast, in part a later poem that links the Old Testament text to the sorrowing of the Virgin. The church draws a parallel between the plight of King Solomon's deserted mistress and the grief of the Virgin whose son is crucified, a typical manifestation of the medieval belief in the foreshadowing of events in the New Testament by scenes in the Old. To match the sensuousness of his text, Biber created a setting rich in soloistic textures (fig. 6-3). The fourth section of the work, an "aria" of two only slightly varied strophes, comprises that portion of the text not taken from the Song of Solomon.

In two sections of *Quo abiit* the vocal parts are "accompanied" by a choir of four violas, without violins. Here, as in the *Requiem à 15,* the absence of violins means a corresponding lack of virtuoso writing for strings and of the high, bright sonority imparted to the tutti by the first violin. The solo for bass and strings that constitutes the third section of *Quo abiit* reveals this difference particularly well, since the combination of bass voice and elaborate, extraverted violin parts is one of Biber's most characteristic textures. In the "Ideo elegit" duet for basses and violins from the *Lux Perpetua,* for example, the voice parts are doubled by the basso continuo, while the violins perform "divisions" that outrival the voices. On the other hand, in the third section of *Quo abiit* the bass assumes far greater independence of the continuo; it avoids any "display" effects, such as the vocal flourishes in the "deposuit" solo of the *Vesperae à 32,* concentrating rather on expressing a key word of the text, "vincta" ("bound"), with syncopations and tied notes in madrigalesque fashion. Here and in general the violas ensure greater contrapuntal equality among the string parts than the normal string choir. The resultant fullness of sound mirrors the tone of the Old Testament parts of the text.

Compared to most solo sections in Biber's church music, the opening tenor solo of *Quo abiit,* although not long, is treated with a greater sense of breadth. Despite the brevity of its

Figure 6-3. Form of *Quo abiit dilectus tuus*

	Section	Measures	Form, Style, Texture
1	Quo abiit	28	Tenor solo with four violas & continuo; joined by soprano, alto and bass for last five bars
2	Ad montem	11	Alto & tenor duet with continuo
3	Dilectus	11	Bass, four violas and continuo
4	Fulcite	10	a) Soprano, strings & continuo (strophe 1)
	A tu Mater	11	b) Soprano, tenor, strings & continuo (strophe 2)
5	Amen	26	Ripieno chorus & strings

text, or perhaps because of it, Biber allows the setting to expand, to be carried forward by the contrapuntal momentum created by the principle theme of the violas and the falling-fifth harmonies (ex. 6-8). Although not at all operatic in tone, this section exhibits the kind of phrase structure that we have suggested was indebted to Biber's experience in opera. What is more prominent, however, and affective, is the sensuous character that is imparted to the line by the falling-sixth interval that enters with "O pulcherrima mulierum" and dominates the second half of the solo, entering finally in several solo voices. And the alto-tenor duet that follows draws its pictorial figures from variations on the viola accompaniment of the tenor solo ("ad montem myrrhae" and "propera") and the falling sixth ("haerebit").

The fourth section of the offertory, which resembles the arias in two strophes from *Chi la dura la vince,* ties some of these features together into a highly structured grouping of phrases. The text comprises a rhymed, metrical poem of undetermined authorship:

I	III
Fulcite cito floribus	A tu Mater maestissima
Illum malis stipate	Quae dum sub cruce stabas
Nam languet haec a moribus	Mandata nunc haec ultima
Salatia parate	A Filio captabas
II	IV
Succurrito discipule	In Filios nos suscipe
Nam Mater haec est tua	Tu Filiis nos offer
Succurre Matri miserae	Et signa tuae gratiae
Et lachrymantem iuus	O mulier hic confer

These four stanzas might have been composed in Salzburg, perhaps by one of the professors at the university who wrote Latin texts for the schooldramas. The first stanza is adapted from one of the antiphons from the feast of the Seven Sorrows of the Virgin (as the earlier parts of the text might have been) rather than directly from the Song of Solomon. In any case, it seems possible that the poem at least was written expressly for a musical setting. Biber faithfully observes the styles of prose and poetry in his setting, treating the prose with considerable freedom with respect to repeated words and phrases as well as occasionally melismatic writing, but utilizing completely balanced phrase units and syllabic style for the poem.

As in most of the arias of *Chi la dura la vince,* this "aria" divides into two virtually identical strophes; each of these can in turn be divided into five-bar halves, the first half

Example 6-8.   Beginning of Offertorium *Quo abiit dilectus tuus*

Example 6-9.   *Quo abiit dilectus tuus,* First Strophe of Fulcite Solo

cadencing on the relative major, the second on the tonic (ex. 6-9). Each half-strophe consists of four bars of vocal solo with continuo, and one concluding bar in which the strings echo the last measure of the vocal line. The vocal lines of each half-strophe then fall into two-bar units that are themselves composed of one-bar units. Each one-bar unit corresponds to one line of the poem. The two-bar phrase endings bring out the tonal logic of the cadences: dominant, relative major, subdominant, tonic. And in the second strophe the change in scoring outlines the phrase structure: tenor solo (first two-bar phrase); soprano solo (second phrase); tenor (third phrase); and soprano/tenor duet (fourth phrase). The final cadences of the two strophes and their echoing by the strings recall the endings of several arias from Biber's opera.

Because of its aria style, the fourth solo section of *Quo abiit* cannot fail to recall operatic procedure. Perhaps to restore a tone more appropriate to church music, Biber now closes the work with a ripieno, fugal Amen of greater than usual gravity. The principal theme, notated in half-notes and marked adagio, outlines a stepwise descending fifth, like that of the *stile antico* Christi of the *Missa S. Henrici,* while a more active upward-moving line provides a countertheme. On the whole *Quo abiit* can be said to exhibit a dynamic that moves from the sensuous, with powerful overtones of lamentation resembling the *Balletti Lamentabili* for strings of 1670 (both are in E minor), through an ever lighter approach to the text that is finally placed firmly within the perspective of a more conventional sacred atmosphere. No other work of Biber's has a strophic solo such as this one, and the work should probably be dated to the latter part of his career.

Offertorium: *Ne Cedite*

CCATB chorus and soloists, two violins, two violas, colla parte *trombones, basso continuo.* This work, entitled *Offertorium de S: Michaele. Archangelo.,* and preserved in the Salzburg cathedral archive, simply bears the ascription "Di Bibern." Karl August Rosenthal ascribed it

Example 6-10.   Comparison of Themes

(a) Theme of *Ne Cedite*, Final Movement

can-ta - - - te, can-ta-te, can-ta-te li - ba - te

(b) *Requiem in F Minor*, Quam olim Abrahae Countertheme

Et se - - mi-ni, se - - mi-ni e - jus

to Heinrich Biber on the basis of its setting, and the fact that the theme of the fugal last movement bears a very close resemblance to the "et semini ejus" countertheme to the Quam olim Abrahae fugue of the *Requiem in F minor* (ex. 6-10). *Ne Cedite* is a very attractive but not profound work, whose overall plan and style, as well as the evidence of copyist, watermarks and paper type, support Rosenthal's conclusion.[11]

   Ne Cedite and four other compositions discussed in this chapter have structures comprising several contrasted sections, one of which is a refrain that is heard twice in the work.[12] In all but one case (*Lux Perpetua*) the refrain is in triple meter and serves both as a contrast and a means of articulating a larger plan (fig. 6-4). *Ne Cedite* is constructed around the idea of two solo movements leading into or followed by the refrain and a third that leads into the concluding fugue. The composition begins with a solo for tenor and strings that announces the full text and musical basis of the "Ne Cedite" refrain, beginning with a "Devisen"-like echoing of the opening motto between tenor and strings (ex. 6-11). After the tutti refrain the second solo movement features the five vocal soloists, beginning with the sopranos and adding the alto, tenor and bass voices one by one on successive lines of the following text: "Nam Sanctus Michael, unus de Principibus primis, venit in adiutorium, qui animas in morte suscipit ut representat eas Judicio." It seems probable that the patterned entrance of the voices from top to bottom and the E-minor tonality of this movement are related to the image of souls being led to divine judgment (the entrance of the bass is reserved for the words "et representat eas Judici" [and leads them to judgment]. That this image was intended to be a consoling rather than terrifying one, however, is indicated not only by the refrain (Do not give your mind over to fear of death; the shield of the angel will deliver you to safety), but by the very optimistic tone of the words "sed signifer Sanctus Michael representat eas in lucem sanctam" in the two Requiems. The E minor, nevertheless, must recall Biber's use of that key for the affect of lamentation and, in the *Vesperae à 32* for associations of divine judgment. Probably a sense of severity that gives way to the joyful refrain underlies its appearance here.

   The penultimate solo section also moves from high to low voices, beginning with the sopranos and ending with the bass; but now the voices are introduced, overlapped and followed by homophonic writing for the strings. With the exception of the close of the bass solo and the string postlude leading back to A minor, this movement is in F major, a key that might have been chosen here, as in the *Vesperae à 32*, as a tonal counterpoise to E minor. Following the bass solo the strings, becoming more lively move via the circle of fifths to F, then close in A minor, setting up the exultant "Cantate libate, Festum celebrate" finale. In its plan as well as many individual details *Ne Cedite* confirms Heinrich Biber's authorship almost beyond the possibility of doubt.

Figure 6-4. Scheme of *Ne Cedite*

	Section	Meter	Measures	Key	Form, Style, Texture
1	Ne cedite	¢ 6/4	9	a	Tenor solo, strings, continuo.
			13		Tutti, "ne cedite" <u>Refrain</u>
2	Nam sanctus Michael	¢	19	e	SSATB soloists in order, basso continuo
3	Ne cedite	6/4	13	a	<u>Refrain</u>
4	Hinc munera date	¢	17	F-a	SSATB soloists with continuo, framed and punctuated by strings
5	Cantate libate		20	a	Ripieno fugue

Example 6-11. *Ne Cedite,* Beginning

Offertorium: *Huc Poenitentes*

CCATB chorus and soloists, two violins, two violas, three trombones ad libitum, organ and violone. Huc Poenitentes, also an offertory built around a refrain structure, is a more impressive composition than *Ne Cedite.* Now, in connection with the penitential theme (the work was written for the feast of St. Mary Magdalen, July 22), Biber sets the work in C minor, a key reserved for pieces with very particular lamenting affections in his work: the "Mount of Olives" Sonata and the similarly profound, chromatic, and rhetorically conceived sixth sonata from the *Sonatae Violino Solo,* the Crucifixus of the *Missa Catholica* (also chromatic), the *De profundis* of the *Vesperae per Annum necessarii,* the Offertory of the *Requiem in F minor,* and particularly serious moments between the two principal pairs of lovers in *Chi la dura la vince* (including chromaticism in one instance). Thus, although the tutti refrain, "Huc poenitentes animae," is set in triple meter and contrasts with the remainder of the offertory in this respect, it is contrapuntal in nature and its main theme has a descending appoggiatura figure built into its ascending sequences, and this "descent" character is common to almost all the major themes of the work, finally culminating in the somber and profound "quae non auferetur ab ea" final fugue (ex. 6-12).

The overall plan of *Huc Poenitentes* has features in common with that of *Ne Cedite* (fig. 6-5). Following a ripieno introduction of grave character, a tenor solo leads into the refrain. Next a solo section in contrasting meter featuring high voices at first (SSA *bassetgen* trio), then a

Example 6-12.   Offertorium *Huc Poenitentes,* Theme of Final Movement

quae   non au-   fe-   re-tur ab e- _ _ a

Figure 6-5.   Scheme of *Huc Poenitentes*

	Section	Meter	Measures	Form, Style, Texture
1	Introduction: Huc poenitentes	¢	10	Ripieno
	Offende preces	3/2	29	Tenor solo & strings
2	Huc poenitentes	3/2	19	Fugal tutti: <u>Refrain</u>
3	Ecce peccatrix foemina	¢	8	SSA trio
			7	Bass solo & violins
4	Huc poenitentes	3/2	19	Fugal tutti: <u>Refrain</u>
5	Nam sic Maria	3/2	16	Alto solo, later with bass solo
			7	Ripieno
6	Quae non auferetur	¢	13	Presto: ripieno fugue

solo for bass and violins, is followed by the refrain. The next solo group, again emphasizing lower voices (alto solo, then alto and bass) follows from the triple-meter refrain and moves to a ripieno setting that gives way to the presto *alla breve* fugue. Despite the obvious external similarities, the dynamic of *Huc Poenitentes* is, in fact, quite different from that of *Ne Cedite*. There is an equally strong sense of forward motion, but the work maintains an inner seriousness and intensity that is unmistakable in the final fugue; the great emphasis on C minor throughout the work belongs to this conception.

Huc Poenitentes is one of Biber's last works, if not the very last we have; and, as we have found in so many others, it features an extended solo with strings. In fact, Biber's last three offertories, *Quo abiit, Ne Cedite* and now *Huc Poenitentes* all have solos for tenor and strings at or near the beginning. In this case the tenor solo is worthy of closer examination, for it lends the work much of its character (ex. 6-13). The solo falls basically into two halves, in both of which the strings echo the first phrase of the voice. Here, however, there is no further patterning of the solo after the "Devisen-aria" beginning; and, in fact, the first section comprises an extension of the appoggiatura idea of "gementes dicite" that moves to G minor in a manner that—by means of its approach from E-flat and the juxtaposition of A-flat and F-sharp in the melodic line—gives it more of the "Phrygian" character of the mediant than of the dominant. The "gementes dicite" idea will come to serve as the basis for the "Huc poenitentes" refrain, and thus cast a shadow, so to speak, over the affective character of the offertory. The ending of this solo is particularly effective owing to the combining of the strings with the voice on the final phrase and the delaying of the final descent from a″-flat to c″ in the strings until the final cadence. The wonderful "decore" melisma imparts a very satisfying sense of completion

Example 6-13.   *Huc Poenitentes,* Tenor Solo

in its breaking the internal melodic sequence of the vocal line in bar thirty-five with a move up to the note f″, the highest tone in the solo—thereby underscoring the rhythmic accentuation on the second beat with the melodic contour—and from there descending nearly an octave and a half to c′. Prior to this point the note e″-flat seemed to have been designated as the upper melodic limit ("gementes," bar 18; "lacrymarum," bar 28), with the idea of descent as an inevitable result of its appearance. Now the voice, having pushed upward to the f″ and fallen to c′, makes a decisive cadence an octave higher ("ornatis"). In this detail, and in the final fugue, whose theme is subtly related to this passage, the appropriately dark and descending character of the C-minor melodies comes to suggest the positive outcome of repentance that constitutes the "message" of *Huc Poenitentes.*

Muttetum Natale à 6: In Festo Trium Regium

Two sopranos, two recorders, two oboes, and basso continuo. The *Muttetum Natale* is of special importance as a kind of piece that Biber must have composed more often than we know of. We have the names of an *Aria de Nativit[ate] Chr[ist]i D[omi]ni,* scored for alto and two recorders, and an *Aria de Passione Domini: "Wer gibt meinen Augen,"* for two recorders, two viole d'amore and three "instruments" (probably continuo), that are now lost. Beyond these pieces woodwind instruments appear only in Biber's *Sonata pro Tabula* (a choir of five recorders), the ritornelli of an aria from *Chi la dura la vince* (four recorders), the *Missa*

Example 6-14.   *Muttetum Natale In Festo Trium Regium,* Beginning of Alleluia Refrain

Salisburgensis (four recorders and two oboes) and the *Requiem à 15* (two oboes as *colla parte* instruments); a lost *Parthi à 3* for two recorders and bassoon is listed at Michaelbeuern.[13]

The scoring of the *Muttetum Natale* mirrors the event described in the text: for the arrival of the three kings to pay homage to the infant Christ, Biber paints a pastoral scene with the traditional shepherd's instruments. The choirboys who sing the soprano parts were probably intended to represent angels. For important processions in seventeenth-century Salzburg the choirboys were dressed as angels, and they are simply called "Engel" in contemporary descriptions of such processions. Quite possibly the boy soloists of the *Muttetum Natale* were so dressed. On one other occasion, the feast of the Holy Innocents (December 28), it was traditional in Salzburg (and elsewhere) to have the Mass sung by boys alone.[14] Works exclusively for high voices, such as Johann Caspar Kerll's *Missa S. S. Innocentium,* and even Masses by Michael Haydn reflect this practice.[15] The scoring for treble register instruments and voices in the *Muttetum Natale* creates an aura of innocence, just as the Et incarnatus of the *Missa S. Henrici,* while the consistent parallel thirds in the alternating vocal and instrumental pairs in the Alleluia refrain contributes to the effect (ex. 6-14). The work is one of Biber's most immediately attractive, often evoking the atmosphere of Monteverdi.

The *Muttetum Natale* makes greater use of repeated music than any comparable work of Biber's (fig. 6-6). Besides the Alleluia that comprises the first and penultimate sections, there is an adagio/allegro complex in the relative minor, and more or less at the center of the composition. The second soprano sings the adagio "Intrantes simul stabulum" with two recorders, then the allegro Alleluia, followed by which the first soprano sings the music of the preceding Alleluia section to a new text ("In hoc Natali"), accompanied now by oboes. There is an element of symmetrical construction in this work that, along with features of the tonal design, suggests Biber's mature style. The main C-major Alleluia refrain has a balanced structure that moves to the dominant in measure 9, stays in the dominant until measure 20, then returns to the tonic for the last 7 measures. The ground-bass second section is built around five statements in the tonic, five in the dominant and another five in the tonic. Then, after the relative-minor middle section, and the Alleluia refrain in C, the Doxology and Amen comprise a motivically integrated complex of three distinct tonal areas: F major for the plainchant "Deo

Figure 6-6. Scheme of *Muttetum Natale*

	Section	Meter	Measures	Key	Form, Style, Texture
1	Alleluia	₵ 3/4	27	C	Pairs of recorders, oboes & sopranos in parallel thirds, Allegro.
2	Tres Reges	₵	28	C/G/C	Fourteen statements of ground bass; two sopranos & continuo with recorders & oboes in last 4 bars
3	Intrantes	₵	9	a	Soprano 2, recorders & basso continuo. Adagio.
	Alleluia		12	a	Soprano 2, recorders & basso continuo
	In hoc Natali		12	a	Soprano 1, oboes & basso continuo. Same music as preceding twelve bars.
4	Alleluia	3/4	27	C	Pairs of recorders, oboes & sopranos in parallel thirds, Allegro.
5	Laudatur Sancta Trinitas	₵	13	F/C	Plainchant doxology. Sopranos in unison; recorders, oboes & basso continuo
	Amen		21	G/C	Imitative texture. Full scoring.

gratias" Doxology, G major for the main Amen section, and C major for the instrumental postlude, at the end of which the sopranos sing the single word "Amen."[16]

Litaniae Lauretanae

From the Vesperae Longiores ac Breviores, *1693, SATB chorus and soloists, two violins, two violas, continuo.* In any setting of a litany the composer faces the special problem of creating an overall form that does not become intolerably repetitious. Between the opening Kyrie and invocations to the Trinity and the concluding Agnus Dei, the *Litaniae Lauretanae* text as set by Biber (without the last four responses) comprises forty-five separate petitions to the Virgin Mary, each of course ending with the response "ora pro nobis." The problem is to overcome the structure of the text with a musical plan, and in a liturgically viable manner. In an age such as the seventeenth century in which so many church compositions exhibit sectional structures the task is especially urgent. The text itself offers something in the way of aid to the composer through its grouping of invocations under the several forms of address to the Virgin: e.g., beginning with "Sancta" (three), "Mater" (eleven), "Virgo" (six), and especially the eight "Regina" invocations at the end. Biber observes these divisions very closely, although not with absolute strictness, creating a long composition of about eight main sections.

Of these sections the most clearly delineated are the Agnus Dei and the immediately preceding section of the eight "Regina" addresses and responses. The Agnus Dei, as we might expect, is contrapuntally conceived, with separate themes for the Agnus Dei, the Qui tollis and the Miserere nobis; the Qui tollis theme is combined with the Miserere theme in the latter part of the movement, then the Miserere is combined with its own inversion, which ends the work. The preceding "Regina" section is integrated through Biber's use of a single florid "ora pro nobis" melisma that runs throughout the movement. The setting before these two movements is more loosely sectional but nevertheless follows a plan that is based on the idea of internal variation and gradual expansion in several musical dimensions of the work—above all themes, scoring and keys. A running commentary on the succession of musical events makes the underlying procedure clear. Following the block-chordal Kyrie (ending on the dominant), the

Example 6-15.   *Vesperae Longiores ac Breviores, Litaniae Lauretanae,* (1693), mm. 17–32

address to the Trinity begins soloistically, then moves to a ripieno setting; its theme is almost exclusively limited to the fourths and fifths of the tonic chord, while the harmony is built entirely on tonic and dominant chords. From the lower fifth that is stated several times in the soprano ("miserere nobis") the line gradually expands to encompass the upper fourth as well in an unmistakably introductory, almost intrada-like effect (ex. 6-15). The following section (the "Sancta" petitions) now emphasizes the upper fourth in the soprano, placing the first two responses in solo voices and instruments, the third in ripieno. The most interesting feature is the fact that the three responses all move to a firm G-major cadence after the E-minor address, while an appendage to the third one ends the section in E minor. The following section for varied solo textures not only moves strikingly in the direction of greater melismatic elaboration—ending with a virtuosic display for bass and violin (ex. 6-16)—it completes the modulation to G that was subordinated to the tonic in the earlier section. The next movement is back in the tonic for a ripieno setting of the "Virgo" invocations. Then another extended solo section on the string of invocations with varied texts—beginning with "speculum justitiae"— presents the dominant, tonic, relative major and seventh (or relative major of the dominant) in order before returning to the tonic. Finally, an adagio section of the simplest kind of block-chord homophony completes the ambitus of E minor with modulation to C major and A minor; this very moving turn to the subdominant side of the key sets the addresses to the Virgin as "healer of the infirm, refuge of sinners, consoler of the afflicted and aid to the faithful." Once again Biber associates modulation to the flat (or *mollis*) side of the key with weakness; to underscore the affect of this section the final cadence to the subdominant is made with the Neapolitan sixth. The contrast of this section with the subsequent ornate "Regina" invocations—which modulate extensively to the dominant—makes a striking effect. In short Biber's *Litaniae Lauretanae* makes a satisfying structure with a strong sense of inner logic; and once again the careful presentation of related tonal areas is a key to the success of an extended work.

Example 6-16.　*Litaniae Lauretanae, mm.* 60–64

Litania de S. Josepho à 20

Eight-part double chorus and soloists, two trumpets, three trombones, seven-part strings (Violin 1, Violin 2, Violas 1–5), and basso continuo. Our discussion of Biber's vocal music ends, fittingly, with a work composed, like the *Missa Salisburgensis* and the *Plaudite Tympana,* for an occasion of particular connection to Salzburg. St. Joseph was Salzburg's *Landespatron,* declared as such in the time of Max Gandolph (1676), and this litany is the earliest extant setting of a text that was set repeatedly in the eighteenth century.[17] The exact occasion for which the work was written is not known, but the records at Nonnberg for 1700 state that in that year for the first time the feast day of St. Joseph, "esteemed patron and father," was held as an "Abbtey-föst"; among the musical observances a Mass with trumpets was performed.[18] Litanies to various saints were frequently performed in the late seventeenth and early eighteenth centuries; the Nonnberg records for 1700, for example, mention concerted performances of several litanies in the first two months of the year (to St. Sebastian, St. Meinrad and the Virgin, among others).[19] Clearly litanies reflect much the same desire for a sense of nearness to the individual saints that was expressed in the immediacy of counterreformation art in general, and found musical expression in the composition of works for name saints. Possibly Biber's litany was linked in some way to the visit of Joseph I and his bride in 1699. In any case, the style and extravagant dimensions of the work, as well as the link to Joseph as patron of an ecclesiastical Austrian state, all fit with the Austrian nationalistic spirit of the time.

The origin of the text of Biber's litany is unknown. Perhaps the entire text was written in Salzburg for local use; apart from the opening Kyrie, the addresses to the Trinity and the Agnus Dei, the text is entirely different from the regular litany to St. Joseph. And the line "Sancte Joseph, clientum tuorum Salisburgensium tutor et patrone piissime" can only have been composed in and for Salzburg. In a number of respects the *Litania de S. Josepho* is remarkable: it is the only piece of Biber's to use trumpets in D rather than the almost universal C trumpets of the time and region; the string body with its five violas is the largest of any sacred work of the time; and the work is exceptionally long—over four hundred bars—with one single

Figure 6-7. Scheme of *Litania de S. Josepho*

Movement	Meter	Measures	Key	Form, Style, Texture
1 Kyrie	¢	25	D	Ripieno, double-chorus antiphony
2 Pater de coelis Deus		34	D	Short solo duets leading into full tutti (miserere nobis)
3 Sancta Maria sponsa Sancti Joseph	$\frac{3}{4}$	123	b/D	Vocal duets (SS, AA, BB, TT) with instruments, then alternating solo/tutti effects, all based on one main thematic idea
4 Sancte Joseph Christo nascenti praesens	¢	23	G/b	Soloists with strings, arioso style
In Aegyptum profuge		17	b	Ripieno fugue (SATB) with <u>colla parte</u> instruments
5 Sancte Joseph patriarcharum decus	$\frac{3}{4}$	73	D	Vocal duets (AA, TT, BB) with pairs of trumpets & violins, then tutti. Fourteen ground bass statements (5 in D; 5 in A; 2 in D)
6 Obiens inter bracchia Christi	¢	36	b/D	Rapid solo/tutti alternation. Chromatic harmonies & tempo changes.
7 Agnus Dei	$\frac{3}{2}$	58	D	Soloists leading into tutti
Miserere nobis		22	D	Double-chorus antiphony ending tutti

section attaining the length of 123 measures. The absence of cornetti here may represent a perception on Biber's part that these instruments were soon to become outmoded. In terms of vocal doubling the two "extra" violas serve as substitutes; that is, the upper three voices of each choir are doubled by strings (Choir I: Violin 2, Viola 2, Viola 3; Choir II: Viola 1, Viola 4, Viola 5), and the lower three of Choir I by trombones as well. In antiphonal passages for the instrumental choirs (e.g., section II) the trumpets and trombones play together, while violas four and five do not play with the string choir. Like the *Missa Bruxellensis,* this piece takes a step in the direction of the eighteenth century, but with generally greater success. The form of the work is outlined in figure 6-7.

Between the first two movements (Kyrie and address to the Trinity) and the concluding Agnus Dei/miserere nobis Biber divides the work logically into sections that deal with Joseph as spouse of the Virgin Mary (section III), Joseph as earthly father of Christ, a solo section to which is appended the traditional fugue with *colla parte* instruments, suggested here by the last word of the phrase "in Aegyptum profuge" (section IV), Joseph as patron of the church, minister to the Trinity, and the like (section V), and finally, Joseph in his particular relationship to Salzburg and his personal relationship to the individual (section VI). Several of these movements are noteworthy in ways that suggest that the piece belongs with Biber's last works. The very long third section preserves the style of vocal duets in all registers between the two choirs, with changing instrumental accompaniment for string and wind choirs, the grouping followed by the ubiquitous *bassetgen* trio, and leading into homophonic and quasi-fugal tutti. But a striking difference now is the integration of the entire movement by means of a highly patterned motive of a type found more often in the eighteenth century; associated appropriately with the words "ora pro nobis," this idea runs throughout the movement binding the various textural contrasts into one continuous entity. The fourth section opens as an arioso-like solo section with five-part string accompaniment (ex. 6-17). Beginning in the

Example 6-17. *Litania de S. Josepho à 20,* mm. 183–89

subdominant (G) to mark the shift to emphasis on the infant Christ (just as occurs in J. S. Bach's *Christmas Oratorio*), this section moves to the relative minor, ending on its dominant (F-sharp) in order to serve as a kind of prelude to the B-minor "in Aegyptum" fugue. The fifth section, back in D major, is built over a ground bass that contains within each bass unit two statements of the four-note "Mozart" theme that appears so often in Biber's music. Five statements in the tonic, five in the dominant, one back in the tonic and one mingling dominant and tonic comprise the entire bass line, while the four-note theme pervades the vocal and instrumental parts. Section VI begins with a tonal juxtaposition that Biber uses several times in this work: between the tonic and the mediant (with Tierce de Picardie). Now for the first time Biber cadences on the mediant via its dominant, but the section continues on to the dominant for several remarkable and often very quick alternations between a single solo voice and full choir; these distinguish the textual references to St. Joseph's connection to Salzburg. Finally, in an effect very like that of the C-major/A-minor section of the *Litaniae Lauretanae,* the fifth section moves to the subdominant (G) via the relative minor and prolonged Neapolitan harmonies in block chords (i.e., the subdominant of the subdominant) for those addresses to St. Joseph that deal with help in times of human suffering and death. We may recall the "miserere nobis" harmonies in the Agnus Dei of the *Missa Salisburgensis.* The section closes in the tonic, but these harmonies and some additional chromaticism set a subdued tone that continues to the end (marked piano) despite the entrance of the trumpets in the final bars. The Agnus Dei is a gently lyrical triple-meter movement of pastorale character with a static counter theme in dotted whole notes that was probably derived from plainchant (the static line is a further link to the *Missa Salisburgensis* [Et in unum]). The miserere is antiphonal between the choirs; its theme, a rising D-major scale that later falls to the fifth below and finally to the starting tone, is more optimistic and triumphant than entreating in tone; but as in the "propter magnam" of the *Missa Alleluia* and the Dona nobis pacem of the *Missa Bruxellensis,* Biber makes the successive entries fall by thirds to the subdominant before closing the work with a recollection of the "miserere" theme of the first movement.

The *Litania de S. Josepho* is, in short, a major work for the time and of pivotal importance in Biber's career in terms of its formal balance, the ease by which the movements are extended, and its unique expressive devices (in particular the rapid solo/tutti effects). The familiar recurrent movement types of the polychoral style—the *stile antico* fugue, equal-voice duets with instruments, ground bass movement, and the like—are all given a more logical overall relationship here than in any other work. The sense of integration in some of the movements is noteworthy; but we may well still feel the loss of the vivid pictorialism of the shorter sections in the *Vesperae à 32;* the newer style does not permit such a concentration on short-lived style juxtapositions. In the area of tonal organization, however, the litany makes unmistakable and necessary gains over the early works. Biber's *Litania de S. Josepho* is, in the final analysis, an exemplary work of the Austrian mid-baroque style.

Church Sonatas I: Compositions for Solo Violin

Of sixty extant independent sonatas by Biber, only five fall clearly outside the scope of this study: the *Sonata à 6 die pauern-Kirchfarth genandt*, *Sonata di Marche* (*Battalia*), *Sonata violino solo representativa*, *Sonata pro Tabula* and a *Pastorella*; there are in addition some twenty-five instrumental suites that have nothing to do with the performance of music in church. These works are excluded because of their obvious dance functions, their titles, reliance on secular programs or effects and their use of harpsichord continuo. The remaining fifty-five sonatas could have been performed in church, and some of them were unquestionably produced primarily for that purpose:[1]

1–16:	*Mystery Sonatas* (fifteen sonatas and one passacaglia)
17–28:	*Sonatae, tam Aris, quam Aulis servientes*, Salzburg 1676 (twelve sonatas)
29–36:	*Sonatae Violino Solo*, Salzburg 1681 (eight sonatas)
37–48:	*Fidicinium Sacro-Profanum*, Nuremberg 1682 or 1683 (twelve sonatas)
49:	*Sonata à 7*, 1668 (MS. Kroměříž)
50:	*Sonata S. Polycarpi* (1673: MS. Kroměříž)
51:	*Sonata Violino Solo* (after 1670: MS. Kroměříž)
52:	*Sonata* (solo violin; MS. Vienna, Minoritenkonvent)
53:	*Sonata à 6* (1673: MS. Kroměříž)
54:	*Sonata* (earlier version of No. VI of *Sonatae Violino Solo*; MS. Vienna, Minoritenkonvent)
55:	*Fantasia* (earlier version of No. IV of *Sonatae Violino Solo*; MS. Vienna, Minoritenkonvent)

In addition the following twelve works of uncertain authorship must be considered to varying degrees:

1. Two sonatas à 3 and a *Sonata à 4 violis*, all preserved at Kroměříž and ascribed to "H. B."[2]
2. Four anonymous ensemble sonatas at Kroměříž: *Sonata à 5*, *Sonata Paschalis*, *Sonata Jucunda*, *Harmonia Romana*. These works were ascribed to Biber by Paul Nettl.[3]
3. Five anonymous violin sonatas from manuscript 726 of the Minoritenkonvent in Vienna (nos. 4, 5, 6, 76, 81).

Many of Biber's sonatas are not easily categorized as "sacred" or "secular." The very term "church sonata" can be defined only with difficulty, since in seventeenth-century Austria musicians did not draw a sharp distinction between sonatas for court and for church, and very rarely employed the terms *sonata da camera* and *sonata da chiesa.* The designation "sonata," as opposed to "Balletti," "Arien" or "Partia" (the most common names for suites), does not indicate a particular function, since its usage was very broad. Besides its appearance in the titles of works such as the *Sonata di Marche,* which is obviously not a church sonata, the word often heads single movements, especially the opening movement of a dance suite, as well as instrumental introductions and interludes within vocal works (e.g., the *Vesperae à 32*). Nevertheless, when used by Biber and many of his contemporaries as the title of a work in several sections or movements, "sonata" usually indicates a composition containing few, if any, dance movements; when used to designate a single movement (usually the first) of a dance suite, it denotes a movement of nondance character.

Scoring is not a fully reliable criterion for determining which sonatas were performed in church, for church and court often shared the same instruments and instrumentalists. Nor does the presence of an organ continuo part always mean that a sonata served only sacred purposes (e.g., Biber's *Sonata pro Tabula*); the Salzburg court, like many others at the time, provided a positive organ exclusively for performances of court music; and the payment lists sometimes differentiate the court and cathedral organists. On the other hand, works with harpsichord (cembalo) continuo were usually not intended for performance in church. Among Biber's works, only dance music (Balletti, Arien) or obviously secular sonatas, such as the *Sonata di Marche* and the *Sonata à 6 die pauern-Kirchfarth genandt,* specify harpsichord continuo. Sonatas intended for performance in church are often easily recognized by their titles (*Sonata Paschalis,* and the like); similarly, sonatas intended for court performance often bear titles that reveal that fact: e.g., *Sonata à 5 per camera al giorno della corteggia, Sonata pro Tabula,* and so on. Many Austrian sonatas, however, are merely called "Sonata" or "Sonata à 5," etc. Those works entitled "sonata" that are actually dance suites, or that have a definitely secular and programmatic content unquestionably never accompanied church services; but the function of a great number of works remains unclear. In many cases it is probably safe to assume that a dual function was possible, if not actually intended. Schmelzer employs the title *Sonata per chiesa e per camera* in manuscript works; and he explains in the dedication of his published *Sacro-Profanus Concentus Musicus* (1662) that the sonatas contained therein serve sacred and secular purposes equally well.[4] The titles of Biber's collections *Sonatae, tam Aris, quam Aulis servientes* and *Fidicinium Sacro-Profanum, tam Foro, quam Choro,* as well as Schmelzer's *Duodenum Selectarum Sonatarum, tam Foro quam honesto Choro,* indicate the same double function.

There is even some justification for the belief than many seventeenth-century Austrian sonatas with unspecified function, especially polychoral sonatas and sonatas with wind instruments, were intended primarily for performance in church. Throughout the seventeenth century—and not only in Austria—the title "sonata" often means "church sonata" as opposed to *sonata da camera.* Legrenzi uses the word "sonata" in this sense in his Opus 4 (1656); he employs the term *sonata da camera* to designate a short movement that, like many of Biber's single-movement sonatas, serves as an introduction to a dance suite.[5] Thomas Balthasar Janowka mentions only the church sonata under the entry "sonata" in his music dictionary (1701); and in the same year, between his definitions of the *sonata da chiesa* and *sonata da camera,* Sebastian de Brossard wrote: "those [i.e., sonatas *da chiesa*] are what are rightly known as *sonatas.*"[6]

The broad musical traits that distinguish the church sonata from the chamber sonata (Balletti, Arien, etc.) in seventeenth-century Austria are those that differentiate sacred and secular music at that time. The church sonatas are more contrapuntal than the Balletti (with the exception of the many "sonata" opening movements of the latter), utilize organ continuo more often, and contain few movements headed with dance titles (although some composers, including Biber, introduced dance styles and even complete dances, not designated as such). The church sonata is almost always more serious and festive in tone than the chamber sonata, and therefore more often includes trumpets, trombones and cornetti. It is sometimes maintained in scholarly literature (and the *Mystery Sonatas* have been cited in support of the view) that the performance of dance movements in church music would not have conflicted with the spirit of seventeenth- and eighteenth-century Austrian Catholicism. However, although in the seventeenth century music, as well as the visual arts, was increasingly utilized as a means of asserting the glory of the Catholic church, dance music was not readily adopted for that purpose. Georg Muffat makes this clear when he notes in the preface to his *Auserlesene Instrumental-Music* (1701) that the works contained therein are unsuitable for church "because of the ballet airs and airs of other sorts which they include."[7] Whether or not Biber intended all of the *Mystery Sonatas* to be performed in church remains uncertain; they might have been used for private meditational and devotional rather than public liturgical purposes.

We are unfortunately not well supplied with information concerning the execution of church sonatas in the Salzburg cathedral. References to such performances are very general and subordinated to description of the liturgical festivities. We do know, from Nonnberg and from Italian treatises and publications from the early part of the century that sonatas (and organ music) were frequently played at the beginning and ending of services, as well as at favored places within the liturgy: after the Epistle (as substitute for the sung Gradual), in place of the Offertory, for the Communion and after the Postcommunion.[8] Janowka bears witness to the frequent playing of sonatas after the Epistle during the seventeenth century, a practice that is attested to in eighteenth-century Salzburg by Mozart's *Epistle Sonatas*.[9] As was the case with the vocal music, the most lavish sonatas would only have been played for the highest feasts involving the Archbishop himself. And these pieces, such as the *Sonata S. Polycarpi* and the introductory sonatas of the *Missa Christi Resurgentis* and the *Vesperae à 32*, remind us that the most exalted ecclesiastical offices within the church were held by men of noble birth, who were at the same time temporal rulers of high standing; the pomp of ecclesiastical celebrations and the splendor of the court festivities were two sides of the same coin. Aside from differences in scoring, there is little to differentiate the introductory sonatas of the *Missa Christi Resurgentis* and the *Vesperae à 32* from the opening sonata of Biber's *Balletti à 6*; the latter probably sounded while the archbishop and his distinguished retinue took their places at a court banquet or dance. In the preface to his *Sacro-Profanus Concentus Musicus* Schmelzer explains why he considered the dedication of his dual-function sonatas to Archduke Leopold Wilhelm so appropriate: the archduke was bishop of several dioceses as well as prince of the empire. At least in the time of Archbishop Max Gandolph, for whom most of Biber's sonatas were written, music was played at the court for sheer musical enjoyment; and Max Gandolph appears to have particularly enjoyed taking the court musicians to services in churches other than the cathedral.[10] The apparent decline in Biber's sonata production after the change to Archbishop Johann Ernst in 1687 undoubtedly reflects the fact that under this "unmusical archbishop" music was confined to special functions and performed less for its own sake.[11]

The *Mystery Sonatas*

Biber's sonatas for solo violin and continuo are by far the best-known, and most historically significant of all his works. Biber's exploration of the technical and expressive possibilities of the instrument had a far-reaching impact on practically his entire *oeuvre*. Although not all the violin sonatas have been published and studied, their style has been carefully examined from the technical point of view. [12] We may now concentrate on those aspects of Biber's violin music that best illustrate its relationship to the remainder of his church music, on those elements that help define both the general character of the church sonata in Austria and Biber's place in its development.

The *Mystery Sonatas* survive in a carefully prepared presentation manuscript with a small engraving of one of the fifteen mysteries of the Rosary affixed to the beginning of each sonata and a similar engraving of the Guardial Angel heading the final passacaglia for unaccompanied violin. [13] The original title page has been lost; the first page of the manuscript, inside a plain cover, contains the dedication to Archbishop Max Gandolph. Although we do not know the title of Biber's collection, we can be certain that it did not include the word "sonata," for in his dedication Biber uses this designation (along with Allemande, Courante, Prelude, and the like) only as an individual movement heading. Possibly the Virgin Mary's name formed part of the title, since Biber explains the connection between her name and Archbishop Max Gandolph's: their both beginning with the letter "M." [14] Since the collection was never published, it might have been a personal offering to the archbishop, perhaps Biber's first.

Unfortunately, the date of compilation of the set is undetermined. It might have appeared on the missing title page along with mention of Biber's position at the court, as it does in Biber's Salzburg publications. Scholarly opinion has tended toward placing the collection in the early to mid 1670s; the *terminus ante quem* is, of course, 1687, the year of Max Gandolph's death. Erwin Luntz, editor of the first modern edition of the sonatas, concluded from stylistic and technical evidence that the *Mystery Sonatas* preceded the *Sonatae Violino Solo* of 1681, an opinion with which I concur. [15] His suggestion that Biber was not well known at the time the manuscript was prepared, since he signed his full name to the dedication (and not to any of the subsequent prints) implies a date no later than 1676. Eugen Schmitz poses the possibility that the *Mystery Sonatas* were played in church during October, the rosary month, and that the passacaglia that ends the set sounded on the feast day of the Guardian Angel, October 2. [16] But according to an entry in one of the chapter protocol books for the year 1669 the feast of the Guardian Angel was celebrated on the first Sunday in September; this date might not have been firmly established at the time, however, since at different times it was celebrated at Nonnberg in October and September. [17] In any case the Guardian Angel feast was always celebrated as an octave. And the rosary month, too, was a deeply personal concern of Archbishop Max Gandolph's, since he founded a fraternity in honor of the name of the Virgin (celebrated on September 12) and the rosary, became a member of this brotherhood himself, and observed the rosary services very diligently. (Also in the early 1670s Max Gandolph built the pilgrimage church of Maria Plain.) The contemporary historian Joseph Mezger, who could have known Biber and Max Gandolph, alludes to these events in his chronicle for the year 1676 (the same year that St. Joseph was named *Landespatron* and a brotherhood founded in his honor), and associates Max Gandolph's strict observance of the special services of the rosary month with his love of church festivities, especially those involving the court musicians. [18] It seems possible, therefore, that Biber planned the dedication of the *Mystery Sonatas* to coincide with some special occasion involving the archbishop and the brotherhood of the Virgin; a plausible date would be 1676.

The fact that the manuscript of the *Mystery Sonatas* might have been compiled in 1676 by no means indicates that the sonatas were written around that time. Some of them were, no doubt; but it is likely that others, perhaps most of the set, were written at Kroměříž, just as were most of the *Sonatae, tam Aris, quam Aulis servientes*. We know of no particular taste for extravagant solo violin music, program music and *scordatura* on the part of Max Gandolph, whereas these devices were all sought for by Bishop Liechtenstein-Kastelkorn.[19] Biber certainly did not choose the subject of the fifteen mysteries of the rosary and then set about writing sonatas to illustrate them. If he had, the sonatas would exhibit much closer programmatic connections to their subject matter than they do. We are almost compelled, for stylistic as well as historical reasons, to conclude that a number of the *Mystery Sonatas* were conceived as separate works before the compilation of the manuscript. At least two sonatas are now known to have existed independently, although not necessarily before the set was assembled. In the Michaelbeuern inventory a *Sonata Paschalis. Surrexit Christus hodie* was listed; this piece was undoubtedly the eleventh of the *Mystery Sonatas* and, as the title reveals, it was associated with Easter, not the rosary. [20] Since this sonata is perhaps the most specific in the set in terms of the matching of music and program, it is quite likely that other sonatas had diverse origins. And the tenth sonata of the set (representing the crucifixion) survives in a late seventeenth-century manuscript at the Minoritenkonvent, Vienna, under Schmelzer's name, in a different key, and with an extra concluding movement; each movement bears programmatic headings that have nothing to do with the Crucifixion.[21] Quite possible others of the set existed in manuscripts and versions now lost. We know at least the intriguing titles of several lost sonatas by Biber that suggest the kind of violin writing found in the *Mystery Sonatas*: e.g., *Ciaccona Violino Solo* (no. 5 of the set is entitled *Ciacona*), *Sonata seu Lyra speculativa,* and *Sonata a violino solo artificiosa.*[22] Now that earlier versions of two of the *Sonatae Violino Solo* have surfaced (and the only two that feature *scordatura* writing) we know that Biber drew on older compositions more than once in compiling his publications. Bishop Liechtenstein-Kastelkorn's obvious delight at receiving a "Ciaconna ohne ferneres accompagniomento" from Schmelzer might be considered to provide a more valuable clue to the dating of the Passacaglia of Biber's collection than does the dedication to Max Gandolph.[23] The *Mystery Sonatas* then, may well date from Kroměříž, or in some cases even earlier.

The *Mystery Sonatas* are unique in the literature of the violin in two respects: the linking of the sonatas, via the engravings, to religious "programs" illustrating the five joyous, five sorrowful and five glorious events in the life of the Virgin; and the variety of *scordature* required for performance of fourteen of the sonatas (fig. 7-1). These two features are, of course, related: the *scordature* are a form of musical "mystery." In them "sound" and "script" are set in apposition again, in that the notation no longer visually resembles the sound it was designed to produce. In a number of sonatas Biber devised tunings to facilitate, or render possible, the execution of passages related programmatically to the affixed engravings. In such cases the association between musical and liturgical "mysteries" is unmistakable. Sonata eleven, corresponding to one of the greatest mysteries of the church, the resurrection, provides the most outstanding example. Here an Easter chorale played in octaves necessitates the following extraordinary *scordatura*: the A string is tuned down a fifth and the D string up a fourth, so that the former becomes a fourth lower than the latter; then the E string is tuned down a tone. The "mystery" of the tuning (g, g′, d′, d″) was so arcane in this sonata that Erwin Luntz printed the work with the wrong tuning.[24] Seven of the other *scordature* involve the tuning of the four strings to a single chord, and a number of others to open fifths and fourths, thus increasing the sympathetic resonance of the instrument for the programmatic passages; one sonata, the "Mount of Olives" has a deliberately dissonant tuning in keeping with its subject matter.[25] But in only a few of the solos does the music bear an indisputable relationship to the subjects of the engravings. Attempts—some more persuasive than others—have been made to reveal connections between music and program in many of the sonatas. But in many cases that has proven to be very difficult, if not impossible. If these works were intended by Biber to represent

Figure 7-1. Outline of the *Mystery Sonatas*

	Sonata and Program	Violin Tuning	Key	Movement Title and Types
1	The Annunciation	normal	d	Praeludium; Aria with variations; Finale
2	The Visitation	a,e',a',e"	A	Sonata; Allemande; Presto
3	The Nativity	b,f♯,b',d"	b	Sonata; Courante and double; Adagio
4	The Presentation of the Infant Jesus in the Temple	a,d',a',d"	d	Ciacona
5	The Twelve-year-old Jesus in the Temple	a,e',a',c"	A	Praeludium; Allemande; Gigue; Sarabande and double
6	Christ on the Mount of Olives	a♭,e'♭,g',d"	c	Lamento; $\frac{3}{2}$ section in Sarabande rhythm; ¢ Adagio; $\frac{12}{8}$ adagio; $\frac{8}{12}$ echo movement
7	The Scourging	c',f',a",c"	F	Allemande and Variation; Sarabande and three variations
8	The Crown of Thorns	d',f',b'♭,d"	B-flat	Sonata; Gigue and two doubles
9	Jesus Carries the Cross	c',e',a',e"	a	Sonata; Courante and two doubles; Finale
10	The Crucifixion	g,d',a',d"	g	Praeludium; aria and five variations
11	The Resurrection	g,g',d',d"	G	Sonata; Surrexit Christus hodie; Adagio
12	The Ascension	c',e',g',c"	C	Intrada; Aria Tubicinum; Allemande; Courante and double
13	Pentecost	a,e',c"♯,e"	d	Sonata; Gavotte, Gigue; Sarabande
14	The Assumption of the Virgin	a,e',a',d"	D	[Sonata]; Aria with twenty-nine variations (last nine variations called Gigue)
15	The Beatification of the Virgin	g,c',g',d"	C	Sonata; Aria with three variations; Canzone; Sarabande and variation
16	The Guardian Angel	normal	g	Passagaglia (sixty-five variations on the descending minor tetrachord)

more than what is conveyed by mood alone, that fact has yet to be convincingly demonstrated, and may be doubted in light of the literal character of some of Biber's program effects in other compositions.

As Biber indicates in his dedication, the *Mystery Sonatas* offer a great variety of single-movement types: "diversisque Sonatis, Praeludiis, Allemandis, Courent: Sarabund: Ariis, Ciacona, Variationibus, etc." Not specified in his list are Lamento, Gigue, Intrada, Gavotte and Canzona. Despite the diversity of its tunings and musical content, the set as a whole is still remarkably consistent, and different from the *Sonatae Violino Solo* and the *Harmonia Artificiosa-Ariosa*. Each of Biber's three collections of violin music bears its own distinctive formal and stylistic traits. The *Mystery Sonatas* are shorter than the pieces of the two later collections, and contain fewer, briefer movements. The violin writing in virtuoso passages is generally less capricious and improvisational, and less technically demanding than in the *Sonatae Violino Solo*; one might often call the former meditative in character, the latter brilliant and external. These terms are relative, of course: there are plenty of brilliant, external effects in the earlier set as well; and the C minor sonatas of both collections have remarkably similar passages that are meditative in character. But the *Mystery Sonatas* have always impressed commentators with their sense that even the obvious programmatic effects do not rest on a foundation of virtuosic display. The fact that many of the *Mystery Sonatas* do not belong to the "sonata" category at all (as Biber uses the term) accounts for much of the disparity in tone and style between the two collections. There is a markedly greater number of dance movements in the *Mystery Sonatas* than in Biber's published sonata collections, most of the pieces containing at least one, and often several dances. A few works consist of an introductory "sonata" or prelude followed by dance movements, and one consists entirely of an Allemande and Sarabanda (both with variations). Thus, some of the sonatas resemble Biber's dance suites, with significant differences: the dances are fewer in number, ordered freely, and often placed in relation to movements of nondance types.

The structures of some of the *Mystery Sonatas* suggest that they were recast from earlier works, both suites and sonatas. In the *Mensa Sonora* and *Harmonia Artificiosa-Ariosa* as well as the manuscript Balletti and Arien, Biber, while often varying the ordering of movements, still respects the norm for the suite at that time. No suite by Biber ends with a Sarabande, as do four of the *Mystery Sonatas.* In two cases a Gigue precedes the final Sarabande. If these works were composed at an earlier period, Biber might have altered the sequence of movements when compiling the set, perhaps in order to have the sonatas conclude with slow movements (as half the *Mystery Sonatas* do). In the process of preparing the collection Biber probably turned to a stock of pieces written at Kroměříž, perhaps even earlier, revised some movements, omitted some, changed the orders of others and added here and there a descriptive sonata, prelude or finale. Several of the *Mystery Sonatas,* however, reveal well integrated forms with no dance movements, and might have been conceived first and foremost for sacred use (e.g., the "Resurrection" sonata).

The most common type of single movement in the *Mystery Sonatas* is that designated sonata and used only as an opening section. It often discloses a two-part form: a slow introduction cadencing on tonic or dominant, followed by a somewhat longer Presto; occasionally part of the introduction returns at the conclusion of the Presto. The slow section usually features affective writing of rhetorical character often with motivic interplay between the violin and continuo; the tension created in the interaction of violin and bass is dissipated in the Presto, usually a movement of no more than lightly contrapuntal character, slower harmonic rhythm and violin figuration above a supporting bass. Sometimes the Presto resembles the fast section of a French overture, or the second movement of a Corelli church sonata. In one such case (Sonata II) entries in the continuo part ensure a four-part fugal beginning. In contradistinction to the sonata introductions the prelude type often concentrates on the spinning-out of violinistic figuration, sometimes highly motivic in character (Sonatas V and X), sometimes formed of nonrepetitive flourishes and swirls in thirty-second notes (Sonata I). Elements of the prelude style pervade a few of the Sonata introductions as well, one of the latter resembling a prelude more than a sonata (no. XI).

It is chiefly in these opening movements that musico-descriptive associations with the engravings appear. In some cases we recognize the programmatic effects immediately: no one knowing the subject matter could fail to connect the echo patterns of the "Resurrection" Sonata (no. XI) with the empty tomb, or the Intrada and Aria Tubicinum of the "Ascension" Sonata (no. XII) with the arrival or departure of a great personage (the Intrada) and the subsequent representation of Christ in glory (the Aria Tubicinum resembles the fanfare music for six trumpets and two basses at "qui sedes" and "quoniam" in the *Missa Alleluia*). Other less obvious—and less certain—pictorialisms appear. The swirling thirty-second notes in the prelude and finale of the first sonata probably represent the angel of the annunciation. Imitation and dialogue between violin and continuo in the first and last movements of the second sonata (the Visitation) are appropriate to the suggestion of dialogue between Mary and her cousin. The arresting rising-fourth motive and dotted rhythm in the prelude of Sonata III

Example 7-1. *Mystery* or *Rosary Sonatas,* Excerpts from No. VI ("Mount of Olives")

Example 7-2. *Mystery Sonatas,* Beginning of No. XIV ("Assumption of the Virgin")

(a call to attention) fits with the engraving of the twelve-year-old Christ in the temple, seated behind a desk like a teacher. Arnold Schering gave a convincing interpretation of the Lamento first movement of Sonata VI ("Mount of Olives") as a description in tones of Christ's meditation and prayer on the night of His betrayal.[26] The drooping melodies depict Christ's sorrow, while the combination of chromaticism and the well-known "organo tremolante" effect conveys a melancholy religious intensity (ex. 7-1). The Presto section of Sonata IX suggests the pushing of the crown of thorns down onto Jesus' head. In the first movement of the ninth sonata the close interplay between violin and continuo, and the ascending/descending melodic patterns appear to be subtly related to the subject of the sonata (the carrying of the cross). Almost certainly the rapid thirds and sixths of Sonata XIII depict the great wind of Pentecost, while a long rising pattern in Sonata XIV portrays the assumption of the Virgin (ex. 7-2). And the rainbow-shaped "flying staccato" patterns at the end of the last sonata were no doubt associated with the crowning of the Virgin, as shown in the engraving.

The greater popularity of Sonatas VI ("Mount of Olives"), X ("Crucifixion") and XI (Resurrection) can perhaps be explained by the fact that their every movement contributes to a prevailing mood. The Lamento of the "Mount of Olives" Sonata casts its shadow upon the rest of the work. Although Biber employs dance styles, he transforms them into vehicles of elegiac and melancholy affections, carrying musical figures and gestures of unmistakably threnodic import. Between the two dance-like passages Biber introduces a passionate and profoundly expressive interlude that adopts some of the chromaticism of the Lamento. In Sonata XI the first movement depicts the empty tomb, the second contains a set of variations on the Easter hymn "Surrexit Christus hodie," and the third imitates the style of a congregational hymn.

Ironically, the only one of the sonatas to survive in a second manuscript copy, the "Crucifixion" sonata, is preserved under Schmelzer's name. Several of the movements bear

Example 7-3. *Mystery Sonatas,* Final Movement of the Vienna Version of No. X ("Crucifixion")

programmatic titles concerning, not the Crucifixion, but the Turkish siege of Vienna in 1683. The Praeludium is headed "Der Türcken Einmarch," the aria "Der Türcken Belägerung der Stadt Wien," the first variation "Der Türcken stürmen," the third variation (Adagio) "Einmarch der Christen," the fourth variation "Treffen der Christen," and the final variation "Durchgang der Türcken." In addition, this copy contains a concluding movement, headed "Victori der Christen," in homophonic, song-like style consisting of two four-bar periods, each subdivided into clearly marked two-bar phrases. The violin plays mostly in double stops (ex. 7-3). This movement might well have been a setting of a popular melody of the time, one perhaps associated with the defeat of the Turks; it is marked to be repeated three times, an indication, perhaps, of a strophic text. The Vienna version of the sonata is in A minor, a tone higher than the Munich copy; the notation of the basso continuo is in A minor, of course, but that of the violin part does not differ from the Munich version; the *scordatura* is simply set a tone higher. The Vienna score also includes (obviously correct) adagio tempo indications before the Praeludium and the Aria that are lacking in the Munich manuscript.

There is no dispute over the authorship of this sonata; Schmelzer died three years before the defeat of the Turks and the program titles are not really appropriate to the styles of most of the movements. Nevertheless, a number of factual questions arise concerning who gave the movements their titles, who composed the final movement, and when these were done. The dating of the titles can be temporally circumscribed at least; the siege referred to is that of 1683, while the manuscript was copied around the end of the seventeenth century.[27] It hardly seems possible that Biber himself supplied the titles; if we compare the Vienna copy with a well-known battle piece of his, the *Battalia,* or *Sonata di Marche,* we find that Biber had developed a set of techniques for the military style, none of which appears here. The final movement might suggest, however, that the sonata had an origin older than its association with the Crucifixion, although we do not know whether or not this movement was written by Biber.

However, a more important question is highlighted by the existence of the Vienna copy of the "Crucifixion" Sonata: namely, the broader issue of programmatic intent in the *Mystery Sonatas* and its relationship to musical "allegory" as a reflection of spiritual values in the seventeenth century. Although Biber is, as we know, capable of the most literal representation of extra-musical events, and some such pictorialism certainly crop up in the *Mystery Sonatas,* the works have often been praised for their "tasteful" avoidance of such devices. This attitude, which seems, in fact, to be a backhanded compliment, has some validity. And the suggestion made above, that the relatively restrained concentration on musical depiction might be owing in part to the possible origins of some of the sonatas as compilations and reworkings, is intended as a speculation regarding their origins, not as an explanation of their representational qualities. Most of the sonatas are decidedly less "pictorial" than Kuhnau's *Biblical Histories,* with which they are often associated. At the same time, there are quite a number of effects of quasi-allegorical character that bear no obvious relationship to the programs: such, for example, are the echo effects over a dominant pedal at the end of the ninth sonata; the short echo passages in the violin that end the "Mount of Olives" Sonata; the

Ciacona structure of the third sonata; and, of course, the many figurational patterns that appear in the arias with variations and the dance doubles.

This last category of movement in the *Mystery Sonatas,* by far the most common in terms of musical technique, is a large part of the reason for the success of the sonatas. There are three main types of variation movement: dance doubles, arias with variations and ostinato bass variations. The violin figurations in some of the variation movements might have been intended to relate to the program in question: in the concluding Sarabande grouping of the seventh sonata (the scourging), for example, the active patterns of the first and third variations could be said to represent the whipping, while the totally contrasted oscillating figure in the second variation suggests the throbbing pain. More often than not, however, no such association is possible, yet the figuration still stands forth with a very sharp profile. But even the invention of figurational patterns is not the most important feature. Many of the doubles in particular are often written in steady note values (quarters, eighths or sixteenths) and from the visual standpoint they appear to be rhythmically, figurationally and melodically monotonous. To look at these movements it would be difficult to maintain that, in view of their almost abstract character, they could have a role in representing a program, even when in some cases successive doubles are cast in a form of "dynamic crescendo" of progressively shortening note values. What happens in such movements, however, is the main key to Biber's achievement in the *Mystery Sonatas*: the constant asymmetrical shifting from register to register and string to string in virtually unchanging note values creates "melodies" and harmonies that can be apprehended by the ear alone. The eye does not grasp all the performance factors that breathe life into the style; visualisation, which otherwise dominates musico-allegorical devices, is out of the question altogether in these passages. There is, in fact, an element of sheer sensuality in Biber's sonatas that is related to the idea of immediacy in counterreformation art that we have introduced in connection to the vocal works. And this quality—the true meaning of the "pizaria" that Bishop Karl Liechtenstein-Kastelkorn admired so much—is related to the sense of artifice that Biber mentions in his preface and that underlies titles such as *Harmonia Artificiosa-Arioso* and *Sonata seu Lyra speculativa.* The violin represents the sphere of human expression in which the desire for higher meaning is played out in quasi-dramatic fashion. The general allegorical character (echo effects and the like) that arises from the sensuous nature of instrumental technique and that might (or might not) be linked directly to extra-musical events, reflects the fact that in counterreformation art transcendent meaning might be uncertain but is never detached from the physical. This is perhaps the deep underlying mystery of Biber's *scordature.* And the constant watchfulness of the Guardian Angel, symbolized by the ostinato of the final Passacaglia, is a wonderful expression of the desire for physical nearness to the other world, the same impulse that prompted the composition of litanies to the saints and the love of visual representation in the southern baroque churches. [28] In the *Mystery Sonatas* Biber's great achievement is to have extended this quality to the ear in a symbolic fashion.

Sonatae Violino Solo, 1681

Judging from the number of extant copies, the *Sonatae Violino Solo* must have been Biber's best-known and most widely-circulated collection. [29] It was largely on the basis of these sonatas that Biber's reputation as a violinist persisted well into the eighteenth century. Quantz played them as a student and Burney knew and praised their technical accomplishments. [30] Besides their availability these sonatas offered the great advantage over the *Mystery Sonatas* of the normal violin tuning in six of the eight solos: the fourth sonata is in *scordatura,* while the sixth begins with the normal tuning but demands that the E string be retuned a tone lower in the middle of the piece. The last sonata, as if a trio sonata, features a two-stave violin part to be played, of course, on a single instrument. It is no longer possible to consider the presence or absence of *scordatura* a criterion for the dating of Biber's violin works; the early Vienna *Fantasia* demands a *scordatura* tuning, as do some trio sonatas from Biber's last publication, the *Harmonia Artificioso-Arioso* (1696).[31] Still, it may be noted that the two sonatas of the set that are known to descend from earlier versions are the two that feature *scordatura* as well as two of the three that have dance movements. The publication of the *Sonatae Violino Solo* reflects Biber's desire to have a representative collection of his violin music in print, one that would establish his reputation; he had played some of the solos for Emperor Leopold with great success and planned on the strength of those performances to petition the emperor for knighthood.

The *Sonatae Violino Solo* are less rich in sonority than the *Mystery Sonatas*; the *scordature* of the latter often produce enormous alterations in the tone of the violin; in this respect they remind us of the viola d'amore that Biber also played and one composition for which survives in the *Harmonia Artificiosa-Arioso*. The viola d'amore was a six-stringed instrument with a "normal" tuning in fifths, that was apparently played only in *scordatura* in Salzburg. The full register and sympathetic metal strings beneath the fingerboard gave it an extraordinarily rich, shimmering sonority that Biber certainly exploits in the surviving *Partia*. But this is basically not the world of the *Sonatae Violino Solo,* which exhibit more the qualities singled out by Burney: fantasy and technical difficulty. There is much more of the virtuoso in evidence in these works; and the virtuoso element has a great deal to do with the structures as well as the styles of the sonatas. These sonatas offer much in the way of improvisatory passage work of various kinds; they contain few dance movements (a total of three) and dance variations, but a relatively large number of lengthy variations on short ostinato basses: "bassi ostinatissimi," in Adler's words.[32] They are also considerably longer on the average than the *Mystery Sonatas,* and reveal greater tendencies toward the development of consistent formal principles in the solo violin sonata.

One of the regular constructive devices of baroque music, the alternation of "strict" and "free" styles, governs the successions of movements in the *Sonatae Violino Solo* ("closed" and "open" might often be a more accurate way of describing the juxtaposition). The term "free" here denotes a marked emphasis on improvisational style with much latitude in the handling of meter, rhythm, form, and even key. Movements in this style appear in three basic functions: introductions (sonatas and preludes), transitions, and finales. The "strict" movements of the collection comprise chiefly dance movements, sets of variations, or combinations of both (dance doubles, passacaglia, chaconne). They are more self-contained and integrated in terms of the above-mentioned musical aspects, less recitative- or toccata-like and impulsive. With these types as a guide we can see that the movements of the individual sonatas often alternate between the two in a manner that is not very different in principle from the alternation of recitative and aria in the cantata.

Sonata I	(A major)	A: three sections, sonata/prelude complex
		B: ostinato bass variations
		C: finale
Sonata II	(D minor)	A: prelude
		B: aria with variations
		C: finale

Sonata III	(F major)	A: sonata/prelude
		B: aria with two variations
		C: transitional section
		D: ostinato bass variations
		E: finale

Sonata IV	(D major)	A: sonata
		B: gigue and two doubles
		C: sonata-like transitional section
		D: aria with variations
		E: finale

Sonata V	(E minor)	A: sonata
		B: ostinato bass variations
		C: sonata-like transitional section
		D: aria with variations

Sonata VI	(C minor)	A: fugue
		B: passacaglia
		C: transitional movement
		D: gavotte and double
		E: transitional movement
		F: finale

Sonata VII	(G major)	A: sonata/prelude
		B: aria with variations
		C: transitional movement
		D: ciacona

Sonata VIII	(A major)	A: sonata in two sections
		B: aria with variation
		C: sarabande
		D: transitional movement
		E: gigue-like finale

These sonatas give an obviously central place to variation movements; even two of the three dances are varied with doubles. As in the *Mystery Sonatas* the variation movements fall under three types: dance doubles (two), arias with variations (six) and ground bass variations (five, one of which is a passacaglia, another a ciacona). Generally the ostinato bass sets are longest, but based on the shortest themes, often of elemental character. The four-bar ostinati of Sonatas I, III and VI (passacaglia) occur fifty-eight, thirty-one and twenty-five times, respectively; the last of these appears in different forms and keys and the movement includes four eight-bar interludes as well as a thirteen-bar coda. The eight-bar ground of Sonata V is stated thirteen times, and the twelve-bar pattern of Sonata VII (ciacona) six (including a final da capo of the ciacona). The dances with doubles, varied once or twice, make up the shortest variation movements, while the arias average about four statements. Two of the sets of aria variations conclude with contrapuntal sections: in Sonata IV the aria theme ends up in canon between violin and continuo; and the two sections of the binary-form aria theme of Sonata VII combine in double counterpoint in the third variation, while in the fourth they appear as subject and countersubject of a fugue that in several places includes three stretto entries of the subject in the solo violin alone. The ground bass types (usually called Variatio), on the other

Example 7-4.   *Sonatae Violino Solo* (1681), Beginning of Sonata III

hand, are founded on elemental harmonic progressions that crystallize in the bass patterns and include refrain-like melodic elements that return to punctuate, even to interrupt, the momentum of the violinistic elaboration. In two cases (the first and third sonatas) the momentum remains so strong that the variations lead into the finales.

Characteristic of the improvisatory movements are pedal tones (usually tonic pedal at the beginning of the work; dominant or, more often, subdominant at the end), brilliant scalar passage work covering the entire range of the instrument up to the seventh position, sudden changes of rhythm and tempo of rhetorical character, toccata-like chromatic figures, a capricious attitude towards the development of motives, key changes, and the like. While pedal tones appear in the majority of such sections, other elements are incorporated according to the function of the movement. Frequent key changes occur most often in the transitions, while the finales concentrate on impelling momentum with the aid of precipitous toccata-like figures (Sonatas II and VI), rapid alternation of tonic and subdominant (Sonatas I, III, V) and *stile concitato* (Sonata III). A number of the opening movements resemble the sonata and prelude types encountered in the *Mystery Sonatas,* although they are generally more technically elaborate. Occasionally Biber creates a complex of both types. The first sonata begins with three balanced sections: a prelude in which the violin indulges in "display" figuration (thirty-second note passage work, arpeggiation) over a tonic pedal; a "sonata"-type movement with an Adagio/Presto/Adagio plan; finally, a gigue-like movement of the type used elsewhere by Biber as the fast section of a slow/fast sonata movement. From this description it can be sensed that the *Sonatae Violino Solo* is a very ambitious collection in which the dialectic of the totally fantastic and the controlled is central to the overall intention.

Commentary on the third sonata will help to concretize these general remarks. The work begins with a movement that features two contrasted styles: the first comprises a harmonically static "echo" idea that gives way to a Presto elaboration of its main motive, with slightly expanded harmonic scope (ex. 7-4); and, framed by two appearances of this first idea—the second one considerably expanded—is a section of thirty-second-note passage work such as is often found in these sonatas. The second appearance of the first idea builds dynamically towards its final cadence, then breaks off abruptly on a weak beat, with alternation of tonic and subdominant, an idea that will reappear at the end of the sonata. Following the shortest set of aria variations in the collection (in the tonic, F major), the flat drops out of the key signature and the violin begins the central transitional movement with intense Presto arpeggiation of an A-major chord, forming a short section ending Adagio in A minor. Moving up another third to C, an Allegro of still more intense character gradually gives way (after a strong dominant cadence) to a more relaxed D minor (with Tierce de Picardie), then to G minor and, finally, via

Example 7-5. *Sonatae Violino Solo,* Ending of Sonata III

another Adagio to F major. Back in F (with one flat restored) one of the longest of the ground-bass variations begins, above a four-note "basso ostinatissimo." Twice the violin figuration builds dynamically, and twice the *Grave* chaconne-like refrain melody returns to break the momentum. The third time the music following the refrain is marked Adagio, a mere oscillating third (a′ to f′) at first, but expanding in register and building to *stile concitato* repeated notes of a penetrating insistence that are restrained only by the oscillating eighth-note pattern. Finally the variations come to a halt and the oscillation moves into the bass, with eighth-note alternation of the subdominant B-flat (on the beat) and the tonic F (off the beat) from here to the end. Above this the violin breaks loose finally, with nothing but the note f″ at first, more penetrating than ever as it moves to a thirty-second-note rushing climax of uncontrollable ecstatic abandon (ex. 7-5). The final cadence can hardly be called that at all; nowhere else in the violin literature of the age does such an abrupt halt appear, the violin leaping down almost two octaves to end with the basso continuo on the third of the chord, on the weak part of a weak beat, at the peak of its exaltation.

It seems anticlimactic to state now that this music, which seems at the end to be making an attempt to break the bonds of the rationalistic age in which it was conceived, is also a music of some considerable planning. The subdominant that takes over in the final section (not only in the metrical accents but in the final violin rush, with its carefully indicated E-flats) can, of course, be related to the plagal cadences and subdominant pedals of the other sonatas, even if the sense of resolution on the tonic is far more tenuous here.[33] And, in terms of the keys of the sonata as a whole all those that constitute the ambitus of F are included: F, g, a, B-flat, C and d; the B-flat has to wait until the final section to make its presence, although the alternation of F and B-flat at the beginning of the sonata might be said to prefigure its appearance, just as the abrupt ending of the opening section fits by hindsight into an overall design. But even though the elements that go into this piece can all be brought under rational control, Biber goes out of his way to stretch his points: the move from F to A minor for the transitional section, for example, is done by means of the sudden entrance of four bars of aggressively agitated A-*major* chords. In a work such as this the verbal metaphors that come to mind are inevitably religious rather than those of, say, the sphere of the secular drama. We might speak, for example, of the failure of the two rational attempts at climax within the variations, as opposed to the irrational elation of the final aural apotheosis.

A work of quite a different character is the magnificent, rhetorically conceived sixth sonata in C minor that, judging from the number of editions, versions and recordings, has always been the most popular work of the set. This piece projects an affective sphere dominated by a heavy baroque lamentation that is unmistakably cast from the mold of conventional figures, and assembled in highly rationalistic fashion. In this sense the sonata is

Example 7-6. Comparison of Passacaglia Themes

(a) Violin Theme of the "Passagagli" of the Vienna Version of *Sonatae Violino Solo,* Sonata VI

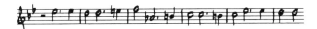

(b) Violin Theme of the Passacaglia, *Sonatae Violino Solo,* Sonata VI

far less original sounding than the F-major sonata; the composer's task, achieved brilliantly here, is to rise above mere conventional figures to a higher, even if still rhetorical plane of expression. In light of this "public" character the C-minor sonata is best approached through its external features, of which easily the most unusual is an "Accordo" indication that appears between the second and third movements, requiring the violinist to lower the pitch of the E string by a tone. In the 1620s Biagio Marini had written a work demanding the retuning of the E string a major third lower during seven measures of rest and its later return to the normal tuning during six measures of rest. Biber's "Accordo" is much less difficult than Marini's since it allows the change to be made between movements, necessitates a lesser degree of alteration, and retains the *scordatura* for the remainder of the sonata. Marini called for the altered tuning to enable the violinist to execute a passage of rapid parallel thirds.[34] And Biber had devised a *scordatura* with a third between the upper strings (and a sixth between the lower) for a similar purpose in the thirteenth of the *Mystery Sonatas.* But no such explanation comes immediately to mind for the *scordatura* in the sixth of the *Sonatae Violino Solo.* On first glance it appears that the only gain for the player is the capacity to play some three-note chords with the note d′ as the highest; apart from these the last four movements can easily be played on a normally tuned instrument. With the introduction of the new "Accordo," however, comes a change of key that renders these chords—especially D major and G minor—more frequent; the third and fourth movements, a "free" section and a Gavotte, are in G minor, the key of the "Crucifixion" *Mystery Sonata,* which utilizes the same tuning. The fifth section then returns to the original key signature and C-minor tonality, but the *scordatura* remains.

Change of key of this type—that is, not merely within the framework of an improvisatory section, but as the new tonic of one or more closed movements—occurs, as we know, very rarely in the church music up to this point; and it appears in only one other place in the *Sonatae Violino Solo*: the aria and variations of the last sonata are in the dominant.[35] It is unlikely, therefore, that the change of key was prompted primarily by tonal-architectural considerations. In light of all we know of the history of this sonata, an external factor comes to mind in the partial derivation of the work from an early sonata of the Vienna manuscript. The manuscript sonata contains two movements only, both in C minor. Except for an adagio tempo marking, a few slight variants in the figured bass, and the absence of a few trills, the first movement of the Vienna copy is identical to the opening movement of the present work. The second movement in the Vienna copy is a C-minor "Passagagli," marked adagissimo, but not the same passacaglia as the second movement of the printed sonata; even the two ground basses are different, although their rhythmic characters (continually accented second beats) and a certain similarity between the opening violin themes of the two movements may be more than coincidental (ex. 7-6). The manuscript work bears no date, but certain factors suggest that it was written earlier than the published sonata. The violin part of the "Passagagli" makes considerably fewer technical demands than most movements of either the *Mystery Sonatas* or the *Sonatae Violino Solo*. It requires no double stopping at all, and extends beyond first position only in the brief concluding cadence; within the limitations of register, some rather difficult string crossings are required now and then, but the somewhat crude style of the counterpoint between violin and bass in a few places invites the opinion that, like the version of the third of the *Sonatae Violino Solo* from the same manuscript, this piece was written at least before Biber's Salzburg years, if not much earlier.

Following the heavily laden opening lamento, the passacaglia of Sonata VI conveys a sense of measured restraint and dignity, almost a sense of moderation of the kind we associate with French baroque music. The movement, in fact, recalls Georg Muffat's style in many features. Such, for example, are the passacaglia-bass type—the rising fifth in minor—the regular modification of the ground bass and the overall modulatory plan in which the ostinato is relieved by free episodes:

a)	40 bars:	Ten statements of the ground in C minor; violin theme varied four times, the ground itself three
b)	8 bars:	Free interlude with violin passage work; modulation to G minor
c)	16 bars:	Four statements of ground in G minor; three variants of theme and ground
d)	8 bars:	Free interlude with violin passage work; ends on dominant of E-flat
e)	16 bars:	Four statements of ground in E-flat; three variants of violin theme and ground
f)	8 bars:	Free interlude; violin passage work; modulation to C minor
g)	8 bars:	Two versions of theme and ground in C minor
h)	8 bars:	Free interlude; violin passage work; ends dominant of B-flat
i)	20 bars:	Five versions of ostinato (B-flat, G minor, C minor, E-flat, C minor); chromaticism in all forms of ground
j)	13 bars:	Coda in C minor; violin passage work; chromaticism at cadence

There is also a lute version of this "new" passacaglia at Kremsmünster in a manuscript that contains only French titles and includes a Muffat passacaglia as well. The lute form of Biber's work has been called a "rewriting rather than an arrangement" of the original, since not only do idiomatic lute patterns transform the violin and continuo parts, but the structure is completely altered, in an equally patterned manner.[36] Now the work comprises a sequence of twenty repeated units ranging from four to twelve bars in length; the arranger follows some passages of the violin sonata fairly faithfully, while with others he adds or omits a few bars. The tonal plan reveals a drastic modification; Biber's complicated harmonic structure is relinquished in favor of a form of tonal ABA plan: the first six units (28 measures) are in C minor, the next nine (54 measures) in G minor, and the last five (26 measures) in C minor. The Kremsmünster version is most likely a very free adaptation made by someone other than Biber from the printed edition, but in light of the resemblance between its tonal plan and the overall plan of Sonata VI we cannot dismiss the possibility that another (presumably earlier) version by Biber served as its model. It is quite possible, therefore, that the change of tuning in Sonata VI reflects a complex origin that might involve two works in C minor and G minor (the Gavotte), the latter a *scordatura* sonata or suite.

But the suggestion implicit in this last remark, that the form of Sonata VI may be judged or even illuminated by its origin, is not our intention. Rather, we note that the manuscript and printed sonatas share a conception that justifies to some extent our describing the former as a "version" of the latter: a fugal lamento built on three figures that are "identifiable" within the

Example 7-7. *Sonatae Violino Solo,* Excerpt from Sonata VI (Transcribed from *Scordatura*)

context of Biber's music, and that of the age generally, sets the tone for a mournful dance of the type that is known from pieces such as the opening movements of Bach's *St. Matthew Passion* and Cantata 78, not to mention the many funeral dance tableaux from French opera of the seventeenth and eighteenth centuries. From this standpoint the Vienna "version" is consistent, but may be considered incomplete, unsatisfactory as the dynamic of any work other than a pure lamento, just as Bach's opening choruses would be without their musico-theological frames of reference. It is the presentation of this kind of more comprehensive affective sphere that Biber intended for Sonata VI. We do not need to invent a program, of course, although that would be quite easy, since the themes of the sonata and the fugue in particular have clear associations throughout Biber's work; but we need to understand how the larger conception of the printed sonata forms a satisfying psychological dynamic in which events such as the *scordatura* and change of key play a part.

The chromaticism that emerges towards the end of the passacaglia is an element from the fugue that runs throughout the entire sonata in various forms, but is absent from the G-minor transitional movement and Gavotte. These latter movements nevertheless play an important role in the "tragic" conception of the work. From its beginning in the bass the G-minor complex is unmistakably linked to the opening theme of the fugue as well as to similar appearances of the theme type that features a rising minor sixth in Biber's work (e.g., a lamenting aria from *Chi la dura la vince,* the Agnus Dei of the *Requiem in F minor,* the "crucifige" theme of the *Stabat Mater,* and so on). The violin enters, arpeggiating the very chords that begin the "Crucifixion" *Mystery Sonata,* their rising- and falling-semitone character recalling for us the recurrent theme of the *Requiem in F minor.* These and related chords will form an important feature of the Gavotte, in the form of support for a melody that has the energetic character of most of Biber's Gavottes. Yet this particular Gavotte, with its chordal injection of energy on the first beat and descending melodic character hints at something of the manner that it ends: with a sense of downward impulse, a little too restrained, perhaps, to be a tragic *catabasis,* but a denial of the initial energy, nevertheless. Biber created a fairly intricate pattern of repeated units for the overall form of the Gavotte and double that comprise only seven bars in variations that bring out more of the catabic character at the end: A (2 measures), A^1, B (2 measures), B^1, C (3 measures), C^1 (the whole repeated), then for the double, A, A^1, B^2, B^2, C^2, C^3.

Within the conception of this sonata as a whole the G-minor complex and the Gavotte in particular can be viewed as an attempt to relieve the tragic coloring of the first two movements, one that is not successful despite the change of key, the absence of chromaticism and the dance element. The return to C minor has a character than can only be described as fateful. The chromaticism returns in the bass along with the familiar "organo tremolante" figure in the violin that suggested fervent prayer in the "Mount of Olives" Sonata; here it bridges the gap between the opening fugue and the close of the passacaglia (ex. 7-7). The Allegro Finale is as remarkable in its way as that of the F-major sonata. Building to a high point, the violin makes a precipitous descent over the last seven measures is unequalled in the violin literature of the

Example 7-8.   *Sonatae Violino Solo,* Ending of Sonata VI (Transcribed from *Scordatura*)

time. There are three changes of time signature and one of tempo, after the violin, wavering between sixteenth-notes and triplets, attains its peak. The final descent plummets, then stops for several intense moments of multiple-stopping (justifying the *scordatura* once again), before the chromaticism turns downward to the final cadence (ex. 7-8). The various shifts in meter, tempo and figuration do not permit the sense of ever-increasing momentum such as ends the F-major sonata from this set. Biber's intention here is to continue the burdening of the work with its heavily rhetorical matter. There is nothing at all of the transcendent about this work; rather, the human and tragic is invoked with the utmost power and conviction. The tragedy is not that of the inevitable and "pure" kind of classical drama, or of the "Appassionata" Sonata, for example, but the baroque rhetorical and allegorical kind, tinged throughout with mourning, perhaps of identification with religious suffering, in light of the multiplicity of its well-known figures.

Biber's *Sonatae Violino Solo* are undoubtedly the most significant solo violin works of the seventeenth century, totally *of* the seventeenth century and unlike the later works of Corelli that ultimately eclipsed them. Along with their increased length and technical demands the dramatic scope of these sonatas is unquestionably greater than that of the *Mystery Sonatas.* In these pieces an individual approach to the questions of style and formal design is found, one that at the same time combines the discipline of the church sonata with the improvisational flights of fancy of the virtuoso soloist and that conveys both the rhetorical (if not programmatic) spirit that permeates Biber's work and the striving for inner musical logic that runs parallel with it.

Manuscript Violin Sonatas

Besides the Vienna *Pastorella* and the Kroměříž *Sonata violino solo representativa,* which are obviously secular in intent, and the Vienna versions of the "Crucifixion" Sonata and the sixth of the *Sonatae Violino Solo,* both of which we have considered, there remain one mature violin sonata at Kroměříž and another in the Vienna manuscript, as well as the early version of the fourth of the *Sonatae Violino Solo* and five anonymous Vienna sonatas whose styles suggest the possibility of Biber's authorship. We will consider these eight compositions according to a plausible chronological sequence after noting something of the general significance of the Vienna collection and its particular problems for the researcher.

The Vienna manuscript (which has never been studied in any detail) provides us with a representative body of German violin music from the second half of the century. Even though a large number of the works contained therein are copies from prints, and not all the great

Example 7-9. Excerpts Transcribed from *Scordatura*

(a) Beginning of *Fantasia* from the Vienna Manuscript

(b) *Sonatae Violino Solo,* Beginning of Sonata IV

violinist-composers of the age are included (no works by Westhoff appear, for example), the forty or so otherwise unknown pieces make clear the fact that technically advanced violin writing was by this time by no means confined to the eminent virtuosi by this time. The sonatas of Rupert Ignaz Mayr (chiefly known for his church music), for example, reveal a firm grasp of violinistic idioms. And we encounter the names of some unknown or little-known composers such as Nikolaus Faber and Johann Voita standing at the head of *scordatura* sonatas of considerable difficulty. This situation makes the ascription of anonymous sonatas problematic, sometimes impossible. From the standpoint of present knowledge concerning the late seventeenth-century German violin school we must conclude that works as demanding as the *Sonatae Violino Solo,* however, could only have been written by violinists of the calibre of Biber and Walther. In such cases the presence of *scordatura* (e.g., No. 81) points to Biber's authorship. The collection contains, however, several anonymous sonatas that might have been composed by Biber, but fall within the capabilities of a fairly wide range of violinists. Probably the most interesting of these works is No. 82, entitled *Contrapunct sopra la Bassigaglos d'Altr.,* a ground-bass sonata incorporating variations on "Wie schön leuchtet der Morgenstern," the exacting violin writing of which, as well as the treatment of the borrowed melody, suggest Biber's style. Yet the chorale tune invites consideration of northern violinist composers as well, such as Nikolaus Adam Strungk and Nikolaus Bruhns, who are not represented in the collection. In the absence of style traits that are particularly associated with Biber's violin music at one or another stage of his career I cannot speculate further concerning his authorship of additional works from this source. Those that are discussed below are, in my estimation, more likely to have been composed by Biber than by any other known violinist of the time.

The third piece in the Vienna manuscript is the *Fantasia* from which Biber drew the Gigue and Variatio and much of the thematic material of the first movement of the fourth sonata of the 1681 collection. Both works begin with a slow chordal introduction followed by a Presto, only the former of which are musically related (ex. 7-9). Besides altering the rhythmic

Example 7-10.   Excerpts Transcribed from *Scordatura*

(a)   Gigue from Sonata IV of the *Sonatae Violino Solo*

(b)   Gigue from the *Fantasia* of the Vienna Manuscript

relationship between the opening bars and the remainder of the passage, the published version makes greater technical demands, and it presents a tighter organization of the material (six bars contain ten of the *Fantasia*), as well as a simpler bass and greater harmonic variety. The expansion of the theme to the multiple stops in bar four and its reiteration just before the cadence in the next two bars give a stronger sense of direction to an opening period that now cadences firmly in the dominant rather than the tonic (the pattern of the tonic cadence of the manuscript work reappears, however, at the close of the otherwise different second transition of the published sonata). The introduction then expands effortlessly to sixteen measures, with the theme moving into the bass as well. The melodic basis of the opening theme—falling fourth from tonic to dominant, then rising a tone before returning to the dominant to continue the descent—must be noted, for it is the same sequence of tones that is common to the *Pastorelle* of Biber and Schmelzer and appears in the Prinner song that Biber used in his *Pastorella*. In the Vienna *Fantasia* this idea reappears in the Presto section of the opening movement as well as the Adagio that follows; and the pattern of its first four tones, with their alternation of tonic and subdominant harmonies, underlies several passages in both sonatas, including the final bars of Sonata IV.

The two versions of the Gigue also differ somewhat (ex. 7-10). The *Fantasia* contains only one double, and the Sonata, two, neither of which follows the manuscript version. Apart from much more imaginative violin writing in the Sonata, most of the changes apply chiefly to the bass, the harmony and melody in the last three bars, and the articulation of the continuo. According to his usual practice, Biber repeats the bass of the Gigue exactly in the two doubles of the Sonata, while in the *Fantasia* he varies the bass of the double. A Minuet ends the Fantasia, so that the work exhibits a structure not unlike the Fantasy Suites of seventeenth-century English music in some respects (fig. 7-2).

Figure 7-2. Scheme of the Vienna *Fantasia*

Movement	Meter	Measures	Form, Style, Texture
1	¢	10	Chordal introduction [adagio]
		55	Presto, contrapuntal
2		21	[Adagio], melody over "walking" bass
3	$\frac{12}{8}$	16	Gigue and Variatio, each eight bars (4 + 4) with repeats
4	$\frac{3}{4}$	18	Minuet, binary form (8 + 10) with repeats

Example 7-11. *Fantasia* from the Vienna Manuscript, Beginning of Presto (Transcribed from *Scordatura*)

The lengthy fugal Presto is at once the most characteristic movement of the *Fantasia* and the least compatible with Biber's later style. The beginning makes this clear immediately: after an initial statement of the long theme by the violin, four bars of non-thematic extension lead to another statement in the continuo (ex. 7-11). This leisurely approach sets the general tone of the Presto, whose overabundance of ideas betrays the youthful composer. In Biber's later fugues the themes contain no such appendages and are always imitated after a short interval. The Presto, on the other hand, contains a profusion of secondary ideas and figurations that give way to one another without ever recurring. Among them we find themes from the introduction and the descending triad figure that appears in many of Biber's works, including the *Salve Regina* (1663), which resembles the *Fantasia* in a number of details.

One of the most unusual aspects of the Presto is the very active bass part with sequences of extraordinary length and range that encompasses a range of more than three octaves, necessitating the use of soprano, alto, tenor and bass clefs (ex. 7-12). When the violin plays in the higher register the bass also rises in pitch; at one point it reaches above the violin part. The bass line seldom behaves like a basso continuo in this movement, and the kind of interaction that occurs here between violin and bass does not figure in any of the later sonatas. Something like it does appear, however, in certain sonatas of the Kroměříž repertoire, including a sonata for two violins, gamba and continuo by "H. B."[37] In the latter sonata, and others like it, the gamba takes up different roles from movement to movement, sometimes doubling the continuo, sometimes emerging as a soloist that may at times reach up into the register of the violin, even crossing with it. Presumably, a gamba was intended for the Presto of the *Fantasia* as well, a further link to the archaic fantasia-suite genre.

This last trait, and one other that appears in the Adagio of the *Fantasia*—the texture of melodic violin part above a "walking" eighth-note bass—provides some of the basis for my

Example 7-12.   *Fantasia* Excerpts Transcribed from *Scordatura*

(a)   Bass Sequences from the *Fantasia* of the Vienna Manuscript

(b)   Excerpt from the Presto of the Vienna *Fantasia*

suggestion that the three following sonatas of the Vienna manuscript might also have been composed by Biber. No. 4 (Sonata) in particular contains so many style traits of the *Fantasia* that their common authorship seems inevitable. The work discloses the following sequence of movements:

I	[Adagio]	29 bars	"Walking" eighth-note bass as support for motivically variegated violin part
II	[Presto]	102 bars	Fugal
III	[Adagio]	40 bars	Aria and one variation

Several motives in the violin part of the first movement are familiar from Biber's instrumental music, especially the Kroměříž dance suites (ex. 7-13). And the fugal movement recalls that of the *Fantasia* in its leisurely approach to melodic style, its superabundance of ideas, bass sequences and active, wide-ranging bass line. The latter reaches from D to a″ (in bass, tenor, alto, soprano and treble clefs) and occasionally crosses over the violin line, just as in the *Fantasia* (ex. 7-14). The Aria features a tranquil melody accompanied by "running" sixteenth notes, while in the *Variatio* the violin adopts the running pattern and the bass slackens its pace.

Sonatas 5 and 6 exhibit many of the same features. The fifth consists of an introduction, allemande, aria with variations and a ciacona, while the sixth requires the following very rare *scordatura*: c′, f′, a′, d″. Biber demands a similar tuning in the seventh of the *Mystery Sonatas*—c′, f′, a′, c″—also in F major. The Vienna sonata consists of an introductory movement, a "fuga" and an aria with two variations. The second movement is designated fuga

Example 7-13.   Anonymous, No. 4 of the Vienna Manuscript (Sonata), Excerpt from Opening Movement

Example 7-14.   Anonymous, No. 4 of the Vienna Manuscript, Excerpt from Presto

Example 7-15.   Anonymous, Beginning of "Fuga" from No. 5 (Sonata) of the Vienna Manuscript (Transcribed from *Scordatura*)

because, unlike the Presto sections of the third and fourth sonatas, it is relatively short and almost entirely monothematic. The bass line is active but narrower in range than that of its companions; at the beginning of the fuga the bass line follows the violin with three successive entries of the theme in different registers and clefs, just as if it were the continuo part of a four-part fugue (ex. 7-15).

As we have said, it is possible that other anonymous sonatas from the Vienna manuscript were composed by Biber, although their styles are general enough to have been produced by other composers whose works appear in the collection. One further work may be considered now, the eighty-first sonata, with the *scordatura* a, e′, a′, d″. This time it is technical and stylistic affinities to the *Sonatae Violino Solo* that suggest Biber's authorship. The opening section features an improvisational violin part in thirty-second notes that recalls Biber's rapid passage work over long pedal tones; but now the introduction is unaccompanied, a device that in a *scordatura* work of this degree of technical elaboration points to Biber more than to any other known violinist (in addition, the sonata follows right after the Biber *Pastorella* and the Vienna version of the "Crucifixion" *Mystery Sonata*).[38] The introduction contains a sequence of three- and four-note chords indicated to be arpeggiated, as well as some patterned elaboration of the four-note motive that appeared in the *Fantasia* and the fourth of the *Sonatae Violino Solo*. Later sections feature elaborate double stopping as well. The final movement is a set of "ostinatissimi" variations over the slow ascending scalar fifth from tonic to dominant.

But from a technical standpoint easily the most impressive work of Biber's from the Vienna collection is No. 84 which is, apart from the *Pastorella,* the only one of the five unpublished Biber works in the manuscript to bear the composer's name. This E-major sonata,

Example 7-16. Beginning of *Sonata* in E Major from the Vienna Manuscript

the only solo by Biber in that key, ranks among the longest and most difficult of all Biber's solos. It has an unusual form: two free, improvisatory movements frame three separate sets of variations. And Biber's improvisational sections very seldom attain the length of the first movement of this sonata (56 measures). Over three successive pedal tones—E (29 measures), A (11 measures) and B (16 measures)—the violin indulges in virtuoso figuration (mainly thirty-second notes) encompassing a three-octave range that extends to the sixth position. Not even the *Sonatae Violino Solo* offer such extravagant swirling and sweeping patterns. Occasionally the momentum is interrupted by a pause, a few bars of triplets, or a touch of Lombard rhythm (ex. 7-16).

The three sets of variations are unlike any others in Biber's output. Two involve mixtures of the ground-bass and aria-with-variations types. The first is based on an aria (not designated as such) in binary form (4 + 7 measures). The bass of the "A" section appears as a ground in two separately repeated groups of variations (3½ and 2½ statements, respectively); then the latter concludes with the last four bars of the "B" section. Another binary-form aria (eight plus eleven bars) serves as the subject of the second set of variations; now the aria (with repeats) frames two variations (repeated with altered endings) on the bass of its "A" section. In the final set of variations two statements of a third ground bass accompany each appearance of the theme (T) and each variation (V):

mm.	1–4:T	(4 measures repeated as a unit)
mm.	5–16:V^1, T, V^2	(12 measures repeated as a unit)
mm.	17–24:V^3, T	(8 measures repeated as a unit)
mm.	25–32:V^4, T, V^4, T	(16 measures repeated as a unit)

A section in improvisatory style over a subdominant pedal concludes the sonata, which, although technically demanding, relies too much on short repeated patterns all of which are in E major. This sonata is, in fact, virtually a framework for violinistic display, a trait that makes it less significant as a rounded composition than the *Sonatae Violino Solo*.

The last manuscript sonata is a composition in A major at Kroměříž, consisting of three movements: 1) an Adagio/Presto "sonata" complex (the Presto a stylized gigue); 2) a long improvisational section built upon pedal points on E, A and D; and 3) an aria with eleven variations. This sonata, dated by Sehnal after 1670, is the sort of piece we might at first glance expect Biber to have included with the *Sonatae Violino Solo*. But on closer examination the reason that he did not (assuming it was written at the time) emerges. The last movement comprises his longest set of aria variations. With each variation a new figuration appears, some of which are very elaborate indeed, and several of which—the "tremolo tardissime," and *stile concitato* thirty-second notes, for example—are familiar from the published set. But once again the very number of such highly patterned units interferes seriously with the creation of a larger dynamic such as governed the forms of the F-major and C-minor sonatas from the 1681 collection. The last movement almost resembles a set of etudes without much of the rhetorical gesture of the *Sonatae Violino Solo*; it seems hardly possible that such a work would have been heard in church, and in this and the preceding composition we are on the border of the church and chamber sonata.

Church Sonatas II: Ensemble Sonatas

Sonatae, tam Aris, quam Aulis servientes, **1676**

These sonatas, Biber's first published work, stand more clearly within the tradition of the seventeenth-century church sonata than any of Biber's other instrumental works, including the *Mystery Sonatas.* Their line of descent extends back through Schmelzer's *Sacro-Profanus Concentus Musicus* (1662) to the Italian sonatas of the early part of the century; even the emblematic rising-arpeggio theme of the first sonata can be found, in both the major and minor forms, as the opening theme of other sonata collections of the age. Nine of the twelve sonatas exist in separate manuscript copies at Kroměříž, all apparently written between 1668 and 1670, and all specifying organ continuo.[1]

The *Sonatae, tam Aris* present five different instrumental combinations for strings with and without one or two clarini. The two framing sonatas, numbers I and XII, *à 8,* feature the most elaborate scoring: two clarini, two violins, and a choir of four violas (in soprano, alto, tenor and bass clefs), plus basso continuo. Sonatas II, III, and V, *à 6,* require the same string body minus the clarini; numbers VI, VIII, IX and XI, all for strings *à 5,* dispense with the soprano viola; and in sonatas IV and X, also *à 5,* a clarino replaces one of the violins. Finally, the seventh sonata, built almost entirely upon a ground-bass, calls for two violins, two clarini and continuo. In all twelve sonatas the fourth viola (basso di viola) plays with the basso continuo independently of the soprano, alto and tenor violas, which usually sound as a choir.

Vital to the conception of these sonatas is the division of their instrumental complement into three contrasted groupings—trumpets, violins and violas—each with its own characteristic styles and making its own unique contributions to the whole. Of these the consistent appearance of the violas as a choir, rather than as soloists of individualistic character such as the violin and trumpet is a conservative feature that, along with the contrapuntal conception of many movements, and the canzona-like single-movement forms of some pieces, distinguishes most of these sonatas from the concertos and trumpet sonatas of contemporary Italian composers. Biber's works have an older pedigree even than the sonatas Georg Muffat wrote for Salzburg, and it is within the framework of the older church sonata that even the more advanced features of their trumpet and violin writing belong. The *Sonatae, tam Aris* represent a high point in the concertato practices and formal principles developed in the early part of the century. Yet into the traditional framework they bring a freshness of imagination with respect to instrumental styles and combinations that puts them beyond the scope of criticism centered on the question of progressive versus conservative elements. In terms of their historical character these works are an approximate equivalent in the area of instrumental music to Biber's polychoral vocal works. And, in fact, some of the sonatas exhibit a comparable degree of variety in the sonorities of successive movements, suggesting mixtures of "solo" and "tutti," archaic and modern styles. Sonata III provides a good example (fig. 8-1).

Although Sonata III is, perhaps, the most varied in textures of the string sonatas, it nevertheless typifies the instrumental conception of most of the sonatas. And we notice that

Figure 8-1. Scheme of *Sonatae, tam Aris,* No. III

Movement	Meter	Measures	Key	Form, Style, Texture
1	¢	19	G minor	Two violins & continuo
	12/8	18	G minor	Two violins & continuo; Presto
2	C	21	B-flat/G minor	Full scoring; alternation between violins and violas; presto, adagio, presto
3		12	G minor	Fugue for violas & continuo
4	3/2	18	E-flat	Full scoring, homophonic, triadic, Allegro
5	C	15	G minor	Violin 1 & continuo; then violin 2 & continuo; recitative-like, improvisatory solo style
6	3/4	46	G minor	Tutti; six-part fugue, presto
	C	5	G minor	Coda; adagio

certain of the movement types—equal-voice duets, fugues for violas alone, antiphonal alternation between violins and violas, virtuoso-like solos for the violin, tutti blocks, and fugal finales—have close counterparts in the polychoral vocal works, such as the *Vesperae à 32.* This is all the more apparent in some of the works with trumpets. The instrumental surface of the *Sonatae, tam Aris* is, like that of the large vocal pieces, designed to be as variegated as possible, in terms both of scoring and styles. Some of the more prominent combinations may be enumerated now, before we consider how they interact at larger structural levels.

TEXTURES	SONATAS
Solo violin and continuo	II, III, VII
Two solo violins and continuo	III, VI, VII, IX, XII
Violas (as a choir) and continuo	III
Violins contrasted with viola choir	II, III, V, IX
Solo clarino and continuo	IV, VII
Two clarini and continuo	I, VII, XII
Clarini and violas (without violins) with continuo	XII
One solo violin, violas and continuo	IV
One clarino, violas and continuo	IV
Two clarini, two violins and continuo	VII
Clarini, violins, and violas in pairs with continuo	I
Clarino, violas, and continuo juxtaposed with violin, violas, and continuo	X

Often entire movements were designed to exhibit one or another of the above combinations; and several sonatas reveal, like No. III, the principle of textural contrast throughout all or most of their sequences of sections. In fact, throughout the first four sonatas Biber introduces the instruments first as a full ensemble made up of separate bodies (No. I), then elaborates on the character of the subdivision of the strings into violins and violas (No. II), further expands on this idea in terms of soloistic textures (No. III) and finally, in the fourth sonata, sets solo trumpet and strings in opposition (first movement), follows this with virtuosic violin writing (second movement); then he presents a movement for solo clarino and violas,

Example 8-1. *Sonatae, tam Aris, quam Aulis servientes* (1676), Ending of Sonata I

and finally, groupings of movements in which both violin and clarino concertize separately and together (Fugue, Adagio, Allegro). Among the many movements of these sonatas some stand out for their particularly systematic textural juxtapositions: the finale of Sonata I intermingles and alternates a melody with its inversion, both presented in parallel thirds by pairs of trumpets, violins and violas; the first movement of Sonata II frames a fugue for the viola choir by short sections featuring elaborate violin writing accompanied by violas; in the first movement of Sonata IV the strings play $\frac{4}{4}$ meter while the clarino is in $\frac{12}{8}$ meter. Although he could have chosen, as many others did, to follow the tonal plan of the gamut (all the keynotes are represented—C (4), D, e, F, G, g (2), A, and B-flat—in jumbled order), Biber undoubtedly grouped the sonatas of most variegated instrumental character at the beginning of the collection in order to present the widest range of concertato possibilities right from the start, an indication that these instrumental factors are central to the overall conception of the set.

Yet, although the attractiveness of these sonatas is undoubtedly owing considerably to the above-mentioned features, the instrumental surface is at the same time a quality that can be found in many Kroměříž sonatas of far lesser value as well as in a collection such as Romanus Weichlein's *Encaenia Musices* (1695) that was undoubtedly highly influenced by Biber's sonatas and that with respect to variegated scoring goes even further than Biber's set.[2] That Biber's sonatas have proven of lasting value while these and many others have not is obviously due to something other than the superficial elements they share. And in the case of the *Sonatae, tam Aris* what differentiates Biber from Vejvanovský or Weichlein is first of all his special grasp of instrumental counterpoint (a quality that encompasses more than the mere fitting together of separate lines), and second, his ability to create a convincing overall dynamic out of a sequence of separate styles. These two qualities are very closely related and exist at the level of the individual movement as well as the overall sonata. The former can be seen in the opening movement of the first sonata, in the gradual expansion of the thematic material to increasingly more intricate culminating points, and the incorporation of two secondary themes of progressively more lively character, all leading to the final triumphant outburst as the instruments toss the majestic first theme and the jubilant third throughout the ensemble, the clarini reaching the high c''' for the first time (ex. 8-1).

A general description of the remaining events to the end of this sonata indicates a logical progression. Following the emphatic C major of this opening movement the Adagio begins with a sustained E-major chord above which the two violins play arpeggio figuration, turning the E into the dominant of A minor; the arpeggiation continues, now Presto, and with the important addition of the note e' in repeated eighth-notes from the trumpets in alternation, cadencing after another seven measures in E minor. The low trumpet tones and A-minor/E-major oscillation may recall the passage Biber used to represent "judicabit in nationibus" in the *Dixit* of the *Vesperae à 32.* As a result of the prolonging of what might be called the "mediant" (or Phrygian) character of the E major sonority, there is a sense of expectancy that is not resolved in this section, and at first the short adagio that follows does little more than lead back to C major, at which point the trumpet tones begin again, now on g'. This time, however, a new theme emerges, that of the preceding Adagio, expanded and turned into a presto dialogue and fanfare for the clarini (10 measures). From this a fugue develops that builds eventually to a full climax of entries in eight parts.

After two such dynamic climaxes the work seems to call for another type of finale, and Biber turns to triple meter, inverting the melodic direction that began the sonata with an opening theme of pronounced arpeggio descent. This idea gives way to the quasi-antiphonal pairing of instruments mentioned above; the constant parallel thirds impart a joyful tone to what is music of lively, but essentially simple character. At the end a new theme begins an upward motion that turns back downward and descends through all the parts in succession while the arpeggio descent of the beginning of the movement returns to end the piece.

In terms of the dynamic of its overall design this sonata takes its primary impetus from the majestic, triadic character of the trumpets that dominates the opening movement with a grandeur that turns to jubilation right at the end. This, the dynamic of the sonatas that introduce the *Vesperae à 32* and *Missa Christi Resurgentis,* is a foreshadowing of the affective progression of the sonata that is completed in the final movement. The jump to the major chord of the mediant for the Adagio is a device that Biber was especially fond of; we have encountered it in the F-major sonata from the 1681 publication, and the mediant key is a preferred contrast tonality in the majority of the major-key sonatas of the *Sonatae, tam Aris.* Despite its familiarity as the dominant of the relative minor, the move up a major third (especially when it is tonicized as well) imparts the sense of a foreign presence (the G-sharp); historically, the mediant—and in a wider sense the key of E minor—was associated with the *cantus durus,* and undoubtedly something of the sense of a move to a "hard" sphere was felt to be conveyed in the major-third relationship. By Biber's time these associations had been weakened by the rationalistic principle of secondary dominants that reduced the conceptual shock of the modulation and subordinated all the keys of the ambitus to the tonic. But the unresolved character of the E is brought out in this case by the failure of the trumpets to move from their single tone; the flurry of activity in the Presto, instead of introducing a new theme, simply intensifies the static alternation of the E-major and A-minor harmonies. The result is, as we said, a sense of expectancy, a weakening of the dynamic after the powerful assertion of C in the opening movement. The ensuing fugue restores the sense of grandeur, but it remains for the finale to move significantly beyond the majestic to give itself over to jubilation by means of its dance rhythm and antiphonal devices. One of the most successful aspects of the movement is the descent of the opening and closing theme of the finale, which shifts the emphasis in the work away from the assertion of glory toward the immediate and physical.

There is nothing routine or shallow even in those works of Biber's that assert the external trappings of splendor that the Catholic church of the counterreformation demanded; the first sonata is such a piece, formal in its structural solidity, but animated from within by the livelier human element. Other sonatas deal in far more immediate terms with the latter, even at times introducing rustic styles. Sonata IX, for example, opens with a movement in which the violin patterns, alternating harmonies, and—from the fourteenth bar—construction on the four-note motive of the Prinner song that seems to have had a profound influence on Biber's earlier work all contribute to create an unmistakable "hoedown" effect that it is difficult to imagine any other composer of the time achieving so successfully. The sonata comprises many short sections with changing styles, several very lively; one passage of a slow, sententiously chromatic character appears three times as a kind of counterbalance to the prevailing exuberance; it introduces a sudden halting of momentum that seems like a reminder of another, pathetic side of life. A highly energetic fugue caps the whole, its theme inverted in the middle with anything but a learned effect, then dying away, piano and adagio, in a five-bar coda.

It is clear that a considerable range of structural possibilities exists in these sonatas. A few of the pieces have as few as three or four movements (nos. I, II, XII), while others that are longer nevertheless offer clear sequences of differentiated textures and styles (nos. IV, X); three sonatas consist of four repeated sections of substantial proportions followed by one or two closing sections (nos. V, VI, VIII). Apart from the ground-bass sonata (VII), the remainder comprise two that are closer to the canzona type (Nos. IX, XI), while No. III (fig. 8-1) merges features of the latter type with the high degree of stylistic differentiation that characterizes the shorter works. In virtually all the sonatas the role of the slow sections is noteworthy; and, in fact, two-thirds of the sonatas end adagio. In spirit some of these adagio endings resemble final brief meditations on the preceding Allegro (Nos. III, IX), while others introduce new ideas of affective character (Nos. VI, VIII, IX). Although it is possible in some cases to consider these endings as a conventional device, a form of braking of the momentum of the finale, it is probable that their presence belongs to the expressive realm of the church sonata, as do the slow endings in many of the *Mystery Sonatas.* And, in fact, the adagio sections throughout the sonatas often tend to counter the tendency toward the extroverted tendency of the surrounding movements. In the major-key sonatas some adagios tend to be in the mediant tonal area (Nos. I, IV, VIII) or to emphasize the relative minor (VI, XI, XII), sometimes by way of its dominant (VI); and in the minor-key works the submediant and dominant (i.e., the keys that exhibit forms of major-third relationship, either to the tonic or relative major) may be used in a similar manner (nos. III, V, X).

Something of what the idea of the combined church/chamber sonata meant to Biber, and his skill in welding musical elements of diverse origins (canzona, suite, concerto) into such a piece may be witnessed in Sonata X in G minor for trumpets and strings; my commentary on this work will conclude discussion of the *Sonatae, tam Aris.* This sonata, not one of those known to have been produced at Kroměříž during Biber's years there, nevertheless owes the theme of its second movement to a sonata of Vejvanovský's; and it is probable that the exact knowledge of the trumpet that enabled Biber to produce one of the fairly rare minor-key trumpet works of the time came from his association with the Kroměříž trumpeter.[3] The sonata comprises five main sections, of which the first, third and fifth are of considerable breadth and feature a noteworthy amount of concertizing between trumpet and violin. The opening bars of the work highlight the two soloists, and the rest of the first movement sets the trumpet in dialogue with the strings; the fourths and fifths that are echoed between the two have an intrada-like introductory character that seems to announce the concerto aspect. Yet the second movement is a canzona-like fugue for strings with an archaic aspect that emerges in the alternation of points of imitation involving the theme with those utilizing its inversion. The violas then recede into an accompanimental background for a triple-meter movement of broad, sweeping character that features much concertizing dialogue between trumpet and violin; a theme of prominent perfect fourths seems almost to round out a tripartite plan with reference back to the opening movement. But there has been no real adagio to this point; and Biber moves now to the submediant for a passage of affective chromatic character. This section continues presto, passing through B-flat, F major and D minor (with Tierce de Picardie),

Figure 8-2. Scheme of *Sonata à 6*

Movement	Meter	Measures	Key	Form, Style, Texture
1	¢	26	C major	Trumpet, strings & continuo; allegro
2		12	A minor	Violin 2 & continuo; [adagio, presto, adagio]
		7	A minor-C major	Violin 2, violas 1 & 2, continuo; 4-part fugal ending
3	$\frac{3}{2}$	29	C major-G major	Trumpet, violins 1 & 2, continuo; ground bass; [allegro]
4	¢	17	C major, ends in E minor	Violin 1 & continuo; [adagio, presto, adagio?]
		18	C major	Trumpet, violas 1 & 2, continuo
5		24	C major	Trumpet, strings & continuo; fugue

before returning to G minor for a gigue-like finale, once again featuring much concertizing between trumpet and violin. Again the fourths and fifths suggested by the use of the trumpet in G minor appear prominently in the theme. work thus exhibits a palpable sense of structural solidity that seems to bring it closer to the sphere of the concerto than its companion sonatas. Once again the secondary keys all make brief appearances, with the subdominant reserved for the brief drawing out of the final adagio cadence. The third movement even features circle-of-fifths treatment of the "fourth" theme covering all the six chords of the ambitus in a chromatic figure that reappears in the early Bach cantatas (e.g., "in ihm sterben wir" from the *Actus Tragicus*). Largely by virtue of the flat minor key with trumpets this sonata, in fact, projects an affect of melancholy that retains the element of grandeur.

Before moving on to the *Fidicinium Sacro-Profanum,* we may consider at this point one of Biber's manuscript sonatas, the Kroměříž *Sonata à 6* for trumpet and strings (now with two violins instead of one); for this piece, written during Biber's early Salzburg years (around 1673 according to Sehnal), has many points in common with the *Sonatae, tam Aris* and in particular with the sonata just described.[4] The *Sonata à 6* has an approximately symmetrical structure (fig. 8-2). The central movement, a ground-bass composition, stands apart as the only one in triple meter, and the one in which the trumpet concertizes with both violins. In terms of ground-bass construction it is unique for Biber, in that the ground—a scalar rising fifth that falls at the end to its starting tone—is announced first as a theme in the trumpet, then passes into the bass in longer note values; later it appears again in the upper parts in its more rhythmically animated form, and at the end this form moves into the bass as well. From the fourth of its twelve statements the movement is in the dominant, in which it closes. The trumpet and violin parts become very lively and animated from the point of the move to the dominant, and the movement as a whole has a very optimistic tone. Before and after this centerpiece are violin solos that lead into continuations for strings in the first instance, and trumpet juxtaposed with violas in the second. The opening movement has some of the same characteristics as the G-minor sonata just described, in particular the rising fourths that are passed back and forth between trumpet and strings. But now the tonic-dominant alternation figure that suggests a call to attention, as it does in the opening section of the fourth of the *Mystery Sonatas* (the twelve-year-old Christ in the temple), passes into the bass as an ostinato, imparting a fanfare character to the entire movement, similar to passages in the *Missa Salisburgensis* ("glorificamus te") and the *Sonata S. Polycarpi.* In the first of the two violin

Example 8-2. *Sonata à 6* (Kroměříž), Descending Triad Themes

solos (for second violin) a new theme is introduced that, along with the rising fourth, will run through the sonata: the descending triad. The solo violin begins with this idea, adagio, and on the chord of the mediant again, as part of a sonata-like passage that continues presto with much development of the rising fourth. Returning to the adagio style, the solo leads into a fugal treatment of the descending triad theme. Following the ground-bass centerpiece, the first violin begins with exactly the same style and thematic material, leading also to a presto elaboration of the rising fourth. This time the continuation, pitting solo trumpet against the violas, gives a sharper thematic profile and a new major-key triumphant character to the descending-triad idea. Finally, the descending triad becomes the core of the theme of the final fugue, with echoes of the rising fourth idea as well (ex. 8-2). Although symmetrical in design, the *Sonata à 6* also exhibits a clear sense of forward motion in the development of the two themes and especially in the manner in which the descending triad moves from what is clearly at first a contrasting idea to becoming the final, and primary statement of the work. This is, unlike the G-minor trumpet sonata, a sonata of glory, everything melancholy and counter to its basic affect transformed step by step into the confident assertion of the basic idea. In some sense this sonata can be considered a metaphor for the primary thrust of counterreformation art.

Fidicinium Sacro-Profanum (1682 [1683])

Biber's last sonata publication, probably intended, like Georg Muffat's *Armonico Tributo,* for special dedication to Archbishop Max Gandolph in connection with the 1682 anniversary of the archdiocese, contains twelve sonatas, six of which are scored for two violins, two violas and continuo (Nos. I–VI), and six with the same forces minus one of the violins (Nos. VII–XII). We note that, while there may be only one violin, the violas never once comprise fewer than two instruments in Biber's music and that of his contemporaries. As is well known, Muffat's *Armonico Tributo* permits dispensing with one or both of the violas in order to perform his five-part works in four parts or as trio sonatas; this variation, along with the additional possibility of their performance as concerti grossi (trio sonata concertino versus orchestrally doubled tutti) indicates a conception of the violas as harmonic fillers, something completely different from the "consort"-like assigning of complete fugues to the violas in Biber's *Sonatae, tam Aris.* Now, in his *Fidicinium,* Biber moves significantly away from the sonata types of his earlier collection; and it is possible that these pieces constitute in some sense a response to Muffat's works. Nevertheless, there is nothing in these sonatas to suggest anything of the kinds of performances Muffat envisaged for his pieces. The sonatas of the *Fidicinium* are pure chamber music; this is one of their most interesting features. No longer do we have sections given over to virtuoso writing for the violin; instead, the technical demands made of the four strings are very nicely and carefully balanced. Although from time to time, as the conception of the individual sonata demands, the violins and violas are polarized, this has nothing to do with the older quasi-antiphonal outlook and, if anything, it indicates that the violas are indispensible, not the reverse. Many of the sonatas project the sense of sheer delight in ensemble string playing in which the two violins saw away as if nothing on earth could be more important while the violas stand apart in high relief, in some cases playing their own independent ideas, in others injecting their version of the main idea. No virtuoso demands are made of the players. The role of accompaniment, even that of filler, is possible for the violas, of course; but these works were not conceived with any such preconceived role for any of the instruments. And as a result the principles of individual styles and overall movement sequences are more abstract (i.e., based on purely musical principles) and representative of up-to-date developments in the sonata than their predecessors.

Although in these sonatas we still have works with canzona-like sequences of varied movement types, and there is no overall formal conception that can be said to govern all the pieces, the slow/fast sequence familiar from Corelli's sonatas has a distinct tendency to play a pivotal role in a considerable number of the sonatas. There is no reason to turn to any particular influence in order to explain Biber's relatively greater reliance on a pattern that was, in fact, developed early in the century; Biber was older than both Corelli and Muffat and his work is generally independent of both. But the presence of what Erich Schenk refers to as "intercalated" Adagios in Muffat's 1682 sonatas—i.e., Adagios that are placed between dance movements, that sometimes create slow/fast sequences out of what would otherwise stack up as dance suites—undoubtedly represents in Muffat's work the influence of Corelli, and might have suggested to Biber a means of normalizing of structural principles in his work.[5] A few of the *Fidicinium Sacro-Profanum* can be described as versions of the slow/fast/slow/fast pattern; and although that does not indicate that those particular works represent something closer to the norm in Biber's conception of the sonata, it does in some cases tend to go along with a more sustained, consistent approach to affective content than usual. As in the *Sonatae, tam Aris,* the Adagios play a very important role in the overall structural conception of many works, and again a considerable number of the sonatas (nine) end with short Adagios.

It is interesting, and may be significant, that the sonata that is nearest to Corelli's scheme, No. XI, is in C minor and bears comparison with Biber's other works in that key in its representation of the sphere of "pathetic" affections. That is, the conspicuous clarity of structural design in this piece might be considered to belong to an attempt to bring a degree of intellectual control to a work featuring so many elements of the lamento style. The sonata exhibits an Adagio, Piu Presto, Adagio, Allegro sequence (with a five-measure Adagio rounding off the final Allegro), with the first and third movements in duple meter ($\frac{2}{2}$), the second in $\frac{3}{4}$, and the fourth in $\frac{12}{8}$. In addition, the first two movements are subtly related thematically in their outlining the tones of the augmented triad, while the final five-bar adagio is derived from the third movement, thereby making the third and fourth movements into a single slow/fast/[slow] complex. All four movements feature some chromatic writing, but it emerges more as a figure only in the two adagios. The final section of the first movement brings in the rising chromatic tetrachord that appears in Biber's other C-minor sonatas (e.g., the "Mount of Olives" Sonata and the sixth of the *Sonatae Violino Solo*), while the third movement extends the relatively mild melodic chromaticism of the opening bars to a figure outlining a diminished seventh, a type used for expressing pathos. In the last movement the chromaticism appears in the bass at the climax of the piece; now it is the means of leading to a dramatic pause on the dominant before the final cadence. And in the brief concluding Adagio the chromaticism is intensified by the turning of the falling diminished seventh downward a semitone instead of upward. In this sonata the rhythmic pacing is very fluent in the second and fourth movements, more halting and intense in the Adagios; yet the idea of an overall affective "sphere" is clearly projected. This is a sonata in which a degree of thematic integration and structural clarity combine to sustain an elegaic tone in a measured, logical manner.

Several other sonatas from the set also exhibit relatively compact structural plans. The third, for example, comprises two slow/fast sonata groupings that frame a gigue; the fourth begins and ends with *alla breves* of a predominantly chordal, homophonic character, between which appear a fast and a slow movement; the fifth deals with the juxtaposition of descending and ascending melodic ideas throughout the movements of a fast, slow, fast, fast sequence. A few sonatas with varied sequences of movements move toward endings with the slow/fast grouping (VI, VII, IX), while one sonata that does not have a real Adagio until the last two measures has a Presto fugal finale whose theme goes back to the opening measures of the work; the two-measure final cadence then brings out the subdominant and tonic minor in a sudden infusion of pathetic affection. The magnificent twelfth sonata opens with a movement of great motivic and contrapuntal ingenuity involving variation, contrapuntal permutation and subtle rhythmic augmentation of its main idea; this movement of considerable intensity gives way to another Allegro in a relaxed triple meter and a continual dotted-rhythmic character. A third Allegro or Presto turns suddenly, after seven bars, to Adagio, then after another fifteen measures followed by a dramatic rest, to a Piu Adagio that introduces borrowing from the minor mode, chromaticism and the Neapolitan sixth chord; the progressive slowing of the tempo within a single span makes a remarkable preparation for the vigorous Allegro fugal finale. One of the more sectional of the sonatas, No. X, uses the varied recall of music to round off a six-movement composition; following an impressive Adagio/Presto sequence, the melodic material of the final section is based on an earlier movement of the sonata (immediately preceding the Adagio/Presto grouping) and resembles the opening movement as well.

But without a doubt the most interesting use of variation technique to integrate one of the longer sequences of movements appears in the first sonata. The core of this piece is an Adagio refrain of lamento-like character, resembling the Kroměříž *Balletti Lamentabili* in its main theme and long, drawn-out plagal cadences (ex. 8-3). The refrain appears twice in its entirety (20 measures), but transposed the second time from B minor to D major, and twice in shortened forms (8 and 9 measures, respectively); the two shortened forms of the refrain change the meter from its original $\frac{3}{2}$ to $\frac{4}{4}$ and $\frac{6}{4}$ respectively, while the third appearance has a pronounced Phrygian character (ex. 8-4). The refrain thus appears in three different meters and three modes, with no two of its four statements in the same combination of both. Between the four refrains appear contrasting sections, the first two of which are Allegro and the third Grave; a two-measure Allegro also precedes the first entrance of the refrain. From all this is is perhaps apparent that what happens throughout the course of this sonata in terms of a musico-rhetorical dynamic is in part an accommodation of the refrain and the contrasting material to one another; whereas the first two appearances of the refrain contrast in tempo and meter with

Example 8-3.   Plagal cadences

(a)   *Balletti Lamentabili*

(b)   *Fidicinium Sacro-Profanum*, Sonata I

the sections that precede and follow them, the last two retain the meter of the preceding sections; and in the final statement the contrast of tempo is also reduced (from Grave to Adagio; all the others from Allegro to Adagio). Whereas the structure of this sonata may be taken to resemble the ritornello structures of the late Baroque, there are obviously some very important differences. The meter changes suggest the archaic variation devices of works such as the *Missa in Albis* and the modal shifts—especially the transposition from B minor to D major—recall the idea of the *catholicon,* or a composition that can be played in several different modes, while the contrasting sections, unrelated to one another, belong to the world of the canzona more than that of the eighteenth-century sonata.[6] In effect, works such as this and the C-minor sonata of this collection illustrate the fluid concept of affect that reigns in many seventeenth-century works, and that we have designated in many cases with the term "affective sphere." The *Fidicinium Sacro-Profanum* represents Biber's once again producing a music that constitutes a personal synthesis of tendencies that were developed in the earlier part of the century with a newer interest in the projection and sustaining of affect that seems to look ahead to the late baroque style, but stands apart from the main currents that were moving in that direction. The variety of possible solutions to the question of musical structure in a short multi-sectional sonata is the strength of these works.

Manuscript Ensemble Sonatas

Besides the Kroměříž *Sonata à 6,* discussed above, only two ensemble sonatas survive in manuscript that are definitely by Biber and intended for use in church: the *Sonata à 7* (1668) for six trumpets, timpani and basso continuo and the *Sonata S. Polycarpi* (1673), for eight trumpets, timpani and continuo. The first of these works, written at Kroměříž, attests to the quality of Bishop Liechtenstein-Kastelkorn's trumpeters and their leader Vejvanovský. The

Example 8-4. *Fidicinium Sacro-Profanum,* Four Versions of the "Refrain" of Sonata I

sumptuous setting reminds us of the bishop's boast to his correspondent at the Vienna court that he could provide "six or seven clarini, ten to twelve strings and seven, eight or more trombones."[7] In fact, although sonatas containing multiple trumpet parts are not exceptional in the Kroměříž repertoire, Biber's composition stands apart in two respects: it contains no string or other wind parts, and all six trumpets are clarino parts reaching to the sixteenth partial: c'''. Even Vejvanovský does not call for more than two virtuoso players. At climactic moments Biber tosses motives of considerable brilliance throughout the ensemble—near the end of the first of the two repeated sections, for example, where each of the six clarini in turn plays to the top note, and for the second half of the second section, where antiphonal writing is used (trumpets 1, 2, 4 versus 3, 5, 6). Given the limitations of the instrumentation the tonal structure can only be simple, but Biber does manage to suggest the dominant and subdominant in the first section (utilizing the seventh [fourteenth] partial, b''-flat, and the eleventh, which must be lipped by the player to f''-sharp); in the second section he modulates with dominant/tonic cadences to D minor (with a lipped c'' sharp) and F.

We have more data concerning the performance of the sonata for eight trumpets, kettledrums and basso continuo that Biber wrote for the feast day of St. Polycarp (January 26, 1673). On the manuscript Biber made the following remark: "N. B. Trumpets 1, 2, 5 and 6 must stand together. And trumpets 3, 4, 7, and 8 also together, for in the triple meter section they divide into two choirs. The Violone, however, and the basso continuo as much as possible must be given to a considerable number of instruments; the *Quartuba* (bass trombone?) might well be used."[8] These instructions were intended for the musicians at Kroměříž, since the Olomouc cathedral did not provide special balconies for the trumpet choirs like those in the Salzburg cathedral. For the Salzburg performance of the work four organs might have accompanied the trumpets as they did at the *pallium* service in 1687.[9] Biber's request for the fullest possible setting of the continuo suggests this, reminding us of the great number of bass register instruments among the parts of the cathedral manuscripts (trombones, bassoons, violoni, besides several organs and, occasionally theorbos).

The *Sonata S. Polycarpi* is longer, grander and more mature than the *Sonata à 7*. Although six of its eight trumpet parts and clarini, only two reach the high c''', and the work generally makes fewer technical demands than the earlier sonata. The Salzburg court retained a stable body of twelve trumpeters and timpanists, for whom Max Gandolph had twelve silver trumpets with gold decoration made; they are shown in various engravings of processions in Salzburg; but they probably had no leader of Vejvanovský's caliber. The repertoire of trumpet intradas at Nonnberg, as well as the trumpet duos that end Biber's *Sonatae, tam Aris* and Weichlein's *Encaenia Musices* (1695), and a considerable number of eighteenth-century trumpet sonatas of various combinations (mostly antiphonal) in the cathedral archive, all attest to the important role played by such music in ecclesiastical festivities. Among these pieces Biber's *Sonata S. Polycarpi* stands out. It may, like most works of its type, be a noisy piece, but there is a considerable amount of skill exhibited in its construction, nevertheless.[10] Apart from the opening nine bars and the beginning of the final Presto, the sonata is limited completely to tonic and dominant harmonies; in fact, the forty-four measures of antiphonal writing before the Presto sound only the tonic harmony. In all such passages the listener is carried along on a wave of sonority, an almost unchanging and undynamic acoustic event, totally unified in its character; the listener either accepts the sound and its associations of glory, triumph, and the like—which was unquestionably the case in the seventeenth century—or he does not; the latter is often the case at the present time, when associations, either historical or aesthetic, may stand between the listener and the music. This does not mean that all such pieces are equally well put together; but the primary skill required is a sense of pacing that ensures that the successive events do not break the momentum, the spell, one might say; this music can shift its sense of direction or affect only within strict limitations. In the forty-four measures of tonic sonority Biber repeats phrases extensively back and forth between the two choirs, always making sure that there are enough slight differences between the successive phrases—in length, rhythm and the high tones of the phrases (g'', then a'', finally c''')—to create the illusion of forward motion that will keep the passage from flagging.

The two short introductory passages (to the sonata as a whole and to the Presto), however, demand more skill, and it is in these that the *Sonata S. Polycarpi* shows the clearest advance over the *Sonata à 7*. In the earlier piece the sonority was built up immediately on the tonic triad from a measure of kettledrum solo to the high c''' in the sixth measure; although very impressive in itself, it left little room for further development. The *Sonata S. Polycarpi,* on the other hand, begins with two clarini only, increasing its rhythmic motion from quarters to eighths and sixteenths, moving upward in pitch to the dominant (m. 5), then reaching its melodic high point and point of greatest harmonic complexity (m. 7), before falling to a thrice-

Example 8-5. *Sonata S. Polycarpi* (1673), Beginning

repeated cadence (ex. 8-5). In this piece we wait until measure 96 for the high c‴. And the Presto has a similar point of climax, also involving the high a″ and the V of V harmony, this time preceded by a move towards D minor, so that the fall to the tonic is underscored by the harmonic motion *A, d,* [C], V_5^6 of G, G, C. Rapid antiphony and a rustic effect (the last five bars) cap the ending to this wonderful fanfare sonata.

A few works of uncertain authorship, all from Kroměříž and all apparently early, bring this study to a close. If, as seems likely, the *Sonata à 4 violis* (for violin, violetta, two violas and organ; copied around 1663 and inscribed with the initials "H. B.") was composed by Biber, then it represents one of his earliest surviving works. Sehnal suggests Biber's authorship, pointing to the striking virtuoso violin part, the long sequences, illogical modulations and inartistic voice leading as characteristics of the young, inexperienced composer; to these we might add the lack of sharps in the key signature of a work that is obviously in D major (with modulations to B minor and A major).[11] Now that at least one very early work of Biber's has turned up in Vienna with many of the same musical characteristics, we have a stronger basis for assigning the Kroměříž sonata to Biber. The title of the work is something of a misnomer, however, for in every significant respect both of instrumental style and formal conception this sonata is dominated by the violin, and at least some of the above-mentioned musical characteristics are owing to that fact. The following scheme (fig. 8-3) indicates a form that is more like a few of the *Sonatae, tam Aris* than any other of Biber's ensemble sonatas. The grouping of repeated sections at the beginning, changes of tempo and style after a few bars, domination of the texture by violin, following of the fugue by a lively homophonic section— these details all appear in some of Biber's first published sonatas, although not in such an exaggerated form as here, and never with such reliance on rhythmic ostinati. The strength of the *Sonata à 4 violis* lies in its grasp of the brilliance and capricious toccata-like character of the seventeenth-century violin style (ex. 8-6), which make it highly likely that the work is one of Biber's.

Two other sonatas signed "H. B." are preserved at Kroměříž, but the question of their authorship is more problematic. Each is entitled *Sonata à 3,* and they both comprise the standard trio sonata instrumentation of two violins and basso continuo (violone, organ), plus an additional tenor-register instrument (in one case trombone, in the other viola da gamba) that sometimes functions as a soloist (either alone or in ensemble) but on other occasions merely doubles the bass line. Sehnal dates the copies around 1679–80, and finds it difficult to

Figure 8-3.　Scheme of *Sonata à 4 violis*

Section	Meter	Measures	Key	Form, Style, Texture
1	¢	19 repeated	D	Three bars (adagio), 2 bars dotted rhythm (presto), ending with 10 bars of syncopated rhythm
2		11 repeated	D	Dominated by virtuoso writing for violin
3		15 repeated	D	Six bars adagio with virtuoso 32nd-note writing for violin; nine bars "tardissime" with ostinato rhythms
4	3/4	41	D/b	Several ostinato rhythms, elaborate string crossings on violin, ending with echo effects (pp/ff/pp)
5	¢	10	D/A	Fugal presto
6	3/4	14	D	Ends with echo effects

Example 8-6.　"H. B.," *Sonata à 4 violis* (1663), Violin Excerpts

believe that the initials "H. B." could refer to Biber, who was already famous at that time. [12] In fact, these two sonatas seem too old-fashioned to have been composed by Biber around 1680; sonatas of precisely their type were written by Bertali, Schmelzer and many others, including northern composers, but not so far as we know by Biber. [13] It is certainly possible, however, that Biber wrote these two works at an earlier stage of his career, while the Kroměříž manuscripts were copier years later. We shall consider the two pieces together in comparison with a similar sonata of Bertali's. [14]

　　H. B.'s and Bertali's *Sonatae à 3* are long, multi-sectional works, containing a great deal of concertante instrumental writing, sometimes interspersed with block-chord homophonic passages. A refrain or ritornello in contrasting meter (the equivalent of a tutti) binds together several movements of Bertali's sonata and the H. B. sonata with trombone, while all three soloists appear separately in quasi-improvisational passages (fig. 8-4). Some important features of the H. B. sonata, however, are the higher degree of the virtuosic element, the basing of the two violin solos on the same harmonic outline (expanded in the second solo), greater degree of tonal contrast, and the logical progression of movements from an introductory slow/fast "sonata" type through the alternation of solos with ritornelli to a finale that combines the adagio/tutti and imitative elements. The conception of the solos in this sonata

Figure 8-4. Antonio Bertali, *Sonata à 3* (No. 1) in D minor and "H. B.,": *Sonata à 3* in D minor

Section	Meter	Measures	Tempo	Form, Style, Texture
			Bertali	
1	¢	22	Allegro	Full scoring
2		14	Adagio [then allegro?]	Full scoring
3		5	[Adagio]	Violin 1, continuo
4	$\frac{3}{2}$	12	Allegro	Full scoring (same as VI)
5	¢	6	Adagio	Violin 2, continuo
6	$\frac{3}{2}$	12	Allegro	Full scoring (same as IV)
7	¢	5	Adagio	Trombone, continuo
8	$\frac{3}{2}$	4	Allegro	Full scoring (same as last four bars of IV and VI)
9	¢	30	Allegro	Full scoring
10	$\frac{3}{2}$	25	Adagio [then allegro?]	Full scoring
			"H. B."	
1	¢	10	[Adagio]	Full scoring
2	$\frac{3}{2}$	23	[Allegro]	Full scoring
3	¢	15	[Adagio]	Violin 1, continuo
4	$\frac{3}{2}$	17	[Allegro]	Full scoring
5	¢	15	[Adagio]	Violin 2, continuo
6	$\frac{3}{2}$	14	[Allegro]	Full scoring (shortened verson of IV)
7	¢	10	[Adagio]	Trombone, continuo
8	$\frac{3}{2}$	10	[Allegro]	Trombone, continuo
9		61	[Allegro]	Full scoring (beginning resembles IV & VI)

compares with that in the Kroměříž *Sonata à 6* for trumpet and strings, discussed above; the ritornello element, however, is entirely different from that of Sonata I from the *Fidicinium Sacro-Profanum,* in that it serves here as a purely homophonic tutti, not a bearer of significant thematic material. These sonatas, in fact, are closer to the *Sonatae, tam Aris* in their emphasis on the concertizing element. The H. B. *Sonata à 3* with viola da gamba, however, is harder to identify as a work of Biber's, since the virtuosic element is far less prominent, and neither the plan of the work nor its stylistic details stand forth with much individuality. On the basis of all Biber's surviving works, however, we would name this last feature as absolutely necessary. And of the five works that bear the initials "H. B." at Kroměříž, only three exhibit the required stylistic traits for ascription to Biber: the *Sonata à 4 violis* and *Congregamini Omnes Populi* (both 1663), and the *Sonata à 3* with trombone. This is not a tidy situation, for one would not expect that two different composers with the same initials would both have been identified by their initials. Yet in the case of the *Sonata à 4 violis* Biber's authorship seems inevitable, while in that of the *Missa in Albis* it seems impossible. It might be, therefore, that unless the copying dates of the *Missa in Albis* (1668) and the *Sonata à 3* with viola da gamba are considerably later than the dates of composition, we must conjecture that for some reason the initials were put on some pieces whose authorship was in doubt even at the time.

Two further Kroměříž sonatas may be considered at this point, although neither is ascribed to anybody at all, and both probably lie outside the range of the church sonata: *Sonata Jucunda* and *Harmonia Romana,* both string sonatas, the former copied shortly before Biber came to Kroměříž and the latter written while he was there, in 1669.[15] These two anonymous sonatas contain elements found in the *Sonata à 6 die pauern-Kirchfarth genandt* and the *Battalia* of Biber's early Salzburg years. They thus serve to delineate some of the major differences between church and chamber sonatas at the time as well as to invite questions concerning the meaning of the two categories for Biber. In the case of the *Sonata Jucunda* the folk-like, quasi-program element suggests Biber's authorship strongly, although Schmelzer might also be considered. As mentioned earlier, the sonata contains a passage featuring the identical dissonances that Biber uses in the *Sonata violino solo representativa* to depict frogs (minor seconds: G-sharp–A); and two sections of the work present a folk-like tune (in two different meters and in octaves between the parts) that resembles one used by both Biber and Schmelzer. In addition there are octaves and several passages of considerable virtuosity for the first violin alone, traits that bear Biber's stamp.

The *Harmonia Romana* is, however, unique in its exploiting of solo/tutti effects, which are presumably the reason for its title. The work is scored for three violins, three violas (i.e., two viole da braccia and one basso di viola) and continuo, the identical scoring of the *Sonata à 6 die pauern-Kirchfarth genandt* and one that may be compared to the three violins, four viole da braccia and continuo (with two violoni) of the *Battalia.*[16] What all these pieces have in common, and that differentiates them from the church sonatas, is the possibility of orchestral scoring, i.e., scoring in which several of the string parts double one another, even including doubling at the octave in the *Battalia.* As a result the solo/tutti effects are all the more pronounced, and the opening Adagio/Presto sonata complex of the *Harmonia Romana* and the *Sonata à 6 die pauern-Kirchfarth genandt* resemble each other in this respect (ex. 8-7). Although a few other works in the Kroměříž archive have three violin parts, none has this kind of design or anything like it. The *Harmonia Romana* is a long suite comprising, after the sonata complex, a Courante, Fuga (in binary form with repeats), Passagio, Saltarello, Allemanda and Gigue. In general, most of the dance movements are in four parts with the two upper parts (and, of course, the continuo) doubled; the Allemanda, however, is in three with only the top part doubled; and while the normal doubling holds for most of the Fuga, in some places the second part divides to produce a fifth contrapuntal line. In the Presto section of the opening sonata complex the six string parts are independent for eleven measures, the continuo

Example 8-7. Comparison of Solo/Tutti Effects

(a) Anonymous, Sonata *Harmonia Romana* (1669), Beginning

(b) *Sonata à 6 die pauern-Kirchfarth genandt,* Beginning

providing a highly elaborated version of the violone for the first six measures; after this unusually rich texture, the sudden adagio interruption in measure five as the first violin plays the minor third of a cadence to the relative major (F) in octaves is an indication of the fantasy-like approach to concerto style that characterizes this piece. In the Saltarello the successive phrases are played first by solo violin and continuo and answered by the usual four-part doubled texture. In the Gigue a similar procedure is followed, except that now the solo violin does not play in these tutti, the result being that the top line is not doubled but the second line is; and in the first group of solo phrases the violin plays the second half in octaves, a device that reappears at the reprise (this is the only nonbinary dance), now intensified with punctuation from the remaining strings. From all these details it is apparent that the *Harmonia Romana* contains a great deal of experimentation with textures, a characteristic, as we have found, of Biber's polychoral works as well.

The Passagio, however, is the most interesting movement in the piece, scored for solo violin accompanied only by two other violin parts (one of them doubled, as it usually is, by soprano viola [fourth violin]) that together never play more than two-note chords until the final cadence; for much of the time the solo violin is left unaccompanied. The manuscript of this movement contains a number of words (deleted from the published edition) indicating changes of style and accompanimental texture: Adagio, Passag., Concerta., Adagio, Concerto, Adagio solo, Tutti. Generally, the "passagio" idea, both as the title and as an internal heading, indicates a more improvisational concept, while adagio represents the kind of writing associated with the slow passages of the introductory sonata movements; "concerta"—and to a lesser extent "tutti"—indicate passages where the solo violin is punctuated by the others violins in similar fashion to the dialogue between violin and orchestra in the opening movement. In fact, the last two terms, so obviously related to concerto style, indicate something that seems clear from the many dangling six-four chords and peculiar voice leadings in the accompanying violins: this movement is not fully transmitted in the manuscript; through some hidden situation in an older source other parts that belong to this movement must have been omitted. Presumably the Passagio was written separately from the other movements for such an error to have been made in it alone; but there is no other means of explaining the crudities of the lower violin parts in this movement, whereas they would make perfect sense as parts in a larger texture (which the modern editor has attempted to remedy with some extra notes in the violins).[17] At the same time the remarkable passages in virtuoso style might have been unaccompanied, or accompanied by basso continuo alone. The movement still has a highly experimental character that is obviously related to the attempt to suggest an Italian concerto of a pre-Corelli type. The obvious link between Italian styles and the concertato character of Austrian sonatas in this period was Antonio Bertali, who died in the year the *Harmonia Romana* was composed; Bertali's work seems to be linked with at least some of Biber's (i.e., the "H. B." *Sonata à 4 violis* appears in manuscript along with a sonata of Bertali's; and the "H. B." *Sonata à 3* with trombone is stylistically very close to Bertali). The early date for this "concerto" (1669), more than a decade before Georg Muffat's description of concerto performances in Rome, indicates at least that something of the newly-emergent style was known at Kroměříž during Biber's years there, although the *Harmonia Romana* must have been a novelty, not a true concerto in the sense of the forms and procedures that arrived in the last quarter of the century, but a striking anticipation within the tradition of the hybrid sonata/suite type of the time. The consistent focus on the solo violinist as concerto protagonist in four of the movements, the highly advanced violin technique and the style features that are shared with Biber's experimental works—even the very idea of such experiment—all make it nearly impossible to conceive of who other than Biber might have written this work (at Kroměříž?) in 1669.

A Catalog of Heinrich Biber's Works

Abbreviations

Baselt	"Die Musikaliensammlung der Schwarzburg-Rudolstädtischen Hofkapelle unter Ph. H. Erlebach (1657–1714)"
Breitenbacher	*Hudební Archiv Kolegiátního Kostela sv. Mořice v Kroměřízi*
Dahms	"Neues zur Chronologie der Opern von Biber und Muffat"
DTÖ	*Denkmäler der Tonkunst in Österreich*
Federhofer/Inventare	"Alte Musikalien-Inventare der Klöster St. Paul (Kärnten) und Göss (Steiermark)"
Federhofer/Michaelbeuern	"Zur Musikpflege im Benediktinerstift Michaelbeuern (Salzburg)"
Fellerer/Mayr	*Rupert Ignaz Mayr und seine Kirchenmusik*
Göhler	*Verzeichnis der in den Frankfurter und Leipziger Messkatalogen der Jahre 1564 bis 1759 angezeigten Musikalien*
Hintermaier	"'Missa Salisburgensis': Neue Erkenntnisse über Entstehung, Autor und Zweckbestimmung"
Keller	"Geschichtliches über die nächsten Vorfahren Mozarts als Kapellmeister im fürsterzbischöflichen Dom zu Salzburg"
Kellner	*Musikgeschichte des Stiftes Kremsmünster*
Lunelli/Meran	"Di alcuni inventari delle musiche già possedute dal coro della parrocchiale di Merano"
Luntz/Biber	"H. I. F. Biber"
Meyer	*Die mehrstimmige Spielmusik des 17. Jahrhunderts in Nord- und Mitteleuropa*
Nettl/Biber	"Heinrich Franz Biber von Bibern"
Nettl/Osegg	"Weltliche Musik des Stiftes Osegg (Böhmen) im 17. Jahrhundert"
Racek	"Inventář hudebnin tovačouského zámku z konce 17. století"
Rosenthal	"Zur Stilistik der Salzburger Kirchenmusik von 1600–1730"

Schaal	*Die Musikhandschriften der Ansbacher Inventare von 1686*
Schenk/Singfundament	"Ein 'Singfundament' von Heinrich Ignaz Franz Biber"
Schneider	"Franz Heinrich Biber als Opernkomponist"
Sehnal	"Die Kompositionen Heinrich Bibers in Kremsier (Kroměříž)"

Introduction to the Catalog

It is impossible today to discover exactly how much music Heinrich Biber composed, but we can be certain that he wrote considerably more than has survived. Inventories of the contents of seventeenth- and eighteenth-century music collections no longer extant frequently provide titles of lost works; and more will undoubtedly turn up. Until now attempts at listing Biber's works have been either lacking in completeness and accuracy (Nettl/Biber; Keller) or confined to works contained in a single archive (Sehnal). No one has included the titles of lost works, even though they shed light on Biber's compositional activity. This catalog is intended to fill a significant lacuna in research on Biber and his music.

Anyone engaged in studying the music of Heinrich Biber must deal with the contents of two archives in particular: the Liechtenstein collection in Kroměříž (Kremsier), Czechoslovakia, and the cathedral archive in Salzburg (Konsistorial-Archiv). These are the chief libraries containing either autograph manuscripts of Biber's music or copies prepared for his own use. The contents of the Liechtenstein (or St. Moritz) collection in Kroměříž were catalogued by Antonin Breitenbacher in 1928.[1] The music had lain in the collegiate church of St. Moritz in Kroměříž for about two hundred years (since the end of the seventeenth century) and was unknown to music history before the late nineteenth century. Breitenbacher organized part of the collection (comprising mostly works dated from shortly before 1660 to 1694) by referring to an inventory of these works dated around 1695. Not all of the compositions listed in the old inventory had survived; but Breitenbacher included the contents of the original listing in his catalog (giving catalog numbers for *all* the works, whether extant or not); the titles of lost works appear in normal print, while those of the surviving manuscripts are printed with wider spacing. Breitenbacher named this part of the St. Moritz archive the Liechtenstein collection, after Bishop Karl Liechtenstein-Kastelkorn, during whose lifetime most of the repertoire was accumulated. In the listing from 1695 we find titles of compositions by Biber that are no longer extant. The archive also contains a large number of anonymous manuscripts and several works signed only with the initials "H. B."; Paul Nettl ascribed works from both of these categories to Biber.[2]

The Salzburg cathedral archive offers a disappointingly small number of Biber manuscripts (not more than eight), considering Biber's thirty-four years of activity in Salzburg. Much of our knowledge of his music must be gained from works preserved in other archives, in some cases from copies of Salzburg manuscripts made either during Biber's lifetime or in the eighteenth century. Biber's music apparently aroused no interest in Salzburg during the latter part of the eighteenth century, and the name Biber became associated with his son Carl. In three old thematic catalogs of the Salzburg cathedral music collection (each entitled *Catalogus musicalis in Ecclesia metropolitana*) the name Heinrich Biber does not appear. The first of these was compiled in the late eighteenth century by Luigi Gatti as well as other copyists active in the 1780s. Rosenthal designated with the letter "A" the unknown compiler of the second catalog (dated 1791); it incorporates several different handwritings, including that of Gatti, principal copyist of the first catalog.[3] Joachim Fuetsch prepared the third catalog in 1822. Today the catalogs give us the titles of works now lost. But the Salzburg cathedral archive contains (and contained in the eighteenth century) a considerable number of works not listed in any of the catalogs. Evidently the compilers did not bother to maintain accuracy or completeness when listing a body of works no longer in use. Although Heinrich Biber's name does not appear in the catalogs, a few works that are ascribed to him in manuscripts of other archives are listed under Carl Biber's name. In addition, one church work (Responsorium *Recessit Pastor Bonus*), attributed to Carl Biber by Fuetsch, was published as a work of Heinrich Biber's in the nineteenth century. The original manuscript no longer resides in the cathedral archive. The question of authorship thus arises whenever a composition bears only the name "Biber"; and sometimes the decision boils down to the choice between an ascription to Carl Biber made in the eighteenth century when Heinrich Biber had been forgotten and one to Heinrich Biber made in the nineteenth century, when Heinrich Biber had been rediscovered and Carl Biber had not.

Fortunately, the identification of the Salzburg watermarks in the last decade or so enables us to eliminate from discussion a considerable number of compositions in the cathedral archive that bear only the name Biber, but whose watermarks date from the eighteenth century.[4] A very few such pieces remain in the area of overlap between Biber father and son; and characteristics of their individual styles usually make the ascription straightforward. The one composition that might have been composed by either Biber is the *Missa in Contrapuncto,* which, because of its composition in the *stile antico,* reveals less of the gap between seventeenth- and eighteenth-century styles; here we must choose between eighteenth- and nineteenth-century ascriptions. The majority of Biber's works that survive in archives other than Salzburg and Kroměříž are preserved in copies from after the composer's death; while the question of authorship is not in doubt, the works cannot be dated on the basis of the manuscripts.

This catalog is divided into two parts: 1) extant works, and 2) an appendix listing lost and doubtful works as well as compositions that have been unnecessarily or falsely attributed to Biber. Information concerning each composition appears in the following order:

Catalog Number and Title

a)   text and author
b)   key
c)   date
d)   contents (= individual movements of suites; single works in collections)
e)   scoring
f)   source(s)
g)   edition(s)
h)   comments

Sources of information concerning lost works are given in square brackets. The titles of lost works are given exactly as they appear in the original sources. As a result the reader will find several different spellings for certain words, for example "Balletti" ("Baletti," "Ballettae," etc.) and "Partita" ("Parthi," "Parthien," "Parthia," etc.). The listing for such titles follows the scoring first (i.e., from smaller to larger forces: *à 2* before *à 3*), the alphabet second (e.g., "Ballettae" before "Balletti," but *Balletti à 2* before *Ballettae à 3*).

Catalog of Heinrich Biber's Works

MASSES

1. *Missa Alleluia*

    a)   Ordinary of the Mass

    b)   C major

    c)   Between 1690 and 1698

    e)   Two four-part choruses (SATB) & soloists, 2 violins, 3 violas, 6 trumpets, kettledrums, 2 cornettos, 3 trombones, 1 theorbo, organ, violone

    f)   (1)   MS parts at the Benedictine monastery in Kremsmünster, Upper Austria

         (2)   Score prepared by Sigismund Keller in Kloster Einsiedeln, Switzerland

    h)   A copy of this work existed at Freising in the eighteenth century [Fellerer/Mayr]. The cover of the original Salzburg parts (now lost) has been preserved and reads as follows: "Missa Alleluja à 26 in Conc. 8 Voci, 6 Viole, 2 Cornetti, 3 Tromboni, 6 Trombe, 1 Timpano (8 Voci in ripieno), et Bassi cont. del Sigre. H. Fr. de Biber Maestro di Capella a Salisburgo" The form of Biber's name gives a *terminus post quem* of 1690 for the date of composition of the Mass. The Kremsmünster title page reads: "Missa Alleluia à 36 voci, 8 voci concerti, 8 voci ripieni, 2 Violini, 3 Viole, 6 Trombe, 1 Timpano, 2 Cornetti, 3 Tromboni, 1 Tiorba, Organo con Violone dal Sign. Biber, sub. P.[ater] T.[heodorich] B.[eer] 1698."

2. *Missa Catholica*

    a)   Ordinary of the Mass

    b)   C major

    c)   After 1680 [Sehnal]

    e)   SATB chorus & soloists, 2 violins, 2 violas, 2 clarinos, organ, violone. Only the string and clarino 2 parts are extant.

    f)   MS parts at Kroměříž (B I 39)

    h)   The chapel of Graf Ferdinand Julius von Salm (1650–97) in Tovacov, Czechoslovakia (16 km. north of Kroměříž) had a copy of this work in the late seventeenth century [Racek]. An anonymous *Missa Catholicca* [*sic*] is listed with many other Masses (which are mostly anonymous but recognizable through their titles as works of Kerll, Hofer, Schmelzer, etc.) in an old inventory of music no longer extant, published in Federhofer/Inventare.

3. *Missa Christi Resurgentis*

a) Ordinary of the Mass
b) C major
c) 1674 [Sehnal]
e) Two four-part choruses (SATB) & soloists (including a third bass part), 2 violins, 2 violas, 2 clarinos, 2 cornettos, 3 trombones, organ, violone
f) MS parts at Kroměříž (B I 103).

4. *Missa ex B*

a) Ordinary of the Mass
b) B-flat major
e) SSATBB chorus (and soloists? see h) below) organ
f) MS parts at Stift Seittenstetten, Lower Austria
h) The original title page reads: "Missa ex B, Canto, Alto, Tenore, Basso, Violini 2 [crossed out] organo L[ocus]: R[epositionis]: Cc, Sig: Biber." The title was copied about 1770. The MS contains two gatherings of parts, the first with parts for Canto I° and II°, Basso I° conc. and II° conc., Alto, Tenore and Passo [*sic*] II^do conc. in duplo, the second with parts for Canto I° and II°, Basso I° conc. and Basso II° conc. At the end of the organ part in the first gathering appears the remark: "Authore Dno Henrico Ignatio Francisco de Bibern. a F[ratre]. Benedicto Calles Seittenstettensi Descripta Anno 1707 die 27 Augusti." Benedictus Calles (1682–1732) was in Salzburg from 1705–8 and later became *Regenschori* at Seitenstetten. The second gathering is in a different hand.

5. *Missa Quadragesimalis*

a) Ordinary of the Mass
b) D minor
e) SATB chorus (with *colla parte* instruments), organ
f) (1) MS parts at Kroměříž (B I 297) under the title *Missa in Contrapuncto*
    (2) MS parts at Prague, Kapitelsbibliothek under the title *Missa Quadragesimalis à 4 voc:*
    (3) MS parts at Stift Seitenstetten (D III 2a) under the title *Missa alla Cappella*
    (4) MS score made by Sigismund Keller (1803–82) in Kloster Einsiedeln, Switzerland
    (5) MS score made by Sigismund Keller in Bayerische Staatsbibliothek, München (1879)
h) Keller's scores contain no Gloria. The Prague MS contains parts for two *colla parte* "Violettis." The Seitenstetten copy has parts for "Violetta," "3 Trompon." and "Violoncello Conc." The titles *Missa in contrapunct* and *Missa sine Gloria in contrapunct* appear under Biber's name in an old inventory of music (now lost) at Stift Michaelbeuern, Salzburg [Federhofer/Michaelbeuern].

6. *Missa S. Henrici*

a) Ordinary of the Mass
b) C major
c) 1696
e) SSATB chorus & soloists, 2 violins, 3 violas, 2 clarinos, 3 trumpets and kettledrums *ad libitum,* 3 trombones, organ, violone

f) (1) MS parts at Stift Kremsmünster, Upper Austria (copied 1701)
    (2) Score made by Sigismund Keller in Kloster Einsiedeln, Switzerland
g) *DTÖ* 49, edited by Guido Adler
h) This Mass was composed for the occasion of Biber's daughter Maria Anna Magdalena's taking the veil at Stift Nonnberg as M. Rosa Henrica; the work was performed on July 11, 1696.

7. *Requiem à 15*

    a) Requiem, Kyrie, Dies irae, Domine Jesu Christe, Sanctus, Agnus Dei, Lux aeterna
    b) A major
    c) After 1690
    e) SSATBB chorus & soloists, 4 *Violette*, 2 *Trombe Basse* (in A), 2 oboes, 3 trombones, bassoon, organ
    f) MS parts in Salzburg cathedral archive (A 181)
    g) Modern edition published in Werner Jaksch, *H. I. F. Biber, Requiem à 15*
    h) Rosenthal states erroneously that the work is published in *DTÖ* [Rosenthal, 86].

8. *Requiem ex F con terza min[ore]*

    a) Requiem, Kyrie, Dies irae, Domine Jesu Christe, Sanctus, Agnus Dei, Lux aeterna
    b) F minor
    c) After 1692
    e) SSATB chorus & soloists, 2 violins, 3 violas, 3 trombones *ad libitum*, organ
    f) (1) MS parts in Salzburg Cathedral archive (A 182)
        (2) MS parts in Augustiner-Chorherrenstift Herzogenburg (Archive No. 51)
    g) *DTÖ* 59, edited by Guido Adler
    h) A *Requiem à 11*, no longer extant, appears under Biber's name in an old inventory of music at Stift Michaelbeuern, Salzburg [Federhofer/Michaelbeuern].

VESPERS MUSIC

9. *Laetatus Sum à 7*

    b) A major
    c) 1676
    e) Two solo basses, solo violin, 3 violas, organ, violone
    f) MS parts at Kroměříž (B III 73).

10. *Nisi Dominus aedificaverit Domum*

    b) G major
    e) Solo bass, solo violin, organ, violone
    f) MS parts in the Sächsische Landesbibliothek, Dresden (Mus. 1851/E/500)
    g) Modern edition: Heinrich Ignaz Franz Biber, *Nisi Dominus aedificaverit domum,* ed. Wolfram Steude. Leipzig: Deutscher Verlag für Musik, 1972.

11.-12. *Vesperae à 32*

    b) C major
    c) 1674

d)   11.   *Dixit Dominus*
      12.   *Magnificat*

e)   Two four-part choruses (SATB) & 8 soloists, 2 violins, 2 violas, 4 trumpets, kettledrums, 2 cornettos, 3 trombones, organ, *Basso di viola* [violone]

f)   (1)   MS parts (autograph) at Kroměříž (B III 89)
      (2)   MS parts at Kroměříž (B III 97)

h)   The autograph title page reads: "A. M. D. G. B. M. V. Assumptae H./ Vesperae à 32:/ 8. Voc in Concert./ 8. in Capella/ 5. Viol./ 2 Cornett./ 3. Trombon:/ 4. Tromb:/ Cum Tympano/ Et 4: bassi Continui:/ Voces in Concerto. 23:/ vom/ Hainrich J. franz biber/ A°. 1674."

13.–42.   *Vesperae Longiores ac Breviores Unacum Litaniis Lauretanis*
      (published by J. B. Mayr, Salzburg, 1693)

d)   *Psalmi Longiores*:
      13.   *Dixit Dominus* (D major)
      14.   *Confitebor* (B minor)
      15.   *Beatus Vir* (G major)
      16.   *Laudate Pueri* (D major)
      17.   *Laudate Dominum* (A major)
      18.   *Magnificat* (D major)

      Psalmi de B. M. Virgine:
      19.   *Dixit Dominus* (G minor)
      20.   *Laudate Pueri* (B-flat major)
      21.   *Laetatus Sum* (F major)
      22.   *Nisi Dominus* (D minor)
      23.   *Lauda Jerusalem* (B-flat major)
      24.   *Magnificat* (G minor)

      Psalmi Breviores:
      25.   *Dixit Dominus* (C major)
      26.   *Confitebor* (A minor)
      27.   *Beatus Vir* (E minor)
      28.   *Laudate Pueri* (C major)
      29.   *Laudate Dominum* (G major)
      30.   *Laudate Pueri* (A minor)
      31.   *Laetatus Sum* (E minor)
      32.   *Nisi Dominus* (C major)
      33.   *Lauda Jerusalem* (G major)
      34.   *Magnificat* (C major)

      Psalmi per Annum Necessarii:
      35.   *Credidi* (D minor)
      36.   *In Convertendo* (A minor)
      37.   *Domine Probasti Me* (F major)
      38.   *De Profundis* (C minor)
      39.   *Memento* (G minor)
      40.   *Beati Omnes* (B-flat major)
      41.   *In Exitu Israel* (D minor)
      42.   *Litaniae Lauretanae* (E minor)

e)   SATB chorus & soloists, 2 violins, 2 violas, 3 trombones *ad libitum,* organ

f)   (1)   Graz, Austria, Musikwissenschaftliches Institut der Universität Graz (MS II; only Alto conc., Tenore conc., Basso conc., Violini 1 & 2, and organ extant). This copy formerly belonged to St. Jakobskirche in Leoben (Austria)

(2)   Kroměříž (A 278–87; A, T, B in concerto, SATB in capella, viola 1, organ extant)

(3)   Kroměříž (B III 61; all vocal parts, violin 2, viola 2 extant)

(4)   München, Bayerische Staatsbibliothek (2° Mus. pr. 169; all parts extant, but printed organ part incomplete; 1 cornetto part, 1 organ and 3 trombone parts in manuscript)

(5)   New Haven, Yale University Library (nine parts extant)

(6)   Ottobeuern, Benediktinerstift (SATB in concerto, 2 violins, viola 1, organ extant)

(7)   Salzburg, cathedral archive (Sop. and Ten. in concerto, Sop. in capella [2 copies], Basso in capella [3 copies], violin 1, 2, viola 1, organ [4 copies]); also MS violin 2 part for the three Dixits and Magnificats, plus MS trombone 1 and 3 and "Organo in Capella" for the whole and MS violone for the Litaniae Lauretanae only. All cataloged under A 173. Some parts formerly in possession of the *Priesterbibliothek.*

(8)   Göttweig, Benediktinerstift (MS copies of seventeen pieces from the set, in seven manuscripts)

h)   Copies, now lost, were in the Damenstift at Hall, Tirol, according to an inventory of about 1720 (W. Senn, *Aus dem Kulturleben einer süddeutschen Kleinstadt,* p. 342) and at the parish church at Meran [Lunelli/Meran].

MISCELLANEOUS VOCAL CHURCH WORKS

43.   *In Festo Trium Regium, Muttetum Natale à 6*

b)   C major

e)   Two solo sopranos, 2 recorders, 2 oboes, organ

f)   MS parts at the Moravske Museum, Brno

h)   The eighteenth-century copy bears the phrase "ex libris Matthiae Altman."

44.   *Litania de S. Josepho à 20*

b)   D major

c)   After 1690

e)   Double chorus (SATB), eight vocal soloists, 2 violins, 5 violas, 2 trumpets in D, 3 trombones, basso continuo

f)   MS parts in the Salzburg cathedral archive (A 435).

45.   *Lux Perpetua*

b)   G major

c)   1673 [Sehnal]

e)   Two four-part choruses (SATB) & 8 vocal soloists, 2 violins, 2 violas, 3 trombones, organ, violone

f)   MS parts at Kroměříž (B II 259), perhaps autograph [Sehnal]

h)   Nettl lists the work erroneously as *Lux Redemptor* [Nettl/Biber, 70].

46.   **Offertorium:** *Huc Poenitentes*

b)   C minor

c)   Around 1700

e)   SSATB chorus & soloists, 2 violins, 2 violas, 3 trombones *ad libitum,* 3 organs, bassoon, violone

f)   MS parts in the Salzburg cathedral archive (A 180)

h)   This is the only work of Biber's to bear the initials H R on the watermark, indicating a date around 1700.

47.   **Offertorium:** *Ne Cedite*

b)   A minor

c)   After 1690

e)   SSATB chorus & soloists, 2 violins, 2 violas, 3 trombones, organo pro Rippien., Organo, Organo o Tiorba, Organo o Viola

f)   MS parts in the Salzburg cathedral archive (A 179)

h)   The manuscript bears only the name Biber and in Luigi Gatti's eighteenth-century catalog of the archive, this work is ascribed to Carl Biber. Rosenthal considers it a work of Heinrich Biber's [Rosenthal, 87]. Judging from its style, it could have been written only by the elder Biber. And the initials FW on the watermark place it in the late seventeenth century, when Carl Biber would have been in his teens or younger.

48.   *Offertorium in Festo 7 dolorum: Quo abiit dilectus tuus*

b)   E minor

e)   SATB chorus & soloists, 4 violas, 4 organs and Organo pro Ripieno

f)   (1)   MS parts in Benediktinerstift, Göttweig, Lower Austria
     (2)   MS parts in Salzburg cathedral archive

h)   The Salzburg manuscript bears only the name Biber. The initials FW on the watermark indicate the elder Biber.

49.   *Salve Regina à 2*

b)   E minor

c)   1663

e)   Soprano solo (not extant), viola da gamba solo, organ

f)   MS parts at Kroměříž (B VI 19).

50.   *Stabat Mater*

b)   E minor

d)   Verses 1, 3, 11, 20 of the sequence

e)   SATB chorus and basso continuo

f)   (1)   MS score in Wachskammer archive of the Salzburg cathedral (Wb. 21); no basso continuo
     (2)   Eighteenth-century set of soprano, alto, tenor, bass, organ and violone parts at Benediktiner Stift St. Peter, Salzburg (1229.55)
     (3)   Score made by Sigismund Keller from the Salzburg cathedral score at Kloster Einsiedeln, Switzerland.

DRAMATIC WORKS

51. *Dramma Musicale: Chi la dura la vince*

   a)   Text by Francesco Maria Raffaelini

   c)   Between Dec. 5, 1690 and the middle of 1692 [Dahms]

   d)   Three-act opera in forty-two scenes (10 + 16 + 16)

   f)   MS score in the Museum Carolino-Augusteum, Salzburg (Hs. 560).

SUITES

52. *Arien à 4*

   b)   E minor

   c)   1673

   d)   Intrada, Aria, Aria, Gigue

   e)   Violin, 2 violas, violone (cembalo part missing)

   f)   MS parts (autograph) at Kroměříž (B XIV 171)

   g)   *DTÖ* 127 (1976), edited by Jiří Sehnal.

53. *Arien à 4*

   b)   A major

   c)   1673–74 [Sehnal]

   d)   Sonata, Allamanda, Amoresca, Gigue, Sonatina

   e)   Violin, 2 violas, cembalo, violone

   f)   MS parts (autograph) at Kroměříž (B XIV 174)

   g)   *DTÖ* 127, ed. Jiří Sehnal.

54. *Ballettae à 4*

   b)   E minor

   c)   Ca. 1680 [Sehnal]

   d)   Brandles, Amener, Montiradar, Courante, Sarabande, Minuet, Retirada, Allegro

   e)   Violin, 2 violas, basso continuo

   f)   MS parts at Kroměříž (B XIV 182)

   g)   *DTÖ* 127, edited by Jiří Sehnal

   h)   Only viola parts extant.

55. *Ballettae à 4*

   b)   D major

   c)   1685 [Sehnal]

   d)   Seven numbered movements, the seventh entitled Minuett

   e)   Violin, 2 violas, violone (cembalo part missing)

   f)   MS parts at Kroměříž (B XIV 30)

   g)   *DTÖ* 127, edited by Jiří Sehnal.

56.   *Balletti à 4*

b)   G major
c)   1673–74 [Sehnal]
d)   Sonata, Allamande, Courente, Sarabande, Aria, Gigue, Sonatina
e)   Violin, 2 violas, violone (cembalo part missing)
f)   MS parts (autograph) at Kroměříž (B XIV 248)
g)   *DTÖ* 127, edited by Jiří Sehnal
h)   The MS is anonymous since there is no title page. Sehnal ascribes the work to Biber because Biber copied it. Besides these *Balletti,* there are three other anonymous works contained under the same catalog number [Sehnal, 24].

57.   *Balletti à 6*

b)   C major
c)   ca. 1690 [Sehnal]
d)   Sonata, Allemande, Amener, Aria, Balletto, Trezza, Gavotte, Canario, Amoresca, Sarabanda, Gagliarda, Ciacona
e)   Violin, 2 violas, 2 trumpets, cembalo, violone
f)   MS parts at Kroměříž (B XIV 241)
g)   *DTÖ* 127, edited by Jiří Sehnal.

58.   *Baletti* [*sic*]

b)   G minor
c)   1670–74 [Sehnal]
d)   Intrada, 2, 3, 4, 5, 6, 7, 8, then an Aria Barbaresca and Aria in D major
e)   2 violins, 2 violas, violone (cembalo part missing)
f)   (1)   MS parts at Kroměříž (B XIV 167)
      (2)   A second Kroměříž copy (anonymous) entitled *Ballettae à 4* (B XIV 107) contains the first eight pieces.
g)   *DTÖ* 127, edited by Jiří Sehnal.

59.   *Balletti Lamentabili à 4*

b)   E minor
c)   "composti Cremsirii 1670"
d)   Allabreve, Allamanda, Sarabande, Gavotte, Gigue, Lamento
e)   Violin, 2 violas, cembalo, violone
f)   MS parts at Kroměříž (B XIV 32; copied by Vejvanovský)
g)   *DTÖ* 127, edited by Jiří Sehnal.

60.   *Balletto*

b)   B minor
c)   1673 [Sehnal]
d)   Intrada, Ballo, Trezza, Aria, Die Werber Aria, Allemanda
e)   Violin, 3 violas, violone (cembalo part missing)
f)   MS parts (autograph) at Kroměříž (B XIV 250)
g)   *DTÖ* 127, edited by Jiří Sehnal
h)   The MS is anonymous. Sehnal ascribes the work to Biber because the MS is in his hand [Sehnal].

61. *Battalia*

b)   D major

c)   1673

d)   Sonata, Allegro: Die liederliche Gesellschaft von allerley Humor, Presto, Der Mars, Presto, Aria, Die Schlacht, Adagio: Lamento der Verwundten Musquetirer

e)   3 violins, 4 violas, 2 violini, cembalo

f)   (1)   MS parts (autograph) at Kroměříž (B XIV 122)

      (2)   A second set of parts is preserved at Kroměříž under the title *Sonata di Marche* (B IV 183)

g)   *Diletto Musicale* No. 357, Vienna: Doblinger, 1971, edited by Nikolaus Harnoncourt

h)   Biber subtitled the work "Das liederliche Schwärmen der Musquetirer, Mars, die Schlacht, Undt Lamento der Verwundten, mit Arien imitirt Und Baccho dedicirt." The manuscript contains the following autograph performance instructions: "NB: wo die Strich sindt mus man anstad des Geigens mit dem Bogen klopfen auf die Geigen, es mus wol probirt werden, der Mars ist schon bekant [a slightly different version appears in the *Sonata violino solo representativa*], aber ich hab ihn nicht bösser wissen zu verwenden, wo die Druml geth im Bass muss man an die Saite ein Papier machen dass es einen *strepitum* gibt, im Mars nur allein." "NB: Die Schlacht muss nit mit dem bogen gestrichen werden, sondern mit der rechten Handt die Saite geschnelt wie die stuck, Undt starck!" The notoriously dissonant second movement bears the following remark: "hic dissonant ubique, nam enim sic diversis cantilenis clamore solent."

62.–68. *Harmonia Artificiosa-Ariosa*

(published 1696 without place and publisher's name; reissued ca. 1712 in Nürnberg by Endtner)

d)   62.   Partia I (D minor): Sonata, Allamande with Variatio I & II, Aria, Sarabande with Variatio I & II, Finale (*scordatura*: both violins tuned a, e′, a′, d″)

      63.   Partia II (B minor): Praeludium, Allamande & Variatio, Balletto, Gigue (*scordatura*: both violins tuned b, f′-sharp, b′, d″)

      64.   Partia III (A major): Praeludium, Allamande, Amener, Balletto, Gigue, Ciacona (*scordatura*: both violins tuned a, e′, a′, e″)

      65.   Partia IV (E-flat major): Sonata, Allamande, Trezza, Aria, Canario, Gigue, Pollicinello (*scordatura*: violin tuned b-flat, e′-flat, b′-flat, e″-flat; viola tuned e-flat, b-flat, e′-flat, b′-flat)

      66.   Partia V (G minor): Intrada, Aria, Balletto, Gigue, Passacaglia (*scordatura*: both violins tuned g, d′, a′, d″)

      67.   Partia VI (D major): Praeludium, Aria with Variatio I–XIII, Finale; both violins in normal tuning

      68.   Partia VII (C minor): Praeludium, Allamande, Sarabande, Gigue, Aria, Trezza, Arietta variata (*scordatura*: both viole d'amore tuned c, g, c′, e′-flat, g′, c″)

e)   Partie I, II, III, V, VI: 2 violins & basso continuo Partia IV: violin, viola da braccio & basso continuo Partia VII: 2 viole d'amore & basso continuo

f)   (1)   Göttingen, Niedersächsische Staats- und Universitäts Bibliothek (1712 ed.)

      (2)   Warsaw, Biblioteka Universytecka (1712 ed.)

      (3)   Würzburg, Graf von Schönborn'sche Archiv (1696 ed.)

(4)   MS copy of Partia VII (transposed up a tone) in Staatsbibliothek, Berlin (Mus. MS 1775)

g) (1)   *DTÖ* 92 (1956), edited by Paul Nettl and Friedrich Reidinger

(2)   *Partia VII,* ed. C. Kint, Leipzig: Günther, 1937

h)   The second edition of this work can be dated 1712 because it appears in the Frankfurt *Messkatalog* for that year [Göhler].

69.–74.   *Mensa Sonora seu Musica Instrumentalis*
(published in Salzburg by J. B. Mayr, 1680)

d) 69.   Pars I (D major): Sonata, Allamanda, Courante, Sarabanda, Gavotte, Gigue, Sonatina

70.   Pars II (F major): Intrada, Balletto, Sarabanda, Balletto, Sarabanda, Balletto

71.   Pars III (A minor): Gagliarda, Sarabanda, Aria, Ciacona, Sonatina

72.   Pars IV (B-flat major): Sonata, Allamanda, Courante, Balletto, Sarabanda, Gigue, Sonatina

73.   Pars V (A major): Intrada, Balletto, Trezza, Gigue, Gavotte, Gigue, Retirada

74.   Pars VI (G minor): Sonata, Aria, Canario, Amener, Trezza, Ciacona, Sonatina

e)   Violin, 2 violas, violone, cembalo

f) (1)   Kroměříž (A 273–277)

(2)   Munich, Bayerische Staatsbibliothek (2° Mus. pr. 113; only violin part extant)

(3)   Washington, Library of Congress (only violin, viola 2, cembalo extant)

(4)   Paderborn, West Germany, Akademische Bibliothek (only violin, viola 1, violone, cembalo extant)

g)   *DTÖ* 96 (1960), edited by Erich Schenk.

75.   *Serenada à 5*

b)   C major

c)   1673

d)   Serenada, Allamanda, Aria, Ciacona, Gavotte, Retirada

e)   2 violins, 2 violas, violone, cembalo. The Ciacona contains no continuo part but has a part for a bass voice (which sings the nightwatchman's call).

f)   MS parts (notes autograph; movement headings by an unknown copyist) at Kroměříž (B XIV 169)

g)   *Nagels Musik Archiv,* No. 112, Kassel, 1934, edited by Paul Nettl; reprinted in *DTÖ* 127 (1956).

h)   Biber included the following performance instructions: "Die Serenada, Allemanda, Aria, Gavotte, Retirada werden alle nicht repetirt. Vom anfang wie sonsten andere Ballett man zu reproduciren pflegt. Aber wohl besetzt, sonderlich die viola brazza 2, welche das *Fundament* zumeist ausführt. In der Ciacona kombt der Nachtwächter, wie man jetziger Zeit die uhr alhier ausrueffen pflegt. Und die andern Instrumente werden alle ohne Bogen gespielt wie auf der lauten auch in der Gavotte, es kombt schön heraus, nemblich die geigen unter die armen."

76.   *Trombet- und musikalischer Taffeldienst à 4*

b)   C major

c)   1673–74 [Sehnal]

d)   Intrada (Tromba luditur in Violino Solo), Sonata, Allamanda, Sarabanda, Gavotte, Gigue, Sonatina

e) 2 violins, 2 violas, violone, cembalo

f) MS parts (autograph?) at Kroměříž (B XIV 173)

g) *DTÖ* 127, edited by Jiří Sehnal

h) Violin 2 and cembalo *tacent* in the Intrada. The Latin phrase heading this movement refers to the style of the first violin part, which imitates a trumpet fanfare, while the lower strings sustain a C-major chord.

SONATAS

77. *Fantasia*

b) D major

d) [Adagio]; Presto; [Adagio]; Gigue and Variatio; Minuet

e) Solo violin & continuo

f) MS 726 of the music archive of the Minoritenkonvent, Vienna, No. 3

h) This work (anonymous) is in part an earlier version of Sonata IV of the *Sonatae Violino Solo,* 1681; it requires the same *scordatura* as Sonata IV.

78.–89. *Fidicinium Sacro-Profanum, tam Choro, quam Foro, Pluribus Fidibus concinnatum et concini aptum*
(Nürnberg: Endter, ca. 1683)

d) 78. Sonata I (B minor)
    79. Sonata II (F major)
    80. Sonata III (D minor)
    81. Sonata IV (G minor)
    82. Sonata V (C major)
    83. Sonata VI (A minor)
    84. Sonata VII (D major)
    85. Sonata VIII (B-flat major)
    86. Sonata IX (G major)
    87. Sonata X (E major)
    88. Sonata XI (C minor)
    89. Sonata XII (A major)

e) Sonatas I–VI: 2 violins, 2 violas, basso continuo
Sonatas VII–XII: 1 violin, 2 violas, basso continuo

f) (1) Durham Cathedral Library (No. 415)
   (2) Warsaw, Biblioteka Universytecka (only violin 2, violone & organ extant)
   (3) Zürich, Zentralbibliothek (AGM XIII 122 & a–e)

g) (1) *DTÖ* 97 (1960), edited by Erich Schenk
   (2) Sonata X, edited by Karl Nef in *Zur Geschichte der deutschen Instrumentalmusik in der zweiten Hälfte des 17. Jahrhunderts* (*Publikationen der internationalen Musikgesellschaft,* V).

h) A copy, now lost, was owned by Stift Osegg in Bohemia in the seventeenth century [Nettl/Osegg]. The collection is undated but was listed in the Frankfurt and Leipzig *Messkatalogen* for 1683 [Göhler]: thus Schenk suggests that year as the date of publication. Erwin Luntz suggests 1682 because in that year the anniversary of the founding of the archdiocese prompted the dedication of other collections to Archbishop Max Gandolph [Luntz/Biber].

90.–105.   *Mystery Sonatas*

c)   ca. 1676?

d)   90.   Sonata I (D minor)
    91.   Sonata II (A major); *scordatura* (a, e′, a′, e″)
    92.   Sonata III (B minor); *scordatura* (b, f′-sharp, b′, d″)
    93.   Sonata IV (D minor); *scordatura* (a, d′, a′, d″)
    94.   Sonata V (A major); *scordatura* (a, e′, a′, c″-sharp)
    95.   Sonata VI (C minor); *scordatura* (a-flat, e′-flat, g′, d″)
    96.   Sonata VII (F major); *scordatura* (c′, f′, a′, c″)
    97.   Sonata VIII (B-flat major); *scordatura* (d′, f′, b′-flat, d″)
    98.   Sonata IX (A minor); *scordatura* (c′, e′, a′, e″)
    99.   Sonata X (G minor); *scordatura* (g, d′, a′, d″)
   100.   Sonata XI (G major); *scordatura* (g, g′, d′, d″)
   101.   Sonata XII (C major); *scordatura* (c′, e′, g′, c″)
   102.   Sonata XIII (d minor); *scordatura* (a, e′, c″-sharp, e″)
   103.   Sonata XIV (D major); *scordatura* (a, e′, a′, d″)
   104.   Sonata XV (C major); *scordatura* (g, c′, g′, d″)
   105.   Passacaglia (G minor)

e)   Sonatas I–XV: solo violin & continuo
   No. XVI: Passacaglia for unaccompanied violin

f)   (1)   MS in München, Bayerische Staatsbibliothek (Mus. MS 4123)
   (2)   MS copy of Sonata X in MS 726 of the music archive of the Minoritenkonvent, Vienna (see (h) below)

g)   (1)   *DTÖ* 25 (1905), edited by Erwin Luntz
   (2)   Universal Edition, 1923; edited by Robert Reitz after the *DTÖ* edition
   (3)   Wilhelm-Hansen Edition, Frankfurt am Main, 2 vols.
   (4)   Passacaglia in *Deutsche Meisterwerke für Violine allein,* No. 1, Köln: Tischer, 1921
   (5)   Passacaglia edited by Karl Gerhartz. Starnberg: Wunderhorn-Verlag (ca. 1921)
   (6)   Sonata VI, edited by F. David. Leipzig: Breitkopf und Härtel; newly revised edition by Henri Petri, 1950
   (7)   Sonata VI in Schering, *Geschichte der Musik in Beispielen,* Leipzig, 1931
   (8)   Sonata VI, Augsburg-Vienna: Böhm (ca. 1930)
   (9)   Sonata VI in *Alte Salzburger Meister der kirchlichen Kunst,* Vol. VIII. Ed. Joseph Messner
  (10)   Sonata XI, second movement, in *Historical Anthology of Music,* vol. 2, no. 238. Edited by Archibald Davison and Willi Apel. Cambridge, 1962.

h)   The copy of Sonata X in the Minoritenkonvent, Vienna is preserved under Schmelzer's name. It is in A minor, contains programmatic titles to the movements (concerning the Turkish siege of Vienna) and includes an additional final movement not found in the Munich MS (see chapter 7 of this study). A *Sonata Paschalis. Surrexit Christus hodie,* undoubtedly Sonata XI of this set, was preserved at Stift Michaelbeuern, Salzburg in the early eighteenth century; it is now lost [Federhofer/Michaelbeuern].

106. *Pastorella*

b) A major
e) Solo violin & continuo
f) MS 726 of the music archive of the Minoritenkonvent, Vienna, No. 79.
h) The last movement is based upon a song by J. J. Prinner, "Nambli wol kann ich ietzt glauben." Biber also used this song in the *Battalia*. This piece is very closely related to a *Pastorella* of Johann Heinrich Schmelzer (see chapter 1).

107. *Sonata*

b) C minor
e) Solo violin & continuo
f) MS 726 of the music archive of the Minoritenkonvent, Vienna, Sonata No. 75
h) Anonymous earlier version of Sonata VI of the *Sonatae Violino Solo,* 1681. See chapter 7 of the present study.

108. *Sonata*

b) E major
e) Solo violin & continuo
f) MS 726 of the music archive of the Minoritenkonvent, Vienna, Sonata No. 84.

109. *Sonata à 6*

b) C major
c) 1673 [Sehnal]
e) 2 violins, 2 violas, trumpet, organ, violone
f) MS parts (autograph) at Kroměříž (B IV 110)
g) (1) Edited by Kurt Janetzky. London: Musica Rara, 1958
   (2) Musica da Camera. New York: Schirmer, n.d. Reprint of (1)
h) In both editions, which are identical, the sonata is transposed to B-flat major. Janetzky's preface to the *Musica Rara* publication refers to a second, C-major, version of the sonata. In reality the only original version is in C, and the B-flat version is Janetzky's transposition.

110. *Sonata à 6 die pauern-Kirchfarth genandt*

b) B-flat
c) 1673 [Sehnal]
e) 3 violins, 2 violas, cembalo, violone
f) MS parts (autograph) at Kroměříž (B XIV 162)
g) *Diletto Musicale* No. 258, ed. Nikolaus Harnoncourt. Vienna: Doblinger, 1971.
h) The Salm chapel at Tovacov owned a copy of this work in the late seventeenth century [Racek].

111. *Sonata à 7*

b) C major
c) 1668
e) 6 trumpets (clarinos), kettledrums, organ
f) MS parts at Kroměříž (B IV 172); probably autograph [Sehnal]
g) *Diletto Musicale,* No. 463, ed. Nikolaus Harnoncourt. Vienna: Doblinger, 1971.

112.   *Sonata pro Tabula à 10*

b)   C major
c)   After 1670 [Sehnal]
e)   5 "flautae" (recorders), 2 violins, 3 violas, organ
f)   MS parts at Kroměříž (B XIV 206)
g)   Edited by Heinz Zirnbauer. Wolfenbüttel/Zürich: Möscher Verlag, 1963.

113.   *Sonata S. Polycarpi à 9*

b)   C major
c)   1673 [Sehnal]
e)   8 trumpets, kettledrums, basso continuo, violone
f)   MS parts (autograph) at Kroměříž (B IV 187)
g)   Edited by Edward H. Tarr. Edward H. Tarr Series: No. 14. The Brass Press, 1978.
h)   The work was written for the installation of Polykarp von Khuenburg as provost of the Salzburg cathedral in January 1673 and presumably performed on St. Polycarp's day, Jan. 26. The manuscript bears the following autograph performance instructions: "NB das Tromba 1. et 2. auch 5. undt 6. alle Vier müssen beysammen stehen. Undt Tromba 3. 4. 7. 8. auch beysammen, dan sie gehen in Tripla ad duos choros. Der violon aber undt der Bass Continuus so vil es sein kan müssen starck besetzt werden, die Quartuba kan wol gebraucht werden."

114.–137.   *Sonatae, tam Aris, quam Aulis servientes*
     (Salzburg: J. B. Mayr, 1676)

d)   114.   Sonata I (C major)
     115.   Sonata II (D major)
     116.   Sonata III (G minor)
     117.   Sonata IV (C major)
     118.   Sonata V (E minor)
     119.   Sonata VI (F major)
     120.   Sonata VII (C major)
     121.   Sonata VIII (G major)
     122.   Sonata IX (B-flat major)
     123.   Sonata X (G minor)
     124.   Sonata XI (A major)
     125.   Sonata XII (C major)
     126.   Trumpet duo I (C major)
     127.   Trumpet duo II (C major)
     128.   Trumpet duo III (C major)
     129.   Trumpet duo IV (C major)
     130.   Trumpet duo V (C major)
     131.   Trumpet duo VI (C major)
     132.   Trumpet duo VII (C major)
     133.   Trumpet duo VIII (C major)
     134.   Trumpet duo IX (C major)
     135.   Trumpet duo X (C major)
     136.   Trumpet duo XI (G minor)
     137.   Trumpet duo XII (G minor)

e)   Sonatas I & XII *à 8*: 2 trumpets, 2 violins, 3 violas, basso continuo, violone
     Sonatas II, III & V *à 6*: 2 violins, 3 violas, basso continuo, violone
     Sonatas VI, VII, IX, XI *à 5*: 2 violins, 2 violas, basso continuo, violone
     Sonatas IV & X *à 5*: trumpet, violin, 2 violas, basso continuo, violone
     Sonata VII *à 5*: 2 trumpets, 2 violins, basso continuo, basso di viola [violone]

f)   (1)   Kroměříž (A 270–72; only part books for violin 2, viola 1 & viola 4 survive)
     (2)   Berlin, Staatliche Hochschule für Musik und Darstellende Kunst (only viola 1 part extant)
     (3)   MS parts for Sonatas I & XII entitled *Sonatae duae* at Kroměříž (B IV 72); dated 1668–70 by Sehnal [Sehnal]
     (4)   MS parts for Sonatas II, III & V entitled *3 Sonatae à 6* at Kroměříž (B IV 93); dated 1668–70 by Sehnal [Sehnal]
     (5)   MS parts for Sonatas VI, VIII, IX & XI entitled *4 Sonatae* at Kroměříž (B IV 92); dated 1670 by Sehnal [Sehnal]
     (6)   Duo No. XI was published in J. E. Altenburg, *Versuch einer Anleitung zur heroisch-musikalischen Trompeter- und Pauker-Kunst* (1795), p. 104.

g)   (1)   *DTÖ* 106–7 (1963), edited by Erich Schenk. This publication is based upon parts (now lost) which were formerly at Kroměříž.
     (2)   Sonata II published as *Sonata 1 à 6 in D* in *Diletto Musicale* No. 359. Ed. Nikolaus Harnoncourt. Vienna: Doblinger, 1971. This edition is based upon the MS source *3 Sonatae à 6* [see f) (4)].
     (3)   Sonata III published as *Sonata II à 6 in g* in *Diletto Musicale* No. 515. Ed. Nikolaus Harnoncourt. Vienna: Doblinger, 1971. See f) (4).
     (4)   Sonata V published as *Sonata IV à 6 in e* in *Diletto Musicale* No. 516. Ed. Nikolaus Harnoncourt. Vienna: Doblinger, 1971. See f) (4).
     (5)   The twelve trumpet duos have been published by The Brass Press (BP-701) 1970, edited by Stephen L. Glover.

h)   A publication entitled *Sonate à 5, 6, 8.*, Nürnberg, 1681, is listed in the Leipzig and Frankfurt *Messkatalogen* for 1681 [Göhler]. This print was probably a new edition of the *Sonatae tam aris quam aulis servientes*. Several old inventories of lost music list copies of Biber's sonatas in a set of nine part-books; these refer to the *Sonatae, tam Aris, quam Aulis servientes* [Racek, Schaal, Baselt].

138.–145. *Sonatae Violino Solo*

(engraved in Salzburg by Thomas Georg Höger; published in Nürnberg by Lohner, 1681)

d)   138.   Sonata I (A major)
     139.   Sonata II (D minor)
     140.   Sonata III (F major)
     141.   Sonata IV (D major); *scordatura* (a, e′, a′, d″)
     142.   Sonata V (E minor)
     143.   Sonata VI (C minor); *scordatura* (g, d′, a′, d″)
     144.   Sonata VII (G major)
     145.   Sonata VIII (A major)

e)   Solo violin & continuo; the violin part of Sonata VIII is notated on two staves.

f)   (1)   Dresden, Sächsische Landesbibliothek (Mus. 1851 R/1)
     (2)   Hamburg, Stadtbibliothek (according to Adler, *DTÖ* 11, *Revisionsbericht*)
     (3)   Kremsmünster, Benediktinerstift

    (4)   Leipzig, Musikbibliothek der Stadt Leipzig

    (5)   München, Bayerische Staatsbibliothek

    (6)   Paderborn, West Germany, Akademische Bibliothek

    (7)   Salzburg, Stift Nonnberg (3 copies: XV 31, 32A, 32B)

    (8)   Vienna, Minoritenkonvent MS 726, Nos. 7–14. (a MS copy apparently made from the print)

    (9)   Würzburg, Graf von Schönborn'sche Archiv

g)   (1)   *DTÖ* 11 (1898), edited by Guido Adler

    (2)   Sonata VI, first movement in Max Steinitzer, *Musikgeschichtliches Atlas Freiburg i. B.* (1908) No. 86, p. 89

    (3)   Sonata VI, Gavotte, edited by C. von Radecki in *Lyrische Stücke für Violine und Pianoforte,* No. 5, Vol. III, No. 9. Leipzig: Breitkopf und Härtel

    (4)   Sonata VI edited by Maxim Jakobsen, Leipzig: Peters, 1931

h)   Listed under Biber's name in the Frankfurt *Messkatalog* for 1684 is the publication *Sonatae, violino, aeri incisae,* probably a new edition of the *Sonatae Violino Solo* [Göhler]. Earlier versions of Sonatas IV and VI appear in MS 726 of the music archive of the Minoritenkonvent, Vienna. A lute arrangement of the Passacaglia of Sonata VI (considerably altered) appears in a MS at the Benedictine monastery, Kremsmünster, Upper Austria. This version is published in *DTÖ* 50 (1918), ed. A. Koczirz. One of the Nonnberg copies of the print is inscribed as having belonged to Biber's daughter M. Caecilia a Bibern.

146. *Sonata violino solo representativa (Representatio Avium)*

b)   A major

c)   1669 [Sehnal]

d)   [allegro]; Nachtigal; [allegro]; Cu Cu; Fresch; Adagio; Die Henn/Der Han; Presto; Adagio: Die Wachtel; Die Katz; Musquetir Mars; Allemande

e)   Solo violin & continuo

f)   Kroměříž (B IV 184)

g)   *DTÖ* 127, edited by Jiří Sehnal

h)   One of the movements of this programmatic sonata, "Musquetir Mars," reappears, somewhat altered and entitled "Der Mars," in the *Battalia* (1673). The sonata ends with the autograph inscription "A. H. D. P. B. V. M. S. Caeliae. Finis" (To the Honor of God the Father, the Blessed Virgin Mary and Saint Caecilia.)

147. *Sonata Violino Solo*

b)   A major

c)   After 1670 [Sehnal]

e)   Solo violin & continuo

f)   MS (autograph) at Kroměříž (B IV 22)

g)   *DTÖ* 127, edited by Jiří Sehnal.

THEORETICAL WORKS

148. Untitled Singing Instruction Manual
    (written by Biber in 1694 for his daughter Maria Anna Magdalena (1677–1742), 28 pp.

f)   MS at Stift Nonnberg, Salzburg (8 175 Ca)

h)   Described in Schenk/Singfundament.

Appendix to Catalog

(In all sections of the appendix, categories of compositions follow the same order used for the main part of the catalog: Masses, Vespers music, miscellaneous church compositions, dramatic works, suites, sonatas)

LOST WORKS

App. 1. *Missa*
[Federhofer / Michaelbeuern]

App. 2. *Missa à 9*
[Federhofer / Michaelbeuern]

App. 3. *Missa in contrapunct*
[Federhofer / Michaelbeuern]

This mass might have been either Biber's *Missa à 4 voci in Contrapuncto* (see **App. 98**) or his *Missa Quadragesimalis* (see **No. 5**).

App. 4. *Missa Praecursoris D[omi]ni*
[Federhofer / Michaelbeuern]

App. 5. *Missa S. Clarae*
[Federhofer / Michaelbeuern]

App. 6. *Missa Sine Gloria in contrapunct*
[Federhofer / Michaelbeuern]

Perhaps Biber's *Missa Quadragesimalis* (**No. 5**).

App. 7. *Requiem à 11*
[Federhofer / Michaelbeuern]

Perhaps one of Biber's two surviving Requiems (see **Nos. 7 & 8**)

App. 8. *Dixit D[omi]nus à 8*
[Fellerer / Mavr]

Possibly the Dixit Dominus of the *Vesperae à 32,* since the same inventory from which this title is taken lists a *Missa Alleluia 8 voc.* and *Magnificat à 8* under Biber's name.

App. 9.   *Magnificat à 8*
[Fellerer/Mayr]

Possibly the Magnificat from the *Vesperae à 32* (see preceding entry)

App. 10.   *Vesperae*

The Kroměříž inventory of about 1695 lists this work with the subscript: "in turcica charta compactae" [Breitenbacher, B III 4, p. 100]

App. 11.   *Alleluja! Celebrabo Jehovam à 12*
"8 Strom., 4 voci" [Baselt]

App. 12.   *Alma Redemptoris à 6*
[Breitenbacher, B VII 16, p. 121]

App. 13.   *Aria de Nativit[atis] Chr[sti] D[omi]ni*
"Alt: 2 flaut:" [Federhofer/Michaelbeuern]

App. 14.   *Aria de Passione Domini: Wer gibt meinen Augen*
"Alt. Sol., 2 Viola di amor, 2 Flauten, 3 Instr. [continuo?]" [Federhofer/Michael-beuern]

App. 15.   *Litaniae Lauretanae ab 8*
[Breitenbacher, B V I, p. 118]

App. 16.   *Lyt[aniae] Lau[retanae]à 9*
[Federhofer/Michaelbeuern]

App. 17.   *Miserere à 9*
[Federhofer/Michaelbeuern]

App. 18.   *Regina coeli à 4*
[Federhofer/Michaelbeuern]

App. 19.   *Regnum Mundi*
organ, two sopranos, two violins. [Benediktiner Frauenstift Nonnberg: Protokoll. Sept. 30, 1703]

App. 20.   *Alesandro in Pietra*
"Dramma per musica." Opera

a)   Text by Francesco Maria Raffaelini; published by J. B. Mayr, Salzburg
c)   Performed January/February 1689
f)   Copies of the textbook are preserved in the Austrian National Library, Vienna, and the Benediktinerstift at Kremsmünster, Upper Austria.

App. 21.   *Alfonsus hujus nominis decimus Hisparniarum rex*
"superbiae vindicatae luculentum exemplum...in theatrum productus ab...juventute academi Salisburgensi...mixto cothurno actus die 3. mensis Septembris. Anno 1696." Schooldrama

a)   Text by Augustin Kendlinger; published by J. B. Mayr, Salzburg, 1696

f)   A copy of the textbook is preserved in the library of the University of Salzburg (4007 I).

App. 22.   *Boni corvinon dissimilia. Seu optimi Corvini genuini filii Ladislaus et Matthias*
"In scenam producti a . . . studiosa juventute Salisburgensi . . . anno 1688."
Schooldrama

a)   Text by Vitus Kaltenkrauter; published by J. B. Mayr, Salzburg, 1688

f)   A copy of the textbook is preserved in the library of the University of Salzburg (4001 I).

App. 23.   *Infelix parentum amor in Fernando filio*
"ab . . . academica juventute pro proemiorum distributione in scenam productus;
P. P. Benedictinos Salisburgi, anno 1697." Schooldrama

a)   Text by Wolfgang Rinswerger; published by J. B. Mayr, Salzburg, 1697

f)   A copy of the textbook is preserved in the library of the University of Salzburg (4008 I).

App. 24.   *Fastus confusus seu a Juditha proprio ense fusus Holofernes*
"tragico-commoedia . . . in scenam productus a . . . studiosa juventute Salisburgensi . . . anno 1691. die 28. Novembris." Schooldrama

a)   Text by Vitus Kaltenkrauter; published by J. B. Mayr, Salzburg, 1691

f)   A copy of the textbook is preserved in the library of the University of Salzburg (4003 I).

App. 25.   *Fastus fumosus famosus ad focum Babilonicum defervescens, seu Nabuchodonosor*
Schooldrama. Performed February 1685 [Schneider]

a)   Author of text unknown

f)   The text is preserved at the Salzburg Government Archives [Schneider, 285].

App. 26.   *Fidei, ac perfidiae exampla in Pertharito ab Unulfo et Garibaldo demonstrata*
"ac . . . in scenam producta a . . . studiosa juventute universitatis Salisburgensis . . . anno 1694." Schooldrama

a)   Text by Vitus Kaltenkrauter; published by J. B. Mayr, Salzburg, 1694

f)   A copy of the textbook is preserved in the library of the University of Salzburg (4005 I).

App. 27.   *Honor divinus de respectu humano triumphans, seu S. Thomas cancellarius, archi-episcopus, martyr*
". . . ab . . . juventute Salisburgensi in scenam productus die [?] mensis [?] Anno 1698." Schooldrama

a)   Text by Wolfgang Rinswerger; published by J. B. Mayr, Salzburg, 1698

f)   A copy of the textbook is preserved in the library of the University of Salzburg (4011 I).

App. 28. *Invidia gloriae umbra in C. Julio Caesare repraesentata*
"...ab ...academica juventute Salisburgensi in scenam producta Anno 1697."
Schooldrama

a)   Text by Wolfgang Rinswerger; published by J. B. Mayr, Salzburg, 1697
f)   A copy of the textbook is preserved in the library of the University of Salzburg (4009 I).

App. 29. *Rex catholicus seu S. Hermenegildus rex, et martyr*
"...in scenam productus a...studiosa juventute Salisburgensi...anno 1689 die [?] Novembris." Schooldrama

a)   Text by Vitus Kaltenkrauter; published by J. B. Mayr, Salzburg, 1689
f)   A copy of the textbook is preserved in the library of the University of Salzburg (4002 I).

App. 30. *Rex invitus martyr invictus coronam terrestrem recusans coelestem martyrio adeptus. Seu D. Wenceslaus Bohemiae rex, et martyr*
"...in scenam productus a...academica juventute...anno 1692 die VI. Augusti."
Schooldrama

a)   Text by Vitus Kaltenkrauter; published by J. B. Mayr, Salzburg, 1692 (4004 I)
f)   A copy of the textbook is preserved in the library of the University of Salzburg (4004 I).

App. 31. *Tratenimento musicale del'ossequio di Salisburgi*
"di rapresentarsi nella grande Sala di Corte in applauso del felice arrivo dell' Augustissima Regina Wilhelmina Amalia Duchessa di Brunsvvich, Luneburg, Sposa dell' Augustissimo Re de' Romani & d' Hongaria Guiseppe I. per Commando di S. A. R.ma' Giovanni Ernesto Arcivescovo & Prencipe di Salisburgo, Composta in Musica a Henrico Franc. a Bibern, Suae Celsitudinis Dapifero & Capellae Magistro in Salisburgo li 8. di Febraro l'anno 1699." A dramatic entertainment divided into three parts designated *Cantata Prima, Cantata Seconda* and *Cantata Terza*. Performed February 1699 in honor of the visit of the Duchess Wilhelmina Amalia, wife of Joseph I., King of Rome and Hungary.

a)   Author of text unknown; text published by J. B. Mayr, Salzburg, 1699
f)   Copies of the textbook are preserved at the following institutions:
(1)   Brussels Conservatory
(2)   Salzburg Government Archives
(3)   Salzburg, Museum Carolino-Augusteum
(4)   Salzburg, University of Salzburg library (4237 I).

App. 32. *Valerianus Romanorum Imperator, barbarorum ludibrium, regiae infelicitatis exemplum*
"...in theatrum productus, et a... juventute academica Salisburgensi...tragico cothurno actus. Die [?] Augusti, Anno 1684." Schooldrama

a)   Text by Otto Aicher; published by J. B. Mayr, Salzburg, 1684
f)   The *scenarium* and text are preserved in the Salzburg Museum Carolino-Augusteum. A copy of the textbook is preserved in the library of the University of Salzburg (3996 I).

App. 33. *Virtus pressa, non opressa. Seu Daniel*
"idolorum eversor, verae pietatis propugnator, aulici favoris exemplum et indiviae...in scenam productus a...iuventute academica Salisburgensi...anno 1686. die 10. Septembr." Schooldrama

a) Text by Otto Aicher; published by J. B. Mayr, Salzburg, 1686

f) The *scenarium* and text are preserved in the Salzburg Museum Carolino-Augusteum. A copy of the textbook is preserved in the library of the University of Salzburg (3999 I).

App. 34. *Virtutis triumphus, sive Ulysses*
"virtute duce, sapientia comite, victor discriminum...Joanni Ernesto, ex comitibus de Thun, archiepiscopo Salisburgensi...die XXX. Juny 1687 concordibus suffrogiis electi, dedicatus...ab academica juventute applaudente in theatro publico exhibitus...." Schooldrama. Performed June 30, 1687 for the celebration of the choice of Johann Ernst von Thun as Archbishop of Salzburg [Schneider]

a) Text by Otto Aicher; published by J. B. Mayr, Salzburg, 1687

f) A copy of the textbook is preserved in the library of the University of Salzburg (4000 I).

App. 35. **Feriis Bacchanaliorum: Nemesis variata seu Fridericus Dux Saxoniae unacum aulico suo Conrado Kaufungo.*
Schooldrama

a) Author of text unknown

c) Performed 1679 [Schneider]

f) The textbook is preserved at the Salzburg Government Archives [Schneider, 285]

h) The number of dances induced Schneider to suggest the possibility of Biber's authorship rather than Hofer's. Georg Muffat is also a possible composer.

App. 36. **Innocentia fidei conjugalis seu Genovefa*
with German title *Unschuld der Ehelichen Threu oder unschuldig und gethreue Genovefa.* Schooldrama

a) Author of text unknown

c) Performed 1681 [Schneider]

f) The textbook is preserved at the Salzburg Government Archives [Schneider, 285].

h) The number of dances induced Schneider to suggest the possibility of Biber's authorship rather than Hofer's. Georg Muffat is also a possible composer.

App. 37.–38. *2 Ariae Variat: p[artes] 8*
Copied at Kremsmünster in 1686 [Kellner]

App. 39. *Ballet à 4*
[Federhofer/Michaelbeuern]

(* of uncertain authorship)

App. 40. *Ballet à 4*
[Federhofer/Michaelbeuern]

App. 41. *Ballet à 4*
[Federhofer/Michaelbeuern]

App. 42. *Ballet à 4*
[Federhofer/Michaelbeuern]

App. 43. *Ballet à 4*
[Federhofer/Michaelbeuern]

App. 44. *Balleti à 4*
[Federhofer/Michaelbeuern]

App. 45. *Balleti à 4*
"Alla Itagliana. Ex E, partes 4" [Racek]

App. 46. *Balleti à 4*
"ex G, partes 4," violin, 2 violas, cembalo [Racek]

App. 47. *Balleti à 4 Voci*
[Federhofer/Michaelbeuern]

App. 48. *Balleto à 4*
[Federhofer/Michaelbeuern]

App. 49. *Balleto à 4*
[Federhofer/Michaelbeuern]

App. 50. *Ballettae à 4*
"ex E, partes 4," violin, 2 violas, cembalo [Racek]

App. 51. *Balletti à 4*
"4 partes, Ex G," violin, 2 violas, violone [Racek]

App. 52. *Balleti p[artes] 4*

Copied at Kremsmünster in 1686 [Kellner]

App. 53. *Balleti à 5*
[Federhofer/Michaelbeuern]

App. 54. *Balleto à 5*
[Federhofer/Michaelbeuern]

App. 55. *Ballettae à 5*
"partes 5, ex C," 2 violins, 2 violas, violone [Racek]

App. 56. *Diversi Balletti*
"p[artes] 5"

Copied at Kremsmünster in 1686 [Kellner]

App. 57. *Ballettae à 6 sopra il cu cu*
[Nettl/Osegg]

App. 58. *Ballettae in turcica charta*
[Breitenbacher, B IV 161, p. 133]

App. 59. *Balletti in turcica charta*
[Breitenbacher, B XIV 33, p. 128]

App. 60. *Ciaccona violino solo*
[Breitenbacher, B XIV 135, p. 132]

App. 61. *Lamento à 4*
[Breitenbacher, B IV 170, p. 114]

A lost copy of the *Balletti Lamentabili?*

App. 62. *Parthi à 3*
"2 Flauten con Fagoto" [Federhofer/Michaelbeuern]

App. 63. *Parthia à 4*
[Federhofer/Michaelbeuern]

App. 64.–65. *2 Parthia à 4*
[Federhofer/Michaelbeuern]

App. 66.–67. *2 Parthin à 4*
[Federhofer/Michaelbeuern]

App. 68. *Parthia à 4 o 5*
[Federhofer/Michaelbeuern]

App. 69. *Parthia à 5*
[Federhofer/Michaelbeuern]

App. 70.–73. *4 Parthien à 5*
[Federhofer/Michaelbeuern]

App. 74. *Parthia à 6*
[Federhofer/Michaelbeuern]

App. 75. *Sonata*

Copied at Kremsmünster in 1687 [Kellner]

App. 76.   *Sonata*
[Nettl/Osegg]

App. 77.   *Sonata à 2. Viol. con Organo*
[Federhofer/Michaelbeuern]

App. 78.   *Sonata à 3*
[Federhofer/Michaelbeuern]

App. 79.   *Sonata à 4*
[Federhofer/Michaelbeuern]

App. 80.   *Sonata à 4*
[Federhofer/Michaelbeuern]

App. 81.   *Sonata à 5*
[Federhofer/Michaelbeuern]

App. 82.   *Sonata à 5*
[Breitenbacher, B IV 107, p. 111]

App. 83.   *Sonata à 5*
[Breitenbacher, B IV 73, p. 110]

App. 84.   *Sonata*
"p[artes] 5."

Copied at Kremsmünster in 1686 [Kellner]

App. 85.   *Sonata*
"p[artes] 5."

Copied at Kremsmünster in 1686 [Kellner]

App. 86.   *Sonata à 7*
[Federhofer/Michaelbeuern]

App. 87.   *Sonata 8*
"ex C, voces seu partes: 9, 8 Concert voces" [Racek]

App. 88.   *Sonata à violino solo artificiosa*
[Nettl/Osegg]

App. 89.   *Sonata: B. M. V.*
"p[artes] 7."

Copied at Kremsmünster in 1686 [Kellner]

App. 90.   *Sonata Paschalis. Surrexit Christus hodie*
[Federhofer/Michaelbeuern]

Probably no. XI of the *Mystery Sonatas*

App. 91.   *Sonata S. Appolloniae*
[Breitenbacher, B IV 152, p. 113]

App. 92.   *Sonata seu Lyra speculativa*
[Breitenbacher, B IV 171, p. 114]

App. 93.   *Sonata Violini et altri*
[Nettl/Osegg]

App. 94.–95.   *2 Sonatas*
"2 Stück del Sigr. Biber," under the heading "Sonatas" [Baselt]

App. 96.   *Sonatina à 5*
[Federhofer/Michaelbeuern]

App. 97.   *Violino Solo*
"1 p[ars]:" [Fellerer/Mayr]

The following eleven entries have not been included with the numbered lost sonatas because either the number of pieces referred to is unknown or the set appears to be a copy of one of Biber's printed collections:

Sonatae
[Fellerer/Mayr]

Sonatae
"2 Partes, ein Theill in türkhischen papier, der andere in angeschribnen Pergame" [Federhofer/Alte Musikalien-Inventare]

Sonatae Violino aeri incisae
Nürnberg, 1684 [Göhler]

Probably a new edition of the *Sonatae Violino Solo,* 1681

12 Biberische Sonaten
[Federhofer/Michaelbeuern]

Possibly a copy of either *Fidicinium Sacro-Profanum,* or *Sonatae, tam Aris, quam Aulis servientes*

12 Sonatae in viridi pargamena compactae
[Breitenbacher, B IV 153, p. 113]

Possibly a copy of either *Fidicinium Sacro-Profanum,* or *Sonatae, tam Aris, quam Aulis servientes*

8 Sonatae impressae et in turcica charta compactae
[Breitenbacher, B IV 220, p. 116]

Probably a copy of the *Sonatae Violino Solo,* 1681

Sonatae impressae, in rubra charta compactae
[Breitenbacher, B IV 1, p. 106]

One of Biber's printed collections of sonatas

Sonate à 5. 6. 8.
Nürnberg, 1681 [Göhler]

Probably a new edition of the *Sonatae, tam Aris, quam Aulis servientes*

"17 Stück Sonate a Viol., e Viola da gamba Solo di Biber, Schütz, Torelli, Fierentio, Conti, Fiorelli & Pez."
[Baselt]

*6 Sonaten à 2 V. & B. c.

*Sonata à 2 Va. d'amore & B. c.

EXTANT WORKS OF UNCERTAIN AUTHORSHIP

App. 98. *Missa à 4 voci in Contrapuncto*

  a)   Ordinary of the Mass
  b)   D minor
  e)   SATB chorus, organ
  f)   MS score at the Gesellschaft der Musikfreunde, Vienna (I 7966, Q 46)
  h)   The work is attributed to Carl Biber in the music catalog at St. Peter's in Salzburg, which is an older source than the Vienna score. The work could have been written by either Heinrich or Carl Biber. See the bibliography (Salzburg. St. Peter's) and the discussion of the work in chapter 4.

App. 99. *Missa in Albis*

  a)   Ordinary of the Mass
  b)   C major
  e)   SSATBB chorus & soloists, 2 violins, 2 violas, 2 trumpets, 3 trombones, organ
  f)   MS parts at Kroměříž (B I 74)
  h)   The manuscript bears the following inscription: "A. d. H. B. Scripta Kremsirii anno 1668, in Septembri." Breitenbacher (p. 67) ascribes the work to Heinrich Brückner, Nettl/Biber (p. 69) to Heinrich Biber. See chapter 4 of the present study.

App. 100. *Missa Bruxellensis*

  a)   Ordinary of the Mass
  b)   C major
  c)   Around 1700 (between 1696 and 1704?) [Hintermaier]
  e)   SATB double chorus, 4 trumpets, tympani, 2 cornetti, 3 trombones, 2 violins, 3 violas, basso continuo

---

*These two MSS are mentioned by Meyer [p. 189], who claims that they are preserved at the Herzog August Bibliothek in Wolfenbüttel. The library does not possess the works at present and their whereabouts is unknown. The titles suggest copies of pieces from the *Harmonia Artificiosa-Ariosa*.

f) Brussels: Bibliotheque Royale Albert 1ᵉʳ. MS II 3862.

g) Modern ed. *Missa Bruxellensis XXIII vocum. Horatii Benevoli operum omnium* VIIa. Edited by Laurence Feininger. Vienna-Salzburg, 1970.

h) The title page of the Brussels manuscript reads *Messa à 8: Voci reali à piu stromenti Del Sig' Orazio Benevoli.* See Hintermaier, and the discussion in chapters 3 and 4 of the present study.

App. 101. *Missa Salisburgensis*

a) Ordinary of the Mass

b) C major

c) Between 1654 and 1696 (1682?)

e) Two eight-part (SSAATTBB) double choruses (plus sixteen soloists), two string choirs (each with 2 violins and 4 violas), two cornetti and four trombones, two oboes and four recorders, two clarini and two trumpet choirs (each four trumpets and tympani), two organ continuo parts and basso continuo

f) (1) MS score in the Museum Carolino Augusteum, Salzburg (Hs. 751)

   (2) Two-part score (*Missa a quatuor Coris in Sexdecim vocibus cum aliis Instrumentis*) in Brussels: Bibliotheque Royale Albert 1er (MS I 3864). Vocal score with violins, and supplementary score for winds.

g) (1) *DTÖ* 20 (1903), edited by Guido Adler

   (2) *Missa Salisburgensis 1628.* Facsim. of Salzburg score. Ed. Laurence Feininger. *Horatii Benevoli operum omnium* VIIb. Vienna-Salzburg, 1969.

h) See Hintermaier and the discussions in chapters 2 and 3 of the present study.

App. 102. *Congregamini Omnes Populi à 15*

b) G major

c) 1663 [Sehnal]

e) SSATBB chorus & soloists, 2 violins, 2 violas, 3 trombones, organ

f) MS parts at Kroměříž (B II 137)

h) The MS designates "H. B." as author; see discussion in chapter 6 of the present study.

App. 103. *Magna es Domine*

e) SATB chorus and soloists, 2 violins and basso continuo

f) MS parts in Salzburg cathedral archive

h) The work is anonymous. Rosenthal (p. 87) ascribed it to Heinrich Biber, presumably because it was copied by the copyist of the Offertoria *Ne cedite mentes* and *Quo abiit dilectus tuis* that are almost certainly works of Heinrich Biber, although ascribed merely to "Bibern." However, unlike these other compositions, *Magna es Domine* offers very little in the way of stylistic support for Heinrich Biber's authorship.

App. 104. *Offertorium venerabili Sacramenta*

b) A major

e) SATB chorus & soloists, 2 violins, 3 trombones, organ

f) MS score at Gesellschaft der Musikfreunde, Vienna (I 8354 Q 47)

h) The work survives in the Salzburg cathedral archive in a set of parts under Carl Biber's name; copyist and watermark confirm the son's authorship. The Vienna score was made in the nineteenth century and carries far less weight.

App. 105. *Recessit Pastor Bonus*

b) G minor

e) SATB chorus (& continuo?)

f) Original source unknown

g) Sigismund Keller published this work in *Zeitschrift für Katholische Kirchenmusik,* IV (1871), as Beilage No. 8 to his article "Geschichtliches über die nächsten Vorfahren Mozarts als Kapellmeister im fürsterzbischöflichen Dom zu Salzburg." It is headed *Responsorium*/"Recessit Pastor bonus"/ à/ 4 Voci/ pro/ Septimana Sancta (Sabbato Sancto)./ Authore/ Fr. Heinrich de Biber./ (1684–98). [*sic*]

h) Joachim Fuetsch's catalog of the Salzburg cathedral music archive (1822) ascribes the work to Carl Biber. There are, therefore, scant grounds for Keller's ascription.

App. 106. *Plaudite Tympana*
[Hymn to St. Rupert]

b), c), e), f(1), g), and h): same as **App. 101**

App. 107. *Allemanda, Gigue*
"À 3 violini verstümbt"

e) Three *scordatura* violins & continuo

f) MS parts at Kroměříž (B XIV 78)

h) Nettl [Nettl/Biber] ascribes this anonymous work to Biber.

App. 108. *Balettae ad duos choros ab 8*

b) C major

d) Intrada, Trezza, Courant, Sarabande, Gavotte, Gigue, Ciacona

e) 1st chorus: violin, 2 violas, Basso viola [violone]
2nd chorus: Violin, 2 violas, Basso [violone]
& Basso continuo

f) MS parts at Kroměříž (B XIV 81)

h) The words "A. d. Henrico Biber" are crossed out on the title page and replaced by "Dal signore Hugi."

App. 109. *Balletti ad duos choros*

b) A minor

c) ca. 1669 [Sehnal]

e) 1st choir: 2 violins, 2 violas, Basso [violone]
2nd choir: 2 violins, 2 violas, Basso [violone]
& Basso continuo

f) MS parts at Kroměříž (B XIV 106)

h) The MS is anonymous. Biber copied the first violin part of the first choir. Sehnal believes that Biber copied only the part he played and did not write the work [Sehnal].

App. 110. *Balletti à 2 violini discordati*

d) Allemanda, Sarabanda, Courante, Gigue
e) Two *scordatura* violins & basso continuo
f) MS parts at Kroměříž (B XIV 80)
h) The MS is anonymous. Nettl [Nettl/Biber] ascribes it to Biber, apparently because of the use of *scordatura*. Schmelzer's authorship should also be considered. A work of his entitled *Balletae discordatae à 2 violini e basso* is preserved at Kroměříž (B XIV 3a). In addition, the archive contains the following anonymous suites, with similar titles, for *scordatura* violins:
   (1) *Balletti à 4: 2 violini discordati, 1 viola, con basso* (B XIV 57)
   (2) *Ballettae discordatae à 4. W. M. S.* (B XIV 102)
   (3) *Balletti discordati* (B XIV 110)
   (4) *Balletti à 2 violini verstümbt* (B XIV 215)
The original late seventeenth-century inventory of the Kroměříž collection listed another anonymous work entitled *Balletti à 2 violini discordati* (B XIV 88); this manuscript has not survived.

App. 111. *Harmonia Romana*

b) D minor
c) 1669
d) Sonata, Courante, Fuga, Passagio, Saltarello, Allemanda, Gigue
e) 3 violins, 3 violas, violone, cembalo
f) MS parts at Kroměříž (b XIV 201)
g) Published as a work of Vejvanovský's in *Musica Antiqua Bohemica*, 48, No. XIX (1961), edited by Jaroslav Pohanka
h) This anonymous work was copied by Vejvanovský. Both Nettl [Nettl/Biber] and Sehnal [Sehnal] ascribe the suite to Biber. Several movements feature solo/tutti contrasts. The Passagio is scored for solo violin accompanied by the remaining two violins; the harmonically incomplete accompaniment suggests that the copyist omitted the continuo part (if not other parts as well). The published edition is generally poor and lacks several indications found in the manuscript. The virtuoso violin writing in the Passagio and the overall style of the work point to Heinrich Biber's authorship more than to Vejvanovský's.

App. 112. *Intrada, Menuete, Boure, Courant, Saraband et Gigue*
"D. Augustini Biber Salisburgensi. Anno 1681"

b) D major
e) Organ solo
f) MS organ tablature in the Musikbibliothek der Stadt Leipzig (II. 6. 19)
h) The manuscript in which this work is found is apparently of Viennese provenance, and contains works by Froberger, Schmelzer, Wagenseil (both) and anonymous composers. No Augustini Biber is known to have worked in Salzburg (or elsewhere) at any period. In 1681 the eldest of Biber's children, Arnold, was eight years of age. The date coincides, however, with one of Heinrich Biber's most active periods in the composition of instrumental music; the organ solo could be an arrangement of another work.

App. 113. *Sonata*

  b) B minor
  e) Solo violin & basso continuo
  f) MS 726 of the music archive of the Minoritenkonvent, Vienna; no. 5
  h) The work is anonymous; see chapter 7 of the present study.

App. 114. *Sonata*

  b) F major
  e) Solo violin & basso continuo; *scordatura* (c′, f′, a′, d″)
  f) MS 726 of the music archive of the Minoritenkonvent, Vienna; no. 6
  h) The work is anonymous; see chapter 7 of the present study.

App. 115. *Sonata*

  b) D major
  e) Solo violin & basso continuo
  f) MS 726 of the music archive of the Minoritenkonvent, Vienna; no. 4
  h) The work is anonymous; see chapter 7 of the present study.

App. 116. *Sonata*

  b) A major
  e) Solo violin & basso continuo; *scordatura* (a, e′, a′, d″)
  f) MS 726 of the music archive of the Minoritenkonvent, Vienna; no. 81
  h) The work is anonymous; see chapter 7 of the present study. There is no continuo part written on the bass staff of the first forty-four bars; the bass enters in bar forty-five.

App. 117. *Sonata à 3*

  b) D minor
  c) 1679–80 [Sehnal]
  e) 2 violins, trombone, violone, organ
  f) MS parts at Kroměříž (B XIV 130)
  g) Published as a work of Biber's. Edited by Kurt Janetzky London: Musica Rara, 1958
  h) The MS bears the initials "H. B." See chapter 8 of the present study.

App. 118. *Sonata à 3*

  b) G minor
  c) 1679–80 [Sehnal]
  e) 2 violins, solo viola da gamba, violone, organ
  f) MS parts at Kroměříž (B IV 215)
  g) Published as a work of Biber's in *Edition Pro Musica,* edited by Kurt Janetzky. Leipzig-Berlin: Pro Musica Verlag, n.d.
  h) The MS bears only the composer's initials, "H. B." Nettl ascribes it to Biber [Nettl/Biber].

App. 119. *Sonata à 4 violis*

   b)   D major
   c)   1663 [Sehnal]
   e)   Violin, violetta, 2 violas, organ
   f)   MS parts at Kroměříž (B IV 117)
   h)   The MS bears the initials "H. B." In addition to the *Sonata à 4 violis,* it contains a six-part string sonata by Antonio Bertali. The copyist of this MS also copied Biber's *Salve Regina à 2* (1663). See chapter 8 of the present study.

App. 120. *Sonata à 5*

   b)   D minor
   c)   "A° 1667/ Die 12. 8bris Scripta"
   e)   2 violins, 3 violas (one a violone), organ
   f)   MS parts at Kroměříž (B IV 47)
   h)   The MS (anonymous) was copied by Pavel Vejvanovský. Nettl ascribes it to Biber [Nettl/Biber]; Sehnal disagrees [Sehnal]. There are no stylistic grounds for Nettl's ascription.

App. 121. *Sonata Jucunda*

   b)   D major
   c)   After 1670 [Sehnal]
   e)   2 violins, 3 violas, basso continuo
   f)   MS parts at Kroměříž (B IV 100)
   h)   The MS is anonymous. Nettl ascribes this work to Biber [Nettl/Biber]. See chapter 8 of the present study.

App. 122. *Sonata Paschalis*

   b)   C major
   c)   "A° 1666/ Die 15. Marti"
   e)   2 violins, 2 violas, violone
   f)   MS parts at Kroměříž (B IV 25)
   g)   Published as a work of Vejvanovský's in *Musica Antiqua Bohemica,* 47, No. V (1960), edited by Jaroslav Pohanka
   h)   The MS is anonymous. Nettl ascribes this work to Biber [Nettl/Biber]; Sehnal disagrees [Sehnal]. The MS was copied by Pavel Vejvanovský. There are insufficient grounds to support Nettl's ascription in the face of Vejvanovský's having copied the work.

WORKS FALSELY ATTRIBUTED TO BIBER

App. 123.   *Hymni Sacri. 1684 Salisb. ex Typographeo Joa. Bapt. Mayr*

h)   This collection was attributed to Biber by Keller (p. 66), who said it was preserved in the upper sacristry of the Salzburg cathedral. The only work that resembles Keller's description bears the following full title: "*Hymni Sacri Breviarii Romani Urbani Papae VIII.* Auctoritate recogniti Festa nova omnia In hunc usque Annum a Summis Pontificibus concessa, Officium Defunctorum, Psalmi Graduales et Poenitentiales, Omnia pro majori commoditate Psallentium ad longum exposita, & novo Typo adornata. Jussu et Promotione . . . Maximiliani Gandolphi Ex Comit. de Küenburg Archi-Episcopi Salisb . . . Salisburgi 1685: Ex Typographeo Joannis Bapt. Mayr." It is thus a liturgical work. Keller probably never saw the publication itself, which is in large folio format and very heavy, or he could never have made such an ascription. It is well known, nevertheless, that Keller attributed anonymous works to whomever he believed was Kapellmeister at the time; and he published a work of Carl Biber's as Heinrich Biber's composition (see **App. 105**).

App. 124.   *Sonata à 6 Campanarum*

b)   G major
c)   1666
e)   3 violins, 3 violas, organ, violone
f)   Two sets of MS parts at Kroměříž (B IV 26 and 28)
g)   Published as a work of Vejvanovský's in *Musica Antiqua Bohemica*, 48, No. XIV (1961), edited by Jaroslav Pohanka
h)   The MS (anonymous) was copied by Vejvanovský. Nettl ascribes the work to Biber [Nettl/Biber]. As Sehnal has discovered, a second copy of this work, which was composed by Philip Jakob Rittler, exists at Kroměříž under the title *Sonata 5 vocum, vulgo Glockeriana* (B IV 26).

Notes

Preface

1. Manfred Bukofzer, *Music in the Baroque Era.* New York: W. W. Norton and Co. Inc., 1947, 13–16.

2. See pp. 100–105 and pp. 159–65.

Chapter 1

1. The baptismal record is quoted with a facsimile in Paul Nettl, "Heinrich Franz Biber von Bibern," 61–62.

2. Nettl, "Biber," 61.

3. Nettl, "Biber," 62. Nettl's source was Wilhelm Feistner, *Geschichte der Stadt Wartenburg* (Reichenberg, 1928).

4. Nettl, "Biber," 63.

5. His *Salve Regina* of 1663 contains an agile part for solo viola da gamba; a *Sonata à 4 violis* of 1663, preserved at Kroměříž in the same handwriting as that of the *Salve Regina,* and ascribed to "H. B.," and some newly discovered violin works that may well be from the same period all exhibit virtuoso violin writing.

6. Nettl, "Biber," 63.

7. See Nettl, "Biber," 63; Guido Adler, Introduction to *DTÖ* 11: v.

8. Nettl, "Die Wiener Tanzkomposition in der zweiten Hälfte des 17. Jahrhunderts," 119–49, remains the basic study of the composer's life and works; see also Adolf Koczirz, "Zur Lebensgeschichte Johann Heinrich Schmelzers," 59–60.

9. Jiří Sehnal, "Die Kompositionen Heinrich Bibers in Kremsier (Kroměříž)," 25–26, 37; idem, Introduction to *DTÖ* 127 (Heinrich Ignaz Franz Biber, *Instrumentalwerke handschriftlicher Überlieferung* [1976]), v–viii.

10. Sehnal, "Die Kompositionen," 37.

11. Ibid.

12. Biber's letter is published in facsimile and in modern transcription in Sehnal, "Ze života hudebníkú Kroměřížské biskupske Kapely v 17. století," 130–31.

13. "Wan nun Gdigister Fürst undt Herr etc. ich zu besserer beförderung meines, auch meiner angehörigen aufnehmens ich von Ihr Hochfürstl Gnd. ein Testimonium peracti Servitii von Nöthen habe." Ibid., 131.

14. "Des Bibers qualiten sein ihme ser wol bekannt, dan er auch bey seiner des Prinners Zeit bey obgedachtem fürsten von Eggenberg gedient solt haben." Quoted from Nettl, "Die Wiener Tanzkomposition," 169.

15. Nettl, "Biber," 64.

16. Helmut Federhofer, "Biographische Beiträge zu Georg Muffat und Johann Joseph Fux," 140.

17. Ibid.

18. Sehnal assumes that Rittler and Biber served together at Graz ("Die Kompositionen," 37).

19. Sehnal, Introduction, v.

20. Nettl, "Biber," 70; Sehnal, "Die Musikkapelle des Olmützer Bischofs Karl Liechtenstein-Castelcorn in Kremsier," 108; idem, "Die Kompositionen," 21–22. The sonata is published as a work of Vejvanovský's in *Musica Antiqua Bohemica,* vol. 48, ed. Jaroslav Pohanka, 21–17.

21. Prinner's treatise is owned by the Library of Congress, Washington. See Helmut Federhofer, "Eine Musiklehre von J. J. Prinner."

22. Nettl, *Das Wiener Lied im Zeitalter des Barock,* 22–28 and *Notenanhang,* 6–12 ("Nambli wol kann ich jetzt glauben" is published on pp. 11–12).

23. Sehnal, "Die Kompositionen," 34.

24. The *Pastorella* is No. 79 in MS. 726 of the Minoritenkonvent, Vienna; the manuscript is discussed in Friedrich Wilhelm Riedel, *Das Musikarchiv im Minoritenkonvent zu Wien. Katalog des älteren Bestandes vor 1784,* 80–82.

25. Nos. 7–14 are Biber's *Sonatae Violino Solo* (1681); Nos. 15–26 are Johann Jakob Walther's *Scherzi da violino solo* (1676); Nos. 27–54 are Walther's *Hortulus chelicus* (1688); Nos. 55–66 are Ignatius Albertin's *Sonatinae XII. violino solo* (1692).

26. See pp. 197–98 and 201–4.

27. Sehnal (Introduction, vii) suggests that since Bishop Liechtenstein-Kastelkorn's references to *scordatura* works begin in the year 1673, and Biber's works of that type (the *Mystery Sonatas* above all) are not known to date before his Salzburg years, it is likely that Biber developed his interest in *scordatura* in Salzburg. However, the Olomouc bishop's references to *scordatura* in letters to Schmelzer belong to a broader interest in a kind of violin music that Schmelzer called "pizaria"; and this interest dates from the exact time that Biber left Kroměříž. The following discussion (and that of the violin works in chapter 8) presumes that, as the Vienna manuscript proves, Biber's involvement in *scordatura* goes back to the beginning of his career.

28. See pp. 201–4.

29. It often happens in the Vienna manuscript that works in very closely related styles are grouped together, suggesting either common authorship or their having been copied from older manuscripts containing works from different time periods.

30. Paris, Bibliothèque Nationale, Vm^7 697, xiii.

31. At times it appears possible that Schmelzer's ritornello might have been derived from Prinner's song or another like it even though the relationship is not explicit; in measure 28 of Schmelzer's piece the first violin melody is very closely related to the beginning of Prinner's song, and the violin writing immediately before that point develops the idea of the alternating of the fifth and sixth degrees of the scale, one of the links between Prinner's song and Schmelzer's ritornello. The first triple-meter section in the Schmelzer *Pastorella* could easily have been quoted from a song either of Prinner's or of Schmelzer's; similar melodic types appear in songs of both men (see Nettl, *Das Wiener Lied, Notenanhang,* 6–17).

32. See Nettl, "Die Wiener Tanzkomposition," 168.

33. Ibid., 168: "Fünftens hab ich dem herrn Schmeltzer zu mir zum Essen geladen und allen fleiss das begehrte Vogelgesang zu überkhomben angewendt; so er vermeldt, dasz er zwar in noten die arien habe, die in bedeuten Vogelgesang zwischen aller der Thier heillen gepell und geschrey, aber die stimb der Vögel und Geschrey der anderen thier müesten aus dem kopf studiert werden;..." (from a letter of Wenzel Cunibert von Wenzelsberg, "Generalquartiermeister" at the Vienna court to Bishop Liechtenstein-Kastelkorn). Wenzelsberg reports his having made known to Schmelzer that he did not believe that everything had been composed. It is possible, therefore, that Biber's *Sonata violino solo representativa,* instead of having been influenced or inspired by Schmelzer's, was composed as a substitute for a work the bishop never received.

34. Nettl, "Die Wiener Tanzkomposition," 170; see also Antonin Breitenbacher, *Hudební Archiv Kolegiátního Kostela sv. Mořice v Kroměříži,* 132 (No. 135).

35. Constantin Schneider, "Franz Heinrich von Biber als Opernkomponist," 332–33.

36. Most of the works cited can be found in *DTÖ*, vols. 11, 25, 56, 93, 97, 105, 106–7, 111–12, and 127. Several are unpublished; editions of the remaining works by Biber are listed in the catalog at the end of this study.

37. The collection is associated with the town of Kroměříž rather than Olomouc, where the cathedral was located, because Kroměříž was for centuries the seat of the bishop's residence and of the collegiate church of St. Moritz; the Liechtenstein collection was preserved in this church, although performances took place in the residence and the cathedral at Olomouc. In addition to Breitenbacher (*Hudební Archiv*) and Sehnal ("Die Musikkapelle"), see Nettl, "Zur Geschichte der Musik-kapelle der Fürstbischofs Karl Liechtenstein-Kastelkorn von Olmütz," Ernst H. Meyer, "Die Bedeutung der Instrumentalmusik am Fürstbischöflichen Hofe zu Olomouc (Olmütz)," and Don Smithers, "Music for the Prince-Bishop." The library of Syracuse University, New York, has a great deal of the Liechtenstein collection on microfilm; a catalog compiled by Craig A. Otto has been issued (1977).

38. Nettl, "Biber," 63; Sehnal, "Die Kompositionen," 21.

39. He is referred to in a contemporary letter as *Cammerdiener* (Nettl, "Die Wiener Tanzkomposition," 168–69).

40. Ibid., 167.

41. Ibid.

42. Ibid., 168, 170.

43. Ibid., 169. The bishop's sentence "Es hat der entwichene Biber den Violin Bass und Viola da gamba gespilt, noch zimblicher gestalt auch etwas componirt," might, with the addition of a comma, be taken to refer to "violin, bass (i.e., violone) and viola da gamba"; but it was not at all usual to refer to the violone simply with the word bass, whereas cello was often referred to as *Bass-Geigen*.

44. Ibid., 170.

45. The bishop first mentions his desire to have *scordatura* works in a letter of March 9, 1673, and in June of that year he refers to a violinist and "Camerdiener" named Heger, who wished to perfect his playing with further study; correspondence with Schmelzer concerning Heger's studying at Graz continues to the end of the year (Nettl, "Die Wiener Tanzkomposition," 170–71).

46. Sehnal, "Die Musikkapelle," 106. Vejvanovský's instrumental works are published in *MAB*, 36, 47, 48, 49, edited by Jaroslav Pohanka.

47. Sehnal, "Die Kompositionen," 23.

48. The correspondence is published in Nettl, "Zur Geschichte," 490–96; Stainer's letter appears on p. 494.

49. Sehnal, "Die Musikkapelle," 97, note 130.

50. Walter Senn, *Jakob Stainer: der Geigenmacher zu Absam*.

51. Nettl, "Die Wiener Tanzkomposition," 169: "ist aber er Biber in person nit ankhomen, sondern hat ein so vormals auch bey hegst gedachter F. gn. Lagey gewest, aniczt aber in Salzburgischen diensten sich befindet, um einen discant geigen besagten geigenmacher abgeordnet und jüngstlich ein Cremoneser Violin zu richten überschickt, auch bedeuten lassen, dasz Herr Erzbischof mit negsten ein völliges stimmwerkh anzufrimben resolviert sei." (Quoted from a letter of J. F. Khuen von Auer dated Jan. 3, 1671).

52. Senn, *Jakob Stainer*, 124. An inventory from the year 1805 lists string instruments of Amati, Stradavarius and Stainer (two alto violas characterized as old and unusable; two contrabassi, one unusable); see Ernst Hintermaier, "Die Salzburger Hofkapelle von 1700 bis 1806: Organisation und Personal," 546–55.

53. Schmelzer's letter of November 2, 1670 is published in Nettl, "Die Wiener Tanzkomposition," 168.

54. Ibid., 169.

55. Sehnal, "Die Musikkapelle," 107.

56. The letter, quoted in Nettl, "Die Wiener Tanzkomposition," 175, contains the following sentence: "Dessen Schreiben vom 21. July samt beygeschlossener Serenada ist dem Herrn Paul Trompeter [Vejvanovský] zurecht zukhommen." Nettl identifies the Serenada with a work of Biber's of that title that is still preserved in an autograph manuscript at Kroměříž (*Serenada à 5,* 1673) and thus dates the letter 1673.

57. The dates in parentheses are Sehnal's ("Die Kompositionen," 23–24). On the authorship of the *Missa in Albis* see chapter 4 of the present study.

58. See chapter 8 of the present study.

59. Sehnal, "Die Musikkapelle," 104; idem, "Die Kompositionen," 29.

60. Domenico Gisberti, *Il viaggio dell'AA. SS. di Baviera à Salzburgo in giornate diviso e all'Altezza Real di Savoia in littere di Ravaglio descritto* (Munich 1670); Franz Martin, *Salzburgs Fürsten in der Barockzeit*, 132.

61. Salzburg, *Landesarchiv* (henceforth Sb. LA), *Geheimes Archiv* XXIV/2$\frac{1}{2}$.

62. Alfred Loewenburg, *Annals of Opera 1597–1940*, col. 39 (1661); a copy of the printed description of the visit to Munich (*La Reception faite a l'Archevesque de Salzbourg, dans la Cour de l'Electeur de Baviere* [Paris, Oct. 2, 1671]) is preserved at Sb. LA (*Geheimes Archiv*, XXIV/2$\frac{1}{2}$).

63. Johann Mattheson, *Grundlage einer Ehrenpforte*, 24.

64. Sb. LA, *Geheimes Archiv*, XXIII 4, (*Besoldungsliste*), *passim*.

65. Ibid., lists for Jan. 1672, May 1672, July 1673, Jan. 1674.

66. Nettl, "Biber," 66.

67. All the documents are preserved at Sb. LA, Hof-Kammer, Hallein X/625 (Pfleg.).

68. The dates in parentheses are Sehnal's ("Die Kompositionen," 23–24).

69. This ground appears in minor form in the Passacaglia second movement of the earlier version of the sixth of the *Sonatae Violino Solo* that is preserved in the Minoritenkonvent, Vienna. But its most impressive setting by far is as the bass of the wonderful chaconne finale of the second Partia of the *Harmonia Artificioso-Ariosa* (1696), in which the two *scordatura* violin parts play in canon at the unison, with many virtuoso runs, the movement ending with a section in which the meter changes from simple to compound triple above the ground.

70. The "Capriccio stravagante" was published in Farina's *Libro della pavane, gagliarde, . . .* (Dresden, 1626); like Biber's *Battalia* and *Sonata violino solo representativa*, it makes various imitations of animals and birds, other musical instruments (lira variata, la trombetta, la clarino, il flautino, tremulanto, fiferino della Soldatesca, etc.), has folk-like themes and special musical devices (col legno bowing, multiple stopping, pizzicato, dissonance). Johann Jakob Walther's famous "Serenata a un Coro di Violini, Organo Tremolante, Chirarrino, Piva, Due Trombe e timpani, Lira Todesca, et Harpa Smorzata, per un Violino Solo" (with basso continuo) from the *Hortulus Chelicus* (1688) is the most obvious descendant of such pieces.

71. David Boyden, *The History of Violin Playing from its Origins to 1761*, 121–25.

72. Modern editions in *DTÖ* 127, ed. Jiří Sehnal, pp. 3–15, 47–60.

73. The *Sonata S. Polycarpi*, *Serenada* and *Battalia* all have performance remarks written by Biber (see the catalog at the end of the present study).

74. See the reports by André Maugars and several witnesses to the 1628 consecration service cited below (chapter 3, note 12).

75. See the discussion on pp. 56–58 and 63–66.

76. Manfred Bukofzer, *Music in the Baroque Era*, 68–69.

77. Ludovico Zacconi, *Prattica di musica*, vol. 1, fol. 8–9.

78. Warren Dwight Allen, *Philosophies of Music History*, 3–28.

79. Walter Benjamin, *The Origin of German Tragic Drama*, 176.

80. Sources cited in notes 64 and 65, above.

81. See p. 60.

82. See p. 61.

83. Johannes Peregrinus, *Geschichte der Salzburgischen Dom-Sängerknaben oder schlechthin des Kapellhauses,* 101–7, 193–95.

84. Details concerning the court musicians in chapter 2.

85. Owing to the loss of the court payments lists from this period, the exact date of Muffat's entry into the archbishop's service is unknown, but he was certainly there in 1678 (C. Schneider, *Geschichte,* 56; Federhofer, "Biographische Beiträge," 140–42; idem, article "Muffat" in *MGG* IX, 915–19).

86. Muffat's sonata remains unpublished; the call number at Kroměříž is IV/118. In general, very little documentary material concerning Muffat and no manuscript compositions of his can be found in Salzburg today. However, a manuscript treatise, dated 1710, is preserved in the convent at Nonnberg (VI 152 II i). This generally unknown work is in two parts, the first entitled *Regulae fundamentales* (Von dem General=Bass, partiturae oder Basso Continuo solches wohl und recht nach ordnung deren Reglen mag erlehrnet werden. Zusammen verfast durch dem Edl: und kunstreichen auch weltberimten Virtuosen der edlen Schlag Kunst Georgium Muffat Organista et Capellae Magister Passavii. 2 Jan: 1710), and the second headed *Praxis* (supra Regulas partiturae Eximii D[omi]ni Georgii Muffat Ziffris exposita. Das ist wollgegrindte Unterweisung, wie die Regln sambt denen Exempln und praxi der partiturae des berimbtesten Maisters H: Georgii Muffat zu verstehen seye: wirdt deroselben gegenwertigen praxis mit denen Ziffern erkhleret, wie er muss geschlagen werdten.) As the description of the *Praxis* part makes clear, the treatise uses numbers to indicate more fully and precisely than the ordinary figured bass symbols the exact voicing of basso continuo chords. This eminently practical work is completely different from the basso continuo treatise of Muffat's (1699) preserved at the Minoritenkonvent, Vienna, and edited by Federhofer (*Georg Muffat: An Essay on Thoroughbass*), although the latter, too, is in two parts (*Regulae Concentuum Partiturae*... and *Exempla der vornehmbsten Greiffen der Partitur*...). The date of the Nonnberg treatise is that of the copying of the manuscript, since Muffat died in 1704; and although he is referred to as Kapellmeister at Passau, the treatise might well represent a work produced at Salzburg for teaching purposes; comparison with the Vienna treatise, whose *terminus ante quem* is 1699, suggests that the Nonnberg work is earlier.

87. Andreas Werckmeister, *Harmonologia Musica oder Kurze Anleitung zur Musicalischen Composition,* 5–6.

88. Muffat's prefaces are published in Oliver Strunk, *Source Readings in Music History,* pp. 442–52.

89. Ibid., 443, 447.

90. Franz Martin, *Salzburgs Fürsten,* 145, 155–58. Archbishop Johann Ernst turned away from the Italian architect Casparo Zucalli, who had built for Max Gandolph, in favor of Viennese court architect Johann Bernhard Fischer von Erlach, an action that reflected his "leaning away from anything foreign" (Martin, 145).

91. See note 98, below.

92. Salzburg, *E.b. Konsistorialarchiv* (henceforth Sb. KA), *Prothocollum Consistoriale* (*Prot. Const.*), Jan. 16, 1679.

93. Sb. LA, *Geheimes Archiv* XXIV. 4.

94. These three publications of Biber's were announced in the catalogues for the Frankfurt fairs of those years as well as their years of publication (Albert Göhler, *Verzeichnis der in den Frankfurter und Leipziger Messkatalogen der Jahre 1564 bis 1759 angezeigten Musikalien. Zweiter Teil. 17. Jahrhundert,* 6).

95. Altmann Kellner, *Musikgeschichte des Stiftes Kremsmünster,* 272.

96. Ibid., 273.

97. Johann Caspar Kerll and Georg Muffat were among the musicians who received knighthoods from Leopold.

98. The letter is preserved at the Allgemeine Verwaltungs Archiv, Vienna.

99. Nettl, "Biber," 66; idem, "Heinrich Franz Biber, A Great Austrian Violinist of the Baroque" (*Forgotten Musicians*), 21.

100. Oswald Redlich, *Weltmacht des Barock,* 230, 241.

101. For many years the date of the founding of the archdiocese was erroneously believed to have taken place in 582 rather than the correct date in the eighth century; following the newer date the 1200th anniversary was celebrated in 1974.

102. A copy of the printed program is preserved at Sb. LA: *Ordnung der Gottesdienst/ So/ Dise bevorstehende Octav hindurch so wohl in/ in [sic] dem Hochfürstl./ Thum Stifft/ Als auch bey/ St. Peter und auff dem Nunberg von Tag/ zu Tag gehalten werden.*

103. Georg Muffat's *Armonico tributo* (1682); Andreas Christophorus Clamer's *Mensa harmonica* (1682); and possibly also Biber's *Fidicinium Sacro-Profanum* (1682 [1683]).

104. Muffat relates this fact in the preface to the *Armonico tributo.*

105. Mattheson, *Grundlage einer Ehrenpforte,* 24–25.

106. Sb. LA: *Ordnung der Gottesdienst,* 6.

107. See pp. 63–66.

108. Küsel's engraving (preserved in the Salzburg Museum Carolino-Augusteum) is reproduced on p. 44 of this study.

109. Two *Te Deum*s and a *Missa Archiepiscopalis* by Andreas Hofer have survived that correspond closely to the scoring shown in Küsel's engraving; since the *Ordnung der Gottesdienst* (Sb. LA) states that Max Gandolph himself sang the High Mass on October 18, Hofer's work must be seriously considered for that occasion.

110. Sb. KA, *Prot. Const.* 1684, fol. 251.

111. See note 83, above.

112. "Hainrich Franz Piber, Hochfrstl. Capellmaister alhier, in namben der gesambten Music im Hochfrstl. Thumb Stüftt. [margin]
      Auf diesen schrüftliches Einlangen und erind hat man genedig Verwilligt, dass in Ansehen derfür die sambentlich in Gott ruhenden Hfl. Capitulares vollsten fundirten Jahrtag Nunmehro nicht mehr im und[teren] Chor, wie vormahls gehalten, sond[ern] auf sein Capellmaisters zu mehreren Respect Aines Hochfr:ⁿ Thumb Capitels und Bischofen Verordnung mit der Orgel und zun gehörigen Musicis condecorirt würdet, ermelter Music hinkünfttig über die ehevor genossenen 6 F: noch andern 6: und also in Allem 12 F—aussgevolgt, auch ain solches wohl dem Praesenzmaister als Anwaldtschaft zur Nachricht und Verhaltnuss per Decreta angesteigt werden solle." (Sb. LA, *Prothocollum capitulare* book for the year 1685, fol. 107v–108r).

113. Constantin Schneider, "Franz Heinrich von Biber als Opernkomponist," 281–347; Sibylle Dahms, "Das Musiktheater des Salzburger Hochbarocks (1668–1709), Teil I: Das Benediktinerdrama"; idem, "Neues zur Chronologie der Opern von Biber und Muffat," 365–67; idem, "Opern und Festkantaten des Salzburger Hochbarock," 382–83.

114. Erwin Luntz introduced this idea, along with the notion that Biber travelled extensively as a performer ("H. I. F. Biber"); Nettl ("Biber," 67) showed that the picture of Biber as a travelling virtuoso did not rest on a foundation of fact, but did not contradict the view that Biber's productivity fell off in the 1680s.

115. The sources are given in the catalog of Biber's works.

116. That is, the aria with motto beginning in the voice that is repeated by the basso continuo (or other instruments) then begun again by the voice, which now continues the vocal line.

117. Even within the entire corpus of the Bach cantatas and Passions these limits are respected; only one single movement of the cantatas—the alto solo "In deine Hände" of the *Actus Tragicus*—is in B-flat minor, while no single movement exceeds four sharps.

118. The historian Markus Hansiz (*Germaniae sacrae,* tomus 2, 846) said of Johann Ernst: "Musicos in gratiam rei Divinae conductos habebat in obsequio, non deliciis."

119. Sb. LA, *Prothocollum capitulare* book for the year 1687, fol. 273v–275r.

120. Ibid., fol. 62

121. The documents relating to Biber's knighthood, including Biber's letter, the design for the coat of arms and Emperor Leopold's lengthy decree are preserved in the Allgemeine Verwaltungs Archiv, Vienna.

122. As noted above (note 114), the image of Biber as a travelling virtuoso is inaccurate. Apart from the places where Biber worked (Graz, Kroměříž and Salzburg), we can be fairly sure that Biber was well known in Vienna (he played for Leopold three times, including at Laxenburg, near Vienna, and he was certainly well known to Schmelzer), Munich (from Karl Biber's report in Mattheson's *Ehrenpforte*) and Nuremberg (from the congratulatory poem from the "Philomusici" of that city that heads the *Fidicinium Sacro-Profanum*). Certain information regarding other visits of his is not forthcoming.

123. See note 121.

124. Sb. LA, *Geheimes Archiv*, Rub 25. litt. B. No. 11.

125. Sb. KA, *Prot. Const.*, Dec. 12, 1690, fol. 876.

126. Sb. LA, *Hofrat Katenichl*, fol. 96.

127. Sb. LA, *Geheimes Archiv*, XXIII 4, *Besoldungsliste*, Jan. 1674, July 1694.

128. Sb. LA, *Geheimes Archiv*, "Beschreibung der Personen welche in der Statt Salzburg wohnen," fol. 37v.

129. See pp. 25–26.

130. Kloster Mondsee, *Cod. Lunaelac*, fol. 167; cited in Nettl, "Biber," 69.

131. Peregrinus, *Geschichte der Salzburgischen Dom Sängerknaben*, 193.

132. See p. 28.

133. The manual is preserved at Stift Nonnberg (8 175 Ca); it is described in Erich Schenk, "Ein 'Singfundament' von Heinrich Ignaz Franz Biber."

134. As Schenk notes (ibid., 280), the many rests in the twelve melodies suggest that they are only one part of a set of traditional two-part *bicinia*.

135. The Nonnberg *Protocol* books are mostly very small (approx. 4 x 6 in.), diary-like volumes catalogued by year under the title *lit: Dom: A [B, C*, etc.]; entries are usually short, often two or three per page, except for special occasions (quite frequent) when descriptions of events may run to several pages (in small handwriting).

136. Nonnberg, *Prot.*, April 25, 1700; Nov. 3, 1700; June 6, 1702; Mar. 31, 1704.

137. References to the performance of "Aufzügen," "Larmae" and "Mezzopunte" are far too numerous to cite. On August 15, 1695, for the feast of the ascension of the Virgin, we find the following description: "Am Unser Lieben Frauen Himmelfarth hat gebrödiget R. B. Angelidus Capuc: Er hat zu Anfang und zu dem beschluss der Prödtig zu dem Einzug der Seeligsten Jungfrau in das Himmlische Jerusalem die Trombeten und Hörpauggen eingeladten und berüeften, haben also zwen mezopunt gemacht...."

138. Nonnberg, *Prot.*, Sept. 21, 1672; Oct. 28 1676.

139. Nonnberg, *Prot.*, June 16, 1691.

140. Nonnberg, *Prot.*, Feb. 10, 1696.

141. Nonnberg was founded around the turn of the eighth century by St. Rupert for his niece Erentraud; in the early eleventh century Emperor Heinrich II had a Romanesque basilica built.

142. Nonnberg, *Prot.*, July 15, 1696: "Den 15 Julii Dom: 5 Pent: sein offentlich eingeführt und eingekhleidt worden die freÿlä gräfin von Ÿberäkher, und woll Edl gebohrne Jungfraw M: A: Magdalena von Bibern. Die erste ist genent worden M Margarita Caelestina die andere M Rosa Henerica ihr Profession ist auf den 20 Julii verschoben worden. Umb 6 Uhr haben wür 3 Tageiten Psal: und nach der Convent Mäss haben wür auf den Music Chor das Asperg: und Stella Caeli Musiciert darauf ins Capitl gangen als dan die Non Psal: und der einführung erwarth Herr B. Paris von Lerchenfeld Prior zu S: Peter hats eingesegnet und das Ambt von S: Henerici gesungen, die Hoff=Musig hat Musiciert Herr Capellm: V Bibern hats bestölt hernach ist in der Canzleÿ ein Mallzeit gewesten von etlich 20 Persohnen welche alle die Unser gnedl Fr Abbtissin auss gehalten. Die Vesp: hat man heunt umb 3. gehalten. Ursach weill man so spatt zum Essen hat khönnen gehen."

143. The *Missa S. Henrici* is scored for five-part choir (SSATB) and soloists with strings and ad libitum trombones, plus basso continuo.

144. The Michaelbeuern inventory is transcribed in Helmut Federhofer, "Zur Musikpflege im Benediktinerstift Michaelbeuern (Salzburg)."

145. Nonnberg, *Prot.,* June 2, 1692.

146. A number of vocal compositions with one or two viole d'amore (sometimes with substitute parts for violins) are preserved at Nonnberg; almost invariably the *scordatura* indicated is F, A, c, f, a, d'.

147. Karl Geiringer, *Alte Musik-Instrumente im Museum Carolino Augusteum Salzburg,* 20; illustrations of three instruments dated 1673, 1700 and 1738 on Tafel II (p. 48).

148. Federhofer, "Zur Musikpflege."

149. Nonnberg, *Prot.,* May 2, 4, 1693. On both these days the court musicians played; on the fourth a Requiem performed by the court musicians is mentioned, and there is a later reference to three Requiems performed by the court musicians. Biber's *Requiem à 15* and *Requiem in F minor* were both written after 1690.

150. Nonnberg, *Prot.,* August 27, 1703; on the following day for a wedding at Nonnberg the party brought their own musicians and once again "beautiful music was heard, with singing voices, lutes, recorders and "Toba" [?]; the countess of Mondfort herself sang an Italian piece."

151. Nonnberg, *Prot.,* September 8, 30, 1703.

152. Nonnberg, *Prot.,* September 11, 1703.

153. Nonnberg, *Prot.,* September 4, 1704.

154. The documents relating to Biber's summer house (Sb. LA, *Hofkammer,* ca. 1695/6) can no longer be found. See Schneider, *Geschichte,* 83; Nettl, "Biber," 67–68.

155. Walter Hummel, "Das Bruderschaftsbüchl der Hl. Kreuz-Bruderschaft an der Bürgerspitalskirche in Salzburg," 205–8.

156. Sb. LA, *Prot. Cap.,* 1700, fol. 251–67; Peregrinus, *Geschichte der Salzburgischen Dom-Sängerknaben,* 193.

157. Sb. KA, *Prot. Const.,* 1699, fol. 557v., 570, 599, 664.

158. Peregrinus, *Geschichte der Salzburger Dom-Sängerknaben,* 114.

159. *Zwey-Einiger/ Hymenaeus,/ Oder Oesterreich-Lüneburgischer/ Frid=* und Freuden=voller/ Vermählungs=Gott (copy at Sb. LA).

160. See pp. 101–7.

161. *TRATENIMENTO MUSICALE/ del'Ossequio di Salisburgo,/ da rapresentarsi/ Nella grande Sala di Corte/ In applauso del felice arrivo/ Dell' AUGUSTISSIMA REGINA/ WILHELMINA/ AMALIA/ Duchessa di Brunsvvich, Luneburg,/ SPOSA/ Dell' AUGUSTISSIMO/ RE de' ROMANI & d' HONGARIA/ GIUSEPPE I./ per Commando/ Di S. A. R.*[ma]*/ GIOVANNI ERNESTO/* arcivescovo & Prencipe di Salisburgo,/ Composta in Musica/ a Henrico Franc. a Bibern, Suae Celsitudinis/ dapifero & Capellae Magistro/ In Salisburgo li 8. di Fevraro l'anno 1699. (copy at Sb. LA).

162. Sb. LA, *Geheimes Archiv,* XXIII/14. The "Maudthaus" in which Biber lived at the expense of the court is today the "Thalhammerhaus" (Rathausplatz 2).

163. Sehnal, "Die Musikkapelle," 107; Ludwig von Köchel, *Die Kaiserliche Hof-Musikkapelle in Wien von 1543 bis 1876.*

164. The dating of the Kroměříž *Balletti à 6* is from Sehnal ("Die Kompositionen," 26); the dating of the Salzburg works is based on the form of Biber's name on the manuscript (i.e., whether he is named *"di* Bibern," *dapifer,* or simply "Kapellmeister") plus the watermarks (which provide only very broad temporal boundaries) and the style; on the dating of the *Missa St. Henrici* see p. 43; on the dating of *Chi la dura la vince* see Sibylle Dahms, "Neues zur Chronologie," 365–67.

165. And some of these manuscripts bear the same watermarks as the compositions by Biber in the cathedral archive. For example, a strophic-song version in German of the Dies irae bears the inscription "componirt und gesungen A^{no} 1680 A. F. V. G. V. H. B.; it might be that the last initials stand for "von Heinrich Biber." But the composition is so simple that it would add nothing to our knowledge of Biber's work other than the fact that he could toss off such a thing. On the other hand, a composition of similarly simple character, entitled *Aria Alto Solo: "bey Jesu nur allein,"* is inscribed "vom Herrn Capel-Maister"; but the watermark is not identifiable from other compositions by Biber, although the work probably dates from the seventeenth century. A few compositions of considerably higher quality also date from this time, including a printed set of thirty aria-with-ritornello pieces and a manuscript set of twenty-five hymns; these cannot be definitively ascribed at present.

166. On the opera see p. 20; the key plan of the *Vesperae Longiores ac Breviores* is given in chapter 7; the *Balletti à 6* sets movements 1, 4, 8, and 12 with two clarini in addition to the strings of the remaining movements; these movements are like pillars in C major between which Biber modulates to closely related keys according to a plan that groups the dominant and mediant as well as the relative minor and subdominant to one another (see fig. 4-5).

167. Sources cited in notes 142 and 150.

168. Franz Martin, *Salzburgs Fürsten,* 155–58.

169. Hermann Spies, *Die Salzburger grossen Domorgeln,* 19; idem, "Geschichtliches über das Salzburger Glockenspiel."

170. Franz Martin, *Salzburgs Fürsten,* 152–53.

171. Nonnberg, *Prot.,* May 3, 1704: "Den 3. Dito. Sabbatho. An dem H: ✠ tag in der Nacht zwischen 12. und 1 Uhr ist der fr: M: Rosa herr Vatter gewester CapellMaister alhier nach 4. Tägiger aussgestandtner Krankheit mit empfangenen H H: *Sacramenten* und schönster Resignation in den Göttlichen Willen ganz sanfft entschlaffen. Gott gebe ihme die Ewige Ruehe. Das Ambt haben sie drauf gesungen, auch S: Joannes Evangeli heünt widerumb angefangen zusingen."

172. Because Biber died in the hour after midnight some of the records of his death place it on the second rather than the third: "Herr franz hainrich von Pibern gewester Cammerdiener und Capelmaister ist den. 2 Maii verstorben und dahero vor demselben nicht mehr abgevolgt worden" (Sb. LA, *Geheimes Archiv,* XXIII 4/2; May, 1704). The burial record at St. Peter's simply states that "den 4. Maii ist H. biber Capellmaister Eingraben worden" (Archive of St. Peter's, *Sepulturae, etc:/ Ad Ecclesias, Capellas, et Coemeterium Monasterii/ S. Petri Salisburgi,* fol. 77v.).

173. Sb. LA, *Frank Beamtenkartei;* Martin, "Beiträge zur Salzburger Familiengeschichte."

174. Anton Heinrich Biber's letters are preserved at Sb. LA (*Gen. Einehmer und Hofzahlamt,* 1706/lit F).

175. Martin, "Beiträge zur Salzburger Familiengeschichte."

176. Nonnberg, *Prot.,* Sept. 13, 1705.

177. Sigismund Keller, "Geschichtliches über die nächsten Vorfahren Mozarts als Kapellmeister im fürsterzbischöflichen Dom zu Salzburg," 65.

178. Nonnberg, XV: 31, 32A, 32B.

179. Maria Magdalena Karolina, daughter of Karl Biber, for example, entered the convent at Nonnberg; like her aunt, she was an outstanding singer and played violin and viola d'amore (Keller, "Geschichtliches," 72).

180. Peregrinus, *Geschichte der Salzburgischen Dom-Sängerknaben,* 194–95.

181. "Herrn Johann Joachim Quantzens Lebenslauf, von ihm selbst entworfen," in F. W. Marpurg, *Historisch-kritische Beyträge zur Aufnahme der Musik,* 197–250; English translation in Nettl, *Forgotten Musicians,* 280–319.

182. Schneider, *Geschichte,* 95.

183. Helene Wessely-Kropik, ed., *Romanus Weichlein (1652-1706): Encaenia Musices (1695). Erster Teil (DTÖ 128), Zweiter Teil (DTÖ 130);* Introduction 128: vii–viii.

184. See, for example, chapter 3, notes 56 and 63.

185. Clamer's name appears in the payments lists under the *vicarii chori* and, from time to time, in the chapter protocoll books.

186. In his treatise (*Manuductio ad organum*, 1704) Samber refers to having studied with Muffat; his name appears regularly in the court payments lists of the late seventeenth and early eighteenth centuries as cathedral organist, usually with extra remuneration for tuning the instruments (Sb. LA, *Geheimes Archiv*, XXIII 4).

187. The theme appears prominently in Biber's *Missa S. Henrici* (Agnus Dei), *Requiem à 15*, *Missa ex B* (Et unam sanctam), *Litania de S. Josepho, Missa in Contrapuncto* (Christe; this Mass, however, is probably a work of Karl Biber's). It had, however, an extraordinarily widespread use and, perhaps, a particular association with the *stile antico*, for it appears as model *cantus firmus* in the Fux *Gradus ad Parnassum* and Kircher's *Musurgia Universalis*, as well as in Monteverdi's vocal Masses, and the *stile antico* E-major fugue of Bach's *Well-tempered Clavier*, Book II. The Mozart examples are discussed in Hermann Abert, *W. A. Mozart* 1: 310; 2: 496–97. Abert also refers to the theme that accompanies the chorale of the armed men in The Magic Flute as "ein Stück katholisches gutes: das Kyrie der Missa S. Henrici (1701) von Hch. Biber" (2: 675–76). The latter theme was also widespread and the connection to Mozart mentioned by Abert is highly doubtful.

188. See the introduction to the catalog of Biber's works.

Chapter 2

1. Franz Martin, *Salzburgs Fürsten*, 106.

2. Martin, *Salzburgs Fürsten*, 146–51, 155–59, 162–63.

3. Martin, *Salzburgs Fürsten*, 132, 164. The Italian visitors were Alberto Priami (see chapter 3, note 12) and Lorenzo Gisberti (see chapter 1, note 60).

4. Schneider, *Geschichte*, 64–67.

5. Hermann Spies, "Die Tonkunst in Salzburg in der Regierungszeit des Fürsten und Erzbischofs Wolf Dietrich von Raitenau (1587–1612)," 36–42.

6. "Die Reformation des Chores und Fundation der fürstlichen Chormusik am Dom," cited in ibid., 47–51.

7. It is now virtually certain that the Mass was composed in the second half of the seventeenth century, perhaps for the great "Jubeljahr" of 1682, and most likely by Biber. See the discussion on pp. 56–58 and 63–66, and the sources cited in chapter 3, note 11.

8. Peregrinus (*Geschichte der Salzburgischen Dom-Sängerknaben*, 93) quotes the description of the contemporary chronicler Steinhauser: at this "allerstattlichsten *solemnisten Actum* sich auch die Hochfürstl: Hof *Musica* mit der allerkhünstlichsten und lieblichsten concerten, in unterschidliche Chöre abgetheilt, darunter sich auch Trometen, Lauten, Violen, Tiorben, Zünggen und Possaunen hören lassen, zu unterthänigsten gefallen, lobwürdigist gebrauchet."

9. "Zweyen wolgezierten Orgelln schönen Gemählen" (Gregor Kyrner), quoted from Herman Spies, *Die Salzburger Grossen Domorgeln*, 13.

10. See pp. 40–47 of the present study.

11. Ernst Tittel (*Österreichische Kirchenmusik*, 155) suggests 1668, and Sigismund Keller ("Geschichtliches über die nächsten Vorfahren Mozarts als Kapellmeister im fürsterzbischöflichen Dom zu Salzburg," 27) indicates 1670. Guido Adler (*DTÖ*, 20, ix) and Franz Martin (*Salzburgs Fürsten*, 134) state 1675.

12. Sb. LA, *Protocollum capitulare* book for 1668, fol. 262v. Quoted in Karl Weinmann, "Andreas Hofer," 73–74.

13. Judas Thaddäus Zauner, *Chronik von Salzburg*, 450.

14. "[A]uch die 2 kleineren Orgeln, welche mit den anderen 2 am Chore symmetrisch erbaut wurden, vollendet waren." (Hübner, *Beschreibung der Stadt Salzburg*, 1: 218).

15. Ibid., 198: "An den 4 Hauptschwibbogen, worauf die grosse Kuppel ruht, sind 4 ganz gleiche Orgeln; die Hauptorgen aber, ein Meisterstück dieser Kunst, steht auf dem grossen Musikchore des Schiffes ruckwärts; alle 5 sind vom Erzbischof Paris, und unter Erzbischofe Jakob Ernst Lichtenstein erneuert und neu gefasset worden."

16. Spies, *Die Salzburger grossen Domorgeln*, 14.

17. Ibid., 13–16.

18. J. B. Samber, *Continuatio ad manuductionem organicam*, 145–52. Samber's remarks are discussed in Spies, *Die Salzburger grossen Domorgeln*, 32–37. Samber gives registrations for accompanying one, two or several voices, for preluding, playing fugues, responses, versetts, toccatas, playing in tutti, improvising, *Sub elevatione, galanten Spiel*, etc.

19. Ernst Hintermaier ("Die fürsterzbischöfliche Musik in Salzburg zur Zeit Mozarts"; "Die Dommusik im 18. Jahrhundert") cites several descriptions and reports from the eighteenth and early nineteenth centuries that demonstrate the basic continuity of performance locations in the cathedral.

20. Schneider, *Geschichte*, 85.

21. Spies, "Vergangenheit," 332.

22. Sb. LA, *Geheimes Archiv*, XXIII 4 (Payments lists from the late seventeenth and early eighteenth centuries); Schneider, "Franz Heinrich Biber," 289.

23. Martin, *Salzburgs Fürsten*, 119–20; Sb. LA, *Geheimes Archiv*, XXIII 4.

24. Sb. LA, *Geheimes Archiv*, XXIII 4.

25. Peregrinus, *Geschichte der Salzburgischen Dom-Sängerknaben*, 101, 178–83.

26. Ibid., 180.

27. Spies, "Die Tonkunst," 99.

28. Ibid., 98–105; also Spies, "Vergangenheit," 330–34.

29. Spies, "Die Tonkunst," 103.

30. Ibid., 99–100.

31. Ibid., 100–101.

32. Ibid., 29–30.

33. Spies, "Vergangenheit," 334.

34. Franz Dückher von Haslau zu Winkl, *Saltzburgische Chronica*, 317–18.

35. Sb. LA, *Prothocollum Capitulare*, 1654, fol. 28v.

36. Martin, *Salzburgs Fürsten*, 139.

37. Joseph Mezger, *Historia Salisburgensis* (1692), 920.

38. Hofer's *Ara Musica* (1677), Biber's *Mystery Sonatas* (unpublished), *Sonatae, tam Aris, quam Aulis servientes* (1676), *Mensa Sonora* (1680), *Sonatae Violino Solo* (1681), *Fidicinium Sacro-Profanum* (ca. 1683), Andreas Christophorus Clamer's *Mensa Harmonica* (1682) and Georg Muffat's *Armonico Tributo* (1682); all but the first are instrumental works.

39. Not all the payments lists have been preserved. This statement is based on those that survive: 1671, 1672, 1673, 1674, 1694, 1697, 1698, 1700, 1701, 1702, 1703, 1704.

40. Sb. LA, *Prothocollum Capitulare*, 1672, fol. 120.

41. See chapter 1, note 51.

42. See pp. 60–61; Hintermaier, "Die fürsterzbischöfliche Musik," 397.

43. Archbishop Max Gandolph made clear in the provisions for his anniversary services (established in 1674, and held annually in November) that the terms began in 1674 (see p. 61).

44. Nonnberg, XI 17.

45. See Hummel, "Das Bruderschaftsbüchl" and Schneider, "Franz Heinrich Biber." Also the biographical information contained in Dahms, "Das Musiktheater," 317–45, and Hintermaier, "Die Salzburger Hofkapelle" has been especially helpful in identifying musicians named in the payments lists.

46. Sb. LA, *Geheimes Archiv*, XXIII. 14.

47. Schneider, "Franz Heinrich Biber," 287–88, 306–7.

48. Published in F. W. Marpurg, *Historisch-kritische Beyträge zur Aufnahme der Musik* vol. 3. English translation in R. Donington, *The Interpretation of Early Music*, 589–90. The same situation prevailed in Kroměříž under Bishop Liechtenstein-Kastelkorn (Nettl, "Die Wiener," 169).

49. Paul Winter, for example (*Der mehrchörige Stil*, 87), describes the right balcony nearer the altar as containing five singers, a conductor and organist, although string players are clearly visible; there is likewise no mention of the cornetto in the right choir, and the figure standing in the foreground of the left choir is described as a singer. Klaus Haller (*Partituranordnung u. musikalischer Satz*, 106) speaks of a positive and a theorbo in the choir.

50. "Astitere in dextro Chori latere DD. Canonici Metropolitici, in sinistro Conventus S. Petri. Inter utrumque Chorum medio loco in subselliis honorifice paratis extranei DD. Praesules mytrati consedere." Mezger, *Historia Salisburgensis*, 942.

51. The *Missa Alleluia* has not survived in the original parts of the Salzburg cathedral archive, but the title page is extant, in which the work is called *Missa Alleluia à 26*; the Kremsmünster copy of 1698 is entitled *Missa Alleluia à 36*.

52. Hintermaier ("Die Dommusik") cites several reports to this effect from the eighteenth and nineteenth centuries; in the seventeenth century the practice is confirmed by the layout of the score of the *Missa Salisburgensis* (trumpets divided into loco 1 and loco 2), by Biber's remarks on the performance of the *Sonata S. Polycarpi*, and by the alternating character of the trumpets in the works themselves.

53. Sb. LA, *Geheimes Archiv* XXIII. 14 (1700); this more detailed breakdown of the payments to court employees (from which we know Biber's full salary with benefits) speccifies in the case of two trumpeters the sum of eighteen florins per year "von der im Domb verrichtenden Music" and *"Praesens* wegen der Domb-Music."

54. Michael Praetorius, *Syntagma musicum* 3: 171.

55. Even the two largest of the *Sonatae, tam Aris, quam Aulis servientes* (Nos. I and XII) have been recorded with good effect with the addition of timpani for the most obvious fanfare-like passages (*Heinrich Biber: Twelve Sonatas for trumpets, strings, timpani and continuo,* "The Parley of Instruments," directed by Roy Goodman and Peter Holman, *Hyperion* A66145, 1985).

56. This detail is confirmed by the documents cited in Hintermaier, "Die Dommusik."

57. See *DTÖ* 59, ed. Guido Adler, p. 102.

58. Hintermaier, "Die Dommusik," 149–53.

59. The eighteenth-century reports (see the preceeding footnote) in referring to balconies on the left and right sides of the cathedral do not make clear the viewer's position in relation to these balconies. Hintermaier takes the positioning to refer to someone looking into the nave from the altar—i.e., the opposite from someone looking at Küsel's engraving; if this is correct then the strings remained on the Epistle side throughout the seventeenth and eighteenth centuries, while the solo singers were on the Gospel side.

60. The latter is suggested as a secondary meaning by Charles Sherman in the foreword to his edition of Hofer's *Magnificat*.

61. The published score of this work (ed. Charles Sherman) makes no allusion whatever to the possibility of solo performance.

62. "Der Buchstabe S kennzeichnet Einzel oder Konzertante Stimmen, im Gegensatz hiezu bezeichnet R einen stärkeren Gesangschor, wenn die grössere Zahl der musiker einen solchen gestattet und was jener, der an Sängermangel leidet, bleiben lassen muss." See K. A. Rosenthal, "Zur Stilistik der Salzburger Kirchenmusik von 1600–1730," 86, note 48.

63. In the choir, eighteen or nineteen singers are visible. Assuming that the four soloists of chorus I share the balcony with the strings, while those of chorus II are located with the trombones and cornetti, we arrive at eight additional voices.

64. Hans T. David and Arthur Mendel, eds., *The Bach Reader,* 120–24.

65. Hintermaier ("Die fürsterzbischöfliche Musik," 396) gives this figure; in "Die Dommusik im 18. Jahrhundert," p. 151, on the basis of plans preserved at the Salzburg Museum Carolino-Augusteum, he estimates the size of each balcony as fifteen square meters; the height of the balconies can be estimated from the fact that they were reached via a staircase of thirteen steps (visible in the church, but eliminated from Küsel's engraving, presumably for aesthetic reasons).

66. The title page of this work enumerates the vocal parts incorrectly as 2C, 2A, 2T, 2B instead of 2C, A, T, B, an error that undoubtedly arose from a misunderstanding of the eight ripieno parts.

67. That is, the *Requiem à 15* has single parts for the six voices of the chorus (besides parts for the six soloists). In the case of the six-part *Missa ex B* the number of parts reflects the situation at Seitenstetten, not Salzburg; but at times the work features alternation of the soprano and bass parts. Johann Caspar Kerll's *Triumphate sidera,* for SSATTB chorus, has doubled ripieno parts only for the voices that do not divide (altos and basses), indicating SAT and STB groupings within the chorus.

68. According to persons present at the performance in certain places within the cathedral parts of the work were virtually inaudible; the commercial recording (*Harmonia Mundi* 25 22073-7) was made in the Kollegien-Kirche instead of the cathedral.

69. *Justus ut palma/ Offertorium/ a/ 2 Canto conc:/ Alto Tenore/ Basso/ 2 Violini/ 2 Cornetti Ripp.*[ni]*/ 2 Viole/ e/ Organo/ desunt 2 Violini dup:*[ti]*/ Del Sig:*[re] *Casparo Kerl. (A 209)*

70. Guido Adler, "Zur Geschichte der Wiener Messkomposition in der zweiten Hälfte des XVII. Jahrhunderts," 11. It is clear that Adler the scholar knew the seventeenth-century usage of the word "Capella" (see pp. 17–18); Adler the editor (*DTÖ* 49) apparently disregarded this knowledge.

71. Meuer's work is discussed, with examples, in Max Schneider, "Die Besetzung der vielstimmigen Musik des 17. und 16. Jahrhunderts." Kerll's Mass is published in *DTÖ,* 49, ed. Guido Adler.

72. Adler, "Zur Geschichte," 22.

73. Max Schneider, "Die Besetzung," 223.

Chapter 3

1. Friedrich Daniel, "Die Konzertanten Messen Johann Stadlmayrs." Unpublished dissertation. Vienna, 1928.

2. Michael Praetorius, *Syntagma musicum* 3: 169–97.

3. Hintermaier, "Die Dommusik," 149, 151.

4. Daniel, "Stadlmayr," pp. 10–27, 43–47, 107–13.

5. *DTÖ,* vol. 46, ed. Guido Adler.

6. *Dixit Dominus à 14,* MS Kroměříž, B III 77.

7. Karl August Rosenthal, "Zur Stilistik der Salzburger Kirchenmusik von 1600–1730)," 18.1: 80, n. 17.

8. See *DTÖ,* vol. 45, ed. Anton Maria Klafsky, pp. 110–40; Haydn's *Missa in Dominica Palmarum,* in particular, contains sections (Kyrie, Et incarnatus, Crucifixus, Sanctus, Benedictus, Agnus Dei) in four-part note-against-note cantus firmus settings in free chant rhythm (notated entirely in whole notes with bars of varying lengths).

9. That is, the cathedral archive consisted traditionally of two parts: the "Dom-Chor" repertoire of concerted works after 1650 and the so-called "Wachskammer" repertoire of vocal works mostly before 1650 (See Rosenthal, "Zur Stilistik," 78).

10. Orazio Benevoli, *Festmesse und Hymnus, DTÖ* 20, ed. Guido Adler; the manuscript, owned by the Salzburg Museum Carolino-Augusteum (MS 751) was published in facsimile as Vol. 7b of the Benevoli *Omnia Opera* under the title *Missa Salisburgensis,* ed., Laurence Feininger.

11. See Ernst Hintermaier, "'Missa Salisburgensis': Neue Erkentnisse über Entstehung, Autor und Zweckbestimmung"; Werner Jaksch, "Missa Salisburgensis: Neuzuschreibung der Salzburger Domweihmesse von O. Benevoli."

12. The four accounts are: Martin Harlander's manuscript description (1628) published in *Kirchenmusikalisches Vierteljahrschrift* (1900), 79; Gregor Kyrner, *Relation und Beschreibung über die Translation der Reliquien beeder heyligen SS. Ruperti & Virgilii....* (Salzburg, 1628); Alberto Priami, *Ordine della solennissima et sontuosissima processione....* (Bracciano, 1628); Thomas Weiss, *Basilicae Metropolitaniae Salisburgensis Dedicatio* (Salzburg, 1629). See Spies, "Vergangenheit," 337. The accounts of later Salzburg chroniclers (Dückher, 1666; Mezger, 1692, etc.) add nothing to the four eyewitness reports and are mostly derived from them.

13. Spies, "Vergangenheit," 338.

14. Rolf Damann, *Der Musikbegriff im deutschen Barock,* 201.

15. "Auff zwelff unterschiedlichen Chören" (Kyrner); "auf allen Kören" (Harlander).

16. Guido Adler, *Der Stil in der Musik.*

17. Manfred Bukofzer, *Music in the Baroque Era,* 68.

18. Ibid., 69.

19. Charlotte Brontë, *Villette* (1853); see chapters 19 and 23 (pp. 275–76, 340 of the Penguin Classics edition; related viewpoints on singing of a "baroque" kind and of the pomp of Rome appear on pp. 293 and 515–16 of the above-mentioned edition).

20. Benjamin, *The Origin of German Tragic Drama,* 176.

21. Rosenthal, "Zur Stilistik," 83–84.

22. Heinrich Albert, "Leben und Werke der Komponisten und Dirigenten Abraham Megerle, 1607–1680," 62.

23. Ibid., 74–90.

24. Ibid., 60.

25. Schneider, *Geschichte,* 80.

26. Mezger, *Historia Salisburgensis,* 810. Sb. LA, *Geheimes Archiv,* 1653, XXIV/10.

27. Mezger, *Historia Salisburgensis,* 845, 876, 973, 974. Sb. LA, *Prothocollum Capitulare* book, 1673, fol. 21v.

28. Mezger, *Historia Salisburgensis,* 980. Sb. LA, *Geheimes Archiv,* XXIV/5.

29. Sb. LA, *Prot. Cap.,* 1673, fol. 20r–22r.

30. On the dating of the *Sonata S. Polycarpi* see Sehnal, "Die Kompositionen," 24.

31. See chapter 2, note 40.

32. Sb. LA, *Prot. Cap.,* 1674, fol. 92v–96v.

33. Sb. LA, *Prot. Cap.,* 1695, fol. 199–21.

34. Sb. LA, *Prot. Cap.,* 1697, fol. 128v–29r; 1699, fol. 194–95; 1700, fol. 36v–37r.

35. Sb. LA, *Prot. Cap.,* 1699, fol. 194–95. Werner Jaksch (*H. I. F. Biber, Requiem à 15: Untersuchungen zur höfischen, liturgischen und musikalischen Topik einer barocken Totenmesse,* pp. 57–64) discusses the funerals of Dean Fürstenberg and Archbishop Max Gandolph.

36. Sb. LA, *Prot. Cap.,* 1696, fol. 102.

37. Alois Josef Hammerle, *Chronik des Gesanges und der Musik in Salzburg,* 3: 210.

38. Sb. LA, *Prot. Cap.,* 1775, contains a huge chart of all the *Anniversaria* that had been established to that point.

39. Johann Caspar Kerll, "De B: M: V: Assumptione Triumphate sidera la Madonna à 18"; "Justus ut palma: Offertorium"; "Exultent justi: Offertorium"; "Tota pulchra es O Maria." Maurizio Cazzati, eight motets for eight-voice double chorus and basso continuo: "Coeli laetentur"; "Non vos"; "Christus resurgens"; "Dies Sanctificatus"; "O Sacramentum"; "Hodie in Jordane"; "Charitas Pater est"; "Agimus tibi gratias." Antonio Bertali, "O Virginum Virgo: Offertorium De B: M: V:"; "Offertorium: De Trinitate Benedictus"; "De B: M: V: In deserto iuxta torrentem à 10." There are also several anonymous works from this period; and a few of Karl Biber's and Matthias Biechteler's works date from the late seventeenth century. The number of Biber's works contained in the archive is disappointingly small, and must reflect lack of interest in them during the eighteenth century. Of Hofer's there is almost nothing at all. And the late eighteenth-century cataloguers of the archive knew little or nothing of Hofer's and Biber's works; even Biber's works that were in the archive at the time are not listed.

40. See Karl Weinmann, "Andreas Hofer"; Miriam Wagoner Barndt-Webb, "Andreas Hofer: His Life and Music," 50–86, 160–81.

41. Breitenbacher, *Hudební Archiv*; Barndt-Webb, "Andreas Hofer," 87–159, 182–208.

42. Charles Sherman, foreword to Andreas Hofer, *Te Deum*; Barndt-Webb, "Andreas Hofer," 189–90.

43. See the catalog at the end of this study.

44. Barndt-Webb, "Andreas Hofer," 166–79.

45. Hintermaier, "Missa Salisburgensis," 165–66.

46. Bibliothèque Royale de Belgique, Brussels, MS II 3864 (the *Missa Bruxellensis* is MS II 3862). The use of the word "Pausen" identifies the copyist of the *Missa Salisburgensis* reduction as a German. We determine that the reduced score was made from the Salzburg score from the copying of errors and characteristic details from the one score into the other: e.g., at certain points in the Salzburg score the copyist had to double the size of a bar since the barline came right at the division between left and right pages; the Brussels score has double-size bars at the same places although they never once occur at divisions between pages. Fétis had already noticed that the reduction score was "instrumentée par un compositeur allemand" (*Biographie universelle des musiciens et bibliographie générale de la musique,* second edition [1860], 343), and it seems possible that his ascribing the two Biber Masses to Benevoli ("composée par Benevoli, à Prague") came about as the result of an aquisition of the two compositions along with two polychoral Masses of Benevoli and the fact that one or another of the Biber pieces might have borne the initials "H. B." (See Hintermaier, "Missa Salisburgensis," 195). Fétis, associating the sixteen-voice *Missa Salisburgensis* with the two sixteen-voice Masses of Benevoli (all of which came into the Brussels library together from the Fétis bequest) and noting that most of the instrumental parts seemed to be "extra" to the work (in a separate score with the word "Pausen"), concluded that Benevoli wrote the works during his two-years at Prague while the instrumentation was done by someone else; this explanation would have helped to account for the obvious disparities between the Biber Mass and those of Benevoli. The nineteenth-century ascription of the Salzburg score of the *Missa Salisburgensis* to Benevoli has been explained by Hintermaier (ibid., 155) as an addition of the Salzburg Archivist Jelinek that probably came about from the Ambros *Geschichte der Musik,* where the work is first discussed in music-historical terms. Ambros himself might have made the association between the Fétis and Salzburg manuscripts. Since the connection of the former to Benevoli was made before the *Missa Salisburgensis* was rediscovered in the 1870s (Spies, "Vergangenheit," 336), and it can hardly be possible that two independent mis-ascriptions were made, it must be the case that Ambros saw the Fétis score and recognized the work in Salzburg; it might even be possible that the connection of the Fétis manuscripts to Prague, early though it is, goes back to Ambros (who was, of course, a native of Prague and active there for many years).

47. Guido Adler, "Zur Geschichte der Wiener Messkomposition in der zweiten Hälfte des XVII. Jahrhunderts," 37.

48. The *Muttetum Natale* and *Litania de S. Josepho,* for example, both contain ground-bass movements organized in tonic/dominant/tonic schemes, while the Doxology of the Dresden *Nisi Dominus* is built upon eight statements in the tonic.

49. Ibid., 39.

50. The word "Bassetgen" (or "Bassetchen"; Italian *bassett, bassetto*; French, *petit basse*) indicates "any part or instrument that, instead of the true bass, leads the *fundament* into an upper-register harmony" ("Diejenige Stimme, oder auch Instrument, so an statt das rechten Basses das Fundament zu einer harmonie in der Höhe": Johann Gottfried Walther, *Musikalisches Lexicon,* 78–79). See also Praetorius, *Syntagma musicum* 3: 112–13; Friedrich Niedt, *Musikalische Handleitung,* chapter 3; Johann David Heinichen, *Der General-Bass in der Composition,* 515; Johann Quantz, *Versuch einer Anweisung die Flöte traversiere zu spielen,* 205.

51. See p. 24, also chapter 1, note 144.

52. Nonnberg, *Prot.,* Sept 10, 1704.

53. As noted above (note 39), the eighteenth-century catalogs of the cathedral music archive make no reference to Biber.

54. Nonnberg, XIV 12, XI 8.

55. Nonnberg, *Prot.,* 18 Feb. 1668.

56. Ibid., April 12, 13, 1700.

57. Ibid., Aug. 4, Nov. 21, 1700.

58. Ibid., July 4, 1698, June 25, 1700.

59. Ibid., Feb. 16, 1670, Mar. 10, June 21, 24, 25, 1699.

60. Ibid., Sept. 10, 1704.

61. Ibid., June 24, 1700.

62. Ibid., Dec. 7, 1704.

63. Ibid., Nov. 21, 1670, Aug. 15, 1695, Aug. 15, 21, 1698.

64. Ibid., Oct 28, 1676.

65. Nonnberg, XIII 6; I 18; XV 2; XV 5.

66. Sigismund Keller, "Geschichtliches über die nächsten Vorfahren," 66. In his study Keller accurately lists a considerable number of Biber's works in all categories, all of which were unknown at the time. Unfortunately, however, his statement that "the themes of several Masses and circa 8 *Regina coeli"* are listed in the catalogue of the Dom-Chore" reveals that he sometimes confused Heinrich Biber with his son Carl; and Keller published a *Responsorium* of Carl Biber's as a work of the father's. The *"Hymni Sacri.* gr. Fol. *Salisb. ex. Typographeo Joa. Bapt. Mayr 1684"* that Keller claims to have seen is not known as a work of either Biber. Perhaps Keller either mistook the title of a liturgical work for that of a musical work (e.g. *Hymni Sacri Breviarii Romani Urbani Papae VIII. Auctoritate... Salisburgi 1685: Ex Typographeo Joannis Bapt. Mayr*), which hardly seems possible since Keller was a priest and should have recognized such a volume right away, or he confused such a title with the *Hymnus-Buch* that contains Biber's *Stabat Mater.* Either explanation requires that he not have seen the volume, whereas he did see the others he listed.

67. Nonnberg, XI 4.

Chapter 4

1. For the titles see the catalog at the end of this study.

2. The *Missa in Contrapuncto* is preserved at the archive of the Gesellschaft der Musikfreunde, Vienna (I 7966, Q 46), in a score made in the nineteenth century; it is catalogued with a musical incipit in the archive of St. Peter's, Salzburg as a work of Carl Biber's.

3. On the dating of the *Missa Christi Resurgentis* and *Missa Catholica* see Sehnal, "Die Kompositionen," 23–24; the original title page of the *Missa Alleluia* refers to Biber (de Bibern) as "Kapellmeister" but not *dapifer*, indicating perhaps a date soon after 1690; the *Missa S. Henrici* can now be dated 1696 (see p. 43, chapter 1, note 142); see Hintermaier, "Missa Salisburgensis" on the dating of that work and the *Missa Bruxellensis*.

4. Since none of the manuscript copies of these works can be traced directly to Biber or the Salzburg copyists' circle, the copies cannot be used to date the works.

5. The *Missa Quadragesimalis* is, of course, in D minor (occasionally Dorian), but there is a large number of A-major (Tierce de Picardie) cadences that are approached from the flat sixth degree (B-flat).

6. See chapter 1, note 187.

7. Johann Kuhnau describes his use of this effect for the words "Wohl dem" (blessed is he), in his preface to a cycle of church cantatas for the year 1709: "Man könnte auch bei dem haisch huius viri, oder huic viro, und folgendlich bey dem Teutschen Worte, *dem*, einen sonderlichen Nachdruck andeuten, in dem man das *dem* wiederholte, in unvermuthete und den Auditorem zur Attention bringende Tonos setzete, das also dieser Verstand herauskäme: wohl dem, dem, sage ich, der, so zu reden, auf dem Theatro der Welt (laut des aus der Frantzösischen Version angeführten Wortes, personnage) eine grosse und ansehenliche Person praesentiret, und mit Bestande der Wahrheit unter die Glückseligsten kan gerechnet werden,..." (reprinted in B. F. Richter, "Eine Abhandlung Joh. Kuhnau's," 151.

8. See chapter 3, note 49.

9. Bukofzer, *Music in the Baroque Era*, 117.

10. Nettl, "Biber," 69; Breitenbacher, *Hudební Archiv*, 67, note 35; Sehnal, "Die Kompositionen," 25.

11. Breitenbacher, *Hudební Archiv*, 67. The *Missa in Albis* is No. 74 among the Masses listed; while Nos. 73 and 75 are anonymous, Nos. 70, 71, 72, and 76 are works of Heinrich Brückner. And this kind of grouping of the works of a single composer in succession is characteristic of the entire collection.

12. Johann Caspar Kerll, *Missa Pro Defunctis*, from *Missae Sex* (Munich, 1689); original parts and MS scores from the nineteenth century at the Bayerische Staatsbibliothek, Munich. In the Dies irae the same music is heard several times in triple and quadruple meter: Dies irae, Liber scriptus, Juste judex, Oro supplex (all quadruple meter); Judex ergo, Quaerens me, Ingemisco, Huic ergo (all triple meter).

13. Biber uses the former instead of quarter notes in the duet "In pegno d'Amore" from *Chi la dura la vince* as well as in "Canto 10" of the singing manual he wrote for his daughter. The latter (black whole notes) was a common means of notating hemiola rhythms and was still used by Hofer and Kerll, although not by Biber.

14. Sehnal, "Die Kompositionen," 26; see the discussion in chapter 6.

15. Martin, *Salzburgs Fürsten*, 138.

16. That is, the Masses before 1690—*Missa Christi Resurgentis*, *Missa Catholica* and *Missa Salisburgensis*—have ABC Kyries, while the vocal Masses and those after 1690—the *Missa Quadragesimalis*, *Missa Alleluia*, *Missa S. Henrici*, *Missa ex B* and *Missa Bruxellensis*—have ABA Kyrie forms; it is doubtful, however, if this feature can be considered to reflect their chronology.

17. Claudio Monteverdi, *Opere*, ed. G. Francesco Malipiero, 15: 55–56; 9: 17–20.

18. See pp. 13 and 26 for discussion of two compositions by Biber that utilize this ostinato bass.

19. Since the third viola part doubles the basso continuo in many places the loss of the latter is not as great as it seems at first; in many places the rhythms of the text are closely reflected in the string parts, enabling a fair degree of certainty in the identification of sections; also, *colla parte* string writing in other sections even permits complete reconstruction of the vocal parts.

20. Martin, *Salzburgs Fürsten*, 120–23.

21. See pp. 100–101.

22. The surviving title page from the cathedral archive only lists basso continuo, while the theorbo is specified in the Kremsmünster copy; however, theorbo parts can be found among the cathedral manuscripts of other works.

23. The statement that this was the "usual" arrangement is based on Hofer's works, Biber's earlier works (*Lux Perpetua, Vesperae à 32, Missa Christi Resurgentis*) and the average procedure in his later works with similar scoring. Adler cites a different doubling for the lower parts that is, in fact, by no means usual in this Mass ("Die Wiener Messkomposition," 27).

24. It may be noted that in this passage Biber demands the note e''' twice from the first cornetto. This note was hardly ever written for the instrument at that time; the upper register usually ends a tone lower.

25. Adler, "Wiener Messkomposition," 39.

26. The *Musicalischer Schlissl* (1677) of Biber's former colleague, J. J. Prinner, bears witness to the number and variety of themes that could be derived from a single plainchant melody.

27. Hintermaier, "Missa Salisburgensis," 165.

28. There are scores of no other Masses by Biber; and scores of Masses are exceptionally rare for the period. The only other score of a work by Biber to have survived is that of the opera *Chi la dura la vince* which is bound with the archbishop's coat of arms and was clearly kept as a souvenir or presentation copy.

29. Martin, *Salzburgs Fürsten*, 148–49.

30. Bach marks the alternation of styles Vivace/Adagio; as is well known, the movement descends from the sixth movement ("Der Friede sei mit Euch") of *Cantata 67*.

31. See, for example, the descriptions of the funeral rites for Archbishop Max Gandolph and Dean Wilhelm von Fürstenberg in Jaksch, *H. I. F. Biber*, 57–64.

32. The quintessential manifestation of this quality is, of course, the Benedictine abbey church of Weltenburg, built by the Asam brothers around the year 1721.

33. See chapter 1, note 117.

34. The first printed presentation of the circle of keys was that of Johann David Heinichen (*Neu-erfundene und gründliche Anweisung* [1711], 261–62). In the seventeenth century the incipient musical circles of Lorenzo Penna reflected the fact that key signatures were conceived as the successive changing of "mi" into "fa" and vice versa; the flat was called b-molle because it rendered the composition "soft, sad or languid"; likewise, the introduction of the b-quadro or of sharps rendered the composition harsh ("aspra") or hard ("duro"). See Penna, *Li primi albori musicali*, 174–83, 26–29. By Heinichen's time the terms *dur* and *moll* had been taken to signify major and minor; but Heinichen retains the idea of *genera* by referring to the sharps and flats as chromatic and enharmonic, respectively.

35. Johann Mattheson, *Das neu-eröffnete Orchestre*, 231–53; translated in George Buelow, "An Evaluation of Johann Mattheson's Opera, *Cleopatra*," 92–107; summary in idem, "Mattheson and the *Affektenlehre*, 401–2.

36. Also, the *Requiem à 15* has been made the subject of a full study (Jaksch, *H. I. F. Biber*).

37. See the source cited in note 7 above.

Chapter 5

1. Further details on the sources in the catalog of Biber's works.

2. Five sonatas of Carl Biber have been published as Nos. 2–6 in the series *Accademia Musicale*, ed. Charles Sherman; the Nonnberg trumpet intradas appear in *Denkmäler der Musik in Salzburg*, vol. 1, ed. Gerhard Walterskirchen.

3. That is, it appears that the composer planned the setting in terms of where the traditional types of movement could be most suitably placed: e.g., double-chorus antiphony for "Domine à dextris tuis" in the Dixit and "dispersit" in the Magnificat, *stile antico* for "sede a dextris," bass solo for "deposuit," etc.

4. Joseph Kerman describes the music of the classical period as "psychologically complex" in relation to that of the baroque period in *Music as Drama*, 75.

5. Benjamin, *The Origin*, 174–85.

6. Eric Chafe, "Key Structure and 'Tonal Allegory' in the Passions of J. S. Bach: An Introduction," *Current Musicology* 31, 39–54.

7. The word "ambitus" is presented in this sense in Heinichen, *Neu-erfundene und gründliche Anweisung*, 261–62.

8. See Karl Dahlhaus, *Untersuchungen über die Entstehung der harmonischen Tonalität*, 259–66.

9. *Das Erbe deutscher Musik* 2/1.

10. See the sources listed in the catalog of Biber's works.

11. This fact is easily determined from their style as well as from the fact that at times they double the violins, a detail that never occurs in Biber's music.

12. Act I, scene 6: aria "Pur ch'io possa trionfante dominare" of Seiano. Violins are frequently heard in the ritornelli of Biber's arias, of course; in this solo they are incorporated into the two strophes (without ritornelli).

13. This rhythm appears also in the section "Quid sum miser" of the *Requiem in F minor* as well as in the magnificent passacaglia from Sonata V of Muffat's *Armonico Tributo*.

14. Schmelzer's *Vesperae brevissimae* are preserved in the music collection of the Austrian National Library (MS 17329).

15. See pp. 162–63.

Chapter 6

1. The document is preserved in the Allgemeine Verwaltungs Archiv, Vienna.

2. The *Huc Poenitentes* bears the watermark with initials H. R.; this watermark is commonly found on works of the early eighteenth century only.

3. The dates of Nos. 1, 2, and 3 are Sehnal's ("Die Kompositionen," 24–25); the remaining pieces have been dated by the watermarks and the title that appears with Biber's name. Only the *Muttetum Natale* cannot be dated by these means; its style suggests a relatively late date of composition.

4. Christopher Simpson, *The Division-Viol*; Thomas Mace, *Musick's Monument*.

5. Sehnal, "Die Kompositionen," 26.

6. See the discussion of the Vienna *Fantasia* on pp. 201–4.

7. Sehnal, "Die Kompositionen," 26.

8. In particular, the sixteenth-note pattern in measure fifteen of the gamba part and elsewhere (see ex. 6-2) appears in *Congregamini* in parallel thirds between the upper voices.

9. Sb. KA, *Hymnus/ Buch/ Ano/ MDCCCXXCIII/ Renovirt (WC XXI). In Festo/ Septum Dolorum/ B. Mariae. V./ Ad Vesp: Hymnus/ Auctore/ Sig: Francisco Henerico De Bibern,/ Capell: Maestro.*

10. *"Hymnus/ in Festum 7 dolorum B. V. M./ a/ 4 Voci/ Organo/ e/ Violone. Di Sign. Francesco/ Henrico de Bibern/ Maestro di Capella/ Ad Chorum Monasterii S. Petri hic Salisburgi"* (1229.55); the soprano part is doubled. Since both copies refer to Biber as Kapellmeister but not *dapifer*, and with the aristocratic "de" before his name the piece might have been composed around 1690 or soon thereafter.

11. Rosenthal, "Zur Stilistik," 1887; the copyist of *Ne Cedite* also copied Biber's Offertorium *Quo abiit dilectus tuus*; the watermarks of both pieces contain the initials FW (Franz Wörz) and should, according to Hintermaier ("Missa Salisburgensis," 163), be dated before 1696.

12. The *Muttetum Natale, Lux Perpetua*, and *Huc Poenitentes* all have refrain structures.

13. Federhofer, "Zur Musikpflege."

14. Franz Martin, "Vom Salzburger Fürstenhof um die Mitte des 18. Jahrhunderts," 35.

15. Hintermaier, "Die Salzburger Hofkapelle," xxviii. Kerll's *Missa S. S. Innocentium* (source cited in chapter 4, note 12) is scored for four sopranos and alto with two violins and trombone (an alternate scoring of two sopranos, two tenors and bass with two violins and bassoon is mentioned also, presumably to give the work greater applicability).

16. The *Muttetum Natale* is the only work of Biber's to quote directly from plainchant, although both Requiems derive themes from chant.

17. Franz Martin, *Salzburgs Fürsten,* 124.

18. Nonnberg, *Prot.,* Mar. 19, 1700.

19. Ibid., Jan. 19, 22, 23, Feb. 21.

Chapter 7

1. Of the undated manuscript solos on this list, one (No. 51) has been dated after 1670 by Sehnal ("Die Kompositionen," 23); the others, all from the Vienna manuscript, can be dated only on the basis of their styles, which suggest time periods ranging from that of the earlist known works of Biber to his full maturity as a violinist (see the discussion of the individual works).

2. The two sonatas à 3 have been published as works of Biber by Kurt Janetzky (*Musica Rara,* 1958; *Edition Pro Musica,* n.d.).

3. Nettl, "Biber," 70. The *Sonata Jucunda* remains unpublished; the other sonatas have been published in *Musica Antiqua Bohemica,* vols. 47 and 48, ed. Jaroslav Pohanka, as works of Vejvanovský, who copied them. Within the broader context of Biber's instrumental work, which was not available to Nettl, it is impossible any longer to consider the *Sonata Paschalis* and *Sonata à 5* as potential works of Biber. Not only did Vejvanovský copy and date the two pieces before Biber was present at Kroměříž, but the sonatas are too weak to have been composed by Biber. They will not be discussed any further. The *Harmonia Romana* and *Sonata Jucunda,* however, might have been composed by Biber and are discussed in chapter 8.

4. See *DTÖ,* vol. 111-12, ed. Erich Schenk, p. 153.

5. Ernest Newman, *The Sonata in the Baroque Era,* 130.

6. Ibid., 24.

7. Translation in Strunk, *Source Readings,* 449.

8. Nonnberg, *Prot.,* Feb. 18, 1668, Aug. 4, 1693, Nov. 21, 1693, July 4, 1698, June 25, 1700, Sept. 10, 1704. For a summary of the performance of church sonatas in Italy see William Klenz, *Giovanni Maria Bononcini of Modena,* 125-32.

9. Newman, *The Sonata in the Baroque Era,* 24.

10. See note 18.

11. See chapter 1, note 118; also Franz Martin, *Salzburgs Fürsten,* 162.

12. See Rudolf Aschmann, *Das deutsche polyphone Violinspiel im 17. Jahrhundert;* Gustave Beckmann, *Das Violinspiel in Deutschland vor 1700;* David Boyden, *The History of Violin Playing;* Elias Dann, "Heinrich Biber and the Seventeenth-Century Violin"; A. Moser, *Geschichte des Violinspiels;* E. Van der Straeten, *The History of the Violin;* J. W. von Wasielewski, *Die Violine und ihre Meister.*

13. The traditional belief that it is an autograph can be neither affirmed nor denied, since the painstakingly copied manuscript reveals little in the way of personal handwriting characteristics.

14. "Quae primam de suo beatissimo Nomine sumens Litteram, primam Tuo Celsissimo Nomini imposuit. Sic Maria Maximilianum condecoravit." See the facsimile in *DTÖ* 25: 1.

15. *DTÖ* 25: v.

16. Eugen Schmitz, "Bibers Rosenkranzsonaten," 235-36.

17. Sb. LA, *Prot. Cap.,* 1669, fol. 84; Nonnberg, *Prot.,* Oct. 22, 1672, Sept. 1695.

18. Mezger, *Historia Salisburgensis,* 920: "Principis frequentia in Sacris solemnitatibus [margin]. Nulla erat celebrios festivitas, in qua non oves concreditae vultum sui Pastoris agnoscerent. Intererat Divinis tanquam suis, frequentissime sacrum facere, et ordinandos sacro charactere initiare ipse solitus. In aliis quoque Ecclesiis nullam alicuius nominis celebritatem praetermisit, quin illam suae praesentiae et totius Aulae splendore, suorum phonascorum vocibus, buccinis, tympanis redderet celebriorem. Menstruas supplicationes S. Rosarii (cuius Archifraternitatis Albo sua se manu inscripsit) diligentissime comitabatus, quamdiu vires, et anni permisere." A little later (p. 920) he adds: "Ad majus devotionis incrementum instituta simul sodalitus, et undique propagata S. S. Rosarii, titulo Beatissimae Virgini devota, eaque sacris signis, labaris, aliusque instrumentis et insignibus pietatis exculta."

19. See pp. 7–8.

20. Federhofer, "Zur Musikpflege."

21. See p. 4.

22. Breitenbacher, *Hudební Archiv,* 114 (No. 171), 132 (No. 135); Nettl, "Weltliche Musik des Stiftes Osegg (Böhmen) im 17. Jahrhundert."

23. See p. 6.

24. *DTÖ* 25: 49–57. The score in the *DTÖ* edition therefore contains three different violin lines, none of which contains the notes we hear: 1) the original *scordatura* notation, 2) the incorrect realization of the line according to the wrong *scordatura,* and 3) a "corrected" version of the faulty realization. When the error was discovered the *DTÖ* re-issued a correct violin part, but the score remains uncorrected.

25. That is, the lower fifth is tuned a-flat–e'-flat, and the upper g'-d".

26. Arnold Schering, *Beethoven und die Dichtung,* 78–80.

27. Riedel, *Das Musikarchiv,* 80–82.

28. Eugen Schmitz ("Bibers Rosenkranzsonaten," 235–36) argues that Biber used the descending tetrachord ostinato in this piece because it recalls the beginning of a guardian angel song published in 1666, "Einen Engel Gott mir geben." But the ostinato is by no means identical to the beginning of the song, which is in major instead of the minor of the passacaglia. The descending tetrachord was too widespread as an ostinato for such a conclusion to have any meaning.

29. At least eleven copies of the print have survived; see the catalog of Biber's works.

30. Chapter 1, note 181; Charles Burney, *A General History of Music,* 2:462.

31. Beckmann (*Das Violinspiel,* 71) considered that the *scordatura* works were written later than those for normal tuning, while Nettl ("Biber," 75) asserted the reverse. It now appears that Biber wrote works in *scordatura* at the beginning of his career (the Vienna *Fantasia* is probably no later than the early 1660s), in the 1670s and early 1680s (the *Mystery Sonatas* and *Sonatae Violino Solo*) and again in the 1690s.

32. *DTÖ* 11: xiii.

33. And it might well be felt that the sonata ends on the dominant of B-flat rather than the F major tonic. Such a conclusion was not unheard of: Johann Kuhnau, in the preface to his *Musicalischer Vorstellung einiger Biblischer Historien* (*DDT* 4: 123), says the following of a program sonata that appeared to end in the wrong key (the subdominant): "Die Sonata gieng aus dem D.moll. Und in der *Gique* liesse sich immer die *Modulation* in dem G.mol hören. Wenn nun endlich das *Final* wieder in das D. gemacht wurde, so wolte das Ohr noch nicht *Satisfaction* haben, und hätte lieber die Schluss-Cadence im G. gehöret." Kuhnau praises the device as appropriate to his interpretation of the program (incomplete recovery from an illness).

34. Biagio Marini, *Sonata seconda per il violino d'inventione* (Op. 8, 1626–29); see Boyden, *The History of Violin Playing,* 130–31.

35. Although, as noted earlier, there is a key signature change in Sonata III, it is made only in conjunction with a continually modulating transitional section. And in all the many movements of the *Mystery Sonatas* not a single one—not even a single ostinato statement—is in a key other than that of the sonata (a fact that both reflects their suite-like character and confirms their early date of composition).

36. *DTÖ* 50: 90.

37. Published in *Edition Pro Musica,* ed. Kurt Janetzky.

38. Paris, Bibliothèque Nationale, Vm[7] 697, xiii.

Chapter 8

1. Sehnal, "Die Kompositionen," 23. Thus the two sonatas *à 8,* the three *à 6,* and the four string sonatas *à 5* appear in three sets of parts grouped according to their scoring. In the late seventeenth century two other works of Biber entitled *Sonata à 5* existed at Kroměříž; they are now lost, but might have been Sonatas IV and X of the *Sonatae, tam Aris* (Breitenbacher, *Hudební Archiv,* 110–11, Nos. 73, 107).

2. *DTÖ* 128: 130.

3. See Don Smithers, *The Music and History of the Baroque Trumpet Before 1721,* 187.

4. Sehnal, "Die Kompositionen," 24. This sonata was published in an edition by Kurt Janetzky (*Musica Rara,* 1958) transposed from its original C major to B-flat; Janetzky's statement that there are two versions of the sonata in C and B-flat is misleading since there are no works for trumpet in B-flat from this period.

5. *Introduction* to *DTÖ* 89: xvii.

6. See Gustave Reese, *Music in the Renaissance,* 120, 133.

7. See p. 8.

8. "N. B. Das Tromba 1. et 2. auch 5. und 6. all viere müssen beysamen stehen. Undt Tromba 3., 4., 7., 8. auch beysamen, dann sie gehen in tripla ad duos choros. Der Violon aber und der Bass continuus, so vil es sein kan, müssen starck besetzt werden, die quartuba kan wohl braucht werden."

9. See p. 60.

10. Don Smithers, *The Music and History of the Baroque Trumpet,* 186.

11. Sehnal, "Die Kompositionen," 26.

12. Sehnal, "Die Kompositionen," 26.

13. Eva Linfield, "Dietrich Buxtehude's Sonatas: A Historical and Analytical Study," 66–79.

14. Two sonatas of Bertali for two violins, trombone and basso continuo have been published (ed. John D. Hill and Robert Paul Block, *Musica Rara* 1971); the work referred to here is *Sonata à 3 no. 1 in D minor.*

15. See chapter 7, note 3.

16. The *Battalia* and *Sonata à 6 die pauern-Kirchfarth genandt* have been published in *Diletto Musicale* Nos. 357 and 258, ed. Nikolaus Harnoncourt.

17. See pp. 63–64 of the *Musica Antiqua Bohemica* edition (cited in chapter 7, note 3).

Catalog

1. Breitenbacher, Antonin. *Hudební Archiv Kolegiátního Kostela Sv. Mořice v Kroměříži.* Kroměříž, 1928.

2. Nettl, Paul. "Heinrich Franz Biber von Bibern." *Studien zur Musikwissenschaft* 24 (1960): 70–71.

3. Rosenthal, Karl August. "Zur Stilistik der Salzburger Kirchenmusik von 1600–1730." *Studien zur Musikwissenschaft* 18 (1930): p. 88, note 68.

4. See Hintermaier, Ernst. "'Missa Salisburgensis': Neue Erkenntnisse über Entstehung, Autor und Zweckbestimmung." *Musicologica Austriaca* 1 (1977): 163–65.

Bibliography

Archive Material

Salzburg, *Dompfarrei: Heirats-Buch.*

Salzburg Government Archives (Landesarchiv): *Domkapitel-Protokolle* (*Prothocollum capitulare*) 1653–1704. The minutes of the cathedral chapter.

———. *Frank Beamten-Kartei:* (A card catalogue compiled by Adolf Frank in the first quarter of the present century containing biographical data on Salzburg musicians).

———. *Geheimes Archiv:* a large (mostly financial) segment of the Salzburg court archive material, containing various payments lists and decrees such as the *Praecedenz Ordnung, Tafel-Ordnung* and enumeration of horses and personnel for the Archbishop's 1671 trip to Munich, the "Beschreibung der Personen welche in der Stadt Salzburg wohnen," etc.

———. *Gen. Einehmer und Hofzahlamt,* 1706/lit F: documents relating to Anton Heinrich Biber's seeking a position at the court.

———. *Hof-Kammer,* Hallein X/625 (Pfleg.); ca. 1695/6: documents (1673) relating to property in Hallein that Biber's wife inherited from her father, and to Biber's construction of a summer house.

———. *Hofrat Katenichl:* Biber's promotion to *Truchsess.*

———. *Schlachtner Chronik:* A manuscript account of events in Salzburg by late seventeenth-century chronicler Johann Benignus Schlachtner. Hs. 17.

———. *Weihnachts-Salzlisten:* The record of annual gifts of salt from the court to the various employees; useful as a means of identifying and enumerating the court musicians.

Salzburg, Konsistorial-Archiv: *Catalogus musicalis in Ecclesia Metropolitana,* compiled by Luigi Gatti in the last quarter of the eighteenth century.

———. *Catalogus musicalis in Ecclesia Metropolitana,* complied in the year 1791.

———. *Catalogus musicalis in Ecclesia Metropolitana,* compiled by Joachim Fuetsch in 1822.

———. *Consistorial-Protokoll* (*Prothocollum consistoriale*) 1670–1704. Appointments, promotions, the *Capellhaus,* and other matters relating to the cathedral.

———. *Jahrtags Verzeichnis* (Hs. A 238).

———. *Notata miscellanea im Stift und Land: 1664–1758* Hs. A 168.

———. *Ordo Officiorum solenniorum et de Requiem et vigil simulac Missarum quotidian in Ecclesia Cathedr. Salisb. 1678.* Hs. A 422.

———. *Protocollum capitulare conventus 1657–73.* Hs. A 114. *1674–1732.* Hs. A 115.

———. *Was das ganze Jahr in der Kirche gehalten wird, 1690.* Hs. A 175.

Salzburg Museum Carolino-Augusteum: *Bürgerverzeichnis*

———. *Stadtrats-Protokoll* 1670–1704.

Salzburg, Benediktiner Frauenstift Nonnberg: *Protokolle* 1668–1705.

Salzburg, St. Peter: *Catalogus rerum musicarum pro choro figurato Ecclesiae S. Petrensis. 1822,* compiled by P. Martin Bischofreiter, O. S. B.

———. *Sepulturae, etc: Ad Ecclesias, Capellas, et Coemeterium Monasterii S. Petri Salisburgi.*

Vienna, Allgemeine Verwaltungs Archiv: Adelsarchiv.

Books and Articles

Abert, Hermann. *W. A. Mozart.* Newly revised and expanded version of Otto Jahns Mozart. 2 vols. 8th ed. Leipzig: Breitkopf und Härtel, 1973.

Adler, Guido, ed. *Handbuch der Musikgeschichte.* 2d rev. ed. 3 vols. Berlin: H. Keller, 1930. Reprint. Munich: Deutsche Taschenbuch Verlag, 1975.

————. Introduction to *Heinrich Franz Biber: Acht Violinsonaten 1681.* Denkmäler der Tonkunst in Österreich 11. Vienna, 1898, v–xvii.

————. Introduction to *O. Benevoli: Festmesse und Hymnus.* Denkmäler der Tonkunst in Österreich 20. Vienna, 1903, ix–xviii.

————. Introduction to H. I. F. Biber, J. H. Schmelzer, J. C. Kerll: *Vier Messen für Soli, Chor und Orchester aus dem letzten Viertel des 17. Jahrhunderts.* Denkmäler der Tonkunst in Österreich 49. Vienna, 1918, vii–ix.

————. *Der Stil in der Musik.* 2d ed. Leipzig, 1929.

————. "Zu Bibers Violinsonaten." *Zeitschrift der internationalen Musikgesellschaft* 9 (1907–8), 29ff.

————. "Zur Geschichte der Wiener Messkomposition in der zweiten Hälfte des XVII. Jahrhunderts." *Studien zur Musikwissenschaft* 4 (1916): 5–45.

Aicher, Otto. *Saeculum aureum Ecclesiae et provinciae Salisburgensis.* Salzburg: Johann Baptist Mayr, 1682.

Albert, Heinrich. "Leben und Werke des Komponisten und Dirigenten Abraham Megerle, 1607–80, Beitrag zur Geschichte der bayrisch-österreichischen Kirchenmusik." Ph.D. diss., Munich, 1927.

Allen, Warren Dwight. *Philosophies of Music History.* 1939. Reprint. New York: Dover Publications, 1962.

Ambros, August Wilhelm. *Geschichte der Musik.* 5 vols. Breslau: F. E. C. Leuckart, 1862–78.

Antonicek, Theophil. "Das Salzburger Ordensdrama." *Österreichische Musikzeitschrift* 25 (1970): 370–77.

Arnold, Frank T. *The Art of Accompaniment from a Thorough-Bass as Practised in the XVIIth and XVIIIth Centuries.* London: Oxford University Press, 1931.

Aschmann, Rudolf. *Das deutsche polyphone Violinspiel im 17. Jahrhundert.* Zurich, 1962.

Barndt-Webb, Miriam Wagoner. "Andreas Hofer: His Life and Music (1629–1684)." Ph.D. diss. University of Illinois, 1972.

Bäumker, Wilhelm. *Das Katholische deutsche Kirchenlied in seinen Singweisen, von den frühesten Zeiten bis gegen Ende des 17. Jahrhunderts.* 4 vols. Freiburg: Herder'sche Verlagshandlung, 1883–1911.

Baselt, B. "Der Rudolstädter Hofkapellmeister Ph. H. Erlebach." Ph.D. diss. Halle, 1963.

————. "Die Musikaliensammlung der Schwarzburg-Rudolstädtischen Hofkapelle unter Ph. H. Erlebach (1657–1714)." *Traditionen und Aufgaben der Hallischen Musikwissenschaft.* Sonderband der Wissenschaftlichen Zeitschriften der Martin-Luther-Universität. Halle, Wittenberg, 1963, 105ff.

Beckmann, Gustav. *Das Violinspiel in Deutschland vor 1700.* Leipzig: N. Simrock, 1918.

Beer, Johann. *Sein Leben, von ihm selbst er zählt.* Ed. Adolf Schmiedecke. Göttingen: Vanderhoeck & Ruprecht, 1965.

Benjamin, Walter. *The Origin of German Tragic Drama.* Trans. John Osborne. London: New Left Books, 1977.

Berend, Fritz. *Nicolaus Adam Strungk (1648–1700): Sein Leben und seine Werke.* Hannover, 1913.

Birsak, Kurt. *Die Holzblasinstrumente im Salzburger Museum Carolino Augusteum: Verzeichnis und entwicklungsgeschichtliche Untersuchungen.* Salzburger Museum Carolino Augusteum: Jahresschrift 18 (1972). Salzburg, 1973.

Blume, Friedrich, ed. *Die Musik in Geschichte und Gegenwart: Allgemeine Enzyklopädie der Musik.* 14 vols. Kassel und Basel: Bärenreiter-Verlag: 1949–68. Supplements: 1973, 1979.

Böhme, F. M. *Altdeutsches Liederbuch.* Leipzig: Breitkopf und Härtel, 1877.

Bonta, Stephen. "The Uses of the Sonata da Chiesa." *Journal of the American Musicological Society* 22 (1969): 54–84.

Boyden, David D. *The History of Violin Playing from its origins to 1761.* London: Oxford University Press, 1967.

Breitenbacher, Antonin. *Hudební Archiv Kolegiátního Kostela sv. Mořice v. Kroměříži. Kroměříž,* 1928.

Brontë, Charlotte. *Villette* (originally published in 1853 under the pseudonym Currer Bell). Penguin Classics. Ed. Mark Lilly; intro. Tony Tanner. London: Penguin Books, 1985.

Brook, Barry, ed. *The Breitkopf Thematic Catalogue.* The Six Parts and Sixteen Supplements: 1762–87. Ed. with an Introduction and Indexes by Barry S. Brook. New York: Dover Publications, 1966.

Brossard, Sebastian de. *Dictionnaire de Musique* (1703). 2d ed. Paris 1705. Facsim. ed. Hilversum, 1965.

Bukofzer, Manfred F. "Allegory in Baroque Music." *Journal of the Warburg and Courtauld Institutes* 3, (1939–40): 1–21.

————. *Music in the Baroque Era.* New York: W. W. Norton & Company Inc., 1947.

Burney, Charles. *A General History of Music from the Earliest Ages to the Present Period.* 4 vols. London 1776–89. Ed. with critical and historical notes by Frank Mercer, 1935. Reprint. New York: Dover Publications, 1957.

Chafe, Eric. "Key Structure and Tonal Allegory in the Passions of J. S. Bach: An Introduction." *Current Musicology* 31 (1981): 39–54.

————. "The Church Music of Heinrich Biber." 2 vols. Ph.D. diss. University of Toronto, 1975.

Dahms, Sibylle. "Das Musiktheater des Salzburger Hochbarocks (1668–1709), Teil I: Das Benediktinerdrama." Ph.D. diss. Salzburg, 1972.

————. "Ignaz Franz Heinrich Biber" ("Musikergedenkstätten in Stadt und Land Salzburg"). *Österreichische Musikzeitschrift* 26 (1971): 414.

————. "Neues zur Chronologie der Opern von Biber und Muffat." *Österreichische Musikzeitschrift* 29 (1974): 365–67.

————. "Opern und Festkantaten des Salzburger Hochbarock." *Österreichische Musikzeitschrift* 25 (1970): 377–84.

Dammann, Rolf. *Der Musikbegriff im deutschen Barock.* Köln: Arno Volk Verlag, 1967.

Daniel, Friedrich, "Die Konzertanten Messen Johann Stadlmayrs." Ph.D. diss. Vienna, 1928.

Dann, Elias. "Biber." *The New Grove Dictionary of Music and Musicians.* Ed. Stanlie Sadie. Vol. 2. London: Macmillan, 1980, 678–82.

————. "Heinrich Biber and the Seventeenth-Century Violin." Ph.D. diss., Columbia University, 1968.

Donington, Robert. *The Interpretation of Early Music,* 1963. 2d ed. rev. and reprinted with corrections. London: Faber and Faber, 1975.

Dückher von Haslau zu Winkl, Franz. *Saltzburgische Chronica.* Salzburg, 1666.

Eineder, Georg. *The Ancient Paper-Mills of the Former Austro-Hungarian Empire and Their Watermarks.* Monumenta chartae papyraceae historiam illustrantia 8. Gen. ed. E. S. Labarre. Hilversum: The Paper Publications Society, 1960.

Eitner, Robert. *Biographisch-Bibliographisches Quellen-Lexicon der Musiker und Musikgelehrten.* 10 vols. Leipzig: Breitkopf und Härtel, 1900–1904.

Elsinger, D. "Der Salzburger Chronist J. B. Schlachtner." Ph.D. diss. Salzburg, 1970.

Esterl, P. Franz. *Chronik des adeligen Benediktiner-Frauen-Stiftes Nonnberg in Salzburg.* Salzburg: Franz Xaver Duyle, 1841.

Federhofer, Helmut. "Alte Musikalien-Inventare der Klöster St. Paul (Kärnten) und Göss (Steiermark)." *Kirchenmusikalisches Jahrbuch* 35 (1951): 97–112.

————. "Biographische Beiträge zu Georg Muffat und Johann Joseph Fux." *Die Musikforschung* 13 (1960): 130–42.

————. "Eine Musiklehre von Johann Jakob Prinner." *Festschrift Alfred Orel zum 70. Geburtstag.* Vienna-Wiesbaden, 1960. 47–57.

————. "Muffat." *Die Musik in Geschichte und Gegenwart* 9 (1961): 915–19.

————. "Die Musikpflege an der St. Jakobskirche in Leoben." *Die Musikforschung* 4 (1951): 333–41.

————. "Ein Salzburger Theoretikerkreis." *Acta Musicologica* 36 (1964): 50–79.

————. "Zur handschriftlicher Überlieferung der Musiktheorie in Österreich in der zweiten Hälfte des 17. Jahrhunderts." *Die Musikforschung* 11 (1958): 264–79.

————. "Zur Musikpflege im Benediktinerstift Michaelbeuern (Salzburg)." *Festschrift Karl Gustav Fellerer zum sechzigsten Geburtstag.* Ed. H. Hüschen. Regensburg: Gustav Bosse Verlag, 1962, 106–27.

Feistner, Wilhelm. *Geschichte der Stadt Wartenberg.* Reichenberg, 1928.

Fellerer, Karl Gustav. *Der Palestrinastil und seine Bedeutung in der vokalen Kirchenmusik des achtzehnten Jahrhunderts.* Augsburg: Dr. Benno Filser Verlag, 1929.

————. *Geschichte der Katholischen Kirchenmusik.* 2d ed. Düsseldorf: Musikverlag Schwann, 1949.

————. *Rupert Ignaz Mayr und seine Kirchenmusik.* Leipzig: Breitkopf und Härtel, 1936.

————. "Zur Geschichte der Kirchenmusik um die Wende des 17. Jahrhunderts in Deutschland." *Musica Divina* 16 (1928).

Fétis, François. *Biographie universelle des musiciens et bibliographie générale de la musique.* 2d ed. Paris, 1860.

Flotzinger, Rudolf. "Johann Heinrich Schmelzers Sonata 'Lanterly'." *Studien zur Musikwissenschaft* 26 (1964): 67–78.

Flotzinger, Rudolf and Gruber, Gernot. *Musikgeschichte Österreichs* Vol. 1: *Von den Anfängen zum Barock.* Graz: Verlag Styria, 1977.

Gassner, Josef. *Beiträge zu einer Bibliographie der Geschichte des Salzburger Domes.* Reprinted from *Der Dom zu Salzburg: Symbol und Wirklichkeit.* Salzburg, 1959, 135–53.

————. *Die Musiksammlung im Salzburger Museum Carolino Augusteum.* Salzburg: Salzburger Museum Carolino Augusteum, 1962.

Geiringer, Karl. *Alte Musik-Instrumente im Museum Carolino Augusteum Salzburg.* Edited by the direction of the Museum Carolino Augusteum. Leipzig: Breitkopf und Härtel, 1932.

Giebler, Albert C., "The Masses of Johann Caspar Kerll." Ph.D. diss., University of Michigan, 1957.

Gisberti, L. *Il viaggio dell'AA. SS. EE. di Baviera à Salzburgo in giornate diviso e all'Altezza Real di Savoia in littere di Ravaglio descritto.* Munich, 1670.

Göhler, Albert. *Verzeichnis der in den Frankfurter und Leipziger Messkatalogen der Jahre 1564 bis 1759 angezeigten Musikalien.* Leipzig: C. F. Kahnt, 1902. Reprint (4 vols. in 1). Hilversum, 1965.

Greinz, Christian. "Die fürsterbischöfliche Kurie und das Stadtdekanat zu Salzburg." *Fürsterzbischöfliche Konsistorium* 8 (1929): 109–46.

Gugl, Matthias. *Fundamenta partiturae.* Salzburg, 1719.

Haas, Robert M. *Die Musik des Barocks.* Handbuch der Musikwissenschaft. Vol. 3. Ed. Ernst Bücken. Wildpark-Potsdam: Akademische Verlagsgesellschaft, 1928.

Haberl, F. X. "Über Abraham Megerle, Kapellmeister und Komponist, zuletzt Stiftskanonikus in Altötting." *Kirchenmusikalisches Jahrbuch* 12 (1897): 72–91.

Haller, Klaus. *Partituranordnung und musikalischer Satz.* Münchner Veröffentlichungen zur Musikgeschichte 18. Tutzing: Hans Schneider, 1970.

Hammerle, A. J. *Chronik des Gesanges und der Musik in Salzburg.* 4 vols. Salzburg, 1874–77.

Hansiz, Markus. *Germaniae sacrae,* Tomus II. Archiepiscopatus Salisburgensis Chronologice propositus auctore P. Marco Hansizio, Soc. Jesu., 1729.

Harnoncourt, Nikolaus. Jacket notes for Telefunken recording SAWT 9537 - A Ex (Biber: *Sonata St. Polycarpi, Laetatus Sum, Epiphany Cantata, Requiem*), 1968.

Haslberger, Adauctus. "Historiae Ecclesiae Salisburgensis" (1782). MS. 27077/III. Bayerische Staatsbibliothek, Munich.

Heinichen, Johann David. *Neu-erfundene und gründliche Anweisung.* Hamburg, 1711.

Heuss, Alfred. "Eine instrumentale Passionsschilderung aus dem 17. Jahrhundert." *Musikbuch aus Österreich* 8 (1911): 3–11.

Hintermaier, Ernst. "Die Dommusik im 18. Jahrhundert." in *1200 Jahre Dom zu Salzburg. Festschrift zum 1200jährigen Jubiläum des Domes zu Salzburg.* Salzburg, 1974, 448–53.

_____. "Die fürsterzbischöfliche Musik in Salzburg zur Zeit Mozarts." *Österreichische Musikzeitschrift* 27 (1972): 395–400.

_____. "Die Salzburger Hofkapelle von 1700 bis 1806. Organisation und Personal." Ph.D. diss. Salzburg, 1972.

_____. "'Missa Salisburgensis': Neue Erkenntnisse über Entstehung, Autor und Zweckbestimmung." *Musicologica Austriaca* 1 (1977): 154–96.

_____. "The Missa Salisburgensis." *Musical Times.* November 1975, 965–66.

Högler, Fritz. "Die Kirchensonaten in Kremsier." Ph.D. diss. Vienna, 1926.

Hofer, Norbert. "Beide Reutter als Kirchenkomponisten." Ph.D. diss. Vienna, 1915.

Hübner, Lorenz. *Beschreibung der hochfürstlich-erzbischöflichen Haupt- und Residenz-Stadt Salzburg und Ihrer Gegenden.* 2 vols. Salzburg, 1792–93.

Hummel, Walter, "Das Bruderschaftsbüchl der hl. Kreuz-Bruderschaft an der Bürgerspitalskirche in Salzburg." *Jahresschrift des Salzburger Museum Carolino-Augusteum.* Salzburg, 1959–60, 205–21.

Iselin, Dora J. *Biagio Marini: sein Leben und seine Instrumentalwerke.* Hildburghausen, 1931.

Jaksch, Werner. *H. I. F. Biber, Requiem à 15. Untersuchungen zur höfischen, liturgischen und musikalischen Topik einer barocken Totenmesse.* Beiträge zur Musikforschung 5. Ed. Reinhold Hammerstein and Wilhelm Seidel. Munich: Emil Katzbichler, 1977.

_____. "Missa Salisburgensis. Neuzuschreibung der Salzburger Domweihmesse von O. Benevoli." *Archiv für Musikwissenschaft* 35, no. 4 (1978): 239–50.

Janowka, Thomas Balthasar. *Clavis ad thesaurum magnae artis musicae.* Prague, 1701.

Keller, Sigismund. "Geschichtliches über die nächsten Vorfahren Mozarts als Kapellmeister im fürsterzbischöflichen Dom zu Salzburg." *Haberls Zeitschrift für Katholische Kirchenmusik* 4 (1871): 2–3, 19–22, 26–29, 51–52, 55–57, 63–66, 72–73. With supplement *Kirchliche Compositionen* (works of Salzburg composers). Ed. S. Keller. Leipzig: Breitkopf und Härtel, 1871.

Kellner, Altmann. *Musikgeschichte des Stiftes Kremsmünster.* Kassel: Bärenreiter, 1956.

Kerll, Johann Caspar. *Ein Compendiose Relation von dem Contrapunct.* Vienna: Gesellschaft der Musikfreunde. (MS 1307, 49 pp.)

Klein, H. "Die Feierlichkeiten der Domweihe des Jahres 1628." *Der Dom von Salzburg, zum 300-jährigen Jubiläum* (1928): 105ff.

Koczirz, Adolf. "Zur Lebensgeschichte Johann Heinrich Schmelzers." *Studien zur Musikwissenschaft* 26 (1964): 47–66.

Köchel, Ludwig von. *Die Kaiserliche Hof-Musikkapelle in Wien von 1543 bis 1876.* Vienna, 1869.

Kolneder, Walter. *Georg Muffat zur Aufführungspraxis.* Sammlung Musikwissenschaftlicher Abhandlungungen 50. Strasbourg/Baden-Baden, 1970.

Kutscher, A. *Das Salzburg Barocktheater.* Vienna: Rikola, 1924.

Liess, Andreas. "Biber." *Die Musik in Geschichte und Gegenwart* 1 (1949–51): 1828–31.

————. *Wiener Barockmusik.* Wien: Doblinger, 1946.

Linfield, Eva. "Dietrich Buxtehude's Sonatas: A Historical and Analytical Study." Ph.D. diss., Brandeis University, 1984.

Loewenburg, Alfred. *Annals of Opera: 1597–1940,* 1943. 2d ed. revised and corrected. Geneva: Societas bibliographica, 1955.

Lunelli, Renato. "Di alcuni inventari delle musiche gia possedute dal coro della parrocchiale di Merano." *Studien zur Musikwissenschaft* 25 (1962): 347–62.

Luntz, E. "H. I. F. Biber." *Musikbuch aus Österreich* IV. Ed. Dr. Hugo Botstiber. Vienna/Leipzig: Fromme, 1906, 19–28.

————. Introduction to *Heinrich Franz Biber: Sechzehn Violinsonaten. Denkmäler der Tonkunst in Österreich* 25. Vienna, 1905, v–vii.

Mace, Thomas. *Musick's Monument.* London, 1676. Facsim. eds. Paris, 1958, New York, 1966.

Maier, J. J. *Die Musikalischen handschriften der K. Hof und Staatsbibliothek in München. Erstes Theil: die Handschriften bis zum Ende des 17. Jahrhunderts.* Munich, 1879.

Marpurg. F. W. *Historisch-Kritische Beyträge zur Aufnahme der Musik* 3 (5 vols). Berlin, 1754–78.

Martin, Franz. "Barockfeste in Salzburg." In *Bergland* 12, no. 6 (1930): 11–16, 43–52.

————. "Die Salzburger Chronik des Felix Adauctus Haslberger." *Mitteilungen der Gesellschaft für Salzburger Landeskunde* 67 (1927), 68 (1928), 69 (1929), 74 (1934).

————. "Beiträge zur Salzburger Familiengeschichte." *Mitteilungen der Gesellschaft für Salzburger Landeskunde* 78 (1938).

————. *Salzburgs Fürsten in der Barockzeit, 1578 bis 1812* (1949). 3d ed. Salzburg: Verlag das Bergland-Buch, 1966.

————. "Vom Salzburger Fürstenhof um die Mitte des 18. Jahrhunderts." *Mitteilungen der Gesellschaft für Salzburger Landeskunde* 77 (1937), 78 (1938), 80 (1940); also reprinted separately (Salzburg, n.d.).

Mattheson, Johann. *Das Neu-eröffnete Orchestre.* Hamburg, 1713.

————. *Grundlage einer Ehrenpforte.* Hamburg, 1740. Reprint. Ed. Max Schneider. Berlin: Leo Leipmannssohn Antiquariat, 1910.

Maugars, André. "Reponse faite à ein curieux sur le sentiment de la musique en Italie, escrite à Rome le 1er Octobre 1639." English trans. Carol MacClintock, *Readings in the History of Music in Performance.* Bloomington and London, 1979, 116–26.

Mayr, Johann Baptist. *Zwey-Einiger Hymenäus oder Österreich-Lunebürgischer Frid- und Freudenvoller Vermählungs-Gott.* Salzburg: J. B. Mayr, 1699.

Meyer, Ernst H. "Die Bedeutung der Instrumentalmusik am Fürstbischöflichen Hofe zu Olomouc (Olmütz) in Kroměříž (Kremsier)." *Die Musikforschung* 9 (1956): 388–411.

————. "Kremsier." *Die Musik in Geschichte und Gegenwart* 7 (1958): 1753–55.

————. *Die mehrstimmige Spielmusik des 17. Jahrhunderts in Nord- und Mitteleuropa.* Kassel: Bärenreiter, 1934.

Mezger, Joseph. *Historia Salisburgensis.* Salzburg: J. B. Mayr, 1692.

Mitterwieser, A. "Geschichte der Papiermühle zu Lengfelden bei Salzburg." *Der Papier-Fabrikant,* 48 (1938): 485–87.

Moissl, F. "F. H. I. Biber, ein Wartenberger Grossmeister des Violinspiels." *Mitteil. d. Ver. f. Heimatk.* Eberswalde: Eberswalde Buch, 1907.

Moser, Andreas. "Die Violin-Skordatur." *Archiv für Musikwissenschaft* 1 (1918–19): 573–89.

————. *Geschichte des Violinspiels* (Berlin, 1923). 2d edition revised and expanded by Hans-Joachim Nössel. 2 vols. Tutzing: Hans Schneider, 1966.

Moser, H. J. "Eine Pariser Quelle zur Wiener Triosonate des ausgehenden 17. Jahrhunderts: Der Kodex Rost." *Festschrift Wilhelm Fischer.* Innsbruck, 1956, 76–82.

————. *Geschichte der deutschen Musik.* 3 vols. Cotta, Berlin and Stuttgart, 1921–28.

Müller, Johannes. *Das Jesuitendrama in den Ländern Deutscher Zunge vom Anfang (1555) bis zum Hochbarock (1665).* Augsburg: Dr. Benno Filser Verlag, 1930.

Nef, Karl, "Zur Geschichte der deutschen Instrumentalmusik in der zweiten Hälfte des 17. Jahrhunderts." *Publikationen der internationalen Musikgesellschaft* 5, 1902.

Nettl, Paul. *Beiträge zur böhmischen und mährischen Musikgeschichte.* Brno, 1927.

————. "Der deutsch-böhmische Geiger Biber und die Quellen seiner Kunst." *Sudetendeutsches Jahrbuch.* Ed. O. Kletzl. Egerkassel: Stauda, 1926, 57ff.

_____. "Heinrich Franz Biber, A Great Austrian Violinist of the Baroque." *Forgotten Musicians*. New York: Philosophical Library, n.d., 17–27.

_____. "Heinrich Franz Biber von Bibern." *Studien zur Musikwissenschaft* 24 (1960): 61–86.

_____. *Heinrich Franz Biber von Bibern*. Sudetendeutsche Lebensbilder 1. Reichenberg: Stingl, 1926.

_____. *Story of Dance Music*. New York: Philosophical Library, 1947.

_____. "Weltliche Musik des Stiftes Osegg (Böhmen) im 17. Jahrhundert." *Zeitschrift für Musikwissenschaft* 4, no. 2 (1922): 351–57.

_____. *Das Wiener Lied im Zeitalter des Barock*. Vienna/Leipzig: Verlag Dr. Rolf Passer, 1934.

_____. "Die Wiener Tanzkomposition in der zweiten Hälfte des 17. Jahrhunderts." *Studien zur Musikwissenschaft* 8 (1921): 45–175.

_____. "Zur Geschichte der Musik-Kapelle des Fürstbischofs Liechtenstein." *Zeitschrift für Musikwissenschaft* 4 (1921–22): 485–96.

Newmann, William S. *The Sonata in the Baroque Era*. 1959. Rev. ed. Chapel Hill: University of North Carolina Press, 1966.

Niedt, F. E. *Musikalische Handleitung* 1–3. Hamburg, 1700; 1706; 1717.

Orel, Alfred. "Die Katholische Kirchenmusik von 1600–1750." *Handbuch der Musikgeschichte* 1. Ed. by Guido Adler. Berlin: H. Keller, 1930, 507–36.

Otto, Craig A. *Seventeenth-Century Music from Kroměříž, Czechoslovakia: A Catalog of the Liechtenstein Music Collection on Microfilm at Syracuse University*. Syracuse: Syracuse University Libraries, 1977.

Peregrinus, Johannes. "Geschichte der Salzburgischen Dom-Sängerknaben oder schlechthin des Kapellhauses." *Mitteilungen der Gesellschaft für Salz-burger Landeskunde* 28 (1888): 357–416; 29 (1889): 87–212.

Pillwein, Benedikt. *Biographische Schilderungen oder Lexicon Salzburgischer theils verstorbener, theils lebender Künstler, auch solcher, welche Kunstwerke für Salzburg lieferten.* . . . Salzburg, 1821.

Planyavsky, Alfred. *Geschichte des Kontrabasses*. Tutzing: H. Schneider, 1970.

Pletzger, Hans. "Ein Stück Salzburger Kirchenmusikgeschichte." *Kirchenmusikalisches Vierteljahrsschrift* 15, no. 3 (1900): 78ff.

Praetorius, Michael, *Syntagma Musicum*. 3 vols., 1619. Facsimile ed. Wilibald Gurlitt, Kassel: Bärenreiter, 1958.

Priami, Alberto, *Ordine della solennissima, et sumtuosissima Processione fatta per la dedicazione del Domo, e chiesa cattedrale dall illustrissimo e reverendessimo Principe Paris* . . . Bracciano, 1628. *Beiträge zum Quellenstudium Salzburgischer Landeskunde*. Ed. J. V. Doblhoff (1893): 312.

Prinner, J. J. "Musikalischer Schlissl," 1677. MS treatise in The Library of Congress, Washington.

Printz, Wolfgang Caspar. *Historische Beschreibung der Edelen Sing- und Kling-Kunst*. Dresden, 1690. Facsim. ed. Graz, 1964.

Quantz, Johann Joachim. *Versuch einer Anweisung die Flöte traversiere zu spielen*. 3d ed. Breslau 1789. Facsim. ed. Hans-Peter Schmitz, Kassel: Bärenreiter, 1953. English trans. (*On Playing the Flute*) ed. Edward R. Reilly. New York: Schirmer Books, 1966.

Quoika, Rudolf. *Die Musik der Deutschen in Böhmen und Mähren*. Berlin, 1956.

Racek, Jan. "Inventář hudebnin tovačouského zamku z Konce 17. století." (Music inventory of castle Tovacov from the end of the seventeenth century). *Musikologie* 1 (1938): 61–66.

Redlich, Oswald. *Weltmacht des Barock*. 4th ed. Vienna: Rudolf M. Rohrer Verlag, 1961.

Reese, Gustav. *Music in the Renaissance*. New York: W. W. Norton & Co. Inc., 1954.

Reichlin von Meldegg, Regintrudis. *Stift Nonnberg zu Salzburg* (Salzburg, n.d.).

Richter, B. F. "Eine Abhandlung Joh. Kuhnau's," *Monatshefte für Musik-Geschichte* 34, no. 9 (1902): 148–54.

Riedel, Friedrich Wilhelm. *Das Musikarchiv im Minoritenkonvent zu Wien. Katalog des älteren Bestandes vor 1784*. Catalogus Musicus 1. Kassel, 1963.

Rosenthal, Karl August. "Musikaustellung im Salzburger Dom." *Musica Divina* 16, no. 9–10 (1928): 182ff.

_____. "The Salzburg Church Music of Mozart and his Predecessors." *The Musical Quarterly* 18 (1932): 559–77.

_____. "Steffano Bernardis Kirchenwerke." *Studien zur Musikwissenschaft* 15 (1928): 46–61.

_____. "Zur Stilistik der Salzburger Kirchenmusik von 1600–1730." *Studien zur Musikwissenschaft* 18 (1930): 77–94; 19 (1932): 3–32.

Samber, J. B. *Continuatio ad manuductionem organicum*. Salzburg: J. B. Mayr, 1707.

_____. *Elucidatio musicae choralis*. Salzburg: J. B. Mayr, 1710.

_____. *Manuductio ad organum, Anleitung zur edlen Schlagkunst*. Salzburg: J. B. Mayr, 1704.

Sander, Hans Adolf. "Beiträge zur Geschichte der Barockmesse." *Kirchenmusikalisches Jahrbuch* 28 (1933): 80–96.

_____. "Italienische Messkompositionen des 17. Jahrhunderts aus der Breslauer Sammlung des Daniel Sartorius (1671)." Ph.D. diss. Breslau, 1932.

Schaal, R. *Die Musikhandschriften der Ansbacher Inventare von 1686*. Quellen-Katalog zur Musikgeschichte 1. Wilhelmshaven: Heinrichshofen, 1966.

Schenk, Erich. "Beobachtungen über die Modenesische Instrumentalschule des 17. Jahrhunderts." *Studien zur Musikwissenschaft* 26 (1964): 25–46.

———. "Ein 'Singfundament' von Heinrich Ignaz Franz Biber." *Speculum musicae artis. Festschrift Heinrich Husmann.* Munich, 1970, 277–83.

———. Introduction to *Georg Muffat: "Armonico Tributo" 1682, Sechs Concerti Grossi 1701. Denkmäler der Tonkunst in Österreich* 89. Vienna, 1953, vii–xxi.

Schering, A. *Beethoven und die Dichtung.* Neue Deutsche Forschungen 77. Berlin: Junker und Dünnhaupt Verlag, 1936.

Schmitz, E. "Bibers Rosenkrantzsonaten." *Musica* 5 (1951): 235–36.

Schneider, C. "Franz Heinrich Biber als Opernkomponist." *Archiv für Musikwissenschaft* 8 (1925): 281–347.

———. *Geschichte der Musik in Salzburg.* Salzburg: Kiesel, 1935.

———. "Die Salzburger Domweihe 1628: Ein Kirchenmusikalisches Fest des Barockzeit." *Musica Divina* 16, no. 7–8 (1928): 141ff.

Schneider, Max. "Die Besetzung der vielstimmigen Musik des 17. und 16. Jahrhunderts." *Archiv für Musikwissenschaft* 1 (1918–19): 205–34.

———. "Zu Bibers Violinsonaten." *Zeitschrift der internationalen Musik Gesellschaft* 8 (1906–7): 471–74.

Sehnal, Jiří. "Die Kompositionen Heinrich Bibers in Kremsier (Kroměříž)." *Sborník Praci Filosofické Fakulty Brněnské University* (1970), 21–39.

———. "Die Musikkapelle des Olmützer Bischofs Karl Liechtenstein-Castelcorn in Kremsier." *Kirchenmusikalisches Jahrbuch* 51 (1967): 79–123.

———. Introduction to *Heinrich Ignaz Franz Biber: Instrumentalwerke Hand-schriftlicher Überlieferung. Denkmäler der Tonkunst in Österreich* 127. Graz, 1976, v–viii.

———. "Pohled do instrumentáře kroměřížské kapely 17. a 18. století" (A look at the instrumentarium of the Kroměříž chapel in the seventeenth and eighteenth centuries). *Umění a svět* 1 (1956): 30–45.

———. "Ze života hudebníků Kroměřížské biskupské Kapely v 17. století." (From the lives of musicians of the Kroměříž episcopal chapel of the seventeenth century.) *Hudobnovedne studie* 7 (1966): 122–34.

Senn, Walter. *Aus dem Kulturleben einer süddeutschen Kleinstadt: Musik, Schule und Theater der Stadt Hall in Tirol in der Zeit vom 15. bis zum 19. Jahrhundert.* Innsbruck, Vienna, and Munich: Tyrola-Verlag, 1938.

———. *Jakob Stainer: der Geigenmacher zu Absam.* Innsbruck, 1951.

———. *Musik und Theater am Hofe zu Innsbruck.* Innsbruck, 1954.

Simpson, Christopher. *The Division Viol* (London 1659). 2d ed. 1665. Facsim. ed. London, 1965.

Smithers, Don. *The Music and History of the Baroque Trumpet Before 1721.* Syracuse: Syracuse University Press, 1973.

———. "Music for the Prince-Bishop." *Music and Musicians* 18, no. 8 (1970): 24–27.

Spies, Hermann. "Aus der musikalischen Vergangenheit Salzburgs bis 1634." *Musica Divina* (1914): 314–40.

———. "Beiträge zur Geschichte der Kirchenmusik in Salzburg im Spätmittelalter und zu Anfang der Renaissancezeit." *Mitteilungen der Gesellschaft für Salzburger Landeskunde* 90 (1950): 142–59.

———. *Die Salzburger grossen Domorgeln.* Augsburg: Dr. Benno Filser Verlag, 1929.

———. "Die Tonkunst in Salzburg in der Regierungszeit des Fürsten und Erzbischofs Wolf Dietrich von Raitenau (1587–1612)." *Mitteilungen der Gesellschaft für Salzburger Landeskunde* 71: (1931), 1–64; 72 (1932), 65–105.

———. "Geschichte der Domschule zu Salzburg." *Mitteilungen der Gesellschaft für Salzburger Landeskunde* 78 (1936).

———. "Geschichtliches über das Salzburger Glockenspiel." *Mitteilungen der Gesellschaft für Salzburger Landeskunde* 86 (1946) and 87 (1947).

———. *Musik bei der Domweihe im Jahre 1628.* Salzburg, 1928.

———. "Steffano Bernardi." *Salzburger Chronik* 11/12 (1899).

Stainhauser, Johann. "Das Leben, Regierung und Wandel Erzbischof Wolf Dietrichs." Ed. W. Hauthaler. *Mitteilungen der Gesellschaft für Salzburger Landeskunde* 13 (1873).

Stephenson, Kurt. *Johann Schop: sein Leben und sein Werk.* Halle, 1924.

Strunk, Oliver. *Source Readings in Music History.* New York: W. W. Norton & Co. Inc., 1950.

Tietze, H. *Die Kirchliche Denkmäler der Stadt Salzburg.* Österreichische Kunsttopographie 9. Vienna, 1912.

Tittel, Ernst. *Österreichische Kirchenmusik.* Vienna: Verlag Herder, 1961.

Tomek, Ernst. *Kirchengeschichte Österreichs.* Vol. 2, *Humanismus, Reformation und Gegenreformation.* Innsbruck and Vienna: Tyrolia-Verlag, 1949.

Trolda, Emil. "Tote Musik." *Musica Divina,* (1919), 71–72.

Ursprung, Otto. *Die Katholischen Kirchenmusik.* Handbuch der Musikwissenschaft 9, ed. E. Bücken. Potsdam: Akademische Verlagsgesellschaft Athenaion, 1929–31.

Vetter, Walther. *Das Frühdeutsche Lied*. Ausgewählte Kapitel aus der Entwicklungsgeschichte und Aesthetik ein- und mehrstimmigen deutschen Kunstliedes im 17. Jahrhundert. 2 vols. Universitas-Archiv. Eine Sammlung wissenschaftlicher Untersuchungen und Abhandlungen 8. Münster i. W.: Helios-Verlag, 1928.

Wagner, H. F. "Theaterwesen in Salzburg." *Mitteilungen der Gesellschaft für Salzburger Landeskunde* 33 (1893): 247–329.

Wagner, Peter. *Geschichte der Messe*. Leipzig: Breitkopf und Härtel, 1913.

_____. "Die Konzertierende Messe in Bologna." *Hermann Kretzschmar Festschrift*. Leipzig: C. F. Peters, 1918, 163–68.

Waldt, Julius. "Vom Salzburger Domchor (Beiträge zur Geschichte der Musik in Salzburg)." *Salzburger Zeitung* 129 (1907).

Walterskirchen, Gerhard. Preface to *Denkmäler der Musik in Salzburg* 1. Ed. Maria Michaela Schneider-Cuvay, Ernst Hintermaier und Gerhard Walterskirchen. München and Salzburg: Emil Katzbichler, 1977, vii–x.

Walther, Johann Gottfried. *Musikalisches Lexikon*. Leipzig, 1732. Facsim. ed. Richard Schaal. Kassel: Bärenreiter, 1953.

Wasielewski, Wilhelm Joseph von. *Die Violine im XVII. Jahrhundert und die Anfänge der Instrumental-Composition*. Bonn, 1874; with separately published supplement *Instrumentalsätze vom Ende des XVI. bis Ende des XVII Jahrhunderts* (Berlin, n.d.).

_____. *Die Violine und ihre Meister*. rev. and enlarged by Waldemar von Wasielewski. Leipzig: Breitkopf und Härtel, 1920.

Weinmann, Karl. "Andreas Hofer." *Archiv für Musikwissenschaft*. 1 (1918): 68–83.

Weiss, Thomas. *Basilicae metropolitanae Salisburgensis dedicatio*. Salzburg, 1629.

Werckmeister, Andreas. *Harmonologia musica*. Frankfurt and Leipzig, 1702.

Wessely-Kropik, Helene. Introduction to *Romanus Weichlein (1652–1706): Encaenia Musices* (*Denkmäler der Tonkunst in Österreich* 128). Graz-Vienna, 1976, vii–viii.

_____. "Romanus Weichlein. Ein vergessener österreichischer Instrumentalkomponist des 17. Jahrhunderts." *Bericht über den Internationalen Musikwissenschaftlichen Kongress Wien 1956*. Graz, 1958, 689–707.

Widmann, Hans. *Geschichte Salzburgs*. 3 vols. Gotha, 1914.

Winter, Paul. *Der mehrchörige Stil*. Frankfurt: C. F. Peters, 1964.

Zauner, Judas Thaddäus. *Chronik von Salzburg*. Salzburg, 1796–1826.

Zobeley, Fritz. *Die Musikalien der Grafen von Schönborn-Wiesentheid*. Thematisch-bibliographischer Katalog. Tutzing, 1967.

Music

(The works of Heinrich Biber are not listed in this bibliography. See the catalogue of his compositions on pp. 305–65. Anonymous manuscript compositions are listed here under the archive in which they are found).

Benevoli, Orazio. *Festmesse und Hymnus*. (i.e., *Missa Salisburgensis* and *Plaudite Tympana*). *Denkmäler der Tonkunst in Österreich* 20. Ed. Guido Adler. Vienna, 1903.

_____. *Missa à 8 Voci Reali à piu stromenti*. Brussels: Bibliothèque Royale Albert 1er. MS. II 3862. Modern ed. (*Missa Bruxellensis XXIII vocum*) in *Horatii Benevoli operum omnium* VIIa. Ed. Laurence Feininger, Vienna and Salzburg, 1970.

_____. *Missa à quatuor coris in sexdecim vocibus cum aliis instrumentis*. MS copy of the *Missa Salisburgensis* in two parts: 1) vocal score with violins; 2) supplementary score for wind instruments. Brussels: Bibliothèque Royale Albert 1er. MS. II 3864.

_____. *Missa Salisburgensis* 1628. Facsimile ed. of score in Salzburg Museum Carolino Augusteum (Hs. 751). *Horatii Benevoli operum omnium* VIIb. Ed. Laurence Feininger. Vienna and Salzburg, 1969.

Bernardi, Steffano. *Kirchenwerke*. *Denkmäler der Tonkunst in Österreich* 69. Ed. Karl August Rosenthal. Vienna, 1929.

Bertali, Antonio. *Capricio*. (solo violin and basso continuo). Vienna: Minoritenkonvent. MS 726, No. 97.

_____. *Offertorium de B. M. V.: In deserto iuxta torrentem* (SATBB, violas and basso continuo). Salzburg: Konsistorial-Archiv. MS. A 184.

_____. *Offertorium de B. V. M.: O Virginum Virgo* (SSATTB chorus and soloists, strings, trombones and basso continuo). Salzburg: Konsistorial-Archiv. MS. A 183.

_____. *Offertorium de Trinitate: Benedictus* (SSAATTBB chorus and soloists, strings, trombones and basso continuo). Salzburg: Konsistorial-Archiv. MS. A 182.

_____. *Sonata à 6*. Kroměříž: MS. B IV 117.

———. *Sonata à 3.* Ed. J. D. Hill and R. P. Block. London: Musica Rara, 1971.

———. *Sonata à 3.* Ed. J. D. Hill and R. P. Block. London: Musica Rara, 1971.

Biber, Carl Heinrich. Church works in *Salzburger Kirchenkomponisten. Denkmäler der Tonkunst in Österreich* 80. Ed. Constantin Schneider. Vienna, 1936.

———. *Dixit Dominus* (SATB chorus and soloists, strings trombones and basso continuo). Salzburg: Konsistorial-Archiv. MS. A 168.

———. *Due sonate per clarino.* Ed. Charles H. Sherman. *Accademia Musicale,* no. 3. Mainz: Universal Edition, 1969.

———. *Due sonate per trombe.* Ed. Charles H. Sherman. *Accademia musicale,* No. 4. Mainz: Universal Edition, 1969.

———. *Missa à dupplici choro* (SSAATTBB chorus and soloists, 2 violins, 2 violas, 4 trumpets, timpani, trombones and basso continuo). Salzburg: Konsistorial-Archiv. MS. A 114.

———. *Missa brevis à 4 voci* (SATB chorus and soloists, 2 violins, 2 violas, trombones and basso continuo). Salzburg: Konsistorial-Archiv. MS. A 118.

———. *Missa Resurrectionis Domini à 4 voci* (SATB chorus and soloists, 2 violins, 4 trumpets, tympani, trombones and basso continuo). Salzburg: Konsistorial-Archiv. MS. A 131.

———. *Missa S. Henrici à 4 voci* (SATB chorus and soloists, 2 violins, trombones and basso continuo). Salzburg: Konsistorial-Archiv. MS. A 123.

———. *Missa S. Josephi à 4 voci* (SATB chorus and coloists, 2 violins, trombones and basso continuo). Salzburg: Konsistorial-Archiv. MS. A 126.

———. *Missa S. Leopoldi In contrapuncto à 4* (SATB chorus and basso continuo). Salzburg: Konsistorial-Archiv. MS. A 125.

———. *Missa Sanct: M: Magdalena* (SATB chorus and soloists, 2 violins, 2 clarini, tympani and basso continuo). Salzburg: Stift Nonnberg. MS. I 49.

———. *Offertorium de Venerabili Sacramento* (SATB chorus and soloists, trombones and basso continuo). Salzburg: Konsistorial-Archiv. MS. A 169.

———. *Offertorium de Vener: Sacram: Salve praetiosum, à 4 Voci* (SATB chorus and soloists, trombones and basso continuo). Salzburg: Konsistorial-Archiv. MS. A 147.

———. *Regina Coeli* (Tenor solo, clarino solo, 2 violins and basso continuo). Salzburg: Konsistorial-Archiv. MS. A 142.

———. *Regina Coeli à 4 voci* (SATB chorus and soloists, strings, 2 clarini, tympani, trombones and basso continuo). Salzburg: Konsistorial-Archiv. MS. A 137.

———. *Requiem à 4 voci* ("Violino principale," 2 violins, 2 violas, 4 trumpets, timpani, trombones and basso continuo). Salzburg: Konsistorial-Archiv. MS. A 132.

———. *Sonata per due corni inglesi.* Ed. Charles H. Sherman. *Accademia Musicale,* No. 5. Mainz: Universal Edition, 1969.

———. *Sonata per due oboi.* Ed. Charles H. Sherman. *Accademia musicale,* No. 5. Mainz: Universal Edition, 1969.

———. *Sonata Sancti Joannis Nepomuceni.* Ed. Charles H. Sherman. *Accademia musicale,* No. 6. Universal Edition, 1969.

———. *Te Deum à 10* (SSATB chorus and soloists, 2 violins, 4 trumpets, tympani, trombones and basso continuo). Salzburg: Konsistorial-Archiv. MS. A 135.

———. *Te Deum laudamus a due chori* (SSAATTBB chorus and soloists, 4 violins, 4 violas, 2 cornetti, 6 trombones, 8 trumpets, tympani and basso continuo). Salzburg: Konsistorial-Archiv. MS. A 133.

———. *Tenebrae à 4.* Munich: Bayerische Staatsbibliothek. MS. 4317.

Bruhns, Nikolaus. *Mein Herz ist bereit.* In *Das Erbe deutscher Musik* Series 2, Vol. 1 (Landschaftsdenkmale. Schleswig-Holstein und Hansestädte). Ed. Fritz Stein. Braunschweig: Henry Litolff Verlag, 1937.

Cazzati, Maurizio. *Motetto à 8 voci pro omni tempore* ("Agimus tibi gratias": SSAATTBB single parts and basso continuo). Salzburg: Konsistorial-Archiv. MS. 221 c.

———. *Per il giorno dell'Epiphania: Motetto à 8 voci* ("Hodie in Jordane babtizato Domino": SSAATTBB single parts and basso continuo). Salzburg: Konsistorial-Archiv. MS. A 221 a.

———. *Per il giorno della Pentecoste: Motetto à 8 voci* ("Non vos relinquam orphanos": SSAATTBB single parts and basso continuo). Salzburg: Konsistorial-Archiv. MS. A 220 a.

———. *Per il giorno della Resurrectione di nostro Sig.:ʳᵉ : Motetto à 8 voci* ("Christus resurgens ex mortuis": SSAATTBB single parts and basso continuo). Salzburg: Konsistorial-Archiv. MS. A 220 d.

———. *Per il giorno della Santtissima Trinita: Motetto à 8 voci* ("Charitas Pater est": SSAATTBB single parts and basso continuo). Salzburg: Konsistorial-Archiv. MS. A 221 d.

_____. *Per la Nativita di Nostro Sig:*^re *e per il primo giorno dell'anno: Motetto à 8 voci* ("Dies sanctificatus illuxit nobis": SSAATTBB single parts and basso continuo). Salzburg: Konsistorial-Archiv. MS. A 220 c.

_____. *Per l' Assensione di N: Sig:*^re*: Motetto à 8 voci* ("Coeli laetentur, terra exultet": SSAATTBB single parts and basso continuo). Salzburg: Konsistorial-Archiv. MS. A 220 a.

_____. *Per ogni Tempo e per Funerali: Motetto à 8 voci* ("O Sacramentum, o grande misterium": SSAATTBB single parts and basso continuo). Salzburg: Konsistorial-Archiv. MS. A 221 b.

Clamer, Andreas Christophorus. *Mensa harmonica.* Salzburg: J. B. Mayr, 1682.

Draghi, Antonio. *Kirchenwerke. Denkmäler der Tonkunst in Österreich* 46. Ed. Guido Adler. Vienna, 1916.

Hofer, Andreas. *De sancta Caecilia. Virgo prudentissima à 14.* Kroměříž: MS. B II 35.

_____. *Dixit Domini à 17.* Kroměříž: MS. B II 34.

_____. *Laetatus sum à 4.* Kroměříž: MS. B III 78.

_____. *Laudate pueri à 4.* Kroměříž: MS. B III 80.

_____. *Magnificat à 17.* Ed. Charles Sherman. *Accademia musicale,* No. 10. Mainz: Universal Edition, 1969.

_____. *Missa Archiepiscopalis.* MS parts at Stift Kremsmünster, Upper Austria.

_____. *Nisi Dominus, à 7.* Kroměříž: MS. B III 79.

_____. *Te Deum Laudamus à 23.* Ed. Charles H. Sherman. *Accademia musicale,* No. 1. Mainz: Universal Edition, 1969.

_____. *Tenebrae factae sunt in F.* Ed. Sigimund Keller. *Beilage No. 7* to S. Keller, "Geschichtliches über die nächsten Vorfahren Mozarts als Kapellmeister im fürsterzbischöflichen Dom zu Salzburg." *Zeitschrift für Katholische Kirchenmusik.* Leipzig: Breitkopf und Härtel, 1871.

Kerll, Johann Caspar. *De B. M. V. Assumptione: Triumphate sidera la Madonna à 18* (SSATTB chorus and soloists, 2 violins, 3 violas, 2 cornetti, 4 trombones and basso continuo). Salzburg: Konsistorial-Archiv. MS. A 210.

_____. *Exultent justi: Offertorium à 5 voci* (SSATB chorus and soloists, strings and basso continuo). Salzburg: Konsistorial-Archiv. MS. A 211.

_____. *Justus ut palma: Offertorium* (SSATB chorus and soloists, 2 cornetti, trombones, 2 violas, and basso continuo). Salzburg: Konsistorial-Archiv. MS. A 209.

_____. *Missa à 3 cori. Denkmäler der Tonkunst in Österreich* 49. Ed. Guido Adler. Vienna, 1918.

_____. *Missae sex* (*Missa non sine quare*; *Missa patientiae et spei*; *Missa S. S. Innocentium*; *Missa corona Virginum*; *Missa in fletu solatium*; *Missa renovationis*; *Missa pro defunctis*). MS. score prepared by Joseph Maier. 1866. Munich: Bayerische Staatsbibliothek.

_____. *Requiem à 5 vocibus.* Munich: Bayerische Staatsbibliothek.

_____. *Responsoria Hebd: S:*^tae *Feria V. in Cena Domini.* MS. score at the Minoritenkonvent, Vienna (XII B18).

_____. *Tota pulchra es o Maria à 5 Voc* (SSATB chorus and soloists, strings and basso continuo). Salzburg: Konsistorial-Archiv. MS. A 212.

Kuhnau, Johann. *Johann Kuhnaus Klavierwerke.* Ed. Karl Päsler. *Denkmäler Deutscher Tonkunst* 4. Leipzig: Breitkopf und Härtel, 1901.

Monteverdi, Claudio. *Tutte le opere di Claudio Monteverdi* 1–16. Ed. Gian Francesco Malipiero. Asolo, 1926–42.

Muffat, Georg. *Apparatus Musico-organisticus.* Vienna, 1690.

_____. *Armonico tributo* and *Concerti Grossi* II. *Denkmäler der Tonkunst in Österreich* 89. Ed. Erich Schenk. Graz and Vienna, 1953.

_____. *Concerti Grossi* I. *Denkmäler der Tonkunst in Österreich* 23. Ed. Guido Adler. Vienna, 1904.

_____. *Florilegium* I. *Denkmäler der Tonkunst in Österreich* 2. Ed. Guido Adler. Vienna, 1894.

_____. *Florilegium* II. *Denkmäler der Tonkunst in Österreich* 4. Ed. Guido Adler. Vienna, 1895.

_____. *Sonata violino solo.* 1677. Kroměříž: MS. B IV 118.

Müller, P. Romanus. *Alles was Nisten thuet soll machen guete bruet.* 1673. (*"Ad pulpitum* ihr *Domini* geliebte herren *Musici"*: soprano solo, 2 violins, viola, basso continuo). Salzburg: Stift Nonnberg. MS. XI 17.

Paris. Bibliothèque Nationale: Vm^7 697, xiii (Recueil de Rost).

Prinner, Johann Jakob. *Ballettae à 4* (1676). Kroměříž: MS. B XIV 108.

_____. *Balletti Francesi à 4.* Kroměříž: MS. B XIV 63

_____. *Balletti Francesi à 4.* Kroměříž: MS. B XIV 154.

_____. *Balletti Francesi à 4.* Kroměříž: MS. B XIV 155.

_____. *Balletti Francesi à 4.* Kroměříž: MS. B XIV 185.

_____. *Balletti Francesi à 4.* Kroměříž: MS. B XIV 186.

_____. *Manches will gleich aus den Blicken.* In Paul Nettl, *Notenanhang* to *Das Wiener Lied im Zeitalter des Barock,* 6–8. Vienna and Leipzig: Verlag Dr. Rolf Passer, 1934.

_____. *Nambli wol kann ich ietz glauben.* In Nettl, *Das Wiener Lied,* 11–12.

_____ . *Was halt man von denen die sich verliebt nennen und wissen doch selbst nichts davon.* In Nettl, *Das Wiener Lied,* 9-10.

_____ . *Serenada à 4.* Kroměříž: MS. B XIV 127.

_____ . *Serenada Canicularis à 4.* Kroměříž: MS. B XIV 128.

Rittler, Philip Jacob. *Aria villanesca à 9.* Kroměříž: MS. B XIV 125.

_____ . *Sonata à 6 Campanarum.* Kroměříž: MS. B IV 28. Anonymous. B IV 26 (Rittler, *Sonata 5 vocum vulgo Glockeriana*). Published as a work of Pavel Josef Vejvanovský in *Musica Antiqua Bohemica* 48. Ed. Jaroslav Pohanka. Prague: Artia, 1961, 21-27.

Salzburg. Benediktiner Frauenstift Nonnberg. Anonymous. *Ach khommet von Himmel, Ihr Göttliche Flammen* (soprano solo, 2 viole d'amore, 2 violins "in deffectu violarum dmour," basso continuo). MS. VI 9.

_____ . *Ave Regina* (soprano solo, 2 violins, basso continuo). MS. X 29.

_____ . *Aria: "Auf! wer stimbt an meiner Wörten"* (soprano solo, 2 violins, basso continuo). MS. IX 13.

_____ . *Aria: "Bey Jesu nur allein"* (alto solo, 2 violins, basso continuo). "Vom Herrn Capel-Maister." MS. XIII 6.

_____ . *Aria de Passione Domine: Jerusalem. à 7* (soprano solo, 2 violins "ad libitum," 2 violae d'Amour, basso continuo). MS. IV 2.

_____ . *Aria: "Khom O Geist."* (soprano solo, basso continuo). MS. VI 10.

_____ . *Aria: "Wer gibt meinen Augen."* (soprano solo, 2 violins, basso continuo). MS. I 18.

_____ . *Ave Regina* (alto solo, 2 violins, basso continuo). MS. X 28.

_____ . *Cantilena de S: Virg: Scholastica à 6* (soprano solo, viola d'amore, oboe or violin, basso continuo). MS. X 28.

_____ . *Canto solo ad Requiem: "Wehe mein betrangten Herzen."* (soprano solo, 2 violins, basso continuo). MS. VII 3.

_____ . *Canto solo ex F: Regnum mundi.* (soprano solo, 2 violins, viola, basso continuo). MS. XIII 34.

_____ . *Cantus à 10: "Mein Herz bequeme dich."* (De Immaculata V: Maria. et in Nativitate Domini). (2 sopranos, 6 clarini, tympani, basso continuo). MS. IX 48.

_____ . *Christus/Die Seel* (dialog; only vocal parts extant). MS. XIV 13.

_____ . *Dies irae: Das ist Zäcker über das strenge Urtheil bosses vergossen und in nachvolgenes trauriges Klaglied verfört* [?], componirt, und gesungen A[no] *1680 A. F. V. G. V. H. B.* (soprano part of a nineteen-strophe German translation of the Dies irae plus a second German version of the Dies irae for soprano, three violas and basso continuo). MS. VII 6.

_____ . *5 secular songs* (soprano and basso continuo). MS. XI 8.

_____ . *Ist aina a Welt Mensch und lebt nur allein* (soprano, alto and *bassetchen* (bassetto) continuo part). MS. XI 22.

_____ . *Liebes Nunberg* (soprano solo, 2 violins, 3 violas, theorbe, organ). MS. XVI 3.

_____ . *Messias venit* ("Ein schöner quodlibet mit einem Alt und Violin, auch zwey Viola con Organo"). MS. XIV 1.

_____ . *Offertorium de Nativitate Xti Domini: "O Jesu, kleines Kündt"* (SATB chorus and soloists, 2 violins, basso continuo). MS. III 20.

_____ . *Profession Gesang: "Ich empfinde"* (soprano solo, 2 violins [not extant], basso continuo). MS. XIII 13.

_____ . *Quodlibet: "O iucunda dies"* (soprano solo, basso continuo). MS. XV 7.

_____ . *Regnum Mundi* (soprano solo, 2 violins, basso continuo). MS. XVI 2.

_____ . *Regnum Mundi* (incomplete parts for two settings). MS. XVI 5.

_____ . *Salve Regina* (alto solo, viola da gamba solo, basso continuo). MS. X 22.

_____ . *30 sacred arias* (print; title page missing. Extant parts: 1) violone vel organo (MS); 2) organo (printed); 3) violino 2[do] (printed). Cover has the pencilled remark "fehlen violino 1 & cantus"). XVII 1 and 2.

_____ . *25 hymns* (title missing. Nineteen hymns for the common of the saints and six for the proper. Varied scorings for 1-3 sopranos, alto, tenor and bass, violins and violas). MS. XI 4.

_____ . *Wan du wirst wie Gott will leben"* (soprano solo, violin, viola d'amore, basso continuo). MS. XIV 13.

_____ . *Wan man thät fragen, und ich solt sagen* (parts of three settings: 1) in D, for soprano, alto and basso continuo; 2) in G, for soprano, 2 violins and basso continuo; 3) in G, for soprano [and ?]). MS. XII 11.

_____ . *Zu einer Geistl: Recreation: "Gott ein Ursprung"* (soprano solo, basso continuo). MS. XIV 12.

Schmelzer, Johann Heinrich. *Ballettae discordatae.* Kroměříž: MS. B XIV 3a.

_____ . *Missa Nuptialis.* In *Denkmäler der Tonkunst in Österreich* 49. Ed. Guido Adler. Vienna, 1918.

_____ . *Pastorella.* 2 violins and basso continuo. Paris. Bibliothèque Nationale: Vm[7] 697, xiii (*Recueil de Rost*).

_____ . *Sacro-Profanus Concentus Musicus. Denkmäler der Tonkunst in Österreich* 111 and 112. Ed. Erich Schenk. Graz and Vienna, 1965.

_____ . *Sonata.* Solo violin and basso continuo. Vienna: Minoritenkonvent, MS. 726, #100.

_____. *Sonata per chiesa et camera.* Kroměříž: MS. B IV 38.

_____. *Sonata per chiesa et camera.* Kroměříž: MS. B IV 207.

_____. *Sonatina l'amorosa.* Solo violin and basso continuo. Vienna: Minoritenkonvent, MS. 726, #1.

_____. *Triosonaten. Denkmäler der Tonkunst in Österreich* 105. Ed. Erich Schenk. Graz and Vienna, 1963.

_____. *Vesperae brevissimae* (SATB chorus and soloists, strings, trombones, basso continuo). Vienna: Austrian National Library. MS. 17329.

_____. *Violinsonaten. Denkmäler der Tonkunst in Österreich* 93. Ed. Erich Schenk. Vienna, 1958.

Stadlmayr, Johann. *Hymnen. Denkmäler der Tonkunst in Österreich* 5. Ed. J. E. Habert. Vienna, 1896.

Tolar, Jan Krtitel. *Balletti e Sonate. Musica Antiqua Bohemica* 40. Ed. Jaroslav Pohanka. Prague: Artia, 1959.

Vejvanovský, Pavel Josef. *Composizioni per Orchestra. Musica Antiqua Bohemica* 47, 48, 49. Ed. Jaroslav Pohanka. Prague: Artia, 1960–61.

_____. *Serenate e Sonate per Orchestra. Musica Antiqua Bohemica* 36. Ed. Jaroslav Pohanka. Prague: Artia, 1958.

Vienna, Minoritenkonvent. MS. 726 (A collection of 102 violin sonatas from the second half of the seventeenth century. Contains works by Albertin, Biber, Voita, Teubner, Mayr, Schmelzer, Bertali, Walther and anonymi).

Walther, Johann Jakob, *Hortulus Chelicus* (1688). Vienna: Minoritenkonvent. MS. 726, no. 27–54.

_____. *Scherzi da Violino Solo* 1676. *Das Erbe deutscher Musik,* series I, vol. 17. Ed. Gustav Beckmann. Kassel: Nagels Verlag, 1953.

Wasilievski, Joseph Wilhelm von, Ed. *Instrumentalsätze vom Ende des XVI. bis Ende des XVII. Jahrhunderts* 1874. Reprint. Berlin: Leo Liepmannssohn Antiquariat, n.d.

Weichlein, Romanus. *Encaenia Musices* 1695. *Denkmäler der Tonkunst in Österreich* 128, 130. Ed. Helene Wessely. Graz and Vienna, 1976.

Westhof, Johann Paul. *6 Suites for solo violin.* Dresden, 1696. Facsimile ed. 1974.

Index

Compositions by Heinrich Biber, and works traditionally attributed to him, are indexed according to their titles. Other compositions are indexed according to composer.

Violin: ability to imitate other instruments, 13–14
Virtuoso writing, 7, 20

Watermarks, Salzburg: as aids in determining authorship, 232
Weichlein, Romanus, *Encaenia Musices:* possible influence of Biber on, 29, 211

Weiss, Maria (Biber's wife), 11
Weiss, Peter (Biber's father-in-law), 11
Werckmeister, Andreas: on Muffat's style, 16

Zacconi, Ludovico: on the effects of music, 15
Zauner, Judas Thaddäus: on organs at Salzburg, 33
"Zefiro torna." *See* Monteverdi, Claudio